UNITED NATIONS CONFERENCE ON TRADE AND DEVELOPMENT

Geneva

The history of

UNCTAD

1964-1984

UNITED NATIONS
New York, 1985

NOTE

The designations employed and the presentation of material in this publication do not imply the expression of any opinion whatsoever on the part of the Secretariat of the United Nations concerning the legal status of any country, territory, city or area or of its authorities, or concerning the delimitation of its frontiers or boundaries.

* * *

Material in this publication may be freely quoted or reprinted, but acknowledgement is requested, together with a reference to the document number. A copy of the publication containing the quotation or reprint should be sent to the UNCTAD secretariat.

UNCTAD/OSG/286

UNITED NATIONS PUBLICATION
Sales No. E.85.II.D.6
ISBN 92-1-112189-2

00500P

PREFACE

This book, prepared to mark the twentieth anniversary of UNCTAD, attempts to portray and assess the achievements of the Organization, as seen by its secretariat. It has been written by staff members of UNCTAD, past and present, in some cases individually and in others collectively. It does not commit the Governments of the member States of UNCTAD, nor does it commit the Secretary-General of UNCTAD.

In a nutshell, perhaps it can best be described as an attempt to review how far member States and the UNCTAD secretariat have together successfully pursued the basic aim of the Organization, as set out by the General Assembly in its founding resolution, namely: to promote international trade, especially with a view to accelerating economic development; to formulate principles and policies on international trade and related problems of economic development; to make proposals for putting such principles and policies into effect: to initiate action for the negotiation and adoption of multilateral legal instruments in the field of trade; and to be available as a centre for harmonizing the trade and related development policies of Governments and regional economic groupings.

The address by Mr. Gamani Corea, Secretary-General of UNCTAD, at the meeting of the Trade and Development Board held to commemorate the 20th anniversary of UNCTAD, serves as an Introduction to the book.

Part One reviews the activities and achievements in the general world economic context and against the background of the interdependence of economies and of activities in different areas. Part Two deals with particular topics, distinguished broadly along the lines of the various programmes adopted by UNCTAD intergovernmental organs and the corresponding work of the secretariat. Part Three covers other specific areas of UNCTAD work within the overall United Nations framework. Part Four contains an organizational chart of the intergovernmental machinery of UNCTAD, a list of selected UNCTAD meetings and a list of selected reports and studies.

CONTENTS

	Page
Address by Mr. Gamani Corea, Secretary-General of UNCTAD, at the commemorative meeting on the 20th anniversary of UNCTAD	1

Part One

THE EVOLUTION, PHILOSOPHY AND ACHIEVEMENTS OF UNCTAD

A general review

A. The economic and political setting	7
B. The philosophical and political origins of UNCTAD	8
C. Evolution of UNCTAD's philosophy and programmes	10
Commodity policy	15
Money and finance	15
Trade and industrialization	16
Shipping	17
Technology	18
D. UNCTAD and its progress towards universalism	18
The fuller participation of the socialist countries of Eastern Europe in the world economy	19
Economic co-operation among developing countries	21
E. Homogeneity versus differentiation of developing countries	23
F. UNCTAD and developing countries' domestic economic policies	29
G. Institutional aspects	32
Internal aspects: evolution of UNCTAD's institutional machinery	32
External aspects: relationship with the General Assembly and other United Nations bodies and specialized agencies	37
Role of the Secretary-General of UNCTAD	41
H. Decision-making and the meaning of consensus	44
I. Conclusion	48

Part Two
TWO DECADES OF ENDEAVOUR (1964-1984)
Major fields of activity

	Page
I. COMMODITIES	53
A. History of UNCTAD commodity policy initiatives	53
The pre-1964 period	53
UNCTAD I (1964)	56
UNCTAD II (1968)	58
UNCTAD III (1972)	61
UNCTAD IV (1976)	63
UNCTAD V (1979)	65
UNCTAD VI (1983)	68
B. Evaluation	70
C. Problems and tasks of the future	73
II. MONEY, FINANCE AND DEVELOPMENT	75
A. Introduction	75
B. International monetary and financial issues	77
International monetary issues	77
Financing of export shortfalls	78
Financing of structural payments imbalances	81
Liquidity needs and reserve asset creation	82
Reform of the international monetary system	83
Financial resources for development	87
Volume terms and conditions of financial flows	88
Multilateral development finance	91
Private flows	92
Debt problems of developing countries	94
Mobilization of domestic resources	97
C. Overall appraisal and tasks for the future	99
III. UNCTAD'S ACTIVITIES IN TRADE AND INDUSTRIALIZATION POLICIES, WITH SPECIAL REFERENCE TO TRADE IN MANUFACTURES	102
A. Nature and evolution of the problems	102
B. Principal policy initiatives and their results	105
The generalized system of preferences	106
Restrictive business practices	112
Non-tariff measures	116
Structural adjustment related to trade	118
Services	122
C. The international trading system: summary of issues and tasks for the future	126

		Page
IV.	SHIPPING	130
	A. The shipping scene prior to UNCTAD I	130
	B. UNCTAD I: the launching of a process	132
	C. Overall view of the development of UNCTAD activities in the field of shipping	135
	The liner conference system and the liner Code	139
	International shipping legislation	142
	Shippers' interests	144
	Merchant fleet development	144
	The open registry issue	146
	Ports	148
	Multimodal transport and containerization	150
	D. Problems and challenges of the future	154
V.	TRANSFER OF TECHNOLOGY: TECHNOLOGY ISSUES—FROM IDEAS TO ACTION IN UNCTAD (1970-1984)	158
	A. Introduction	158
	B. The conceptual framework of UNCTAD's initiatives in technology	158
	C. Technology initiatives in UNCTAD: their evolution	161
	The scene in the early 1970s	161
	UNCTAD's unique role	163
	Selected initiatives of UNCTAD on technology	164
	D. New directives for action during the 1980s	166
	The central role of the Conference	166
	New initiatives of UNCTAD VI (Belgrade 1983)	167
	E. Some concluding reflections	168
VI.	NATURE AND EVOLUTION OF TRADE RELATIONS AMONG COUNTRIES HAVING DIFFERENT ECONOMIC AND SOCIAL SYSTEMS	170
	A. Introduction	170
	B. Principal policy initiatives undertaken in UNCTAD	170
	UNCTAD I	170
	UNCTAD II	172
	UNCTAD III	173
	UNCTAD IV	174
	UNCTAD V	176
	UNCTAD VI	177
	C. Overall evaluation	178

		Page
VII.	ECONOMIC CO-OPERATION AMONG DEVELOPING COUNTRIES	182
	A. Historical evolution of UNCTAD's involvement in economic co-operation among developing countries	182
	The situation before 1964	182
	The introduction of ECDC into UNCTAD's formal work programme	183
	Intergovernmental guidance in the formulation of UNCTAD's work programme prior to 1977	185
	Mexico City Programme on ECDC and the establishment of a Committee on ECDC	186
	The Arusha Programme for Collective Self-Reliance	187
	UNCTAD's deepening involvement with the global system of trade preferences (GSTP)	189
	The Caracas Programme of Action: the decentralization of ECDC activities by the Group of 77	192
	B. Principal policy initiatives: description, results and evolution	194
	Economic integration	194
	Monetary and financial co-operation	198
	Global system of trade preferences among developing countries	202
	Co-operation among State trading organizations (STOs)	204
	Multinational marketing enterprises (MMEs)	205
	Multinational production enterprises (MPEs) and joint ventures (JVs)	206
	C. Problems and tasks for the future	206
VIII.	UNCTAD ACTIVITIES ON BEHALF OF THE LEAST DEVELOPED, LAND-LOCKED AND ISLAND DEVELOPING COUNTRIES	208
	A. Least developed countries	208
	Policy initiatives within UNCTAD	208
	The evolution in the perception of least developed countries' problems	212
	A brief evaluation of the impact of UNCTAD's efforts	213
	Tasks for the future	214
	B. Land-locked and island developing countries	216
	Land-locked developing countries	216
	Island developing countries	218
IX.	INSURANCE	221
	A. Insurance in developing countries prior to 1964	221
	B. The role and activities of UNCTAD in the field of insurance	222
	C. Present market structure and its evolution	223
	D. Future actions	225

Part Three
OTHER ACTIVITIES IN THE FIRST TWENTY YEARS

	Page
I. OPERATIONAL ACTIVITIES	229
A. Background	229
B. Main fields of operational activities	232
II. SPECIAL PROGRAMME ON TRADE FACILITATION (FALPRO)	242
A. Nature and evolution of trade facilitation	242
B. Main results of FALPRO's activities	244
C. Problems faced in carrying out trade facilitation	245
D. Tasks for the future	246
III. UNCTAD AND DISARMAMENT	248
IV. ASSISTANCE TO NATIONAL LIBERATION MOVEMENTS	252
A. Introduction	252
B. Economic and Social Survey of Zimbabwe	252
C. UNCTAD V	253
D. UNCTAD VI	255
E. Concluding remarks	256
V. UNCTAD AND ENVIRONMENTAL PROBLEMS	257

Part Four
ANNEXES

I. ORGANIZATIONAL CHART OF THE INSTITUTIONAL MACHINERY OF UNCTAD	269
II. SELECTED LIST OF UNCTAD MEETINGS	270
III. SELECTED LIST OF REPORTS AND STUDIES	283

THE CHALLENGE OF CHANGE

*Address by Mr. Gamani Corea, Secretary-General of UNCTAD,
at the commemorative meeting on the 20th anniversary of UNCTAD* *

I make these remarks on the twentieth anniversary of the United Nations Conference on Trade and Development, deeply conscious of the enormous privilege I have enjoyed of serving as its Secretary-General over a period of more than half of its existence. I feel this sense of privilege, and indeed of pride, all the more strongly when, on an occasion such as this, I reflect on the nature and role of UNCTAD—what it stands for, and what it has done over these last 20 years.

Before I comment on what UNCTAD is, I wish to pay tribute to those who have helped to shape it. I would like to recall on this twentieth anniversary the contribution of the Secretaries-General of the United Nations—past and present. U Thant was deeply involved in the very creation of UNCTAD. Kurt Waldheim gave it every encouragement. The dedication of the present Secretary-General, Javier Pérez de Cuéllar, is amply evident from his moving message which the Director General for Development and International Economic Co-operation, Jean Ripert, has just read out to us. UNCTAD's great debt to its own Secretaries-General, Raúl Prebisch and Manual Pérez Guerrero, is immeasurable. Prebisch was the pioneer—the dominant figure in the establishment of UNCTAD—and he has put his stamp on the nature of the organization. Pérez Guerrero nurtured its growth and preserved its essence in the sensitive years of growth and adaptation. There were many others who were involved in the growth and evolution of UNCTAD—some happily with us in this room—whom I cannot mention for reasons of time. But I cannot reflect on the origins of UNCTAD and its early years without mentioning one who is not with us any more—Wladek Malinowski. He too played a decisive role in shaping the nature of UNCTAD.

It is the basic mission of UNCTAD that has helped attract to it people of ideals, of dedication, and of ideas. UNCTAD would not have become what it is without the zeal of those who come to UNCTAD meetings to represent their governments and to plead and to articulate their cause or without the support of those—academics, members of non-governmental organizations and others—who encourage and stimulate its work. But also it would not have become what it is without the dedication of those who have chosen to serve on its staff and to contribute their ideas and their expertise to its goals. On this twentieth anniversary it is fitting to pay tribute to all these people, for it is they who have helped to make UNCTAD what it is. UNCTAD is, by any reckoning, an important institution in the family of international organizations. It is important and it is distinctive not only for what it has achieved, but also for what it is. UNCTAD is the one institution in the international

---

* Delivered at the 648th meeting of the Trade and Development Board, 17 September 1984.

system which deals with global economic issues, not merely in narrow sectoral terms, but in terms of their interactions and their interrelationships. This central feature of UNCTAD's basic mandate is vastly enhanced by the universality of UNCTAD's membership which embraces the market economy countries, the socialist countries of Eastern Europe, the developing countries, and China. There is no other forum where the vital issues relating to trade and development can be addressed and pursued in as universal a context as in UNCTAD. Perhaps it is both its mandate and its membership—as well as its origin—that has given to UNCTAD yet another distinctive feature. It is that UNCTAD has been concerned from its very beginning with change—change in the existing state of affairs, change in the status quo. Change is inherent in development. It is inherent in correcting weaknesses and redressing imbalances.

If these dimensions have served to set UNCTAD apart and to underline its unique role, they also explain much of the drama that has characterized the life of the organization over the last 20 years. UNCTAD's task over this period has not been easy, but this is inherent in the very nature of UNCTAD. Agreements to introduce changes in the prevailing order of things do not come about easily; they do not come about only by convening meetings and launching negotiations. They depend on the climate and attitude of the times, on the study and analysis of problems, the mobilization of opinion, and the reconciliation of interests. It is the fact that UNCTAD is, in various ways, concerned with all these processes which helps to bring about progress and change that makes the work of UNCTAD both vital and exciting. Commitment to goals and ideals is an essential part of UNCTAD. It is this commitment that sustains UNCTAD in the face of challenge and of difficulty. In its endeavours and its strivings there is more than a hint of passion.

On this anniversary occasion there will naturally be much reflection on both what UNCTAD has achieved and on what it has failed to achieve. I believe that UNCTAD can take pride in its achievements. The negotiating process in UNCTAD has led to decisions and agreements which have contributed to the making of international law. UNCTAD's activities and negotiations have contributed to the stabilization and strengthening of commodity markets, for products that represent a significant proportion of world commodity trade. UNCTAD has been the source of a major development in the global trading system—the provision of preferential treatment for developing countries on a non-discriminatory and non-reciprocal basis. UNCTAD has also shown itself capable of addressing the specific problems of particular groups of countries and of securing agreements for actions on their behalf. The 1978 agreement on the official debts of the poorer countries, the Substantial New Programme of Action for the Least Developed Countries are examples. If, in the near future, as I hope, the Common Fund comes into existence, UNCTAD will have made a major contribution to institution building in an area of the utmost importance to trade and development. This is by no means the complete picture. In the areas of the transfer of technology, of shipping, of trade between countries with different economic and social systems, of economic co-operation among developing countries, of money and finance, and of insurance, two decades of study, analysis, discussion and negotiation in UNCTAD have forged new perceptions and new concepts and encouraged new approaches and actions.

Behind all this stands UNCTAD's more general but equally important contribution—the role it has played in raising issues, generating ideas, and influencing thoughts and policies and actions in national capitals and in other institutions of the international system. This is a substantial record which marks 20 years of creative endeavour.

UNCTAD has faced its tasks and pursued its goals in a changing international scene. This scene has undoubtedly influenced UNCTAD's experience. UNCTAD came into being at a time of expansion in the world economy, when the industrialized countries were growing rapidly and world trade was expanding at an increasing tempo. In those years there was a broad acceptance of some at least of the major directions of change—the need to enlarge financial flows to developing countries, to strengthen and stabilize commodity markets, and to assist the developing countries in their participation in world trade. Even at that time progress was not easy, but it did come in measured steps. Today we are all conscious of the changed atmosphere—the mounting political tensions, the commitment of massive resources to armaments, the environment of global economic recession and crisis, of inflation and unemployment, of payments problems, and of the slowing down of world economic growth. This is not an environment that has proved conducive to multilateral approaches. It has indeed seen the dangerous weakening of multilateralism, of international economic co-operation, and of the whole institutional system which embodies these objectives. This background has affected negotiating processes in virtually every forum and not only in UNCTAD. It has cast a shadow over the celebration of UNCTAD's 20 years of existence.

Yet, even against this background of crisis UNCTAD has striven to play its role and to make distinctive contributions to the solution of the problems of our time. In this setting of difficulty UNCTAD has been able to develop themes and approaches that are different from the past and have great portent for the future. It was at Belgrade, in this setting of crisis, that the changing character of interdependence came to be highlighted and its logic set out for mutual reinforcing actions to stimulate recovery and to reactivate development. It is against this setting that the implications of the changes that have been taking place in the world economy for the international systems in the area of trade and payments have come to be identified and analysed as a basis for their adaptation and reform. I believe that all this is of tremendous importance to what UNCTAD can and must do in the future.

The international setting in the next decade or two will undoubtedly be different from what it has been in the past. Both the problems and the opportunities that lie ahead constitute a challenge for UNCTAD as it enters upon its third decade. The scenario in respect of the tempo of growth in the industrialized countries appears less propitious than before and this has major implications for the development process in the developing countries. But on the other hand, the latent growth impulses of the developing countries, greater than at any time in history, hold out an exciting promise for the future—a promise that is of significance for the global economy and for the industrialized countries themselves. There is also the fact of technological change and progress, in many new areas, which can profoundly affect the prospects for the future. I believe that the question of promoting and ensuring long-term dynamic growth will be a major issue in the years to come. That is why I have spoken of the need for a new "development consensus"—not so much in the sense of a greater receptivity to development needs but as an underlying premise in the evolution, adaptation and design of the systems of the future. UNCTAD has an exciting and challenging task ahead in contributing to the elaboration, understanding and forging of this consensus. It is a task to which I am confident UNCTAD will respond with increasing strength and vigour.

All this will have its impact on the nature of UNCTAD—the issues that receive attention and the character and style of its negotiating processes in the years ahead. Ten years ago, on celebrating UNCTAD's first decade, I pointed to two forces that could have a decisive impact on the global dialogue on development issues and on the negotiating processes in UNCTAD. These two forces were the progress of international economic co-operation, on the one hand, and the growing strength of the developing countries on the other. The recent crisis has set back each of these forces, but I believe that in the future their momentum can be regained. The imperatives of the world situation and the reality of interdependence demand a return to dialogue and multilateral co-operation.

The adaptation and strengthening of the international system in the fields of trade and payments, and the adoption of national policies that accommodate changes and reduce frictions, will both facilitate and benefit from a return to multilateral co-operation. The international community has therefore to set its sights beyond immediate difficulties, and look forward to the moment when opportunities will arise for strengthening the multilateral system. At the same time, the potential for increased co-operation among developing countries has to be harnessed and translated into concrete schemes and actions that will enhance their collective self-reliance and influence the climate of international negotiations. Each of these forces—multilateral co-operation and the collective self-reliance of the developing countries—would give strength to UNCTAD itself and increase its relevance and capability over the years that lie ahead.

Part One

THE EVOLUTION, PHILOSOPHY AND ACHIEVEMENTS OF UNCTAD

A general review

A. The economic and political setting

The 20 years since the establishment of the United Nations Conference on Trade and Development (UNCTAD) have witnessed profound changes in the international economic and political setting. So many changes have occurred and so many developments have been set in motion and are in a process of evolution, of flux and fluidity, of continuity and discontinuity, of action and interaction. It is therefore next to impossible in this very brief prefatory account to describe them with any pretence to adequacy, or assign to them an order in terms of chronology or importance. All that is attempted here is to mention them, with a view to providing the ambience or milieu in which UNCTAD has been carrying out its tasks during its first two decades.

Nevertheless, as a very rough approximation for this purpose, three phases can be identified in these twenty years:

(*a*) Up to the early 1970s;
(*b*) The years from about the mid-1970s to the end of the decade, and
(*c*) The 1980s.

The first 10 years of UNCTAD—the first phase—may be described as years of relatively high rates of growth of income of developed market-economy countries and of world trade (with the inevitable swings). At the political level, these years were characterized by a relative absence of high international tension, thereby leading to détente (again in an ambience of super-power rivalries and regional conflicts).

The second phase saw the start of the erosion of the multilateral trading system, the breakdown of the Bretton Woods system of money, finance and payments; the slowdown of growth rates and rise in the emergence of structural rigidities and maladjustments, and the recrudescence of protectionism; the emergence of the energy problem as a significant component of world economy, the Organization of the Petroleum Exporting Countries (OPEC) and its economic and financial impact; and the increased interdependence of countries as well as of production, trade, money and finance: all these factors led to a halting and hesitant part-acceptance by the leading Western countries of the inadequacy of the institutional and policy instruments to deal with them in an integral and co-ordinated manner.

Parallel to these developments, and both contributing to as well as resulting from them, other significant forces were at work: the shift in the balance of economic forces among the developed market-economy countries towards Western Europe and Japan, with some diminution of the United States dominance in world trade and money; the near completion of the economic integration of Western Europe, at least of its current possibilities and its process of internal consolidation and realignment; the increased and pervasive weight of transnational corporations in the world economy—in production, technology, trade, finance, marketing, distribution, communications and information systems, etc.; the vastly increased role of private international commercial finance; the opening up of the Council for

Mutual Economic Assistance (CMEA) economies, with their growth, dynamism and increasing participation in the world economy; a steady increase in developing countries' share in world output and trade, even in an adverse milieu, with the significant rise of the new industrial exporters among them; significant rates of growth of trade among developing countries.

The beginning and steady progression of the economic crisis had predictably highly adverse consequences on the growth rates and development programmes of developing countries, with depressed commodity prices, restricted export markets, high interest rates relative to inflation rates, reduced flow of official development assistance (ODA) and limited access to international capital markets, aggravation of the external debt problem, and the like.

The third phase has seen the aggravation and deepening of the world economic crisis, manifested in the stronger operation of all the adverse elements described above, and leading to a grim situation for the world economy as a whole, and particularly for the developing countries. The beginnings of an economic recovery in the industrial world are currently noticeable, but the prospects are clouded by a number of uncertainties in the short run, and the persistence of the structural factor of disequilibrium in the longer run.[1]

Meanwhile, the technological revolution has continued to make giant strides, and diverse technologies have achieved significant breakthroughs unimaginable in the 1950s. These have immense potential for the health and prosperity of the world's peoples, but also for their destruction and death. Important shifts have occurred, and are still in process, in technological leadership in the various fields as between the industrial countries—giving rise to rivalries and tensions. It is fair to say that despite any progress achieved by them developing countries have been left far, far behind.

The deepening of the economic crisis has further coincided with a significant rise in international tension, the recrudescence of the cold war, and an armaments race of unparalleled magnitude and destructive capability. The enormous, ever increasing and wasteful use of material, scientific and human resources on armaments has a most disastrous direct and indirect impact on development: direct because of the denial of resources for development, and indirect because of the negative milieu it creates for world trade, development and international economic co-operation.

B. The philosophical and political origins of UNCTAD[2]

The international economic institutions set up at the end of World War II under United States leadership were mainly designed to avert the recurrence of the

---

[1] For a comprehensive analysis of these issues, see the annual *Trade and Development Report* prepared by the UNCTAD secretariat since 1981.

[2] See in this connection:
R. Prebisch: "Towards a New Trade Policy for Development", reproduced in *Proceedings of the United Nations Conference on Trade and Development, Second Session,* vol. II—*Policy Statements* (United Nations publication, Sales No. 64.II.B.12);

disastrous events of the 1930s and to promote free trade and payments by dismantling restrictions and allowing market forces to bring about the optimum international division of labour and maximum welfare of all countries. Full employment was recognized as a commitment, but there was little or no recognition of the importance of economic development, or of trade as an engine of economic development, despite the inclusion of an element of development in the Charter of the World Bank. There were too few developing countries then either independent or effective enough to articulate their perceptions in this regard. The failure of International Trade Organization (ITO) to come into existence, principally, due to the non-ratification of its charter by the United States, left an institutional gap which was only very partially filled by the General Agreement on Tariffs and Trade (GATT). The trinity—International Monetary Fund, the World Bank and GATT—were in reality the institutions in which decision-making authority, largely in Western control, was vested.

The United Nations Charter indeed embodied the goals of the promotion of the social and economic advancement of all peoples and of international economic co-operation. But the Western powers chose to use the three institutions mentioned above for global decision-making, while retaining their own Organization for European Economic Co-operation (OEEC) and Organization for Economic Co-operation and Development (OECD) institutions for intra-Western decision-making and concerting Western positions on global issues. The Economic and Social Council (ECOSOC), the Charter organ of the United Nations was hardly able to provide the needed initiatives and leadership.

With the emergence and increased participation of a large number of developing countries as members of the United Nations, there was a growing focus on development problems in United Nations bodies and a demand for action by the United Nations. Perhaps the important factor which sparked these efforts was the progressively deteriorating position of developing countries in world trade in the 1950s and early 1960s. It was at this stage that Dr. Prebisch's analysis, under the auspices of the Economic Commission for Latin America (ECLA), of the centre-periphery relationships, the commodity problems and terms of trade of developing countries in the context of economic development focused the searchlight on the inherent defects of the international economy and of the trading system.

At the same time the shortcomings of the GATT system were becoming increasingly manifest. Its lack of a solid institutional basis (the proposal to provide it with one by creating the Organization for Trade Co-operation (OTC) in 1955 failed to materialize for lack of United States support), its omission of major areas of interest to developing countries (viz. non-recognition of the special importance of trade to economic development and exclusion of the Havana Charter provisions for commodity arrangements, its assumption of equality and reciprocity among unequal trading partners, its excessive preoccupation with the reduction of trade barriers among the industrialized market-economy countries, its relative neglect of

---

D. Cordovez: "The Making of UNCTAD" *Journal of World Trade Law*, 1967;
S. Gosovic: *UNCTAD: Conflict and Compromise* (Leiden, 1971);
S. Dell: "The Origins of UNCTAD", in M. Zammit Cutajar (ed), *UNCTAD and the South-North Dialogue* (Pergamon Press, 1985), pp. 10-32.

developing countries and its virtual lack of consideration of the place of the socialist countries of Eastern Europe in the GATT system—these deserve mention.

A political event of importance occurred at that time which galvanized the underlying political and intellectual forces: the Conference on Problems of Developing Countries, held in Cairo in July 1962, which was attended by 36 African, Asian and Latin American countries. Perhaps this was the first joint move of countries covering all the three regional groups, the earlier bloc being the Afro-Asian one in the General Assembly: the joining of Latin American countries was to prove to be an event of the highest significance for the future. The Cairo Declaration called for an international conference on "all vital questions relating to international trade, primary commodity trade and economic relations between developing and developed countries" within the framework of the United Nations.

The socialist countries of Eastern Europe which from the mid-1950s had been pressing for such a conference readily supported the call in the Cairo Declaration. It was, however, not without a great deal of reluctance and resistance that the United States and other major trading nations finally agreed to the ECOSOC decision adopted in August 1962 to convene such a conference.

The General Assembly considered later in the same year details of the proposed conference, viz. the agenda, countries to be invited, the site and other matters, and adopted resolution 1785 (XVII) in December 1962 calling for the conference early in 1964. The role of the General Assembly at that time probably represented its first important steps in the area of international economic co-operation and development—a process which accelerated over the next 20 years in response to developing countries' concerns.

The decision to set up UNCTAD did not come about easily or smoothly. Western powers which had rejected the ITO proposal, and had the strongest objections to the creation of any new United Nations machinery in the field of trade and development, gave in only in the last resort as a compromise arrangement between a non-existent ITO on the one hand and an already established GATT on the other.

The significance of UNCTAD I had been universally attested to at that time. The Secretary-General of the United Nations, U Thant, described it as one of the most important events since the establishment of the United Nations. Developing countries hailed it as the beginning of new era of international co-operation in the field of trade and development. Its Final Act and basic recommendations embodied an international consensus on the dynamic links between international trade and development and marked a major step in parliamentary diplomacy.[3] In institutional terms, UNCTAD I produced two epochal results: (*a*) the establishment of UNCTAD itself as a permanent institution, and (*b*) the emergence of the Group of 77 as a united force of the developing countries.

C. Evolution of UNCTAD's philosophy and programmes

From the very beginning UNCTAD's basic philosophy, in its political and ethical content, has been one of compromise and co-operation, not one of confron-

---

[3] See Diego Cordovez, *op. cit.*

tation and conflict—to promote economic development and trade through international co-operation within the universal United Nations framework. At UNCTAD I its first Secretary-General Dr. Prebisch set out this philosophy of "converging" measures. At UNCTAD II the central theme of Dr. Prebisch's report "Towards a Global Strategy of Development" was the urgent importance of "converging" measures by both developed and developing countries with emphasis on both, and special stress on the need for fundamental reforms in their economic and social structures, and attitudes and discipline in the development planning of developing countries.[4]

The essential points of Dr. Prebisch's philosophy and thesis, as presented at UNCTAD I, may be stated here. Developing countries faced a persistent trend in external imbalance which was associated with the process of development. This imbalance was mainly a manifestation of the disparity between the rate of growth of their primary exports and that of their import of industrial goods. This was "a spontaneous feature of economic development", which was attributable to a number of factors: technological progress in the industrial centres resulting in the increased use of synthetics and the diminished raw material content of the finished products; low income and price elasticity of demand for staple foodstuffs and consumer goods, as compared to the demand for industrial goods and services; the modernization of agriculture in the industrial centres, resulting in enormous increases in agricultural production, which in turn led to agricultural protectionism and farm income support policies at home, and to large increases in exports often supported by subsidies. These were aggravated by the tendency of the terms of trade of developing countries to deteriorate over time relative to the industrial countries. These have had highly adverse effects on the export demand, incomes and growth capabilities of developing countries, which with their internal social structures, low level of technology and domestic resources, are incapable of achieving the high growth rates of output and industrialization required to bring about the enormous adjustments in terms of the introduction of modern technologies and the shift of population from primary to other sectors. Development in the periphery in the past was largely a spontaneous phenomenon of limited scope and social depth; it came about under the dynamic influence of a unique combination of external factors (in the nineteenth century and the early decades of the twentieth), which have since ceased to exist.

The rules and principles on which the post-war international economic institutions were founded and functioned assumed that the expansion of trade to the mutual benefit of all merely required the removal of obstacles to the free play of market forces in the world economy—an assumption of symmetry in a situation that was far from symmetrical, an assumption of equality among partners who were far from equal. There was no recognition of a positive conception of international economic policy designed to modify and influence the course of events with set and clear objectives. In these circumstances, economic development (or growth) in the peripheral countries was essentially a passive response to the impulses emanating from the centre. These impulses from the centre not only failed to impart sufficient dynamism to the periphery, but also aggravated its inherent external imbalance and stifled the generation of dynamic forces in the domestic economy.

---

[4] TD/3/Rev. 1 (United Nations publication, Sales No. E.68.II.D.6).

The new policy for which Dr. Prebisch pleaded was not uni-dimensional or unilateral. The crisis highlighted the need for, and the imperatives of development demanded, action on both the external and the domestic structures and policies by both developing and developed countries. On the external side, the policies called for a variety of measures in the commodity area (including International Community Agreements (ICAs) and compensatory transfer of resources); exports of manufactures (including trade liberalization and preferences); provision of resources for development (including debt adjustments) linked to economic plans and programmes; increased exchanges with the socialist countries of Eastern Europe; and appropriate institutional arrangements and changes in policies and rules for concerted international action. On the domestic side stress was laid on the responsibility of developing countries to bring about the internal changes in social and economic structures (i.e. land tenures, income concentration, ignorance of the masses and limited social mobility), and development planning to give direction to economic and social objectives and to mobilize both domestic resources and international co-operation.

At UNCTAD II, in his address the Secretary-General of the United Nations, U Thant, underlined the same message and said that the assumption of concrete commitments by developed countries should be accompanied by corresponding commitments by developing countries, not in a narrow spirit of reciprocity but in a spirit of concerted and converging action. After 20 years of UNCTAD, the call for a constructive partnership of developed, developing and socialist countries has been made with clarity, balance and objectivity in the current crisis—in the context of the sharpened interdependence of nations, of the linkage of development to recovery and of the interrelationship of trade, finance, payments and development—by Mr. Gamani Corea, the Secretary-General of UNCTAD, in his report[5] to UNCTAD VI.

The Declarations and Action Programmes adopted by the Group of 77 at their pre-UNCTAD Ministerial Meetings at Algiers, Lima, Manila, Arusha and Buenos Aires in 1967, 1971, 1976, 1979 and 1983 respectively, embody the same philosophy and call for partnership. The Buenos Aires Platform of the Group of 77 was indeed a "Message for Dialogue and Consensus", as was the New Delhi Message and the Economic Declaration of the Heads of State or Government of Non-Aligned Countries.

In pursuing this call for partnership and co-operation, UNCTAD's principal aims have been:

To promote international trade and economic development of developing countries;

To promote trade and economic co-operation, particularly between countries at different stages of economic development, between developing countries and between countries with different economic and social systems;

To formulate principles and policies on international trade and development and to facilitate the restructuring and adaptation of those principles and rules and the international institutions concerned;

---

[5] *Development and recovery: The realities of the new interdependence;* TD/271/Rev.1, United Nations publication, Sales No. E.84.II.D.4.

To promote a more equitable international economic order, a larger voice for developing countries in decision-making, and a development dimension and consensus in international institutions and policies.

The universalist, developmental and comprehensive character of UNCTAD's philosophy will be evident from the foregoing.

UNCTAD's efforts to achieve these aims, i.e. its policy initiatives and ideas in various fields of trade and development, have been influenced by and have also been a response to changes in the world economic situation and in the international economic and political setting and to the continually growing and increasingly critically needed developmental imperatives. It is perhaps fair to say—and honesty demands it be said—that despite its conceptual contribution and sustained inter-governmental efforts, UNCTAD as an institution and developing countries as a group have not had very much of a role in determining the course and contours of the world economy, at any rate in the first 10 years of UNCTAD, though from about the mid-1970s their role increased somewhat in world trade and energy markets. Nevertheless, UNCTAD's initiatives and ideas, while responsive to developments in the international economy, have also been autonomous in relation to economic development. These should, therefore, be seen from this twin perspective in order to obtain an appreciation of the priorities, shifts in emphasis, as well as the continuities and discontinuities in the articulation and negotiation of issues.

As long as the growth rates of output of developed market-economy countries and world trade remained reasonably high and protectionist measures did not go to extreme lengths in the 1960s (notwithstanding the discriminatory restrictions on exports of developing countries), UNCTAD's attention was given mainly to securing commodity arrangements and compensatory finance, preferential as well as freer access to developed market-economy country markets and increased volume and improved terms of aid. Other issues were also studied and pursued from the developmental aspects, e.g. shipping, technology, restrictive business practices, monetary issues, the "link" between the Special Drawing Rights (SDRs) in IMF and development finance, etc. However, with the worsening of the world economy, especially from the early 1970s, clearer perceptions were obtained of the long-term structural character of the maladjustments of the world trading and financial systems, and the sharp aggravation of the development crisis led to the search for more adequate, long-term solutions. In this regard the Programme of Action on a New International Economic Order (NIEO)[6] was a landmark in the 1970s, as was UNCTAD I in the 1960s. UNCTAD's initiatives and ideas since mid-1975 have thus had to address the more difficult and less tractable structural problems.

The following paragraphs, which give a brief account of the evolution of UNCTAD's programmes and efforts in the different sectors, bring out the force of the developments and considerations mentioned above.

The policies may be summarized as follows:—

(a) *Commodities:* Initially, commodity stabilization arrangements and compensatory financing, later, a comprehensive and integrated programme of several dimensions—and the recent accent on the short-term programme to meet the crisis.

---

[6] See General Assembly resolution 3202 (S-VI) of 1 May 1974.

(*b*) *Trade and industrialization:* From preferential tariff treatment, liberalization of non-tariff barriers and export promotion to non-reciprocity, preferential treatment, assured and adequate access to markets, a satisfactory "safeguard" system, abolition of restrictive business practices, especially of transnational corporations, structural adjustment and protectionism; reformulation and adaptation of the principles and rules of the international trading system; the services sector.

(*c*) *Money, finance and development:* Resource transfers: initially larger volume and improved terms of aid in the 1960s and early 1970s. Later a stress on massive transfers; a search for an adequate international financial framework, including automatic provisions—attention is now being given to monitoring and surveillance, while pursuing the above goals.

(*d*) *Indebtedness:* In addition to resources transfer, the search for international consensus, guidelines, a comprehensive set of measures, collective agreement—the imperative of short-term crisis measures.

(*e*) *International monetary system:* Initially attention to the Compensatory Financing Facility (CFF), the Supplementary Financing Facility (SFF) and other financial facilities; moving to the "Link", the creation of Special Drawing Rights (SDRs) in the IMF, reallocation of quotas; conditionality; the structural character of balance of payments of developing countries; basic reform of the Bretton Woods system; a larger voice in decision-making for developing countries.

(*f*) *Shipping:* In the initial phases, attention to primary data collection and research; consultative machinery, levels of freight rates, route studies, port improvement, etc. Later a shift to the negotiating phase, the Conventions, registration of ships and bulk trades.

(*g*) *Technology:* The first phases focusing on transfer of technology, shifting later to technology development, Economic Co-operation among Developing Countries (ECDC) in technology, reverse transfer of technology, with continuity in the negotiating programme.

(*h*) *The least-developed countries* (LDCs): The early years were devoted mainly to research and negotiation of the need for a special LDC programme; significant action commenced only from about the mid-1970s, followed by the Immediate Action Programme (IAP) and Substantial New Programme of Action (SNPA) and the United Nations Conference on LDCs under UNCTAD's leadership—now grappling with implementation and monitoring of the SNPA.

(*i*) *Economic Co-operation among Developing Countries (ECDC):* Initially support to regional and subregional integration arrangements of developing countries. With NIEO, major elements of collective self-reliance, such as the Global System of Trade Preferences (GSTP), Multinational Marketing Enterprises (MMEs), State Trading Organizations (STOs) and recently South Bank, and other payments and finance projects.

(*j*) *Economic co-operation among countries belonging to different economic and social systems:* The pursuit of the basic philosophy of universality has been a constant objective. The first phases were devoted to studies, discussions and recommendations on East-West and East-South issues; clarification of issues related to the principles and modalities of foreign trade systems of the socialist countries of Eastern Europe, and their place in the world trading system; bilateral and multilateral consultations in the framework of the Trade and Development Board, as well as outside; technical co-operation programmes.

COMMODITY POLICY

UNCTAD's commodity policy has undergone significant changes in scope and emphasis over the 20 years. At UNCTAD I, Dr. Prebisch formulated his analysis of the long-term deterioration in commodity terms of trade and lack of dynamism and growth for primary products and argued for resource transfers by means of compensatory and supplementary finance, linking the case for these resources with economic development. At UNCTAD II a further step towards a more comprehensive policy was proposed in the secretariat's report on an "integrated commodity policy" calling for increased export earnings, analysing short-term and long-term problems as well as financial measures, and stressing the need for a "general agreement on commodity arrangements" embodying these principles. At the next phase, at UNCTAD III, renewed stress was laid on the importance of a comprehensive strategy and a broad programme of measures including economic diversification and action on synthetics and substitutes.

All these proposals were turned down by the developed countries. Their response in the first 10 years was commodity consultations and a commodity-by-commodity approach. These produced hardly any results. Basically, developed countries stuck to the Havana Charter principles of free market forces and 'laissez-faire' in commodity markets, governmental intervention being justified only in exceptional situations.

The Secretary-General of UNCTAD, Mr. Gamani Corea, brought to UNCTAD IV the Integrated Programme for Commodities (IPC) and its major dimensions in an integrated fashion with powerful substantive and political thrust; and then came the breakthrough, the adoption of the IPC. This marks a signal and decisive international consensus on commodity policy, whose importance should not be underestimated despite the disillusionment generated by the failure to make worthwhile progress in implementation. The firm link of commodity policy to economic development and the need for an integrated set of measures in the context of development, as well as of a healthy international trading system, emerge as important gains to build on in the future. (A detailed history of UNCTAD activities in the field of commodities is contained in part Two, section I.)

MONEY AND FINANCE

The adequate transfer of resources on satisfactory terms and conditions, and reform of the international monetary system have been among UNCTAD's central concerns from the very beginning and continue to be of basic importance. The various elements of these two areas have, however, shifted in importance over time. In the early years, volume and conditions of resource transfers and compensatory and supplementary financial mechanisms received the highest priority. Attention then moved to the need for massive transfers and a search for automatic resource transfer mechanisms and an international framework for that purpose. Unfortunately, these did not achieve adequate results and all the targets, including that relating to Official Development Assistance (ODA), failed to materialize. The transfer of resources is even more urgent now in this crisis than ever before, and

UNCTAD activities include the monitoring and surveillance of progress in this field.

The crisis of external debt, which was forecast by UNCTAD years ahead, has continued to hold the centre of attention for the past seven to eight years, while simultaneously the breakdown of the Bretton Woods monetary arrangements and the erosion of the system of multilateral development finance have brought to the fore the critical and urgent need for the reform of the international monetary system, subsuming thereunder the acceptance of a development dimension in the creation of liquidity, the creation of SDRs in adequate volume and their equitable allocation, and other related matters. To the demands of crisis management have been added those of long-term structural adjustment. (A detailed history of UNCTAD activities in the field of money and finance are contained in part Two, section II.)

TRADE AND INDUSTRIALIZATION

UNCTAD's initiatives and activities in trade and industrialization policies, as in other areas, have undergone significant changes in content as well as in emphasis. A basic continuity from the outset has remained, viz. the reform of the principles and rules of the international trading system. In the early phases the principal activity related to the Generalized System of Preferences (GSP)—a major UNCTAD accomplishment—which was accepted in 1968 (the European Economic Community (EEC) deserves praise for its lead here) and whose implementation was commenced in 1971 and completed in 1976. Review, monitoring and improvement of the GSP remained a major task in the 1970s. While continuation of the GSP is virtually assured, the erosion of its basic characteristics (non-discrimination and non-reciprocity) is now a principal concern.

Recognition of the inadequacy of a policy heavily accented on access to markets led the secretariat at UNCTAD IV to move towards a more comprehensive strategy for the export of manufactures in a broad framework of several elements, and this led to a comprehensive programme including industrial adjustment and other related policy changes (resolution 96 (IV)). Firm pursuit of this was, however, rendered virtually impossible by the preoccupation with the Tokyo Round of Multilateral Trade Negotiations in GATT (MTNs) left in a state of dormancy mixed with high expectations and the deepening of the world's economic troubles.

UNCTAD's considerable analytical work and recommendations adopted on non-tariff measures (largely unimplemented) prior to the Tokyo Round were useful inputs, as were several studies and suggestions on the MTN issues during the negotiations themselves and technical assistance to developing countries. Its monitoring and surveillance tasks on MTN-related codes and decisions currently provide a new accent.

Parallel to the attention given to the MTN issues, a new area gained in importance, viz. restrictive business practices, right through the 1970s, culminating in the successful adoption of the Set of Principles and Rules. The monitoring and implementation of the Set as well as its improvement and revision should be an area of increased effort in the 1980s.

The poor record and results of trade liberalization measures in the 1960s and 1970s and the serious structural maladjustments in the world economy, now more manifest, have since UNCTAD V, led to the focusing of attention on the interlinked character of the industrial restructuring in developed countries, and industrialization in developing countries in the context of maintaining an open, non-discriminatory trading system and curtailing protectionism. UNCTAD's studies and deliberations on this set of issues will figure importantly in the 1980s and beyond.

Other major new areas of focus currently are the study of production and trade in services in the context of development, and recommendations and proposals on principles and policies related to the international trading system, with a view to making it more responsive to the needs of developing countries and supportive of accelerated economic development, and to giving it a more universal character. UNCTAD is once again returning to its fundamental conceptual and institutional challenges in the 1980s. (A detailed history of UNCTAD activities in the field of trade and industrialization are contained in part Two, section III.)

Shipping

UNCTAD's record in shipping is high testimony to its pioneering and path-breaking initiative and courage in challenging the existing regimes and rules, which basically were based on colonial and imperial power structures and remained outside the ambit of any international regulation. At UNCTAD I, Group B countries opposed any consideration of shipping questions. A beginning was, however, made with the "Common Measure of Understanding on Shipping Questions" and the establishment of the Committee on Shipping in 1965. From these modest and small beginnings it is no mean record to have achieved the following in the course of 20 years: the entry into force of the Convention on a Code of Conduct for Liner Conferences; the adoption of the United Nations Convention on International Multimodal Transport of Goods; the adoption of the Hamburg Rules; the progress of negotiations on conditions for the registration of ships; the on-going work in the field of bulk trades, i.e. market practices and procedures, including the role of Transnational Corporations (TNCs); promotion of merchant marines of developing countries and of consultative mechanisms between shippers and the Liner Conferences; technical assistance for the introduction of multimodal operations and port improvements—to list the major items. These speak for themselves.

Certain distinct lines of direction and emphasis are discernible in the pursuit of the above-mentioned programmes. In the early years the main issues concerned the level and structure of freight rates, protection of shippers' interests and consultation machinery. This was followed by the focus on developmental issues, e.g. development of national merchant marines, on international shipping legislation and, subsequently, other issues such as multimodal transport, bulk cargo market and registration of ships. In the early years, the main actions were taken by resolutions and decisions. Failure in implementation and ineffectiveness of appeals to voluntary compliance in a vastly entrenched field of vested interests led to the search for legal instruments: the codes, rules, etc. Secretariat research is underpinning these operations all the time, not only in statistics but also on difficult and complex policy issues: legal, economic, and institutional.

In the face of the strong opposition of some major powers to UNCTAD's entry into certain of these areas, the initial process of launching an investigation or establishing a working group had to be carried out by voted decisions when it proved impossible to reach decisions by consensus. However, subsequent consultations and negotiations in UNCTAD's machinery led to consensus on further work and to negotiations which with skill and patience were successfully carried out (see also section below on "Decision-making and the meaning of consensus"). (A detailed history of UNCTAD activities in the field of shipping is contained in part Two, section IV.)

TECHNOLOGY

The evolution of UNCTAD's work in the field of technology is a dramatic example of how a subject (of such critical importance), which had remained virtually on the periphery for the first 10 years, was brought to the centre of international attention and negotiation by courageous and imaginative initiatives. The negotiation of an international code of conduct on the transfer of technology and UNCTAD's contribution to the revision of the Industrial Property System including the Paris Convention, are important landmarks. Both these negotiations are still going on but, whatever the final outcome, it cannot but be positive in transforming an unsatisfactory and inequitable regime. The initial focus was on the legal and economic aspects of technology transfer, but soon the programme embraced other major elements. UNCTAD's ideas on the reverse transfer of technology, including the possibilities of national and international action to offset and redress the damaging consequences to developing countries of the "brain drain", are again of a path-breaking character, even if the formidable difficulties to effective action are recognized. The addition of new major dimensions in the technology area, such as strategy for the technological transformation of developing countries, co-operative exchange of skilled manpower among the developing countries, new and emerging technologies and the fullest and freest possible access to technology in the public domain are again evidence of UNCTAD's dynamism and daring in charting the areas where the resistance and hostility of powerful interests are likely to remain very strong indeed in the years ahead. (A detailed history of the initiatives undertaken by UNCTAD with regard to the transfer of technology and other technology issues are contained in part Two, section V.)

The development of the ideas and policies in the areas of economic co-operation among developing countries (ECDC) and economic co-operation with socialist countries of Eastern Europe is treated in section D below for reasons stated therein. The problems relating to the least-developed countries (LDCs) is dealt with in section E "Homogeneity and differentiation".

D. UNCTAD and its progress towards universalism

In terms of membership and its aims and goals, UNCTAD's universality has been among its principal strengths. It has as its members all the three groups of states: developed market-economy countries, socialist countries of Eastern Europe and the Group of 77 and, since 1972, the People's Republic of China. It cannot and does not stand for or canvass any particular economic and social system—capitalism, socialism, statism or whatever. It is founded on the United Nations principle that the economic and social system of a country is entirely a matter of that country's choice, not for any external agency, national or international, to impose. It strives to improve and restructure the existing international economic system in such a way as to facilitate the full and effective participation of all States, irrespective of their economic and social systems, or levels of economic development. The major thrust of UNCTAD's endeavours, it hardly needs to be said, has been in relation to the developing countries' economic relations with developed market-economy countries which is understandable, given the latter countries' dominant place in the world economy and the former's very heavy dependence on them for trade, capital, technology, etc. And yet the other two dimensions are essential to a healthy world economy, namely:

(*a*) The fuller participation of the socialist countries of Eastern Europe in the world economy; and

(*b*) The development of the full potential of economic co-operation among the developing countries themselves (ECDC).

Analysis is made here of the factors which have helped and those that have hampered UNCTAD's progress in realizing its universalist goals.

THE FULLER PARTICIPATION OF THE SOCIALIST COUNTRIES OF EASTERN EUROPE IN THE WORLD ECONOMY

First, as regards the fuller participation of the socialist countries of Eastern Europe in the world economy, there are three elements in this which are subject to varying but interacting influences: East-West, East-South and intra-East. Intra-East (CMEA) economic exchanges are covered by a regime different from the present international trading system, though affecting and being affected by it to varying degrees. UNCTAD's attention to intra-East issues has been slight if any (as compared with its significant concern with intra-West economic exchanges and with their important effects on the world economy and the developing countries in particular). World trade being "an interconnected network", "repercussions in any one part are felt inevitably in all others". The negotiation and implementation of policies in East-West-South economic co-operation under UNCTAD's auspices have encountered several difficulties.

In the first place, economic co-operation with the socialist countries of Eastern Europe is particularly vulnerable to a deterioration in the political climate and a rise in international tensions. Variations in this climate, swinging from cold war to détente to renewed cold war, trade restrictions for non-economic reasons applied from time to time, recurrent recessions and monetary crises of varying depth, have been basic factors.

Secondly, in the UNCTAD machinery itself, Western countries have invariably attempted to stall or avoid discussions of East-West economic issues and to deal with them in other forums, not all within the United Nations system; this despite UNCTAD's clearly recognized competence and contributing capability in its comprehensive universal framework. This Western stand has been maintained, irrespective of the political climate; this stand has, however, been hardening with increased international tension.

Thirdly, developing countries themselves have not shown as much support for too deep an involvement by UNCTAD in East-West economic issues as they have in North-South issues, more particularly West-South issues, lest their own problems should otherwise receive reduced attention, and increased trade and credit facilities from the Western countries to the socialist countries of Eastern Europe should be at their own cost.

As regards East-South economic co-operation, both negative and positive factors have been operative. Among the negative factors should be mentioned the ideological/political hesitation of many developing countries to promote economic co-operation with socialist countries even in the 1960s. This attitude has now changed significantly. Over 100 developing countries have developed economic and commercial relations with the socialist countries of Eastern Europe. The principal reason has been the changed political perception on this issue. UNCTAD's conceptual and intergovernmental work (including studies, seminars and consultations) has also had some impact.

A second factor relates to the character and operating methods of the socialist system of foreign trade. For many years, the socialist system of planning, its State monopoly of foreign trade and the mechanisms of its foreign trade organizations and agencies have not been adequately known and understood, in part due to unfamiliarity with them and, in part, due to searching in the socialist economies for yardsticks, criteria and modalities of the market economy. This ideological/analytical attitude is steadily changing. UNCTAD has done a great deal, through its studies, deliberations in the Trade and Development Board sessional committees, confidential consultations between interested parties within the framework of the Trade and Development Board, seminars, expert groups and related technical assistance programmes, to disseminate information and promote understanding of these subjects.

A third issue which is no nearer to a solution now than it was in the 1960s is the demand for 0.7 per cent of Gross National Product (GNP) transfer of resources to developing countries from the socialist countries of Eastern Europe. Related to this are the developing countries' demands concerning the operation of the Special Fund of the International Investment Bank.

In spite of these obstacles, UNCTAD's record in East-South economic co-operation has been steadily progressing through studies, technical assistance and intergovernmental deliberations, pursuant to decisions taken in the first 15 years (i.e. Conference resolutions 15(II), 53(III) and 95(IV) and resolution 112(XIV) of the Trade and Development Board). Useful work has also been done with respect to the possibilities of a multilateral system of payments between socialist countries of Eastern Europe and developing countries, and of utilizing trade opportunities from the multilateral schemes of CMEA member countries.

Over the past 15 to 20 years extensive as well as intensive economic linkages have developed between the socialist countries of Eastern Europe and the market-economy countries (both developed and developing) through a wide variety of new forms and instruments, which are significant and innovative contributions to the institutional and legal modalities of a new international trading system, going beyond the traditional concepts of "free" trade and "market" forces and the GATT framework. UNCTAD's mandates in this field of East-West-South economic co-operation, in conjunction with its mandate in regard to principles and rules of an improved and universally applicable international trading system, present it with a most valuable opportunity to move forward in its universalist goals.

A word about the socialist countries of Eastern Europe *vis-à-vis* the international monetary system. Socialist countries do not take a significant part in the international monetary system (IMF-World Bank group), even if some of them are members. They partake in international money and capital markets and in intergovernmental loans and credits in varying degrees, but basically they remain outside the international monetary system, though much affected by it. This detracts fundamentally from its universality. UNCTAD studies and deliberations have drawn attention to this. The proposal to convene an international conference on international monetary issues under United Nations auspices, should it materialize, would provide an opportunity to remedy this defect. A matter for further study is what changes and adaptations in the present policies, rules and instruments would be required to facilitate the effective participation of the socialist countries of Eastern Europe in the international monetary system (a problem somewhat parallel to that faced in respect of the international trading system and one to which UNCTAD's intellectual and conceptual contribution could be historic). (Section VI of part Two deals in some detail with the nature and evolution of trade relations among countries having different economic and social systems.)

ECONOMIC CO-OPERATION AMONG DEVELOPING COUNTRIES (ECDC)

UNCTAD's philosophy and programme in relation to ECDC falls into two distinct but closely related elements: first, co-operation among developing countries in forging common positions and utilizing their improved leverage in negotiations with the developed countries; and, two, policies and programmes for establishing new and strengthening existing co-operation among themselves in trade, technology, finance and investment. The first, as noted elsewhere, has been an important contribution of UNCTAD since its inception. But it has only been during the second decade of UNCTAD—perhaps in the past seven to eight years—that the second element of ECDC has acquired new and impressive dimensions.

In the first 10 to 12 years, UNCTAD's efforts in ECDC consisted, for the large part, in providing technical assistance to regional and subregional integration schemes of developing countries, supported by secretariat research.

UNCTAD's ECDC role entered a new phase with the establishment of the ECDC Committee following the Mexico City Programme and the decision to concentrate on three main programmes, the global system of trade preferences (GSTP), Multinational Marketing Enterprises (MNMEs) and State Trading Organizations (STOs) in the wake of the Manila and the Arusha Programmes. Recently, projects in the area of finance and credit have been added to these priorities. It is clear, however, from the record of recent years that, despite considerable technical preparation and governmental deliberations, little progress has been made in any of these and that serious difficulties are encountered in UNCTAD. These difficulties are briefly: the dispersed and fragmented character of the Group of 77 machinery of ECDC and its lack of effective leadership and co-ordination; the absence of a permanent Group of 77 secretariat or technical core to assist member governments; major differences among developing countries as to the relative importance and priority of the diverse programme elements (South Bank, GSTP, etc.); a weakening of UNCTAD's leading role in the ECDC field within the United Nations system; the inadequacy of UNCTAD's regular and extra-budgetary resources; the failure of the UNCTAD secretariat to mobilize available resources for priority projects; and, last but not least, the controversy concerning the universality of the United Nations system in relation to the developing countries' demand that the role of the United Nations be limited to support measures of ECDC. (A detailed history of UNCTAD activities in the field of ECDC is contained in part Two, section VII.)

There has been a certain amount of criticism regarding the position taken by the developing countries. On the one hand, according to the critics, these countries call for the support of the international community and international institutions for ECDC programmes. Their demands on industrialized countries for aid, market access and industrial and economic readjustment entail changes in the latter countries' domestic structures and policies. At the same time, developing countries maintain that ECDC programmes are exclusively their affair and cannot be subject to comment or review in any international institution, including UNCTAD, but will be brought to them for support. This further overlooks the possibility that ECDC programmes could have an economic impact on other countries not parties to those programmes, who would have a legitimate interest in studying the possible effects of these programmes on their own economies, especially if they were also called upon to support them.

The concern of developing countries to be free to draw up their own ECDC programmes and to resolve their own regional and intra-regional differences of policies and interests (without the presence of powerful developed countries not averse to interfering in their counsels) is not only understandable, but is perhaps justified by historical experience. The big powers are not lacking in power or opportunities to determine the policies of developing countries by bilateral means, their control over international financial, trading and other institutions, and through international corporations and commercial banks. Given this power equation, developing countries' anxiety to be left alone to negotiate among themselves cannot be contested, subject to their securing subsequent international approval or support (as the case may be) to their programmes in UNCTAD and other institutions where they may have accepted legal obligations.

Developing countries are implementing a great number of ECDC measures in numerous channels and institutions—bilateral, multilateral, regional and sub-regional, much of this outside the framework of United Nations agencies, even though a number of United Nations agencies are involved in some of them directly or indirectly, substantially or marginally. This is not the place to evaluate the progress being made in ECDC in terms of the world economy or of the potential waiting to be tapped. We are concerned here with two specific issues: (*a*) how could UNCTAD effectively increase its ECDC contribution, which is an important element of its universality?, and (*b*) how far does the developing countries' position compromise UNCTAD's universality? The answer to the first would seem to depend in part on the answer to the second. Obviously, steps to overcome many of the limitations of UNCTAD cited earlier would have to come from the Group of 77. Nevertheless, a major step would be taken if the developing countries recognized the strictly defined but obviously legitimate interest of other countries in ECDC programmes in the UNCTAD framework, without any prejudice whatsoever to their autonomy to draw up and implement them.

UNCTAD's image as a universal United Nations organ and its ECDC role would both be enhanced if the residual differences on procedures and principles concerning the ECDC Committee and the meetings of the Group of 77 related thereto could be accommodated by all the groups of States concerned. It is a sad reflection that sterile and counter-productive issues have prevailed so long over substantive programmes of overriding urgency, creating a confrontational situation and casting a shadow over all of UNCTAD's activities. On the other hand, determined efforts to implement even one or two of the principal ECDC projects under UNCTAD auspices will give more credence to the oft-repeated charters of collective self-reliance and UNCTAD's universality.

E. Homogeneity versus differentiation of developing countries

A fundamental aspect of UNCTAD's philosophy, which cuts across nearly every area of its activity, relates to the homogeneity of the developing countries on the one hand and their differentiation on the other. A recurrent misconception is that UNCTAD does not take into account the divergent economic interests and the different levels of economic and industrial development of developing countries, but canvasses unrealistic and inappropriate global solutions which do not meet their needs. Since this kind of criticism can harm the institution's image and credibility, it is necessary to examine this in some detail.

First, as to the homogeneity of developing countries: a historic and epochal contribution of UNCTAD in 1964 to the evolution of world political economy was the creation of the Group of 77, a coalition for the first time of the world's developing countries, banding together, forging common positions and proposals and seeking to apply concerted leverage, so as to increase their bargaining power in the negotiations *vis-à-vis* the industrialized nations. The fact that this group has remained alive and strong and shown considerable unity in dealing with developed countries over the past 20 years, in the face of its own internal differences (political, economic, ideological) and of persistent and powerful pressures to break it up, is perhaps an enduring tribute to its historical validity and rightfulness.[7] The Group of 77 is not exclusively an UNCTAD phenomenon, though originating in it; it has become an important negotiating partner in nearly every international institution.

Western countries, by and large, and the socialist countries of Eastern Europe recognize the validity and usefulness of this grouping in international economic affairs; even when their support of many of its proposals is marginal and meagre.

---

[7] In the felicitous words of the Deputy Secretary-General of the Commonwealth Secretariat, Sir Peter Marshall, in his address to the Colloquium on North-South Negotiations, convened by the Quaker United Nations Office, Geneva, March 1984:

"One of the salient characteristics of the post-war world is the emergence on the international scene of a host of newly independent countries whose joint awareness of their problems, of their prospects and, indeed, of their survival, outweighs the manifest differences between them individually in circumstances of geography or of politics, or of economics, or of culture. A second salient characteristic is the expression of this joint awareness in the multilateral institutions which have grown up since the end of the Second World War, especially, but by no means exclusively, in the United Nations system. It is perhaps the combination of these characteristics which so baffles and disenchants more traditional opinion in the developed world."

They recognize that it has served to provide a focus on the essential issues and needs of the third world and channels for dialogue and negotiation—channels which for over 120 member nations are far from easy to set up on a global scale. The United States has often been the exception in this regard, and its position towards the Group and its activities has varied from indifference and tolerance to negativism and hostility. By virtue of its leading world position, it has influenced the other Western countries negatively on many issues of substance and has blocked or diluted progress on them.

Other Western countries have, from time to time, succeeded in moving the United States to less negative policies, but such success has been meagre. And in the past three years or so, they have evinced a disturbing inability or unwillingness to take a more conciliatory line towards the Group of 77 different from the leader of their own group. The socialist countries of Eastern Europe have not been effective in changing this situation, because they seem primarily concerned with their own East-West and East-South issues in UNCTAD. In any evaluation of the North-South dialogue, including that in UNCTAD, failure to recognize or mention these various factors in clear and candid terms would be a serious omission. However, a positive change in United States attitudes and policies, (brought about whether by its taking a less short-sighted view of its interests and not bringing global political and strategic considerations to the North-South issues in the United Nations, by the the persuasion of its allies, by the pressures of the Group of 77 or the socialist countries of Eastern Europe, by a combination of one or more of these factors, or by the inexorable march of events) is almost a *sine qua non* for significant progress on the global scene.

The Group of 77 is now facing a more serious threat to its unity than perhaps at any time since its emergence: geopolitical pressures; the depth of the economic and financial crisis, and the Group's resulting sharply aggravated dependence on external financial resources; disenchantment with the NIEO and post-NIEO results of multilateral negotiations in the past decade, combined with scepticism as to the advisability of the negotiating modalities so far pursued; and, last but not least, the relatively modest (in relation to both expectations and potentials) progress in mobilizing its own resources for collective self-reliance. The way out of these difficulties lies in continued and determined action over time, including the pursuit—in UNCTAD and other forums—in the short and medium term of more specific and concrete negotiating packages and trade-offs, more flexible coalitions (cutting across group lines) of developed and developing countries, greater utilization of co-operative potentials with the socialist countries of Eastern Europe, and other similar measures but all within a firm (but not rigid) framework of unity. The response is not for the Group of 77 to disband. Clearly, if the member countries do not hang together, they will hang separately.

Within the framework of united action, differentiation has been applied in a number of UNCTAD policies and recommendations. In the first place, the category of the least developed countries has received special recognition and consideration in UNCTAD right from the beginning and has gathered momentum since. In the early years, the importance of non-discrimination among the developing countries was also equally stressed by the developing countries, reflecting the basic difficulty of differentiation; the fear that it might cause disunity in their ranks, without developed countries offering real or substantial benefits to the least developed. This position changed from UNCTAD II onwards, and the need for special measures in their favour was agreed. It is not necessary here to go over the details of the Immediate Action Programme and the Substantial New Programme of Action, and the series of special measures which emerged from the United Nations Conference on the Least Developed Countries held under UNCTAD auspices. The commitment by developed countries to provide 0.15 per cent of their GNP to them, special action to ease their debt burdens, the gradual acceptance of a "least-developed-nation-favoured" clause in the North-South context, the additional concessions offered to their products under GSP schemes over and above those accorded to other developing counties, payment by donors of their contributions to the Common Fund for Commodities special quotas in commodity agreements, implementation and monitoring of their programmes on a country-by-country basis—these are worth listing. Likewise, considerable action to improve the lot of the land-locked developing countries has also been taken, the first legal instrument negotiated under UNCTAD. The problems of island developing countries are under continuing study. For good reasons, many governments recognize the need for caution against the proliferation of additional categories of developing countries, given the limited resources and the overriding common interests of developing countries. (A more detailed history of UNCTAD activities in relation to the least developed, the land-locked and the island developing countries is contained in part Two, section VIII.)

In the field of development finance, while UNCTAD has pursued certain objectives and targets for the benefit of developing countries as a whole (the 1.0 per cent aid target, including 0.7 per cent ODA, and easier terms and conditions of aid), the differential needs of not only the least developed countries, as noted above, but of the low income and the middle income developing countries more dependent respectively on ODA and international capital markets have also been recognized.

Again, in the allocation of ODA the search for global targets and policies in UNCTAD has never militated against regional financial assistance programmes, as under the Yaoundé and Lomé Conventions, regional development banks and the like.

As regards external debt, UNCTAD's analysis of its origins and growth has been remarkable for its far-sightedness and accuracy, just as UNCTAD's prognostication of its serious aggravation was prophetic and Cassandra-like—a crisis whose nature and serious dimensions are not adequately recognized by the creditor countries and international financial institutions even to this day. While UNCTAD has been pleading for far-reaching and comprehensive solutions to this situation (comprising massive resource transfers, debt cancellation, moratoria, additional facilities to take care of structural adjustment needs, relaxation of conditionality, an independent commission on international indebtedness and the like), because piecemeal and small measures would simply not do, it has also been cognizant of and provided specific ideas for solutions to the different types of debt situations faced by the above-mentioned categories of developing countries.

UNCTAD's endeavours to bring about a reform of the international monetary system do not and cannot differentiate between the developing countries, but include measures which would benefit the third world as a whole, a larger voice in the decision-making machinery, the "link", larger allocations of SDRs, assigning to SDR, the role of the key international reserve currency and changed policies of IMF, so as to take adequately into account developmental dimensions in the international monetary system.

A point of importance in the discussion on differentiation is that no single measure can bring (direct) benefit to each and every developing country, let alone equality of benefit for all. For this reason, it is essential to have comprehensive programmes embracing as many areas of interest as possible to benefit the greatest number of countries. Equally, it is essential to endeavour to distribute the advantages accruing under any one measure or programme among all the countries concerned, without in that process distorting or destroying the programme itself. This is seen in areas relating to commodities, manufactures, development finance and the least-developed countries.

The heavy dependence of a very large number of developing countries on the export of commodities and the impact of the weakness of this sector on their ability to cope with their development problems clearly point to this area as one requiring major restructuring for the benefit of most developing countries. Commodity agreements for any one commodity would obviously benefit (directly) only a small number of exporting countries; hence, an integrated and comprehensive coverage of commodities. The strong pressures from many countries to include additional products in the Integrated Programme for Commodities (IPC) are a reflection of this need. Equally, the great importance attached to the "second window" of the Common Fund, particularly by the African countries, evidenced their desire, supported by other developing countries, to benefit from the institution. If all the principal IPC elements were effectively implemented, benefit would accrue to the great majority of developing countries both directly and indirectly.

Similar considerations have played a part in the GSP. Admittedly, sharp differences of view and interest came to the fore in UNCTAD during the GSP negotiating process among developing countries. A large number of them realized that, given their rudimentary industrial structure, they would derive little or no benefit from the GSP. Therefore, developing countries as a whole exerted continuing pressure for the inclusion in the GSP of dutiable processed and semi-processed agricultural products to the greatest extent possible. In principle, this was agreed to, but in practice coverage of processed and semi-processed goods was totally unsatisfactory: domestic agricultural protectionism, particularly in EEC, was the principal hurdle; the pretext that improvements in such coverage would harm their Lomé partners (the African, Pacific and Caribbean (ACP) Countries) was fairly systematically used. Another divisive issue was that of special preferences enjoyed by a number of developing countries in EEC under the Yaoundé and the Lomé Conventions and under the Commonwealth preferential system. Before the United Kingdom joined EEC, one of the difficult negotiations centred around this issue for years even after the GSP became operative. Developing countries as a group, after intense debate, agreed that under the GSP these beneficiaries of special preferences should receive at least equivalent advantages to compensate them for sharing these preferences with other developing countries. This formula has worked satisfactorily on the whole. In the event, however, the special regime of financial and other assistance and preferences embodied in the Lomé Convention, applicable to over 60 developing countries of the ACP group, has been recognized and accepted by other developing countries not ACP members.

Yet another important aspect of differentiation of developing countries is the "graduation" issue, which has assumed great importance, especially within the GATT framework and MTN-related codes and decisions, and under whose guise measures of discrimination and restriction of the GSP, as well as most-favoured-nation (MFN) benefits, are being unilaterally applied. The preference schemes of the United States, EEC, Japan and others apply the "graduation" principle by various means, viz. competitive needs criteria, maximum percentage limits, quotas and the like, whereby countries taking shares of the preferential market in products larger than determined under the criteria are denied preferential treatment for their products. The argument is that these countries have developed a competitive export capability, have "graduated" and are not entitled to preferential treatment. On the basis of a provision in the Enabling Clause of the GATT MTN decision, which stated that developing countries could accept greater obligations with the progressive development of their economies and improvements in their trade situations, support is being sought for "graduation" and for an increasing measure of reciprocity by developing countries in trade negotiations with developed countries in the form of concessions as well as compliance with the GATT codes and obligations. Developing countries have rejected "graduation" in principle, but have had to tolerate it in practice.

As a general principle, it is unexceptionable that a category of developing countries should not qualify for differential or preferential treatment if they cease to be developing.[8] The criteria applied, however, are far from clear: is it per capita income, per capita export of manufactures, share of manufactures in exports, share of manufacturing in GDP or a composite criterion? The real issue is whether the concept of "graduation" is relevant to the situation that confronts the trade of developing countries with the industrialized countries. It is less a question of preferential treatment *vis-à-vis* third parties in the markets of developing countries, and more a question of competition *vis-à-vis* domestic industries. The extent to which developing countries which are successful in gaining significant market shares in specific products/sectors in industrialized countries (it does not matter whether preferential or non-preferential) are denied market access by restrictionist and protectionist measures points to the real nature of the problem.

A word might be added on the possible effect of a contractual or legal acceptance of a category of "graduated" developing countries—should it arise—on the Group of 77: it would seriously divide and weaken the Group, as it has existed and operated thus far, and cause serious damage to the already limited negotiating strength of the "graduates" and, even more, to other members of the Group.

The foregoing paragraphs consider issues of differentiation among developing countries with respect to policies calling for action by developed countries.

---

[8] See the report of the Secretary-General of UNCTAD to UNCTAD VI: *"Development and recovery: the realities of the new interdependence."* (*Op. cit.*, para. 79).

Differentiation in the ECDC context, which is of crucial importance for success, has also received substantial attention in UNCTAD programmes and studies.[9]

This differentiation, often cited as a divisive factor which could undermine their mutual co-operation, holds forth the greatest promise of co-operation in trade (including manufactures, raw materials and minerals), technology skilled manpower, investment, finance and other fields, provided they forge the necessary linkages and create effective institutions and mechanisms to that end, not simply leaving them to market forces alone. The complementarities and mutually advantageous opportunities for exchanges are immense. Here again, it is essential to devise measures of benefit to all of them, especially the least developed and weaker developing countries. Within the regional and subregional economic groupings, special measures to protect and promote the industry and exports of the weaker partners are an essential ingredient, as are measures of assistance in such financial institutions and payments arrangements—and UNCTAD is an active partner in these endeavours. At the intra-regional level, in connection with the GSTP programme, the principles and guidelines for the negotiations take full cognizance of these concerns and needs.

Yet another dimension to differentiation relates to the harmonization and adaptation, where necessary, of the regional and subregional ECDC programmes on the one hand and the global inter-regional programmes on the other. The issues involved are numerous indeed and bristle with complexities and differences—political, economic and, in many cases, simply technical; and their resolution calls for much time, patience, technical expertise and mutual accommodation: qualities which, given the necessary political thrust and impetus, can develop and grow steadily with experience and some first successes. UNCTAD at both intergovernmental and secretariat levels is aware of these great challenges and opportunities.

This discussion would be incomplete without a reference to the differentiation of the oil-exporting from the non-oil-exporting developing countries. UNCTAD analyses and recommendations deal with the diverse economic impacts of this differentiation. They recognize the negative effect of high oil prices on the balance of payments of oil-importing developing countries and also the positive effect of the financial assistance from the oil-exporting countries, which in many cases exceeds 0.7 or 1.0 per cent of the GNP, and of the recycling of their surplus funds. The UNCTAD secretariat does not subscribe to the view which blames high petroleum prices as the main reason for world inflation and the developing countries' payments crisis. Recognition is made of the exhaustible and finite nature of their oil resources, of the damaging eroding effects of inflation in industrialized countries on their foreign exchange assets and, above all, of the fact that they are developing countries with their own urgent needs. Equally, attention has been repeatedly drawn

---

[9] See the reports of the Secretary-General of UNCTAD to UNCTAD IV, *New directions and the structures for trade and development* (TD/183/Rev.1) (United Nations publication, Sales No. E.77.II.D.1), paras. 154-161, to UNCTAD V, *Restructuring the international economic framework* (TD/221/Rev.1) (United Nations publication, Sales No. E.79.II.D.12), paras. 65-73, and to UNCTAD VI. *Development and Recovery ... op. cit.*, paras. 72-75, for a most cogent and admirable presentation of these issues.

to the considerable additional opportunities of South-South financial co-operation, as yet untapped.

F. UNCTAD and developing countries' domestic economic policies

There has frequently been criticism that UNCTAD's approach to trade and development issues has been unilateral and biased, because it has concentrated most of its efforts to demands on developed countries, and has scarcely given any attention to the domestic economic policies of developing countries or to their obligations in the area of international economic co-operation. There is perhaps a grain of truth in this criticism. Basically, however, such a view tends to overlook a number of important considerations. In the first place, UNCTAD's principal responsibility (or competence) is in the area of international economic co-operation, i.e. the external environment in which developing countries pursue their developmental efforts, and it is reasonable, therefore, for UNCTAD to concentrate first and foremost on that task, all the more so given its limited resources.

Secondly, developing countries have remained somewhat sensitive about any international institution (UNCTAD included, despite its special place in their affections) scrutinizing their domestic development and related economic programmes and policies in a multilateral forum, giving rise to the possibility of pressures in favour of one or other pattern of development or policy.

Thirdly, most of the internal development planning, priorities and policies, even if they entail some external aspects, are essentially matters for decision at the national level, and do not fall into the category of problems calling for international negotiation. Questions arise such as: should there be any planning of development or should the economy be left entirely free to private enterprise? In planning, what rates of growth; what ratios of capital formation to GDP; what roles to assign to governmental and private sectors in aggregate resource allocation, as well as in particular sectors of industry, power, agriculture, mining, transport, etc.; what priorities over time to heavy versus light industry, agriculture versus industry, *ad nauseum*? It is for the country concerned to take these decisions in the light of its political and socio-economic circumstances and available resources; and not for any international agency in a multilateral framework to seek to determine, particularly when such issues lend themselves to ideological and political disputations among the big powers.

This does not mean, however, that developing countries are not receptive to advice and assistance at the international level. Indeed, all the extensive technical and financial assistance offered to developing countries by international institutions, including UNCTAD, at the national level (and where feasible even at regional, subregional and interregional levels) in the areas of planning and development over the years answers the point behind the criticism.

UNCTAD has from its very origin been emphasizing that the primary responsibility for the economic development of developing countries is their own, and that development calls for the transformation of their social and economic structures and for a more equitable order of opportunity and distribution, making possible a better development of human resources. But a favourable international environment which would provide aid and access to markets and technology is a critical requirement, if developing countries are not to be thrown back upon their own domestic resources or to be obliged to accept low growth rates. The major reports and addresses of the three Secretaries-General of UNCTAD, whose contributions to the evolution of UNCTAD philosophy have been seminal, would abundantly bear this out.[10]

Developing countries themselves have, at summits and other high level meetings, declared their primary responsibility for economic development, while seeking international assistance, and have committed themselves to pursuing domestic policies for a more just and efficient internal socio-economic order according to their own circumstances and needs, as seen in the Declarations of the Heads of State or Government of the Non-Aligned Countries as, for example, in the Algiers, Lima, Manila, Arusha and Buenos Aires declarations of the Group of 77, and in the Mexico, Manila and Caracas ECDC programmes.

It would be relevant to state briefly UNCTAD's own contribution in this area over the years. For several initial years, secretariat reports on mobilization of domestic resources of developing countries were regularly on the agenda of the Committee on Invisibles and Financing related to Trade (CIFT), as well as the Trade and Development Board. Several individual country studies on balance of payments and mechanisms of adjustment, aid, debt and development finance related to their economic development plans, have been carried out, not omitting domestic fiscal aspects.

Economic performance, in particular the efforts made by developing countries to mobilize internal resources, is recognized as an important element of international development policy and as a legitimate concern of aid-giving countries and institutions for the effective use of external resources. UNCTAD studies analysed quantitative and qualitative indicators for assessing the efforts of developing countries in mobilizing and using internal resources effectively. These studies pointed to their considerable efforts and results, as reflected in the increased importance and improved quality of planning as an indispensable tool, and in the steady rise in the investment and savings ratio until after the 1970s up to the early 1980s. The negative effects of a hostile economic external environment on their self-help efforts have also emerged prominently from these studies.

UNCTAD's contribution in the field of insurance, while dealing with external aspects such as retention of and control over funds in developing countries and saving foreign exchange, has perhaps been more important in internal aspects of the subject such as building up domestic insurance laws, institutions and skilled personnel, and mobilizing domestic funds in developing countries.

Likewise, with regard to developing countries' policies of protection of domestic industries, UNCTAD has not been unaware that some of these policies may not be conducive to efficiency and sound resource allocation, besides hindering competitiveness in external markets. The limitations of an essentially import substitution policy have been stressed from the very beginning. The force of an infant-

---

[10] Dr. Prebisch has been fighting all his life for this philosophy. Most recently, Mr. Gamani Corea has treated this set of issues with admirable clarity in his report to UNCTAD VI: *op. cit.*, chap. II, paras. 91-94.

industry argument cannot, however, be contested in the case of developing countries. Furthermore, for excessive levels of protection which might be required in small countries with domestic markets, the solution lies in the creation of larger, viable markets through regional and subregional trading arrangements and multinational industrial enterprises. UNCTAD has given its support to these programmes. It must also be noted that developing countries employ tariffs and quantitative import restrictions as instruments of macro-economic policy, allocating scarce foreign and domestic resources to priority areas of development. Given their ever-growing import demand, which is far in excess of their export earnings and other available foreign sources (causing structural long-term payments deficits), there is no risk that policies of developing countries will have a restrictive effect on the aggregate level of world trade. Any changes in their import composition would be in response to developmental requirements, not to an idealist dedication to freer trade. Demands for reciprocal concessions in tariff and non-tariff areas in developing countries tend to miss these points. However, these countries take the initiative themselves from time to time to liberalize their protective measures—in order to introduce elements of competition, restrain inflation, meet consumer needs, and finally as some form of *quid pro quo* in trade negotiations.

Developing countries are acutely conscious of the urgent need of export promotion and of improving the quality and competitiveness of their products in international markets. They do not stand in need of sermons on the merits of export-oriented policies, and open trading systems. They are, however, puzzled and daunted by the present situation and future prospect: with their structural maladjustments, social rigidities and protectionist pressures, developed countries are either not ready or not able to absorb the exports of even half a dozen so-called newly industrializing countries (NICs) what disaster would await others if they, too, in large numbers, went in a big way for export-oriented investments and exports? Hence, UNCTAD has been underlining the nexus of structural adjustment and market access in the correct perspective.

In this connection the technical assistance in trade promotion and marketing provided by the International Trade Centre UNCTAD/GATT is of particular importance. It is also relevant to refer to UNCTAD's work in the field of trade facilitation, i.e. assistance in the simplification and rationalization of trade procedures and documents in developing countries—a contribution to both internal and external policies.

UNCTAD's studies on various subjects in the area of environment are useful inputs to the formation of domestic economic policies of developing countries. These relate to self-reliant approaches in resource utilization, environmental aspects of non-renewable resources and pricing of natural resources, reafforestation and conservation, and environmental policies overall and in product sectors in relation to the needs of international trade.

Mention should also be made of UNCTAD's in-depth examination of the economies of each of the least developed countries in connection with the United Nations Conference concerning them, the Substantial New Programme of Action and the follow-up activities in financial and technical assistance to this group of countries. A principal new accent in this work is the recognition of the responsibility of the least developed countries themselves.

UNCTAD's technical assistance and expert advice in a number of areas, including development finance and external debt, commercial policy, ECDC, technology, shipping, etc., has involved the examination of internal economic policies of developing countries, even when UNCTAD cannot wield the leverage of international institutions dispensing large amounts of aid.

Thus, while UNCTAD's record is admittedly not one to be defensive about, some more attention and transparency would redound to the benefit of UNCTAD as an institution, even as it would to the developing countries themselves which, in the framework of UNCTAD, can expect to receive an understanding and appreciation of their developmental needs and aspirations equal at least to that elsewhere.

G. Institutional aspects

UNCTAD's institutional aspects can be conveniently dealt with under three principal headings: (a) internal, (b) external and (c) the role of the Secretary-General of UNCTAD.

Under "internal" the following points are treated: the periodic Conference, the Trade and Development Board, its principal Committees and other subsidiary bodies, negotiating conferences and groups; their evolution since 1964 and some of the issues arising therefrom. Under "external" some of the more important points relating to the place of UNCTAD in the United Nations system, in particular its relationship with the General Assembly and other institutions, including specialized agencies, viz. IMF, the World Bank, the Food and Agriculture Organization of the United Nations (FAO), and the World Intellectual Property Organization (WIPO), as well as GATT, the United Nations Industrial Development Organization (UNIDO) and the regional commissions are touched upon. The role of the Secretary-General of UNCTAD, highly important in both internal and external aspects, is treated in a separate section.

INTERNAL ASPECTS: EVOLUTION OF UNCTAD'S INSTITUTIONAL MACHINERY

Since its establishment in 1964 the machinery of UNCTAD has grown to impressive dimensions, consisting of the Conference as the apex, the Trade and Development Board and its main Committees, and a number of continuing or *ad hoc* intergovernmental groups, expert groups, special or negotiating conferences, and the like. An organizational chart of UNCTAD's institutional machinery is contained in part Four. Starting with the Trade and Development Board, and three permanent Committees, i.e. on commodities, manufactures and invisibles and financing related to trade (as provided for in General Assembly resolution 1995 (XIX), the Board at its first session in 1965 not only set up these three Committees and their terms of reference but a fourth one, the Committee on Shipping. Then, years later, came other Committees: those respectively on preferences, technology, and economic co-operation among developing countries. The process of setting up expert groups, sessional committees, *ad hoc* intergovernmental groups and working groups over a period of time represented a complex process of negotiation within UNCTAD, involving the extension and definition of new areas of study, deliberation and negotiation, and the dynamic interpretation and elaboration of ideas and proposals for trade and development, to mention just a few: there were groups for each of the international development strategies; for supplementary finance, debt operations and international monetary reform; for shipping legislation, and flags of registry, for reverse transfer of technology, for restrictive business practices and for the Integrated Programme for Commodities (IPC), and a sessional Committee of the Trade and Development Board for East-West-South economic issues. The large number of such groups, and their several sessions over years, reflected the evolution of UNCTAD's mandates, competence and negotiating responsibilities. These, in turn, led to special or negotiating conferences, as on the Common Fund, the international code of conduct on the transfer of technology, the code on liner conferences, the code on restrictive business practices, the code on multi-modal transport of goods, and United Nations on the least developed countries, not to mention a number of commodity conferences under UNCTAD both within and outside the IPC framework.

The Conference

First, a word about the periodic Conference itself. The periodic Conference, meeting once every three or four years, has remained a major event in the trade and development dialogue. It is conventional wisdom either to put these Conferences down as failures in terms of the results attained or to fault them for raising undue and unrealistic hopes and expectations. Developing countries tend to take the first view with much justification, but also because admission of success would reduce incentives to further results. Developed countries wish to describe every Conference as successful and fruitful, while grudgingly admitting the scope for further progress, but combined with them a comment that the periodic Conference raises false hopes of big breakthroughs. Some of them would be happy to do away altogether with this periodic event, which, in their view, invariably builds up considerable political pressure and focus; they would prefer to have in its place Ministerial meetings of the Trade and Development Board from time to time to provide the political thrust, with the permanent machinery grappling with the real tasks.

Experience of the six sessions of the Conference, however, would on the whole seem to underline the immense value of the Conference not only for the significant attention and focus at a high political level which it brings to trade and development issues, but also for its considerable intangible and pervasive results. Even when specific or dramatic results cannot be claimed for each session such as, for example, the establishment of UNCTAD itself at the first Conference, the generalized system of preferences (GSP) at the second, the Charter of Economic Rights and Duties, and emphasis on the interdependence of trade, money and finance at the third session, and the Integrated Programme for Commodities (IPC) and the Common Fund at the fourth. This enumeration is by no means comprehensive—each session has provided a measure of impetus to overall progress and movement, even if such impetus has been very small. And yet, without such a periodic event, even this small amount of progress might not have been realized. The periodic Conferences should be seen not as isolated events but as important stages in the on-going process of dialogue and negotiation on the central issues of trade and development and international economic relations.

The institutional aspects of UNCTAD have, from its origin, been the subject of almost continuing consideration by the Conference and the Board, as well as by its Secretary-General. While the first decade was one of building the institutional framework, the infrastructure, in conjunction with the generation of ideas and the accumulation of expertise, steps were also taken to adapt the institution to changing conditions. In this brief review, attention is drawn to five specific decisions and their impact:

(*a*) The decision for UNCTAD to provide technical assistance in its area of competence;

(*b*) The decision taken by UNCTAD III at Santiago in 1972 to enlarge the Board's membership and make the main Committees open-ended;

(*c*) The decision to abolish the seven-member Advisory Committee to the Board and to the Committee on Commodities;

(*d*) Resolution 90 (IV) adopted by UNCTAD IV in Nairobi (1976) which, besides recommending a number of measures to improve the efficiency of the Trade and Development Board and the Committees, recommended to the United Nations General Assembly the strengthening of UNCTAD's role, not only by increased budgetary resources but also by a greater degree of flexibility in budgetary, administrative and personnel matters; and

(*e*) Resolution 114 (V) adopted at UNCTAD V in Manila (1979), on institutional aspects of UNCTAD, strengthening its role in the United Nations system and seeking to restructure and rationalize its machinery.

UNCTAD's role in the provision of technical assistance

Resolution 1995 (XIX) did not make any reference to the possibility of UNCTAD providing technical assistance to developing countries. This lacuna was made good by decisions of the Trade and Development Board taken in 1966 and 1967 (resolutions 21 (IV) and 44 (VII)). Since then, UNCTAD's technical assistance programmes have grown steadily in several areas, taking UNCTAD activities to the field in developing countries. It must nevertheless be stressed that the resources at UNCTAD's disposal for this purpose are in no way commensurate with the magnitude and range of its requirements. Significant augmentation of UNDP and extra-budgetary resources would serve to increase UNCTAD's effectiveness in carrying its ideas and policies to the field. (A detailed description of UNCTAD's activities in the field of technical co-operation is contained in part Three, section I, "Operational activities".)

Increased participation in the Trade and Development Board and the Committees

An important decision was taken by UNCTAD III at Santiago (in resolution 80 (III)) to raise the Trade and Development Board's membership from 55 to 68 and to make the main Committees open-ended so that all member States of UNCTAD could participate if they so wished. The reason was principally the desire of developing countries for broader participation in the UNCTAD machinery. It is debatable, however, whether it has resulted in wider and more active and productive participation of member governments, especially of developing countries, and in the more efficient performance of the Trade and Development Board and the Committees. Membership being had for the asking, the incentive to acquire it and make an effective input not only for the member country concerned but also for the geographical group which it represented, diminished, and the process seems to have detracted significantly from the value or importance of committee membership. The perennial inadequacy of manpower and substantive resources of developing countries has not served to improve the situation.

The Advisory Committee to the Board and to the Committee on Commodities

A brief reference to the Advisory Committee to the Board and to the Committee on Commodities is also of particular relevance. This was a seven-member body set up by the Trade and Development Board at its first session in 1965 to take over the functions of the Interim Co-ordinating Committee for International Commodity Arrangements and to advise the Board, the Committee on Commodities and the Secretary-General of UNCTAD concerning not only commodity arrangements but also any other matters that might be referred to it. This Committee was abolished by the Trade and Development Board after a number of years. During its existence, its members included a number of distinguished development and trade economists and experienced negotiators; however, its contribution did not quite measure up to expectations, largely through no fault of its own. Neither the Secretary-General of UNCTAD nor the Board nor the Committee on Commodities felt impelled, in the then prevailing climate, to entrust the Committee with any challenging or trouble-shooting or specific think-tank or brainstorming tasks, despite the eminent suitability and expressed readiness of some of its members to perform these duties. In retrospect, and looking to the future—a future more complex and difficult than the past—one could consider whether a small group of independent persons of outstanding and distinguished political, academic and business backgrounds would not provide extremely valuable advice to the Secretary-General of UNCTAD as well as the institution itself, provided such a group was chosen with flexibility by rotation and co-option as needed, and met for a sufficient duration (with adequate secretariat preparation) with specific terms of reference.

Institutional issues

Decision 90 (IV) adopted at the fourth session of the Conference on institutional issues was an important landmark which recognized UNCTAD's principal role in the area of international economic co-operation and development, and was a positive response to the Secretary-General of UNCTAD's valuable analysis and suggestions (chapter IV of his report to the Conference). The *Ad Hoc* Committee on Restructuring the Economic and Social Sectors of the United Nations System, which was then in the midst of its labours and finished its report in autumn 1977, fully endorsed the Nairobi decision, as did the General Assembly at both its 1976 and 1977 sessions. Regrettably, however, little action adequately to implement the decision followed, a failure which had unfortunate consequences for UNCTAD, both externally and internally. These very issues and concerns came once again before UNCTAD V at Manila in 1979, resulting in resolution 114 (V), comprising a renewed and even stronger recognition of UNCTAD's central role and a variety of measures for rationalizing the UNCTAD structure.

By the end of the 1970s, it had become increasingly evident that what was required was more extensive and purposeful adaptation of the UNCTAD structure and operating procedures.

The growth in number and variety of UNCTAD bodies, even when this occurred as a genuine response to the unfolding requirements, has given rise to several problems:

It has imposed heavy and often insupportable strains on member governments, especially of the developing countries themselves which have taken the lead in setting up such bodies;

It has exceeded the substantive, technical and logistical resources of the secretariat and strained its budgets;

The concrete results of the meetings and conferences are felt to be far from commensurate with the efforts entailed;

It has led to proliferation and overlapping of activities within UNCTAD bodies themselves;

It has impaired the effectiveness of the permanent Committees and the Trade and Development Board, especially the latter's leadership and co-ordinating function.

The Secretary-General of UNCTAD and the Board have been well aware of these factors and have had them under consideration for some years. It is no surprise that as the institution's activities and operations grow, the need arises for taking stock and introducing reforms aiming at rationalization and restructuring. Pursuant to resolution 114 (V) at Manila, the *Ad Hoc* Intergovernmental Committee on the Rationalization of UNCTAD's Group Machinery considered in 1980 a number of proposals presented by the Group of 77, Group B and Group D, many of which had some common elements. The suggestions themselves, understandably neither dramatic nor original, included the following: strengthening the leadership and co-ordinating function of the Trade and Development Board; making the Committees more effective, especially in their negotiating functions; improved consultations by the Secretary-General of UNCTAD with Governments and regional groups as well as with the bureau of the Board, of its subsidiary bodies, and of the negotiating conferences; control of documentation; a stronger role for the Secretary-General of UNCTAD in internal secretariat management, policy guidance, and co-ordination and improvement of evaluation within the secretariat. Regarding the Board, among the suggestions made was a regular Ministerial Board session once in two years with a limited agenda and, as regards committees, consolidation of one or more of them, e.g. Trade and Technology (for combining manufactures, commodities and technology) or, alternatively, the concentration of the main sessions of the Committees during a certain time of the year, immediately preceding a session of the Board.

The Trade and Development Board took little if any action on these proposals mainly because of the reluctance of member governments to come to grips with them, and after 1981 due to their preoccupation with on-going activities and preparations for UNCTAD VI in 1983. The Secretary-General of UNCTAD, however, continued to stress the need for measures of rationalization and restructuring of UNCTAD machinery not in the narrow budgetary, logistical and mandates-meetings-and-negotiations-cutting terms, in which some of the major industrial powers see the possibilities, but in the context of the need for larger resources, flexibility in operational methods and structural adaptation of an institution which is the principal organ of the General Assembly in the area of international economic co-operation. It is facile and fashionable to talk of wasteful meetings and documentation, but not necessarily wise or responsible.

UNCTAD's 20 years point to one important conclusion concerning mandates and intergovernmental bodies: to establish any and every one of them has been a major effort in overcoming the resistance of developed countries. These gains could be lost by hasty and ill-considered measures put forward in the name of efficiency and rationalization. It would, therefore, seem advisable to adopt a gradual, step-by-step approach to the restructuring of UNCTAD—ensuring at the same time the willingness of member governments to make substantive progress.

External aspects: relationship with the General Assembly, and other United Nations bodies and specialized agencies

UNCTAD as the principal organ of the General Assembly

At UNCTAD I a controversial negotiating point was whether UNCTAD should be an organ of the General Assembly or of the Economic and Social Council (ECOSOC). Western countries, concerned with preserving and reinforcing the Charter role and co-ordinating responsibilities of ECOSOC, made the utmost effort to ensure that UNCTAD should become a subsidiary body of ECOSOC. Developing countries insisted, with success as it turned out, on having UNCTAD as an organ of the General Assembly, principally because ECOSOC membership was limited and unrepresentative, its efforts relating to developing country problems were marginal and ineffective, and the political support and authority of the highest and most democratic United Nations body, the General Assembly—were considered indispensable for promoting the cause of economic development and international economic co-operation. In retrospect, the decision embodied in resolution 1995 (XIX) appears well taken. Apprehensions that a powerful and unrepresentative ECOSOC would frustrate and foil developing countries' initiatives in the United Nations proved unfounded. The enlargement of ECOSOC membership (by Charter amendment) made little difference if any either to the thrust which the Charter organ gave to economic development and international economic co-operation or to its own leadership and co-ordinating role. ECOSOC reviews of UNCTAD Conference and Trade and Development Board reports provided for in resolution 1995 (XIX) were useful, if tame and tiresome, while the addresses by the Secretary-General of UNCTAD were among the highlights. At the same time, it should be stressed that UNCTAD's direct relationship to the General Assembly alone made possible the latter's consistent political and substantive support to UNCTAD over the years, and the nurturing and nourishing of the institution to its present position. This is part of the continuing political process of democratization of international institutions, a process whereby newly independent and developing third world countries began to focus the attention and efforts of the international community on the all important problem of economic development. The increasing concern of the General Assembly with economic development issues from the early

1960s, and its sharply accelerated preoccupation with them since 1974 in the NIEO and its follow-up activities, reflects the same process, with UNCTAD playing a central role.

Initiatives by the General Assembly to conduct economic negotiations itself directly, reflected in its short-lived Committee of the Whole, and the proposed (now static) global negotiations, have thus far made little headway. The uncertain prospects for the launching of global negotiations thus increase all the more the importance of UNCTAD as the General Assembly's arm in the years ahead. Even if global negotiations of one kind or another are conducted directly by the General Assembly, UNCTAD's tasks are unlikely to become less challenging or important. As in the past, the General Assembly is likely to delegate to UNCTAD major issues for study, examination and negotiation at a level of substantive detail and depth, for which UNCTAD is particularly equipped.

Resolution 1995 (XIX) establishing UNCTAD envisaged, albeit somewhat vaguely and in the distant future, the evolution of the institution towards that of an International Trade Organization (ITO), a goal much discussed but not accepted at UNCTAD I. In the 1970s, despite some renewed attempts to consider this idea, with UNCTAD taking on large new areas in the field of trade, finance, money, technology, shipping, etc., efforts to transform UNCTAD into a sectoral trade organization faded away. UNCTAD has now become a *de facto* comprehensive trade and development organization. A great deal would perhaps be lost by seeking to revert or transform it to the position of a trade agency, as is recognized by member States. Developing countries propose from time to time that the General Assembly should formally and *de jure* transform or label UNCTAD as a comprehensive trade and development organization (as proposed at UNCTAD VI), but the move seems to be lacking steam. UNCTAD has thus remained the principal subsidiary organ of the General Assembly without seeking the autonomous status of a specialized agency.

The foregoing analysis underlines the wisdom and desirability of UNCTAD continuing to function as principal subsidiary organ of the General Assembly, the *de facto* comprehensive trade and development organization, within the United Nations structure and under its security and support. It is perhaps not essential to engage in efforts to make it a *de jure* situation. The political and jurisdictional controversies which such attempts would generate would be counter-productive and could weaken UNCTAD without leading to a definitive conclusion. The three successive UNCTAD Secretaries-General have over the past 20 years consistently taken a clear stand in favour of UNCTAD remaining under the auspices of the General Assembly. In the present climate of threats to United Nations bodies, especially the threats to UNCTAD, of curtailing its mandates, resources and independence, the place of the organization is within the United Nations proper.

UNCTAD/GATT

With the establishment of an International Trade Organization (ITO) ruled out, UNCTAD ever since its establishment has had to struggle for recognition as an institution for negotiating trading rules and principles, as well as trade policy questions, because GATT already existed as a contractual framework of rights and obligations and had the full support of major trading countries. This institutional duality has been a crucial and complex factor and is likely to remain an important determinant of UNCTAD's future role.[11] Whereas UNCTAD has successfully developed ideas and policies as well as negotiating mandates covering a broad range of trade, finance, technology, commodities, shipping and other issues going far beyond the international trade sector though not divorced from it, GATT has also accumulated greatly increased responsibilities from its contractual character, recurrent rounds of negotiations and their follow-up. There are differences and often conflicts in regard to which ideologies and policies should govern international economic and trade relations. UNCTAD stresses the development approach, whereas GATT has been promoting a liberal international trading system. There are areas of overlap as well as non-overlapping areas of work; but the independent and distinctive co-existence of the two institutions has now become recognized as both necessary and inevitable.

In certain common areas UNCTAD has successfully exercised principal responsibility, e.g. the generalized system of preferences, restrictive business practices, economic cooperation among developing countries, East-South trade. In certain other areas, for example those relating to textiles in the Kennedy and Tokyo Rounds, UNCTAD's contribution has been significant through secretariat studies, technical assistance to developing countries, and monitoring and review in intergovernmental bodies; but a direct role in negotiations has been lacking. In areas not falling within GATT's competence (shipping, technology, commodity arrangements), UNCTAD has acquired impressive dimensions.

The future prospects point to the likely persistence of this institutional duality, giving rise to some conflicts of policies, as well as of jurisdiction. UNCTAD has been given very important tasks with respect to the following: the services sector, protectionism and structural adjustment, principles and policies related to international trade, and proposals for strengthening and improving the international trading system, with a view to giving it a more dynamic character and making it more responsive to the needs of developing countries. GATT also has a large stake, with the support of the powerful trading nations, in extending its jurisdiction to new areas. The competition of ideas and ideologies is thus likely to continue in a somewhat untidy but none the less necessary and useful institutional duality. Contacts and co-operation at the secretariat level between UNCTAD and GATT have been maintained and developed as necessary within the opportunities set by their overlapping and rival mandates and the character of their on-going negotiations. Finally, special mention needs to be made of a very important area of UNCTAD/GATT co-operation, namely, the operation of the joint International Trade Centre UNCTAD/GATT, whose impressive record has been acknowledged on all sides.

UNCTAD and specialized agencies and other United Nations bodies

(a) *IMF and the World Bank Group*

Right from the beginning, UNCTAD has been deeply involved in the central issues of the international monetary system and development finance covering such

---

[11] For a detailed discussion of the issues involved, see R. Krishnamurti, "UNCTAD as a negotiating instrument on trade policy: the UNCTAD-GATT relationship" in M. Zammit Cutajar (ed), *UNCTAD and the South-North Dialogue: The First Twenty Years* (Pergamon Press, 1985), pp. 33-70.

items as the following: volume and terms of resource transfers; financing of export shortfalls, including improvement in the many IMF facilities; supplementary finance; financing of structural imbalances; the "Link"; inflation; debt problems; SDRs; liquidity needs; and reform of the international monetary system. The UNCTAD secretariat's research and intergovernmental discussions and recommendations in this area are extremely important.

To be sure, there are substantial (and in some issues even fundamental) differences between UNCTAD, on the one hand, and IMF and the World Bank, on the other—in their approach, analysis and recommended measures for reform and improvement. UNCTAD is aware of its continuing impact on these institutions and their policies, even if actual results have fallen short of the needs of the situation.

Co-operation at the level of the secretariat has been maintained right through the years. No jurisdictional difficulty has arisen in the case of UNCTAD secretariat studies on money and finance. UNCTAD itself invited the World Bank to carry out a study on supplementary finance and requested IMF to prepare a study on the "Link" and the need for a longer-term facility for financing stuctural imbalances. IMF and the World Bank participated in both technical and other UNCTAD bodies. The Secretary-General of UNCTAD participates in the IMF Interim Committee and the joint IMF/World Bank Development Committee. He has participated in meetings of the Paris Club concerned with debt rescheduling of developing countries. He is also assisting the Group of 24 of the Group of 77 in the field of money and finance and, at their request, individual developing countries on finance and debt questions. UNCTAD has been pressing for a larger voice for the developing countries in the decision-making processes of these institutions and for an international conference within the United Nations framework.

All these studies and activities have entailed a certain parallelism but no incompatibility with the obligations and competence of the two institutions as set out in their Articles of Agreement. This parallelism has enriched the debates and imparted to them critically needed developmental dimensions. However, as mentioned elsewhere, some of the major developed countries wish to curtail UNCTAD's limited role in this area, especially that of money—presumably because they do not find UNCTAD's ideas and proposals convenient. Such an adverse move in this regard needs to be averted with firmness by the predominant majority of UNCTAD member States, including constructively minded B Group members and the socialist countries of Eastern Europe.

(b) *Other United Nations agencies*

UNCTAD's extensive operations in the area of commodities have been carried out in active co-operation with FAO and international commodity organizations. The UNCTAD and FAO secretariats have maintained close co-operative arrangements. UNCTAD's co-ordinating function in regard to international commodity groups has been discharged, by and large, without giving rise to problems of competence or differences in policies, having regard to the autonomy of these bodies.

UNCTAD and UNIDO activities, with some overlapping in certain areas, have been mutually supportive, complementary and reinforcing, with regard to industrialization and related structural adjustment, export policies and promotion, technology, ECDC, least developed countries, etc. Close co-operation at the secretariat level has also been developed.

UNCTAD's initiatives and operations in the field of technology have spurred action in other international institutions, particularly in the World Intellectual Property Organization (WIPO), which in its strengthened role as a specialized agency has taken in hand the revision of the Paris Convention and is giving increased attention to developing countries' interests; UNCTAD's participation in WIPO's work on the Paris Convention is having a significant impact.

In the area of shipping, UNCTAD has maintained constructive links with the International Maritime Organization (IMO), which after a few initial, confused years has now been recognized as the specialized agency concerned essentially with technical questions of maritime shipping.

Close co-operative links between UNCTAD and the regional commissions have mutually enriched and strengthened their respective activities. Regional commissions and their secretariats made an outstanding contribution to UNCTAD I — in the preparatory stages, at regional developing countries' conferences, in efforts to forge the cohesion of the three regional groups of developing countries and in the substantive preparations. Co-operation has continued over the years but with different emphases. While their contribution to issues of a global character affecting developing countries as a whole have continued to benefit UNCTAD, UNCTAD for its part has assisted by bringing global dimensions to regional consideration of those subjects. With the steady and, in recent years, accelerated decentralization of technical assistance programmes, their joint operational efforts have gained momentum in fields such as regional economic co-operation, the GSP, multilateral trade negotiations (MTNs), technology, shipping and ports and trade with socialist countries, etc.

Role of the Secretary-General of UNCTAD

The Secretary-General of UNCTAD is appointed by the Secretary-General of the United Nations and the appointment is confirmed by the General Assembly. UNCTAD being a world organization of universal membership, of wide and comprehensive competence, as well as challenging tasks, its Secretary-General has a political position and importance which has been recognized by the support provided by the General Assembly.[12] At UNCTAD I some of the Western governments

---

[12] In 1964, the only highest echelon post in the United Nations subject to such a provision was that of the Administrator of UNDP. The UNCTAD precedent was later followed in the case of UNIDO. Years later, when the United Nations Environment Programme (UNEP) was established (General Assembly resolution 2997 (XXVII)) in 1972, the major powers had no difficulty with a provision whereby the Executive Director of UNEP "shall be elected by the General Assembly on the nomination of the Secretary-General for a period of four years". In late 1977 again, when the General Assembly created the second highest post in the United Nations (as it then was described), i.e. that of Director-General for International Economic Co-operation and Development, the post was to be filled by the Secretary-General of the United Nations without confirmation by the General Assembly—a denial of recognition of the importance of the post, which developing countries sought to remedy in the following three years by means of General Assembly resolutions stressing the post's co-ordination and leadership within the United Nations.

opposed the intervention of the General Assembly in the process of the appointment of the Secretary-General of UNCTAD and argued that he should be only an appointee of the Secretary-General of the United Nations; however, they gave way upon the insistence of developing countries. The political importance thus given does not, however, affect the highest authority of the Secretary-General of the United Nations, who is the chief administrative officer.

Secondly, the Secretariat of the United Nations is one of the five principal organs of the Organization—a point stressed by eminent heads of United Nations bodies, including Dag Hammarskjöld, U Thant, Gunnar Myrdal and Raul Prebisch. This does not by any means imply that the secretariat heads act on their own, without regard to governmental mandates and positions; but it does mean that the head of the secretariat has the right and the duty to take initiatives in appropriate situations. In the area of international economic co-operation and development, given the deep commitments of the United Nations system, the secretariat's role and initiative become a dynamic necessity. It is in pursuance of this international commitment, and with the full support of the successive Secretaries-General of the United Nations that the head of the UNCTAD secretariat has been carrying out his tasks.

As will be seen from the 20 years' record, the tasks of the Secretary-General of UNCTAD consist roughly of the following three principal ones: (*a*) to assist the UNCTAD intergovernmental machinery by preparing the necessary studies and providing the needed servicing, that is, putting forward new and innovative ideas, approaches, policies and proposals in regard to the myriad issues within UNCTAD's competence; (*b*) technical assistance to member governments; (*c*) mediation and good offices.

UNCTAD secretariat studies

Over the years, the record speaks for itself: major portions and segments of the three United Nations development decade strategies and the new international economic order (NIEO), as well as a large number and variety of concrete and specific proposals for international action in the area of trade and development, have had their origin and further evolution either directly or indirectly in UNCTAD studies and deliberations. The daring innovativeness of a proposal, the "non-negotiability" of another, the lack of "realism" of a third, the threat posed to vested interests by a fourth—these understandably generate resistance and hostility and preclude objective examination in the short run, especially by governments of some developed countries called upon to transfer resources or open up markets or reduce economic domination. However, as history has shown even in the brief 20 years of UNCTAD, many of the ideas and proposals themselves slowly and steadily gain credibility and acceptability at the political and intellectual levels, even should govermental action on them remain meagre and tardy. Perhaps a highly significant vindication of much of UNCTAD's philosophy and ideas is to be found in the endorsement they have received by the Lester Pearson Commission and the Willy Brandt Commission—the "grand assizes" on development and international co-operation, consisting of outstanding personalities who have held positions of leadership in governments, especially Western governments. Failure of governments to act should, however, be no argument whatsoever against the initiative and duty of the Secretary-General of UNCTAD to perform this task. It would be tempting to seek to reduce the secretariat's independence and initiative in this regard, on the ground that the secretariat should be "neutral". To yield to such a temptation would be one of the greatest disservices to the United Nations; indeed, such a move would in no way help to dissipate the development crisis. In the critical years now and in the future, the continued ability of the Secretary-General of UNCTAD to carry out this task with courage and independence is a *sine qua non* not only of the survival, but also of the success of the UNITED NATIONS machinery.[13]

Technical assistance to member governments and groups in connection with their preparatory work for negotiations

From its very origin, the UNCTAD secretariat has provided not only conference service facilities to the regional groups, but technical substantive advice to the developing countries at their request. This has always been somewhat controversial, it being argued that such secretariat assistance to one group of member governments is incompatible with its international character. None the less, member governments of all groups have tended to accept the practice not only as unavoidable but also useful; given the inadequate substantive and expert resources of developing countries on extremely complex issues. In more recent years, it is true that the objection to this practice has gained considerable strength; major Group B members are taking a firmer line against this role of the secretariat. However, the resources involved are slight indeed, and the help in question contributes considerably to improved clarification of substantive issues and the effectiveness of negotiations. The role of the secretariat is strictly limited and defined, i.e. expert advice, not a role in negotiations as such. It would be no compliment to the developing countries to say that they are taking their negotiating proposals from the UNCTAD secretariat, while at the same time being criticized for engaging in tough posturing. The whole issue requires careful consideration by the objecting member governments as well as by the secretariat: the latter, by strictly defining its tasks and observing, perhaps, a greater measure of self-restraint, could help to dispel exaggerated criticisms and erroneous impressions. This is important both for the image of UNCTAD for the acceptance by governments that UNCTAD should play a mediatory role in negotiations (see below).

Mediation and good offices

The Secretary-General of UNCTAD has played an important role in offering his good offices and promoting agreed decisions and solutions in respect of a large number of subjects. He has done this both at the request of governments and on his own initiative, and invariably in consultation, with and with the approval of, the groups of governments. The weight of the role has varied over time and with the character and complexity of the issues, and the gaps between the different group positions. The Secretary-General of UNCTAD promotes consultations and

---

[13] See in this connection the statement by Ambassador M. Dubey (India) to ECOSOC, on 18 July 1984, in which he referred to the concerted attacks of certain countries on the entire multilateral system (including UNCTAD) and their efforts to make the United Nations institutions the scapegoat of the failures of the policies of those countries. He sounded a timely warning of the dangers ahead, and the urgency of protecting and reinforcing the United Nations system.

negotiations; he is not a party thereto, and there are limits to his role—which are well understood—particularly if the proposals in question originating from or supported by him are not acceptable to developed countries. There need, however, be no inherent incompatibility between the first two tasks of the Secretary-General of UNCTAD and the third, mediatory task, if the distinction is well recognized and respected in practice.

H. Decision-making and the meaning of consensus

Looking back over the years, one notices that a misconception about UNCTAD's decision-making procedures receives publicity and prominence from time to time. It is that in UNCTAD developing countries, being in a majority, often take important decisions of substance by resort to vote, instead of by consensus, and frequently without exhausting the possibilities of negotiating a consensus. The facts relating to the last two decades should, however, serve to dispel this erroneous impression.

An institution such as UNCTAD, which aims at establishing a more equitable and rational international economic system and formulates new policies and measures to that end, is bound to generate hostility from those who control the present system. In this sense, the articulation of sharply different views between the defenders of the *status quo,* on the one hand, and the advocates of change, on the other, is probably unavoidable. This, however, is not necessarily to be regarded as confrontation, nor is it inimical to international co-operation. On the contrary, a clear and cogent presentation of new ideas and proposals is the first essential step in a dialogue leading over time to negotiation, accommodation and consensus.

It was true that at UNCTAD I a number of resolutions and recommendations were adopted by vote. There were, however, certain special circumstances at that time: the Conference was a historic and unique opportunity for a clear and vibrant statement of developing countries' trade and development needs and proposals; the Group of 77 had just been formed and was emerging as a united front. In light of the fact that the issues raised were so numerous and complex, and the negative and hostile posture of Group B as regards both new substantive ideas and the notion of setting up a new United Nations body on trade and development was so strong and given the time constraints, it was perhaps unavoidable that many of the decisions of the Conference were taken by vote. And yet, even at UNCTAD I some of the most vital decisions were the result of informal negotiations among the three groups— either avoiding a vote or following one. The recommendation to the General Assembly to establish UNCTAD as a permanent institution was itself a consensus decision which resulted from the informal negotiations among key delegations of the three groups convened by Dr. Raul Prebisch on his own initiative.

Experience at UNCTAD I led the General Assembly to provide for a formal conciliation procedure in resolution 1995 (XIX)—a device aimed at providing adequate time to negotiate an agreed decision and a cooling-off period before proceeding to a decision by vote. The fact remains that this formal conciliation procedure has not been invoked even once in these 20 years. This bears ample testimony to the permanent use of a variety of informal conciliation and negotiation procedures, and a recognition by all concerned of their efficacy.

The fact is that over the years UNCTAD has succeeded, in a fair measure, in evolving procedures and modalities of negotiation aimed at consensus-building among member States and groups thereof. The group system (of the three groups of member States) for which the legal basis was laid down in resolution 1995 (XIX) forms the essential basis of these modalities and procedures—with the UNCTAD Secretary-General, the President of the Trade and Development Board, the Chairmen of the Committees, the Presidents of the negotiating conferences and groups, the co-ordinators of the three groups—all playing their part. Most of the substantive decisions emerge from these informal negotiations and are formally ratified by the legislative bodies concerned. Given UNCTAD's large membership, a certain degree of unwieldiness, heaviness, cumbrousness and time-consuming processes is inevitable. One should recognize the continuing need to improve these procedures by greater flexibility, and efficiency and more give and take. Yet in efforts to streamline the negotiating process, care should be taken not to impair the participation and support of all interested member governments.

While the great majority of decisions have been adopted by consensus, a number of important decisions [14] have also been taken by vote. It must, however, be stressed in this connection that most, if not all, of the resolutions in question launched a process of secretariat study and/or intergovernmental examination in vital trade and development areas. They did not call for substantive action entailing the transfer of resources, liberalization of trade and shipping restrictions, or other matters of a similar nature. These voted decisions conferring new mandates for UNCTAD's work have been extremely important and have invariably been followed up in the appropriate UNCTAD bodies (the Trade and Development Board or the Committees or others) by intensive and continued negotiations leading successfully, in most instances, to decisions by consensus in the terms of reference and work programme in the fields in question. Important legal or semi-legal

---

[14] Some examples from UNCTAD II onwards are:

Conference resolution 14 (II): Establishment of an intergovernmental working group on International Shipping Legislation;

Conference resolution 66 (III) calling for a conference of plenipotentiaries on a universally applicable code of conduct for liner conferences;

Conference resolution 25 (II) calling for a study on restrictive business practices;

Conference resolution 45 (III) establishing an intergovernmental working group to draft the Charter of Economic Rights and Duties of States;

Board resolution 47 (VII): establishing an intergovernmental group to prepare UNCTAD's contribution to the International Development Strategy;

Conference resolution 81 (III): Study on the establishment of a comprehensive international trade organization;

Conference resolution 78 (III) calling for studies on marketing and distribution of commodities;

Resolution 2 (III) (of the Intergovernmental Group on Transfer of Technology) on the role of patent systems;

Resolution 3 (III) (of the Intergovernmental Group on Transfer of Technology) on the possibility and feasibility of an international code of conduct in the field of transfer of technology;

Conference resolution 125 (V): Study on complementary facility for commodity-related shortfalls in export earnings;

Conference resolution 119 (V): Study on protectionism in the services sector;

Conference resolution 128 (V) setting up a high-level group to study international monetary reform;

Board resolution 264 (XXV): on ECDC work programme;

Board resolution 274 (XXVII): on ECDC work programme.

instruments have had their beginning in these processes and have subsequently been negotiated in conferences of plenipotentiaries: the Code of Conduct for Liner Conferences, the international code of conduct on transfer of technology, the Set of Multilaterally Agreed Equitable Principles and Rules for the Control of Restrictive Business Practices, the Charter of Economic Rights and Duties of States.

It is important to recall here that even the special conciliation procedure contained in resolution 1995 (XIX) designed to avoid a vote and promote consensus decisions does not rule out the resort to vote in regard to certain types of proposals.[15] Proposals relating to a number of specified fields will not require conciliation; these include "any procedural matter; any proposal for study or investigation including such proposals related to the preparation of legal instruments in the field of trade; establishment of subsidiary bodies of the Board within the scope of its competence; recommendations and declarations of a general character not calling for specific action; ...". Proposals appropriate for conciliation listed in the same paragraph are those of "a specific nature for action substantially affecting the economic or financial interests of particular countries" in a number of fields such as "economic plans or programmes, or economic or social readjustments"; trade, monetary or tariff policies, or balance of payments; policies of economic assistance or transfer of resources; levels of employment, income revenue or investment; and rights and obligations under international agreements or treaties.

It will be noted that all the resolutions and decisions adopted by vote in UNCTAD[16] are on matters for which even the conciliation procedure was not intended by UNCTAD's founding fathers, including among them the major powers which insisted on the conciliation procedure and defined its essentials.

Regrettably, in the past five years serious difficulties have been interposed in this process of consensus-building by one or more of the B Group countries—in an unfortunate departure from the practice of the first 15 years. A notable example of this is the non-participation of most, if not all, members of Group D in the *Ad hoc* High-level Intergovernmental Group of Experts on the Evolution of the International Monetary System, convened under Conference resolution 128 (V)— adopted by vote (with 69 for, 17 against and 13 abstentions). A hardening of attitudes is noticeable also in regard to certain other areas. It would seem that a new interpretation is being put on the term "consensus". According to this interpretation, consensus, it seems, is in effect equated with total unanimity, with any major dissenting country virtually exercising a veto over the decision in question, even if it had met with the approval of virtually all the other member governments. This is causing adverse (and confrontational) situations for UNCTAD—for the negotiating process as well as for substantive progress. More dangerously for the institution (and

---

[15] See para. 25 of resolution 1995 (XIX); see also proposals designed to establish a process of conciliation within the United Nations Conference on Trade and Development: "Report of the Special Committee" (A/5749), October 1964.

[16] Two resolutions on ECDC (Board resolutions 264 (XXV) and 274 (XXVII)), though falling in a field to which the conciliation procedure does not apply, raise, nevertheless, issues pertaining to UNCTAD's universality and the access rights of members to certain meetings and documents deriving from universality. These are touched upon in section D on UNCTAD and its progress towards universalism.

potentially for the United Nations as a whole), this novel interpretation of consensus could vitiate and impair the basic constitutional provisions of decision-making embodied in the statutes establishing UNCTAD and other institutions.

At UNCTAD I, during the debate on the institutional question, Group B countries, mainly on the insistence of the United States, pressed very hard for a system of weighted voting or, alternatively for dual voting—meaning a separate majority of developed and developing countries for decision-making. The reason given then for departing from equality of voting of all member States was that because the industrialized countries accounted for the greater proportion of world trade and industrial and financial power, this should be reflected in the decision-making power, and that they were also called upon to offer more aid and market access. (This demand proved unacceptable and it was only then that the conciliation procedure was included.) Whereas in the IMF-World Bank group of institutions voting is weighted, no special unequal voting provisions are embodied in the United Nations, General Assembly, ECOSOC, UNCTAD or other economic bodies (the Security Council is an exception). Even GATT has no provision for weighted or special voting, though in practice GATT decisions are adopted by consensus—that is, in the GATT context, with the consent of the three principal trading nations of the world—the United States, EEC and Japan (there is, however no formal or written text to this effect). In the new specialized agency statutes of UNIDO there are some special voting requirements in regard to budgetary but not to other matters. Even in the Convention on the Law of the Sea (in the negotiation of which, over so many years, several working procedures and modalities were employed in order to avoid voting and to reach decisions by consensus) there are provisions for bodies of restricted membership and special voting requirements for certain specific purposes, but none for either veto or the abrogation or abdication of voting rights.

The current posture in UNCTAD on consensus referred to above runs counter to what might be described as the process of democratizing international institutions, broadening the basis of their participation, and giving developing countries a larger voice in decision-making. The legal validity of a decision by vote is not open to question under the existing law. But given the importance of securing the co-operation of developed countries in carrying out the recommendations, resort to voting is not fruitful. Developing countries have been highly conscious of this. What is therefore disturbing and dangerous is the distortion of the term consensus so as to make it applicable not only to proposals involving substantive economic actions of implementation, but also to procedural decisions calling for an investigation or a committee. The dissenting member government can, to be sure, argue that the decision in question is not binding on it and that it cannot be obliged to abide by or participate in the action taken thereon. This is hardly a useful contribution to international law-making. It is thus critically important and urgent to return to the proven consultative and conciliatory modalities of consensus-building, avoiding the introduction of unconstitutional *de facto* veto or deadlock postures in the UNCTAD machinery.

The merit of a consensus decision, as contrasted with a voted decision, is considered to lie in a certain degree of political and moral commitment to implement it. In practice, however, many important consensus decisions of substance, arrived at after intensive negotiations, remain only very partially or marginally implemented, and in some cases, are even gone back upon. Examples of this are GSP improvements, the principles and rules on restrictive business practices, standstill on tariff and non-tariff barriers, ODA targets, terms and conditions of aid, debt relief measures, important elements of the IPC, and action in favour of the least developed countries. In most areas the consensus has served to water down and dilute the proposals to the lowest possible common denominator of the developed countries, without a concomitant commitment to implement even the watered down resolutions. In defence it is argued that UNCTAD resolutions are only recommendations, not legally binding commitments. Though this might be true in strictly legal terms, the political obligation behind the negotiated agreements cannot be called in question. Besides, the force of the distinction between a recommendation and a legally binding decision, in many areas of trade and development, is greatly exaggerated, as seen from the ease and flexibility with which many GATT provisions are being contravened. UNCTAD's experience indicates that if an obligation to implement goes with a consensus decision, the credibility of the negotiation will be measurably enhanced. Further strengthening of the mechanisms for review, monitoring and surveillance of progress in implementation would also be desirable.

I. Conclusion

Where does this review of UNCTAD's 20 years take us? What are UNCTAD's achievements and failures? What lessons does its experience teach us? This review, while essentially an elucidation of UNCTAD's philosophy, programmes and negotiations, also provides part of the answers. There is little doubt that in terms of specific policy proposals and targets UNCTAD's accomplishments fall far short of its founders' expectations and of the aspirations of the NIEO. And yet it would be somewhat simplistic to pose the question in terms of success and failure. UNCTAD's contribution to the recognition of the interdependence of the world economy and of the development consensus by the international community is not in doubt; nor is its role in the evolution of the world's political economy and of the third world. Its operations and ideas have greatly influenced governments, academia, non-governmental organizations, religious groups, business communities and, above all, other international institutions, even if many of its proposals do not secure ready and sufficient acceptance. However, with the march of events, its ideals and ideas have, over the years acquired an increasing, insistent and even compelling recognition as regards their validity and equity. The power of ideas could be much greater than that of bank balances. UNCTAD's influence will grow as long as it has the independence and courage to continue to present constructive ideas and suggestions according to changing conditions in a genuine spirit of international conciliation and co-operation.

UNCTAD strives to bring about a more rational and equitable international economic order by peaceful, non-confrontational and mutually beneficial policies through the United Nations machinery. Deeply entrenched power structures and interest groups are hard to modify even within a single country, much more so internationally. And yet in this acutely interdependent world in which one cannot even "stir a flower without troubling a star", the alternative to orderly and peaceful change is the collapse of the entire economic system, with its attendant chaos and disaster, and incalculable damage to all. It would be appropriate here to recall poet Rabindranath Tagore's words, quoted by Prime Minister Mrs. Indira Gandhi in her address to UNCTAD II in 1968:

> Power has to be made secure not only against power but also against weakness: for there lies the peril of its losing balance. The weak are as great a danger for the strong as quicksand for an elephant.

Part Two

TWO DECADES OF ENDEAVOUR (1964-1984)

Major fields of activity

I. COMMODITIES

A. History of UNCTAD commodity policy initiatives

THE PRE-1964 PERIOD

This section traces the principal policy initiatives in the field of commodities over the life of UNCTAD, and attempts to provide an assessment of what has been achieved. It also looks briefly to the future issues in prospect over the remainder of the decade, and points to relevant policy initiatives for this future period.

The history of international action in the commodity field is a long one. Attempts to regularize production and sales of some commodities were made in the late nineteenth century and, as transport facilities improved, markets widened and economic interdependence increased, the number of such arrangements tended to rise. But the main proliferation came after the First World War as a reaction initially to the violent fluctuations of the early post-war years and then to the depression of the 1930s.

By and large, the action of the inter-war period was taken by producers in defence of prices or markets. In the first instances, the schemes were in the nature of producer cartels. By means of restrictions on production and a dividing up of the market they sought to sustain or restore prices. Whatever success was achieved was seldom very durable: almost invariably production proved difficult to control even among participants, while in some cases the effect of cut-backs by participants was nullified by expansion in the output of non-members or of new producers. The more closely the arrangement approximated to a producer cartel the more likely was consumer or importer resistance to take the form of transactions with non-participants which often had the effect of undermining the price structure the arrangement was designed to sustain.

This reinforced two tendencies—one towards the closer identification of governments with the schemes and the other towards consultation with or even more direct involvement of consuming or importing interests—both aiming at raising the status and facilitating the enforcement of the commodity arrangement. The movement towards official involvement by the governments of exporting countries also reflects their mounting concern over the impact on revenue of the decline in primary commodity prices after 1927 and the effect on the balance of payments and on economic growth and of the deterioration in the terms of trade of primary exporting countries. Domestically, many governments sponsored or supported schemes for stabilizing prices and incomes in the primary sector. The effectiveness of such schemes tended to vary inversely with the resources that could be officially deployed for the purpose: they were difficult to sustain in countries with low per capita income and also in countries that sold most of their output of the particular commodity on the world market. It was against this background that in a number of cases primary exporting countries turned to one another with a view to organizing the external market. However, only in a few cases was effective control established: wheat, sugar, tea, rubber and tin.

The Second World War altered the commodity situation so completely that almost none of these arrangements was continued. A number of the international bodies that had been created in the 1930s continued to operate, however, though the stabilization problem turned into one of administering a rationalizing system, the quotas being applied to consumers rather than producers and the stimulus being given to production, with as small a rise in price as possible.

Existing and war-time shortages were still matters of concern when world commodity problems were discussed at the United Nations Conference on Trade and Employment at Havana in 1947. That thinking was also influenced by the inter-war experience of stabilization schemes is clearly evidenced by the structure and content of chapter VI of the Havana Charter. According to this chapter, which dealt with intergovernmental commodity agreements, an "international control agreement" was to be regarded as essentially an emergency measure to be entered into only when there was "general agreement" among countries "substantially interested in the commodity" that either a "burdensome surplus" or "widespread unemployment" had developed or was expected to develop in connection with the commodity and that these conditions "could not be corrected by normal market forces".[1] Among the principles governing such agreements, moreover, were several aimed at protecting net-importing (consumer) countries against the risks that had been brought to light from time to time by the stabilization activities of producer cartels in the inter-war period. Control agreements were to ensure the availability of adequate supplies and were to be administered in a manner that gave countries "mainly interested in imports of the commodity concerned" a voice equal to that of exporting countries on all "substantive matters".[2] The life of such an agreement would be limited to five years in the first instance.

The Havana Conference thus endorsed the conclusion of the London Monetary and Economic Conference of 15 years earlier that intergovernmental agreements were preferable to producer cartel arrangements and that the co-operation of consumer interests in importing countries was desirable in their implementation.

Though the Havana Charter was not adopted, chapter VI of it was picked up by the United Nations Economic and Social Council and in resolution 30 (IV) (March 1947), governments were urged to accept the principles it set forth as a general guide to international consultation and action on primary commodity problems. To this end an Interim Co-ordinating Committee for International Commodity Arrangements (ICCICA) was established in 1947 to be responsible for convening commodity study groups, for making recommendations in regard to the calling of United Nations conferences for negotiating commodity agreements and for co-ordinating the activities of study groups and councils administering commodity agreements.

---

[1] United Nations, *Havana Charter for an International Trade Organization* (United Nations publication, Sales No. 48.II.D.4), articles 62 and 63 of the Charter.
[2] *Ibid.*

The setting up of this machinery did not result in a rapid proliferation of commodity agreements. The principal reason for this was undoubtedly the generally more favourable situation in world commodity markets: the real purchasing power of primary products in terms of manufactures was well above the depressed levels of the 1930s and demand was appreciably more stable. But, by making it necessary to reach a consensus among a much larger number of countries than might previously have been involved, the Havana principles inevitably tended to increase the complexity of negotiation. As a result, the agreements concluded in the first 15 years after the war were all based essentially on pre-war forerunners or on a carry-over organizational core. Indeed, not even the pre-war agreements were all re-activated: in the case of rubber, international action was confined to consultation within the framework of a Study Group, while in the case of tea, agreements were negotiated in 1948 and 1950 but thereafter the International Tea Council became a consultative body, concentrating largely on market promotion and data publishing. Thus, it was only in respect of wheat, sugar and tin that fully operative control agreements were concluded in this period.

When the Havana Charter[3] was drawn up in 1948, it was widely believed that the post-war recovery of Western Europe and the pursuit of full employment policies in the industrial countries would lead over the long term to an expanding demand for primary commodities on a scale sufficiently large to remove the need for any intergovernmental intervention in the free working of commodity markets, except under temporary or exceptional circumstances. These, in turn, were largely conceived of in terms of over-supply and depressed prices, or the development of widespread unemployment or under-employment in connection with primary commodities, which could not be corrected within a reasonable time by the normal operation of market forces.[4]

The approach underlying the Havana Charter implicitly assumed that the free working of commodity markets would normally provide an optimum allocation of the world's resources and that the upward trend in demand in the developed countries for primary commodity exports from the developing countries would provide the required motive force for the economic growth of the latter group of countries. The objective of optimum resource allocation could, however, be attained only if these markets were perfectly competitive and resources freely mobile between and within countries; in fact, neither of these conditions is met in practice, affecting with particular force the developing countries whose capacity to adjust to restrictions on the international movement of factors of production and commodity trade is very much weaker than the capacity of the developed countries. Over the post-war period few primary commodity markets have, in fact, been freely competitive; most have reflected, to a greater or lesser extent, the intervention of national governments or the operations of large-scale private enterprises. The resulting imperfections in such commodity markets have been a major factor in preventing the achievement of a rational allocation of resources in world com-

---

[3] Charter for an International Trade Organization, signed at Havana on 24 March 1948. See *United Nations Conference on Trade and Employment. Final Act and Related Documents* (E/CONF.2/78), New York, April 1948.

[4] Havana Charter, article 62.

modity production, which has generally tended to work to the detriment of the developing countries.

UNCTAD I (1964)

It was against this background that the first session of UNCTAD was convened in 1964. The Secretary-General of the Conference, Raúl Prebisch, submitted a major policy statement which contained his own original analysis of the global commodity problem. A brief summary of his arguments are given in this and the following four paragraphs. He argued that external imbalance in the developing countries was mainly a manifestation of the disparity between the rate of growth of their primary exports and that of their imports of industrial goods. The slow growth of primary exports was an inevitable result of technological progress in the industrial centres. On the one hand, there were direct consequences, since technological progress led to the increasing substitution of synthetics for natural products; and was reflected in the smaller raw material content of finished goods. On the other hand, there were indirect consequences, since only a small part of the increased per capita income generated by technological progress went into the demand for foodstuffs and other staple consumer goods, as compared to the demand for industrial goods and services, which tended to rise rapidly.

Moreover, the enormous increase in output of commodities generated by technological progress in some major industrial countries further weakened the demand for imports of a number of agricultural products from the temperate zones and also for some tropical or semi-tropical products. Yet in spite of the huge increase in productivity, domestic prices in the industrial countries concerned usually remained higher—and often much higher—than those on the international market often through governmental action. In this way, or through the payment of subsidies to farmers, the potentially adverse effects of technological progress on prices were countered. But this policy also provided an additional incentive to expand production. If this expansion resulted in exportable surpluses, such surpluses were exported by means of subsidies or other incentives which tended to depress world prices, while other producing countries were unable to follow suit because of the very weakness of their economies.

Thus, the easing or elimination of protectionism in the industrial centres could have a far-reaching effect on the prices of the goods benefiting thereby. But this could not have any decisive effect on the observed downward trend of the terms of trade for primary commodities in relation to industrial products. For, owing to the slowness of the growth of demand for primary commodities, only a dwindling proportion of the increment in the economically active population in the developing countries could be absorbed in their production, and the more productivity in primary activities rose as a result of the assimilation of advanced techniques, the smaller would that proportion be. The economically active population therefore had to be shifted to industry and other activities.

This shift was a lengthy process, even in the industrial countries where the proportion of the economically active population employed in primary production was already relatively small. Hence the phenomenon discussed above. If the switch-over was effected rapidly and primary production was quick to adjust itself to the slow growth of demand, one of the requisites for obviating the deterioration of the terms of trade would be fulfilled. For this to happen, however, industry and other sectors would have to develop very rapidly in the peripheral countries and achieve a rate of growth much higher than that hitherto attained in those countries, particularly if efforts to introduce advanced techniques into primary production and other low productivity activities were intensified.

However, the foreign earnings of the developing countries had suffered severely from the deterioration in the terms of trade which had been caused by *inter alia* the nature of products exported, the lack of co-operation among producing countries and the need for developing countries to increase their exports in order to improve their import capacity. Unless these countries succeeded in obtaining additional resources, they would be unable to achieve even the reasonable rate of growth set as a target in their plans. The situation would be still worse if the terms of trade deteriorated further in the future. Additional resources, then, were indispensable, and it was the purpose of compensatory and supplementary financing to provide them through such a transfer, in so far as the purpose was not achieved through higher prices. This would give economic development plans a large measure of stability which could certainly not be achieved by expedients designed simply to cushion the impact of fluctuations in exports, although such expedients were an important step in the right direction. These plans would have to be reviewed whenever necessary in order to deal with the consequences of deterioration of the terms of trade. In other words, compensatory and supplementary financing operations would need to be an integral part of a more rational policy for financing development.

An explicit and direct link was thus made between action on commodity export earnings and the development process, a link which set the direction for all subsequent policy initiatives on commodities in the succeeding years at UNCTAD. The Secretary-General went on to state clearly that this link involved "a decision to transfer ... to the countries exporting primary commodities the extra income accruing to the industrial countries as a result of the deterioration in the terms of trade".[5] Here, significant resistance from the industrial countries was encountered, a resistance which, like the link mentioned above, has run through all subsequent commodity discussions in UNCTAD. It is also noteworthy that the new approach to international commodity policy adopted at UNCTAD I was generally opposed by many developed market-economy countries based on the laissez-faire philosophy of the Havana Charter, and particularly on the argument that any regulation of the free play of market forces would inevitably lead to a misallocation of resources and eventual economic catastrophe. For this reason 13 of the developed market-economy countries (Australia, Austria, Canada, Denmark, Federal Republic of Germany, Ireland, Japan, Liechtenstein, Norway, South Africa, Switzerland, the United Kingdom and the United States) opposed, for example, the recommendation on the stabilization of primary commodity prices (Special Principle Seven), while most of the remainder abstained. Similarly, for this reason the majority of

---

[5] "Report by the Secretary-General of the Conference", in *Proceedings of the United Nations Conference on Trade and Development,* vol. II—*Policy Statements* (United Nations publication, Sales No. 64.II.B.12), p. 12.

these countries abstained on the recommendation for modification in domestic support policies for primary production by developed countries (Special Principle Five), while one major developed market-economy country (the United States) opposed the recommendation on the regulation of surplus disposals of primary commodities by developed countries (Special Principle Eight).[6] In a very fundamental sense, however, UNCTAD I set the agenda for future work on commodities in UNCTAD.

Indeed, the period between UNCTAD I and UNCTAD IV is largely a record of frustration in intergovernmental attempts to translate the principles enshrined in the UNCTAD I recommendation A.II.7 on "international commodity arrangements and removal of obstacles to, and expansion of, trade"[7] into practical action. A Committee on Commodities of the Trade and Development Board was established in 1965 with a very ambitious mandate, to take over the functions of the ICCICA. It established at its very first session a list of commodities "identified as giving cause for immediate concern" (cocoa, sugar and coffee) and a list of those "which required close attention" (copper, cotton, iron ore, lead and zinc, rice, rubber, tea, tobacco and vegetable oils).[8] Despite lengthy negotiation, virtually nothing was accomplished in regard to these commodities until UNCTAD II.

UNCTAD II (1968)

Reflecting its concern regarding the slow pace of progress on individual commodities, the UNCTAD secretariat issued a major blueprint for an "integrated commodity policy" to be discussed at UNCTAD II (1968). In the secretariat's view, a faster rate of economic growth of the developing countries than had hitherto been found possible would largely depend on an acceleration in the rate of growth of their capacity to import. Since primary commodities were likely to continue to provide by far the greater part of the foreign exchange earnings of the majority of developing countries for a considerable time to come, the successful implementation of policies designed to increase the rate of growth of those countries' revenues deriving from exports of commodities would provide a context within which the attainment of their economic growth targets would become much more practicable. Moreover, since many of these countries were still heavily dependent on one or two commodities for the bulk of their foreign exchange earnings, the successful operation of international measures designed to reduce the short-term fluctuations in the market for these commodities could well have a considerable additional beneficial impact on the rate of growth of the developing countries principally affected.

More specifically, the secretariat argued, to the extent that the actual operation of some commodity markets reflected impediments—such as tariffs or price support for domestic production in the developed countries—to the free flow of trade, intervention by the international community should be designed to reduce, and

---

[6] *Proceedings... op. cit.*, vol. I, *Final Act and Report* (United Nations publication, Sales No. 64.II.B.11), p. 23.

[7] *Ibid.*, p. 26.

[8] *Official Records of the Trade and Development Board, Second Session, Supplement No. 2* (TD/B/21/Rev.1), para. 40.

ultimately to remove, such impediments. In other primary commodity markets intergovernmental intervention would be justified if it were designed specifically to expand the export earnings of the developing countries, or to reduce short-term instability in those earnings. Moreover, such intervention should no longer be conceived purely in terms of temporary measures, designed to cope with emergency situations such as accumulated surpluses, but rather as an integral part of economic development planning.

In the secretariat's view, the attainment of the general objectives of commodity policy—as outlined above—would require, in practice, consideration on a commodity-by-commodity basis, in view of the wide diversity in market structures existing for the different primary commodities. Intergovernmental action, to be successful, would need to be specifically adapted to the particular conditions of the world market for each commodity concerned. It was, nonetheless, useful as an analytical device to group commodities into broad categories with similar market structures in order to explore the different ways in which the achievement of the aims of commodity policy could most effectively be sought in practice.

The relevant grouping of commodities for consideration of possible short-term commodity stabilization schemes would be different from the one most suited to consideration of longer-term issues, such as facilitating market access, harmonization of production of synthetics and substitutes in developed countries with the supply of natural products produced in developing countries or diversification. For short-term stabilization purposes, the relevant grouping would need to be based on some measure of the degree of market instability of the different primary commodities considered. As regards longer term problems of commodity markets, the classification of commodities would need to be related primarily to the underlying factors which most influenced the secular trend of exports from developing countries, factors reflecting economic and technological changes and factors arising directly or indirectly from government policies, as Dr. Prebisch had indicated already at the first session of UNCTAD.

The secretariat concluded that the general case for evolving an integrated international commodity policy was simply that in view of the complex issues involved, and the wide variety of available alternative policies, there was a need to adopt an overall strategy to deal with primary commodities. Such an overall approach would allow international action affecting primary commodity markets to become considerably more effective than in the past. First, it would make possible a rational selection of the most urgent issues requiring remedial action and of the most appropriate policy approaches, which could be welded together into a specific programme. Secondly, while the particular characteristics of individual commodity markets might require the use of different combinations of policies in each, there was a need for an overall review of progress in the commodity trade of developing countries, so that gaps in policy or action could be recognized and suitable remedies sought. Thirdly, the effectiveness of action relating to particular commodities was likely to be enhanced if such action were consciously related to the more general objectives of the economic development of the developing countries. Moreover, rational action in any one commodity market could be taken only when the probable effects on the markets for other commodities had been taken fully into account.

In the secretariat's view, a particular illustration of the close interconnection between different types of commodity trade policy was that of measures dealing specifically with short-term and long-term problems. The stabilization of the world price within prescribed limits, for example, could be expected to affect the rate of investment in new capacity, as well as the rate of growth in world consumption and the level of normal stocks, all of which would powerfully influence the way in which the world economy in general, and the developing producing countries in particular, adjusted to the new situation over the long term. Similarly, to achieve certain desirable "long-term" policy aims, such as diversification of the structure of production in the developing countries, it might be necessary to adopt appropriate "short-term" measures which could help the developing countries concerned to finance such diversification programmes. All the various possible measures whether carried out in the immediate future or over the longer-term would need, therefore, to be integrated within the context of an overall commodity policy.

Another important inter-relationship was that between policy measures which were essentially of a self-financing nature, and those requiring international financial (and technical) support. For example, some policy measures (such as the setting-up of a buffer stock scheme) might require initial financial support but could become self-financing after a period of years. None the less, the division of the whole field of commodity problems into short- and long-term, and the distinction between self-financing and other measures, helped to focus attention both on the period within which the results of policy action were sought, and the balance of cost and benefit which was likely to arise. At the same time, it was important to achieve a fuller co-ordination of international measures of commodity policy with related measures, such as diversification policies or compensatory financing, which were also devoted to improving the trend or offsetting the fluctuations in the export earnings of developing countries. These and related fields of action were, in the secretariat's view, essentially mutually supportive.

Genesis of the commodity by commodity approach

Governments of developed countries were not, however, prepared to follow the secretariat's proposal for an integrated commodity policy. The Conference also failed to reach a consensus on the need for a general agreement on commodity arrangements embodying the main principles of such an integrated policy. Governments of developed countries insisted that progress could be made, not by discussing general principles, but only by considering the problems of each commodity separately, since each market was unique and likely to require its own specially-tailored package of remedial policies. This commodity-by-commodity approach was accepted by the developing countries as a reasonable basis on which to seek appropriate international action, and the Conference identified a range of "problem" commodities for detailed discussion in the various specialized international commodity bodies, with a view to identifying the problems and agreeing on appropriate remedial measures.[9] It called specifically for the conclusion of international agreements in respect of sugar and cocoa. In addition, it recommended the setting

---

[9] Conference resolution 16 (II) listed 19 such commodities, (cocoa, sugar, oilseeds, oils and fats, natural rubber, hard fibres, jute, bananas, citrus fruit, cotton, tungsten, tea, wine, iron ore, tobacco, manganese ore, mica, pepper, shellac and phosphates).

up, at the earliest possible date of an Intergovernmental Consultative Committee on Oilseeds, Oils and Fats and the search for further steps to achieve the objectives of the informal understandings reached on hard fibres, including the possiblity of a formal agreement, and recommended that the FAO Study Group on Jute, Kenaf and Allied Fibres should urgently explore the possibility of setting up an appropriate buffer stock scheme for jute. In the same resolution the Conference recommended that, for a number of other commodities,[10] studies should be made, intergovernmental consultations held and remedial action taken, as appropriate, in order to identify and solve the problems confronting these commodities.

Proposals on access to markets, pricing policy, synthetics and substitutes, diversification and the international commodity trade network, were referred to the permanent machinery of UNCTAD for consideration. Texts on these subjects were later agreed upon by the Committee on Commodities and the Board. However, these texts had little practical effect, just as work on the individual commodities cited above reached only very limited practical conclusions. A new International Sugar Agreement was concluded at the end of 1968, but this was more the culmination of a long series of consultations dating back to 1966, than the result of the resolution adopted at UNCTAD II. Considerable progress toward a new international agreement for cocoa was achieved, but an agreement was not concluded until 1972, following UNCTAD III. Progress was achieved also in relation to tea, for which informal export regulation schemes were negotiated for 1970 and 1971-1972 under the auspices of FAO Consultative Committee on Tea, but no formal commodity agreement could be concluded.

UNCTAD III (1972)

Thus, by the time of the third session of the Conference (1972) the secretariat was moved to argue[11] that, whilst the strategy adopted so far in order to achieve the objective of remunerative and equitable prices—to conduct a series of negotiations on a commodity-by-commodity basis—would seem, in principle, to be a sound approach, since the different circumstances of each commodity market might well require different packages of remedial measures, such negotiations, taking each commodity separately, were inevitably complex and time-consuming. Moreover, remedial action still continued to be assessed by each country in purely commercial terms, and not as a common endeavour forming part of a broad programme for contributing to the development of developing countries. In consequence, the strategy actually adopted had had very limited success, whether one considered the range of commodities still suffering from substantial market instability, or those suffering from unfavourable price trends. This situation created a serious dilemma for the international community, since on the basis of past experience a continuation of the past strategy in this field could not be expected to deal with the major remaining problems of commodity pricing until nearer the end of the century.

---

[10] In particular natural rubber, bananas, citrus fruit, cotton, tungsten, tea, wine, iron ore, tobacco, manganese ore, mica, pepper, shellac and phosphates.

[11] See "The development of international commodity policy" (TD/113), reproduced in *Proceedings of the United Nations Conference on Trade and Development, Third Session*, vol. II—*Merchandise Trade* (United Nations publication, Sales No. E.73.II.D.5).

It seemed to the secretariat, therefore, that at least two new aspects should be added to the existing strategy. First, a higher degree of priority would need to be given by the international community, and by the governments most concerned with particular "problem" commodities, to the need for concluding new international agreements, especially those including price provisions. In some cases, such higher priority would require a more positive attitude to such agreements on the part of importing countries; in other cases, it would involve additional efforts by exporting countries to reach a mutually acceptable arrangement concerning market shares. Second, consideration needed to be given to evolving new international measures which could be applied in a general way to primary commodity trade, or at least to trade in certain well defined groups of commodities of particular export interest to developing countries. Such measures, it was argued, would alleviate the market problems of a wide range of commodities and so complement efforts to negotiate new international agreements for individual commodities. In addition the secretariat appealed to governments to take measures regarding synthetics and substitutes and to safeguard the interests of the international community regarding the resources of the seabed and ocean floor. It emphasized the need for the International Bank for Reconstruction and Development (the World Bank) to assist the diversification, price stabilization and other efforts of the international community in line with the objectives and the strategy underlined in the previous two sessions of the Conference. Lastly, it reiterated the need to look at the marketing and distribution problems of commodities and their products and the need to intensify the intergovernmental consultations on commodities in connection with access to markets and pricing policy.

Once again, however, the secretariat's proposals fell on deaf ears, and the Conference was able to reach agreement only on a resolution calling for a series of commodity-by-commodity intensive intergovernmental consultations "with the aim of reaching concrete and significant results in the matter of trade liberalization and pricing policy early in the 1970s".[12] In the event, during the 1973-1974 period, consultations were held on 15 commodities but little emerged from them in the form of concrete recommendations for action, the consultations basically doing no more than to reaffirm the positions and to make general recommendations which might be considered further by governments.

By this time, however, a change had occurred in both the economic environment (with the oil price increases and a concern that cartelization might spill over into other primary commodity exports) and the general sentiment of governments regarding the commodity-by-commodity approach. The United Nations General Assembly held a special session on problems of raw materials and development in May 1974, out of which sprang a "Programme of Action on the Establishment of a New Intenational Economic Order"[13] which called for the "preparation of an overall integrated programme for a comprehensive range of commodities of export interest to developing countries".[14] This was precisely what the secretariat had been arguing for, unsuccessfully, through three sessions of the Conference. Accordingly,

---

[12] Conference resolution 83 (III), para. 2.
[13] General Assembly resolution 3202 (S-VI).
[14] *Ibid.*, sect. I, para. 3 (*a*) (iv).

as early as the August 1974 session of the Trade and Development Board, an "outline of an overall integrated programme" was put forward by the secretariat.[15] Subsequently, the elements of the programme were elaborated and amplified through a series of studies. The programme was the focus of attention at all three parts of the eighth session of the Committee on Commodities in 1975 and was the centre of informal consultations between the UNCTAD secretariat and governmental representatives. Indeed, at the third part of its eighth session in December 1975, the Committee on Commodities agreed that the stage had been reached where it was possible to take concrete decisions[16] and the programme thus became the main issue at the fourth session of the Conference. A number of factors supported this new momentum. It was evident that if the oil price increase had come to stay, the developing country importers of oil could, in the long run, cope with their rising import bills, not just through emergency assistance, but through enhancement of their export earnings. There was also an idea in the background, seldom directly expressed that the oil producers could themselves help in this through financial support for action to strengthen markets of other commodities. There was at the same time a new receptiveness on the part of the developed consumer countries, partly because of an appreciation of the predicament of the oil importing developing countries, and partly, and perhaps more significantly, because of some uneasy apprehension that the experience of oil might encourage the producers of other commodities along a similar path.[17]

UNCTAD IV (1976)

As the new Secretary-General of UNCTAD, Gamani Corea, put it in his report to UNCTAD IV,[18] the essence of the integrated programme was that, in contrast to previous approaches it aimed at dealing with the problem of commodities in a comprehensive and systematic way. It was not a mere appeal for starting a series of consultations, or even negotiations, on individual projects in an isolated fashion as was the case with such initiatives as the intensive intergovernmental consultations on commodities mentioned above. Nor, was the programme an attempt to provide only a broad framework of objectives and guiding principles that would influence and inspire the negotiations on individual products. It sought, rather, to secure an international consensus to take action on a wide range of products through a set of specific measures which, to a greater or lesser extent, were applicable to each of these products. Certain of the instruments that the programme required would, in fact, be employed to meet the needs of a number of commodities. The programme laid much stress on the comprehensive coverage of commodities reflecting the need to secure adequate balance in the treatment of different commodities. The pro-

---

[15] See TD/B/498.

[16] Paragraph 1 of resolution 16 (VIII) of the Committee on Commodities. See *Official Records of the Trade and Development Board, Seventh Special Session, Supplement No. 5* (TD/B/596), annex I.

[17] An example of this new responsiveness of developed countries can be found in the proposal of a major developed market-economy country for the establishment of an international resources bank which would provide finance for commodity development and stabilization.

[18] *New directions and new structures for trade and development* (TD/183/Rev. 1) (United Nations publication, Sales No. E.74.II.D.1).

gramme, he informed the Conference, also placed emphasis on a multidimensional approach in dealing with the problems of commodities, even when viewed as individual products. Export regulation was the instrument predominantly used in past agreements, but the integrated programme, whilst recognizing the need for export regulation when the situation warranted it, sought also to include a number of other mechanisms that had not in the past been used to a significant degree, but which could contribute greatly towards the attainment of the objectives for individual products.

Thus, the integrated programme for commodities comprised five basic elements. These were:

(*a*) The establishment of internationally-owned stocks covering a wide range of commodities;

(*b*) The establishment of a common financing fund that would make resources available for the acquisition of stocks;

(*c*) The institution, in circumstances which justified it, of a system of medium-term to long-term commitments to purchase and sell commodities at agreed prices;

(*d*) The institution of more adequate measures than were at the time available to provide compensatory financing to producers to cover shortfalls in export earnings;

(*e*) The initiation of an extensive programme of measures to further the processing of commodities by the producing countries themselves.

For the first time since UNCTAD was established, the secretariat's proposals for commodity policy initiatives met a positive response. At the fourth session of the Conference, held in Nairobi in 1976, a resolution (93 IV) on the Integrated Programme for Commodities (IPC) was adopted without dissent, incorporating virtually all of the features proposed by the secretariat. Indeed, the IPC has provided the framework within which all international commodity policy initiatives were developed and assessed from the time of its adoption until the end of the period presently under review.

It provided for a common framework of agreed objectives and principles to guide the negotiations. The international measures required to achieve the objectives were identified. It was expected that the agreements to be negotiated under the Programme would be more multi-dimensional in character than had been the case in the past. The Programme laid down well-defined procedures and a time-frame for implementation. It identified 18 commodities of export interest to developing countries which together accounted for a little over 60 per cent of their exports of commodities, excluding petroleum. And it specified a process for the negotiation of a central commodity financing facility, the Common Fund.

It provided that "with a view to improving the terms of trade of developing countries and in order to eliminate the economic imbalance between developed and developing countries, concerted efforts should be made in favour of the developing countries towards expanding and diversifying their trade, improving and diversifying their productive capacity, improving their productivity and increasing their export earnings, with a view to counteracting the adverse effects of inflation, thereby sustaining real incomes".[19] Apart from these broad objectives, the resolution also listed certain specific objectives. These included the achievement of stable conditions in commodity trade; an increase in real export earnings of developing countries and protection from fluctuations therein; improvement in market access and reliability of supply; diversification of production and expansion of processing in developing countries; improvement in the competitiveness of natural products competing with synthetics and substitutes; and improvements in market structures and in the marketing, distribution and transport systems for commodity exports of developing countries, including an increase in their participation in these activities and their earnings from them.[20]

With the adoption of the IPC, the pace of intergovernmental discussions on a broad range of commodities quickened significantly, since the resolution on the IPC called for meetings preparatory to negotiating conferences to be completed for all 18 of the IPC commodities[21] by February 1978. Moreover, negotiations on the Common Fund, central to the financial coherence of the IPC, were begun at the same time. There was a sense among participants that at long last the commodity problem which had received so much attention at previous sessions of UNCTAD, but on which so little progress had been made, might at last be addressed concretely by the international community. This found expression in statements by leading spokesmen and in pronouncements following meetings of industrialized countries at the highest levels. Support for the regulation of commodity markets was seen not merely as a desirable response to demands from developing countries but also as an instrument helpful to domestic policy in the industrialized countries.

UNCTAD V (1979)

Nevertheless, by the time of UNCTAD V, the Secretary-General of UNCTAD was moved to write[22] that despite this new and vitally important evolution in policy, there had been a relative failure—or at least a long delay—in translating this new commitment into concrete actions. In the period since the fourth session of the Conference, despite several preparatory meetings on as many as 12 commodities included in the Integrated Programme but not covered by international agreements, it had proved possible to bring only one product—rubber—to the stage of a negotiating conference. The traditional feature of commodity discussions—the clouding of the main issues by a mass of technical details, the requests for successive studies, and the avoidance of actual decision—all remained aspects of the post-Nairobi discussion. Often, the basic question whether an international agreement was needed at all for a particular product was left open by developed countries as an issue on which light had to be shed. The alternative approach reflecting a firm

---

[19] Conference resolution 93 (IV) of 30 May 1976, sect. I, preamble.
[20] *Ibid.*, sect. I, paras. 1-7.
[21] Bananas, bauxite, cocoa, coffee, copper, cotton (and cotton yarns), hard fibres (and products), iron ore, jute (and jute products), manganese, meat, phosphates, rubber, sugar, tea, tin, tropical timber, and vegetable oils and seeds.
[22] *Restructuring the international economic framework* (TD/221/Rev.1) (United Nations publication, Sales No. E.79.II.D.12).

commitment to the regulation of the market for a particular commodity and also to appropriate measures of a developmental character and to the search for mechanisms to give effect to them was seldom in evidence. Moreover, he noted, the developing countries did not always succeed in evolving and presenting common proposals in the negotiations on individual commodities.

Another point stressed by the Secretary-General of UNCTAD was that, to a considerable extent, the slow tempo of the negotiating process in respect of individual products had been a reflection of the delay in the establishment of the Common Fund. By serving as an institution able to offer finance for intervention in markets in support of prices through international commodity agreements, and by focusing attention on commodity problems more generally, the Fund was seen as playing the role of a catalyst in bringing about such agreements. Its creation was seen to introduce a new element that would help to avoid the largely negative experience of the past in efforts to arrive at commodity agreements. The uncertainty surrounding the establishment of the Fund inevitably had its impact on the search for solutions for individual commodities. It led to uncertainties about the prospects of finance for buffer stocks and hence to ambiguities regarding the respective roles of stocking and the instruments for market regulation in the mix of possible solutions of individual products.

Thus, as the fifth session of the Conference got under way in 1979, concern had developed that, despite the major new commitments embodied in the IPC resolution, progress in achieving concrete results was not being made at a faster pace than that following earlier sessions of the Conference. Furthermore, what progress had been made had tended to concentrate on the pricing issue, to the neglect of other elements of the IPC. The Secretary-General of UNCTAD stressed the importance of UNCTAD V's turning its attention specially to the other aspects of the IPC.

Marketing, distribution and transportation of commodities

One of these aspects, in his view, was the need for developing countries to increase their share of, and improve their position in, the marketing, distribution and transportation of products. To a considerable extent, the actions needed in this field had to be taken by the developing countries themselves but these could be facilitated by a framework of support and accommodation by the international community. Several commodities continued to be sold through auctions and similar systems whose origins lay in much earlier times, when buyers were less concentrated and more open to the influence of competition. The manner in which these systems should evolve and be adapted was clearly a pertinent issue. Closely related to this was the fact that an increase in the participation of developing countries in marketing and distribution would affect their relationships with transnational corporations which played a major role in commodity trade—relationships which needed to be made more equitable, so as to allow developing countries a more adequate share of the benefits of this trade.

Processing of primary products

Similarly, argued the Secretary-General, a complex of issues surrounded the goal of increasing the participation of developing countries in the processing of their products. These issues were part of the wider question of industrialization and included such aspects as access to markets in industrialized countries, relationships with transnational corporations and trade among the developing countries themselves. The problem of market access had acquired a new urgency against the background of the increasing trend towards protectionism in the industrialized countries and therefore required particular attention. The questions bound up with the objective of enhancing the participation and share of developing countries in the transportation of commodities was particularly linked to the objective of increasing the participation of these countries in world shipping.

Compensatory financing

The Secretary-General reminded the Conference that compensatory financing was also a basic element of the Integrated Programme. The subject had received emphasis in proposals before the Development Committee of the World Bank and International Monetary Fund[23] calling for a study of possibilities relating to a globalized scheme for the stabilization of export earnings—a scheme that would reflect some of the principal elements of the Stabex scheme extended by the European Economic Community to the African, Caribbean and Pacific countries. In terms of the Integrated Programme, however, compensatory financing needed to be viewed as a supplement to, rather than a substitute for, instruments such as commodity agreements which aimed directly at the regulation of prices themselves. When there was a malfunctioning of particular commodity markets, it was important to correct such malfunctioning so that patterns of production, consumption and investment were not unfavourably influenced by extreme and erratic price movements. Compensatory finance could however, usefully play a supporting role in market regulation—both because it might not prove possible to bring all commodities under international agreements that supported prices and also because earnings of producers, which were affected by variations in the volume of exports as much as by price fluctuations, needed also to be stabilized.

The existing compensatory financing facility of IMF was limited in many ways—in respect of its size, the conditions governing its use, and the terms of repayment. In the Secretary-General's view, a major revision of the existing facility was a possible option in the search for an adequate scheme. An alternative was the establishment of a new facility that, unlike the Fund facility, would be specifically commodity-oriented. In such an event, consideration would need to be given to establishing such a new facility as an additional activity—a third window, possibly—of the Common Fund. This would be a plausible course, since the Common Fund would itself be a commodity-oriented financial institution concerned with more than one aspect of the commodity problem. Together with the second window, which would deal with measures of a developmental nature, an additional activity in the form of a compensatory financing facility would round off the character of the Common fund and turn it into a truly comprehensive institution in the commodity arena. It would thus be relevant to view the issue of compensatory financing in that light.

At UNCTAD V, the secretariat had not proposed, and no decisions were taken on, specific initiatives in these neglected fields. Rather, resolutions were adopted authorizing the secretariat to carry out a number of studies in regard to these areas,

---

[23] Joint Ministerial Committee of the Board of Governors of the World Bank and the International Monetary Fund on the Transfer of Real Resources to Developing Countries.

particularly the expansion of processing and product development in developing countries as regards the 18 IPC commodities; the marketing and distribution structures of these commodities; and a complementary facility to compensate for shortfalls in export earnings of individual commodities.

In the succeeding years until the sixth session of the Conference, work proceeded on these studies in parallel with continuing efforts in regard to the negotiation of agreements for commodities not yet so covered, and in regard to the establishment of the Common Fund. In June 1980, a treaty was concluded establishing the Fund,[24] but progress in obtaining the requisite ratifications was very slow, and by the time of UNCTAD VI, the Common Fund had still not come into operation. Progress in concluding international commodity agreements was marginally better, as negotiations were successfully concluded for jute and tropical timber (though with no pricing provisions) and the tin, coffee and cocoa agreements successfully renegotiated. The secretariat's studies on processing, marketing and distribution and on a complementary facility were considered by the Committee on Commodities, but no action was taken.

UNCTAD VI (1983)

By the time of the sixth session of the Conference (1983), the deepening global economic recession, the debt crisis affecting several major developing countries, and the growing fears of increasing protectionism, led to a focus by the Secretary-General of UNCTAD on a plan for recovery which *inter alia* emphasized the catastrophic fall of commodity prices in the early 1980s. As a response to this commodity crisis, he argued in his report to UNCTAD VI,[25] it would not be sufficient merely to urge the speedy implementation of the Integrated Programme, even though this provided an accepted and comprehensive framework for dealing with the commodity problem. There were two reasons for this. First, the negotiation of traditional commodity agreements had proved to be complex and time-consuming. These negotiations involved a host of issues, ranging from the economic provisions of an agreement such as price ranges, export quotas, and the size and cost of stocks, to the constitutions of commodity organizations and, more recently, the identification of measures in the area of marketing and product development. On many of these issues, he noted, there was ground for discord—both between producers and consumers and among producers themselves. Second, the traditional type of commodity agreement paid attention to fluctuations or cycles that were specific to each commodity. It did not provide for a situation of generalized recession in world demand that exerted an exceptionally heavy pressure on commodity prices. As a result, he concluded, the mechanisms established to protect minimum prices, though providing some much-needed support, were often inadequate in achieving their objectives. An emergency programme was therefore required to overcome these limitations.

---

[24] *Agreement Establishing the Common Fund for Commodities* (TD/IPC/CF/CONF/25) (United Nations publication, Sales No. 81.II.D.8 and corrigendum).

[25] *Development and recovery: The realities of the new interdependence* (TD/271/Rev.1) (United Nations publication, Sales No. E.84.II.D.4).

Interim commodity agreements

The Secretary-General therefore proposed a series of "interim agreements"—possibly within the framework of an overall agreement—for a number of commodities which were of critical importance to developing countries and for which agreements were not already in existence. Such agreements would aim essentially at a single objective—the establishment of a safety net taking the form of a minimum support price for each commodity. Such a price would not be determined by time-consuming negotiations. It would be established on the basis of a broad formula that would be acceptable to the international community as constituting a reasonable norm. If market prices exceeded this norm, as adjusted if appropriate, no action would be taken. If they fell below, they would be supported by actions that would include stock-building and export quotas. Stocks would be held nationally by governments of producer countries in the absence of an international authority to intervene in markets, but they would be financed by the Common Fund and other available instruments, including commercial banks. Similarly, countries cutting back exports through quotas would qualify for loan financing, since this would reduce the burden on each country of such cutbacks pending the revival of prices. These arrangements would not involve budgetary outlays by donor countries. The Secretary-General stressed that the interim programme was not, however, a substitute for the conventional commodity agreement. Rather it would be a stepping stone towards it. It derived its rationale from the belief that all governments had a stake in avoiding a collapse in commodity prices and in relieving a situation which hampered the orderly growth of production and investment and brought serious dangers—political, social, and economic—to developing countries.

Role of compensatory financing

The Secretary-General considered that emergency action to deal with the commodity situation should also include compensatory financing. This would be a complement to, rather than a substitute for, price support measures. Indeed, a degree of price support would be needed if compensatory financing requirements were to be kept within practicable limits. The quickest solution would be to improve the present compensatory financing facility of the International Monetary Fund as well as the Stabex scheme of the European Economic Community. The UNCTAD secretariat had already made proposals for a comprehensive commodity-related compensatory financing facility, but pending the examination and negotiation of these proposals, much could be done to improve existing schemes. Greater compensatory financing would, in his view, go far towards bringing relatively quick relief to the many countries that had been affected by the fall in commodity prices.

The Secretary-General stressed that both price support and compensatory financing were aspects of the Integrated Programme for Commodities. But in a situation of crisis the Programme had to be given an emergency dimension. The actions taken in the short term could pave the way for the longer-term measures. In recent times attention had been given to the marketing, distribution, and processing of commodities as part of the Programme. These aspects had already begun to receive attention in individual commodity negotiations with a view to utilizing the Second Window of the Common Fund. The early functioning of the Common Fund was thus, in his view, vital from this perspective as well.

All governments were not prepared, however, to adopt the Secretary-General's proposals for emergency action on commodities. The agreed resolution provided only for the Committee on Commodities to examine the feasibility of the proposed "interim agreements" for commodities "not covered by international agreements or arrangements",[26] and further to examine the role of such international agreements or arrangements in attaining the objectives of the IPC. Another resolution called on the Committee to elaborate the elements of "frameworks for international co-operation in the field of processing, marketing and distribution",[27] frameworks which had been called for already in a resolution of UNCTAD V. As to compensatory financing, the Conference agreed, but not unanimously, to establish an expert group to examine broad aspects of the issue, and particularly whether or not there was a "need for an additional complementary facility to compensate for export earnings shortfalls of developing countries".[28] The expert group was to transmit its report to the Trade and Development Board not later than 31 December 1984.

B. Evaluation

As indicated earlier in this chapter, there has been an essential continuum in the policy proposals of the UNCTAD secretariat on primary commodity issues since the inception of UNCTAD in 1964. The main theme has been the need to deal with such issues in an "integrated" fashion, so that the central role of commodities in the development process may be taken fully into account. It was recognized at UNCTAD I, and is just as true today, after UNCTAD VI, that for all but a handful of developing countries, the flow of foreign exchange earnings so essential to the furthering of the development process depends very heavily indeed on the prices received for, and the quantities supplied of, unprocessed or (in some cases) semi-processed primary commodities.

It is equally true, however, that the first two decades of UNCTAD's history have witnessed a disappointing failure of the international community to act in concrete fashion upon this fundamental perception of the dynamics of development. Thus, essentially nothing was accomplished in the commodity field during the first decade of UNCTAD's life—a series of inconclusive meetings of the Committee on Commodities, followed by a set of "intensive intergovernmental consultations" which, far from paving the way to negotiating conferences for commodity agreements, merely saw governments reiterate the well-established analysis of problems in individual commodity sectors.

The beginning of UNCTAD's second decade saw a major shift in the fortunes of commodity analysis at the intergovernmental level. The oil crisis, and the sharp

---

[26] Resolution 155 (VI), para. 8.

[27] Resolution 156 (VI), para. 3.

[28] Resolution 157 (VI), para. 3 (a). It is noteworthy that one major developed market-economy country (the United States of America) voted against the resolution and three developed market-economy countries (Australia, Canada and New Zealand) and seven socialist countries (Bulgaria, Czechoslovakia, the German Democratic Republic, Hungary, Mongolia, Poland and the Union of Soviet Socialist Republics) abstained from voting.

commodity price boom of the earlier 1970s, followed by an equally sharp collapse in the mid-1970s, brought to the attention of policy-makers everywhere the importance of international commodity policy in the development process. The United Nations General Assembly held a special session in 1974 on raw materials and development out of which emerged a Programme of Action on the Establishment of a New International Economic Order (NIEO) of which a fundamental component was to be an "overall integrated programme for commodities". Subsequently the secretariat's "Integrated Programme for Commodities" (IPC) was formulated, debated and adopted, at the fourth session of the Conference (1976).

The significance of the Integrated Programme for Commodities (IPC)

The previous section of this chapter has described the contents of the IPC and progress made in implementing it. Here it is of interest to evaluate the significance of the IPC, its implementation and its effectiveness. The IPC has been heavily criticized in some quarters as having been too ambitious, and possibly ill-focused since it concentrated on the pricing issue. Yet the "ambition" was certainly shared by governments at the time of the programme's adoption without any dissent. What had perhaps not been anticipated was the strain which the "time-bound" process of negotiation would place on the limited negotiating resources of the developing countries themselves, who therefore often were ill-prepared to face their well-organized and co-ordinated negotiating partners, whose very numbers (two dozen countries) made the adoption when appropriate, of a common negotiating strategy far easier than for the large and disparate group of 120 developing countries.

But more important still than this lack of negotiating capacity was, once again, the failure of governments to translate into action at the day-to-day level, the perception of the crucial linkage of commodities to the development process which had given rise to the adoption of the ambitious IPC. The "integrated" nature of the IPC was quickly dissipated as delegations became bogged down in the detail of preparatory meetings on individual commodities at which, as in the past, it became very difficult indeed to see the wood for the trees. Importantly, too, the slow pace of progress in these meetings sapped the energies and enthusiasm of negotiators, policy-makers and secretariat alike.

Overshadowing all the fervid activity at the individual commodity policy level was an equally arduous and lengthy round of negotiations on the Common Fund, which was to have been the financial linchpin of the system of International Commodity Agreements (ICAs) to be negotiated. The Fund has acquired a political significance as potentially the first concrete manifestation of the NIEO, which increased its importance to the developing countries beyond its original economic significance. But fundamental differences persisted as between the Western industrial countries' conception of the Fund as a pool of monies contributed by pre-existing ICAs and the developing countries' conception (which was also that of the secretariat) of a source of funds to serve as a catalyst to the conclusion for new ICAs, and possibly also as an instrument for the direct stabilization of commodity markets at risk but where no agreements could be reached. The eventual success of the Western industrial countries in imposing their less ambitious vision of the Fund on their negotiating partners certainly also dampened the prospects for a rapid end to the process of preparatory meetings and negotiations of ICAs under the IPC.

The implementation of the IPC must therefore be judged to have been a failure in many respects. Since the programme was adopted in 1976, only one new ICA with pricing provisions has been negotiated (rubber) and two without such provisions (jute and tropical timber). Even the renegotiation of existing agreements has proved more and more arduous than in pre-IPC days. Moreover, the aspects of the IPC dealing with matters other than prices have continued to be neglected in the discussions on individual commodities. Instead quite separate studies have been prepared and meetings have considered, on the one hand, the more general aspects of framework for international co-operation on processing, marketing and distribution, and on the other, a general compensatory financing facility, which would be commodity-specific but not tied to individual commodity agreements. No movement is discernible either in regard to measures to deal with emergency situations which have a cross-commodity impact.

Attitudes of consumers and producers

The reasons for this experience relates to the attitudes of both the consumers and the producers.

(a) *Attitude of consumers*

The consumers did not approach commodity negotiations as believers but rather as agnostics. The developed market-economy governments had not rid themselves of their dislike for market intervention, of their fear of going beyond stabilization of prices and encouraging price increases above the long-term market trend (particularly in an inflationary period such as existed after UNCTAD IV in Nairobi) and of their fear of paving the way for producer cartels. The socialist countries of Eastern Europe, participating in commodity negotiations mostly as consumers, were by and large subscribers to the principle of commodity stabilization through intergovernmental action and were participants in most agreements in being. But they, too, were less comfortable with new approaches to the agreements such as market intervention through stocking, with international intervention in markets and its corollary of financial contributions from participating governments.

(b) *Attitude of producers*

The producer countries had other weaknesses. The lack of confidence in their ability to influence negotiations, their concern as to the impact of international solutions to their particular commodity-specific problems and their difficulty in co-ordinating their position slowed substantially the negotiating process. A further complication is the existence in the case of some products of important developed country producers with their own domestic price support schemes and in the vertical integration of commodity producers. Generally speaking, the producers have come to commodity negotiations in a passive frame of mind relying on the initiative of leading consumers or on international secretariats. Where producers have been able to come together, as in the case of rubber, the results proved to be positive.[29]

---

[29] See also A. Maizels, "Reforming the World Commodity Economy" in M. Zammit Cutajar (ed), *UNCTAD and the South-North Dialogue. The First Twenty Years* (Pergamon Press, 1985), pp. 101-123.

How effective has the IPC been?

As to the effectiveness of the IPC measures which have been agreed, there is very little empirical evidence since the Common Fund has not yet come into operation, and only a few commodity agreements with price provisions are functioning. Of these, the only one negotiated under the IPC, that for rubber, appears to have been very successful in defending the floor price, even during the worst of the recession of the early 1980s, and has now accumulated sufficient stocks to enable it to have a positive impact on ceiling defence when rubber prices eventually recover to challenge that ceiling. Both the tin and coffee agreements have been successful in defending the floor price; as to the ceiling price, the tin agreement has been unsuccessful in the past and the coffee agreement has been untested in that respect. The remaining two agreements—those for sugar and cocoa—have failed quite perceptibly to defend the floor prices, both agreements suffering especially from the non-adhesion of major producing, and (in the case of cocoa) major consuming, countries. Overall, it seems fair to say that when—as for tin and rubber—the major producing and consuming countries participate, and the buffer stock mechanism (which the tin, rubber, and cocoa agreements use) is adequately financed (as was not the case for cocoa), the ICA can be quite effective in defending the agreed price range.

The need for compensatory financing

An ICA focusing on prices only cannot, however, be entirely effective in ensuring—as called for in the resolution on the IPC—the stabilization of developing countries' commodity export earnings around a growing trend. There will always be a need in this regard for residual compensatory finance to smooth out earnings fluctuations caused by unforeseen supply variations. The expert group on compensatory finance is a first step towards action on this aspect of the problem, but only a first step and much remains to be done. Similarly, the Common Fund remains non-operational with the result that finance not only for ICAs with stocking provisions, but also for arrangements dealing with non-stocking measures, is not readily available.

Major areas for future action

There are thus three major areas into which the international community has poured very substantial resources, which have not yet reached fruition, but which could do so with very little further expenditure of resources:

(*a*) the completion of ratification procedures for the Common Fund, so as to make it operational quickly;

(*b*) the completion of preparatory processes for ICAs for a number of commodities (especially copper, cotton and tea) which are already well advanced, together with renewed efforts for the remaining commodities; and

(*c*) the rapid establishment of a mechanism to provide residual compensatory finance for individual commodities.

C. Problems and tasks of the future

The review in earlier sections of the evolution of international commodity policy initiatives indicates clearly that for decades the same basic problems have confronted the world's commodity economies. These problems seem likely to persist over the years to come, and with them, the solutions earlier proposed, which will remain equally valid in the future. In the final analysis, the major task facing developing countries depending upon primary commodity production is to increase the domestic added value of such production so as to generate both employment and higher income for their citizens. This task requires a package of policies relating not only to price and earnings stabilization, but also to the efficient location of production, and to the domestic processing, and subsequent domestic and external marketing and distribution of locally-produced commodities. In turn, external marketing prospects depend in part on the possibilities of access of both primary and processed goods to foreign markets.

Whilst the emphasis in the past in this regard has been on access to the developed market-economy countries, as the largest market, it is clear that in the future more attention will need to be paid not only to the growing markets in the socialist countries of Eastern Europe, but also to the potential for increased intra-developing country trade in both raw and processed commodities. The challenge confronting the developing countries is to ensure that they exploit the potential in these markets before the transnational corporations, with the strength of their marketing experience and financial and managerial resources, pre-empt these markets for themselves. Although these are largely tasks which by their very nature must be addressed by the developing countries themselves, the international community can improve the efficiency of this process by providing for an objective analysis and assessment of policies and options regarding market characteristics and opportunities, a task for which the Common Fund would seem to be suited.

Beyond this, it would seem that there is less a need for new policy initiatives, so much as a need for the effective application of the initiatives already contained in the IPC. Structural developments in the global economy during the remainder of the decade of the 1980s will inevitably lead to greater financial strain on the major borrowing countries; greater risks of protectionist measures such as the recent severe restriction by the United States of the coverage of the generalized system of preferences; and continued, if not increased, volatility in primary commodity markets, as some developing country governments struggle to maintain their foreign exchange earnings in order to meet debt servicing and import requirements and as some industrial country governments take action to protect their domestic agricultural and mining sectors. In such circumstances, the critical importance of international commodity agreements and compensatory finance mechanisms hardly needs repeating. It is to be hoped that the international community will respond more positively and more rapidly to the challenges in the next few years than it has done in the past twenty.

II. MONEY, FINANCE AND DEVELOPMENT

A. Introduction

Throughout the past 20 years UNCTAD's concern with monetary and financial issues related to trade and development has been reflected in intensive activity, consisting of on-going research, the refinement and the formulation of concrete proposals for the resolution of outstanding problems and the pursuit of international agreements. At its very first session, in 1964, the Conference set this process in motion with a series of recommendations in such areas as the international monetary system, compensatory financing of shortfalls in export receipts of developing countries, supplementary assistance to help these countries avoid disruption of development programmes, growth and aid, debt service and debt rescheduling, and mobilization of resources for development.

The emphasis placed on the various elements in the field of money and finance has changed over time reflecting changes in the external environment and in the nature of international relations. Thus, while general continuity may be found in the range of issues dealt with over the years in the various UNCTAD forums reflecting the fundamental development perspective of UNCTAD, the emphasis among issues will be seen to have been subject to certain swings. With respect to monetary issues continuity may be seen in the focus on adequacy of balance-of-payments financing mechanisms and the elaboration of an international monetary system supportive not only of a healthy trading system but also of the development of developing countries. The continuous examination within UNCTAD of the adequacy of the International Monetary Fund's (IMF) Compensatory Financing Facility has contributed, over time, to several reforms of that facility. However, the early UNCTAD work on a Supplementary Financing Facility and on the link between the Special Drawing Rights (SDR) facility of the IMF and development finance did not lead to any concrete results. With respect to the former this idea ran its course by the late 1960s whereas the proposal regarding the SDR link has fallen into the background as support for additional SDR creation itself has run into strong opposition from a few major developed market-economy countries.

With respect to development finance issues the focus of activities has remained broadly constant emphasizing the need for an adequate volume of transfers and appropriate terms and conditions. The period of the 1960s and early 1970s was devoted to refining the ideas and the objective measures of transfers. This aspect has continued but in recognition of the failure to meet already agreed norms and targets it has tended to fall into the background behind appeals for better aid volume performance by the developed countries, strengthening of reviews and the search for mechanisms to ensure increased and more automatic provision of concessional finance. The history with respect to multilateral finance reflects, to some extent, changing fashions and ideas of major donors. Multilateral finance had been seen as a superior form of assistance to bilateral finance in that it provided greater objectivity in assessment of needs and would probably lead to more equitable distribution. These arguments may be disputed but multilateralism was a growing force in international relations through the 1960s and early 1970s and multilateral development finance institutions shared this general mood. Whether as a result of several shocks to the international economy or for other reasons, the fact remains that there has been a growing tendency towards bilateral settlement of issues and a general emphasis on bilateral relations. With respect to aid, multilateral development finance institutions have seen their previously recognized central role under increasing attack by a few major donors. The role and contribution of private finance in supporting development has always been a concern within UNCTAD. As its nature has changed the focus of attention can be seen to have changed. Private finance to developing countries during the 1960s was principally in the form of foreign private direct investment and guaranteed export credits and this was reflected in the discussions within UNCTAD. The 1970s saw an explosion of commercial bank finance in particular through the Euro-currency market. Consideration of these issues within UNCTAD shifted to measures to improve the access of developing countries to these markets and expressions of concern as to the implications of heavy use of such sources of finance. At a very early stage the UNCTAD secretariat was expressing concern with the floating interest rate system and variability over time of maturities on new lending which it felt greatly enhanced the potential debt problems of developing countries. The recent crisis in these markets has regrettably confirmed these concerns. Inadequate aid volume and the diminishing role of commercial bank lending may lie behind the resumed emphasis being given by developed countries to the potential of foreign private direct investment and the increasing interest therein being shown by some developing countries.

As early as the first session of UNCTAD questions of indebtedness were considered. Appropriate terms and conditions of financial flows, effective debt management and adequate balance-of-payments financing mechanisms may be seen as forward looking means to reduce the likelihood of debt crises. While placing emphasis on these matters the UNCTAD secretariat has felt that effective means for treating debt crises when they emerge are necessary both to protect the development process in developing countries and to give greater security to the international financial system. Not until 1978 was international consensus achieved in tackling some aspects of these problems—that of the Official Development Aid (ODA) debt of the poorer developing countries. But this marked the first time in any forum that a collective agreement was able to be reached on such matters. This achievement was followed-up by a further agreement in UNCTAD which set out guidelines or common features to guide debt reorganization exercises. These matters are further examined below but in an overall evaluation of UNCTAD's activities in the field of money and finance they require full recognition.

While "interdependence" has become better defined [1] and now is a regular item on the agenda of the Trade and Development Board, the very concept of UNCTAD includes fundamental notions of the interrelations between trade, finance and the International Monetary System (IMS) and their respective and collective contributions to development. Thus, the nature of the international monetary system can be more or less supportive of trade and development; similarly a healthy and equitable trading system can lessen the burden placed on the International Monetary System, by reducing the need for payments finance. Equally, the financial system plays the role of lubricating trade but also, in a sense, compensating for inadequacies in the trading system. Thus, in examining proposed policy measures addressed to particular areas, it is necessary to keep in mind the possibility that implementation of policy measures in one area may have either beneficial or harmful effects elsewhere. Furthermore, in some cases the most effective way of treating problems in particular sectors may be by implementing policy measures elsewhere. Within UNCTAD this idea of interdependence has evolved to the point where it is seen as the analytical framework within which the whole complex of policy issues of interest to the organization is considered.

B. International monetary and financial issues

INTERNATIONAL MONETARY ISSUES

The principal preoccupation during the early post-war years was to construct a world economic system in which the industrially developed countries would be able to pursue full employment policies while at the same time enjoying the benefits of expanding world trade and the international division of labour. Most of today's sovereign States were still colonies and, consequently, unable to articulate their interests in a system of world trade and payments that would be responsive to the requirements of worldwide development. The rules of international trade and payments that were embodied in the Bretton Woods Agreements and in the General Agreement on Tariffs and Trade (GATT) were, therefore, essentially designed for a world of full employment and stable economic growth which, it was considered, should take full advantage of the benefits of relatively free trade and payments arrangements. The manner in which the system might have been adapted to take into account the needs of the less developed countries was, however, less well understood.

The narrowness of the assumptions implicit in the system became increasingly apparent. In the international monetary field, the experience of many developing countries was characterized by the persistence of internal and external structural imbalance and this made it impossible for these countries to achieve the currency convertibility objectives of the international monetary system as embodied in the Articles of Agreement of the International Monetary Fund (IMF). Many developing

---

[1] The conceptual framework of interdependence has evolved and embraces interdependence among national economies, among sectors and between short-term problems and policies and their longer-term implications.

countries were unable to reconcile the objectives of internal price stability and external equilibrium while maintaining an adequate rate of growth.

In the early 1960s the view gained ground that developing countries needed special treatment and also that the international monetary system should be modified to allow for the different kinds of economic and social systems in existence and for more rational, deliberate and continuous co-operation between them. While UNCTAD in these early years, both at the intergovernmental and secretariat levels, actively pursued the objective of a fundamental reform of the prevailing international monetary system, it also sought to devise and promote counter measures to cyclical disturbances which were endemic to the trade and payments systems and which had deleterious effects on the growth process of developing countries.

Financing of export shortfalls

Since its inception, UNCTAD has given a prominent place in its general analysis of the development problem to the issue of compensation for fluctuations in the export earnings of developing countries. To the extent that economic development depends on imports, particularly of capital goods, it can be programmed only on the assumption that the required foreign exchange will be available. Large and unpredictable fluctuations in export earnings are therefore a serious obstacle to development. The concept of compensatory financing was developed in response to this problem.

UNCTAD's influence on schemes for compensatory financing

Following a suggestion made in 1962 by the United Nations Commission on International Commodity Trade, the IMF, in 1963, established the Compensatory Financing Facility (CFF), which was designed to tide countries over periods of temporary balance of payments disequilibrium arising from export shortfalls. At the same time, however, it was widely felt that something beyond this facility was also needed in order to tackle the problems associated with the deteriorating terms of trade of developing countries. Hence UNCTAD's twofold approach to the stabilization of export earnings: while proposing changes in the scope and terms of the CFF, UNCTAD has also argued the case for the creation of mechanisms designed to address other, mainly longer-term aspects of the problem.

At its inaugural session in 1964 in Geneva, UNCTAD welcomed the CFF as a short-term remedy, but called for its further extension and liberalization. Similar proposals were made in 1965[2] and in the light of these and other relevant considerations, IMF modified certain features of the Facility in 1966, viz: by raising the limit for outstanding drawings, by placing drawings entirely outside the structure of the gold and credit tranches, by accepting the possibility of refinancing drawings on a short-term basis in cases where exports did not recover sufficiently for reasons beyond the drawing country's control, and by taking some account of the rising trend of exports in calculating shortfalls. These modifications permitted a much more extensive use of the Facility at a time when commodity prices tended to be less favourable.

---

[2] See *International Monetary Issues and the Developing Countries. Report of the Group of Experts* (TD/B/32) (United Nations publication, Sales No. 66.II.D.2).

Substantial limitations remained, however, and UNCTAD II, in 1968, put forward a number of proposals, including a suggestion that adverse movements in import prices should also render a developing country eligible for compensation. At the same session, the Conference took up a related issue which had been under study for some time, viz: the lack of an adequate financial mechanism to permit the creation of buffer stocks of commodities. It called on IMF, the World Bank and the International Development Association (IDA), (which were at the time investigating how they could contribute to the stabilization of commodity prices), to concentrate on the problems of financing buffer stocks. The results of these joint endeavours led, in 1969, to the establishment by IMF of the Buffer Stock Financing Facility (BSFF), whereby members could draw on Fund resources to finance their contributions to international buffer stock arrangements.

Work in the area of compensatory financing continued within UNCTAD. In 1969 the second UNCTAD Group of Experts[3] proposed changes in the terms of the CFF, mainly concerning repayments, and UNCTAD III, in 1972, called for adjustments in both the CFF and the BSFF. With regard to buffer stocks, it was also suggested that IMF and the World Bank should finance the establishment of stocks of commodities. Proposals designed to give special IMF assistance to developing countries willing to commit themselves to mutual trade liberalization were proposed at UNCTAD III, but were never followed up in the face of opposition by IMF itself and several of its leading member countries.

At the end of 1975 IMF revised the CFF by improving the formula for calculating shortfalls; raising ceilings on annual and total outstanding drawings; and relaxing the rules regarding the timing of drawings. These changes followed shortly after specific proposals had been made by UNCTAD's Committee on Invisibles and Financing related to Trade (CIFT). Furthermore, earlier in the year the European Economic Community had introduced the so-called STABEX scheme, which provides compensation to its associated African, Caribbean and Pacific (ACP) countries for shortfalls occurring in earnings from any of the commodities covered by the Scheme. Repayment conditions were also more liberal than under the CFF. UNCTAD's continuing work emphasized these and other shortcomings of the CFF, among them the failure to take account of changes in import prices, the exclusion of earnings from services and the fact that the repayment schedule was not tied to the recovery of earnings.

These and other issues were considered by UNCTAD IV in 1976 and UNCTAD V in 1979, and in the latter year the CFF was again modified: the maximum amount of outstanding drawings was raised from 75 per cent to 100 per cent of quota, the existing constraint on annual drawings was removed and coverage was widened to include receipts from travel and workers' remittances. The Facility was further liberalized in 1981, allowing members to make drawings when faced with payments difficulties caused by an excess in the cost of cereal imports.

From the point of view of primary commodity exporters, however, the Facility still offers relatively limited compensation when compared to the size of shortfalls

---

[3] See *International monetary reform and co-operation for development. Report of the Expert Group on International Monetary Issues* (TD/B/285/Rev.1) (United Nations publication, Sales No. E.70.II.D.2).

experienced in recent years. This consideration was reflected in the resolution adopted by UNCTAD VI in 1983, calling on IMF to proceed expeditiously with its review of the CFF.

UNCTAD's role in supplementary financing

As already noted, UNCTAD always regarded the CFF as an answer to only part of the problem. Thus, in 1964, UNCTAD I adopted a recommendation inviting the World Bank to study the feasibility of a scheme that would provide long-term supplementary financial resources to developing countries experiencing shortfalls in export earnings which endangered their development programmes. This scheme would differ from the CFF in that the adverse effects of significant increases in import prices would also give rise to drawing rights. The World Bank scheme[4] provided for prior agreement between a member country and the administering agency on export projections, development programmes and policies and feasible domestic adjustments to offset shortfalls. It was based on the assumption that the necessary finance would be wholly supplementary to existing aid programmes and was widely regarded as a means of filling an important gap in the existing international financial machinery.

The World Bank study was reviewed by the UNCTAD Intergovernmental Group on Supplementary Financing in 1967, and the following year UNCTAD II requested the Group to attempt to resolve the issues it had identified while also working out measures for supplementary finance. This request was later transmitted to the World Bank by UNCTAD, but the Bank in 1971 cast doubts on such a scheme since there seemed to be little prospect of the necessary finance being made available by governments. The Bank, however, announced that should a developing country experience an unexpected shortfall in its export earnings which threatened to disrupt its development programme, it would examine the case on its merits in order to determine whether it could shape or modify its lending to that country to help it overcome its difficulties.

UNCTAD's continuing efforts to create a supplementary financing scheme failed, however, to produce the desired result: in 1973 the World Bank expressed the view that its lending practices in connection with export promotion represented an even better alternative to the proposed supplementary financing scheme. The resultant conflicting opinions within the membership of UNCTAD led to the setting aside of consideration of this proposal.

A commodity-related compensatory facility

As the balance-of-payments situation of developing countries seriously worsened in the second half of the 1970s, UNCTAD renewed its call for a complementary, commodity-related facility. Under such a scheme compensation would not be limited by quotas and the balance of payments criterion. The concept of a commodity-related compensatory facility was developed further and UNCTAD VI decided to create an expert group to study all relevant aspects.[5]

---

[4] *Supplementary Financial Measures — a study requested by the United Nations Conference on Trade and Development, 1964* (International Bank for Reconstruction and Development, Washington D.C., December 1965).

[5] Further details on this commodity-related compensatory facility are contained in section I.

Financing of structural payments imbalances

In the early 1970s the balance-of-payments problems of non-oil exporting developing countries was aggravated by an intensification of the underlying external disequilibrium, so that it became impossible to draw a clear distinction between issues related to the short and longer-term perspectives. This situation also highlighted the inadequacy of the financing facilities available for dealing with such imbalances, and in 1973 UNCTAD made a number of proposals, including some which envisaged a greater flexibility and longer repayment periods connected with the use of IMF resources.

The Extended Fund Facility

A step forward was taken in 1974 with the establishment by IMF of the Extended Fund Facility (EFF), designed to provide conditional assistance to member countries for up to three years in support of comprehensive programmes to correct structural imbalances which prevented the pursuit of an active development policy. Repayment periods were longer than under existing facilities and these were eventually extended to a maximum of 10 years. As the decade progressed, the need of developing countries for additional payments finance increased owing to the adverse impact of rising import prices and of reduced export demand caused by recession in developed countries. The UNCTAD secretariat took the view that externally-induced deficits that were self-reversing should be financed rather than adjusted through internal measures and that those that were structural, rather than self-reversing, would require an adjustment process spread over an extended period. The secretariat thus called for the provision of additional, longer-term support by IMF. A study prepared with United Nations Development Programme (UNDP) support in 1979[6] questioned the efficacy and relevance of short-term financial support in meeting problems of a more enduring structural character and concluded that a gap existed in the prevailing network of facilites which needed to be filled by the creation of a medium-term multilateral facility. While calling for improvements in the EFF, the Conference invited IMF to undertake an in-depth study on the need for such a new facility.

Structural adjustment lending by the World Bank

The growing recognition of the structural nature of the payments problems faced by developing countries at the time was also reflected in the introduction of structural adjustment lending by the World Bank in 1980. The objective here was to provide quick disbursing finance to support measures specifically designed to strengthen countries' balance of payments within five to ten years without holding back economic and social development.

UNCTAD's continuing work in this area included a meeting of a High-level Group of Experts[7] in 1980 the report of which recommended, *inter alia,* the establishment of a medium-term facility designed to respond to the particular adjust-

---

[6] S. Dell and R. Lawrence, *The Balance-of-Payments Adjustment Process in Developing Countries: Report to the Group of Twenty-four* (New York, Pergamon Press, in co-operation with the United Nations, 1980).

[7] *Report of the Ad Hoc Intergovernmental High-level Group of Experts on the Evolution of the International Monetary System* (TD/B/823/Rev.1) (United Nations publication, Sales No. E.82.II.D.2).

ment needs of developing countries. This call, supported by the sixth session of the Conference in 1983, was prompted by the unprecedented size of the payments imbalances, and the relatively limited impact of the EFF and of the World Bank's structural adjustment loans.

Liquidity needs and reserve asset creation

UNCTAD's early concern with international monetary issues related to trade and development was reflected in the report of the Group of Experts of 1965 which made a contribution to the debate on liquidity needs and reserve asset creation in two respects: it envisaged the possibility of a widespread expansion in reserves through the extension of automatic drawing rights in IMF, similar to the type then applied in the gold tranche, into the credit tranches; and it proposed the establishment of a link between the creation of international liquidity and the provision of development finance.

The first proposal met with early success in that some of its features were incorporated into the Special Drawing Right (SDR) facility approved by IMF in 1967 and activated in 1970. Under the scheme SDRs i.e., unconditional liquidity, would be created deliberately in amounts considered necessary in the light of the world's reserve requirements and would constitute a permanent addition to the world supply of reserves. UNCTAD's efforts continued thereafter in the direction of encouraging the establishment of the SDR as the principal reserve asset of the system, as originally intended, as well as calling for regular and increased allocations of SDRs.

The link between SDRs and development finance

The "link" concept (mentioned earlier) was further elaborated by an UNCTAD Group of Experts in 1969, which proposed two alternative approaches: (*a*) a direct contribution of SDRs by the developed countries to IDA out of their allocations; (*b*) contributions in national currencies by these countries to IDA in proportion to their SDR allocations. In each case, the volume and timing of SDR creation would be determined entirely by the monetary requirements of the world economy. The concept received wide endorsement, including that of the United Nations General Assembly in 1971, was studied within IMF and gave rise to an active and long-lasting debate. While some saw the "link" as a technically feasible means of saving resources and of increasing the exports of developed countries to developing countries, others claimed it would be inflationary and that it might even be disruptive for development finance.

Resolutions calling on IMF to continue its studies on the "link" concept were adopted by UNCTAD II in 1968 and UNCTAD III in 1972. The latter year coincided with a period of growing turbulence and uncertainty in the world monetary system. UNCTAD responded with concrete proposals in the areas of, *inter alia*, reserve asset creation, the consolidation of reserve currency balances, and SDR creation and the link with development assistance. The secretariat argued that an enlargement of the collective surplus of the developed countries to the extent implied by individual national current account objectives would require a concomitant increase in the financial resources of the developing countries. It was thus appropriate for an SDR link to be used to enlarge the flow of real resources to developing countries, since this would assist in efforts to provide balanced growth of international trade. This was also seen as a collective contribution to the achievement of the goals of the Second United Nations Development Decade.

The momentum which had been built up in favour of the "link", largely as a result of UNCTAD's efforts, was interrupted when the Committee of Twenty's[8] Outline of Reform in 1974 failed to include even an enabling clause to establish such a mechanism. The creation was, however, announced of a Trust Fund which could be seen as a link between gold revaluation and development finance. At this point UNCTAD studied other modifications in IMF policies designed to increase the availability of unconditional liquidity to developing countries. The accent was placed on securing further allocations of SDRs (none took place during the second basic period, 1973-1977), on the need for international control over the process of liquidity creation, and on the corresponding need for the SDR to replace national currencies as the principal reserve asset.

UNCTAD's work in this area during the past three years—during which no further SDR allocations have been made—has highlighted the urgent need for regular and substantial allocations and for channelling these funds to member countries on appropriate terms through a medium-term facility for enhancing the role of the SDR (between 1973 and 1983 the share of the SDR in total world reserves fell from 5.7 per cent to 3.5 per cent); and for a political decision on the implementation of the "link". These objectives were reflected in resolution 162 (VI) adopted by UNCTAD VI.

Reform of the international monetary system

The concern of UNCTAD with the functioning of the Bretton Woods system found expression, *inter alia,* in the report of the Group of Experts of 1969 which analysed and proposed solutions to current problems in the area of reserve creation, the adjustment process and the multiple reserve asset system. When the 1971 crisis struck, the UNCTAD secretariat stressed the need for a trade and payments system which: was not dependent on the payments deficits of a reserve currency country; was one which promised to foster sustained and balanced growth of the world economy and in which development objectives featured more prominently.

A reformed adjustment process would have to: provide countries with a means of balancing their external accounts at a minimum cost in terms of domestic output and employment; involve the least possible use of trade restrictions by deficit countries; and ensure a greater use of exchange-rate adjustment than in the past.

Consistent with its earlier analysis of the world economy, the UNCTAD secretariat made a case for: preferential treatment of developing countries in the monetary field; an examination of the adequacy of developing countries' reserves and of methods for increasing them; a much closer identification of the reformed system with the problem of commodity price stabilization; and a greater

---

[8] The Committee on Reform of the International Monetary System and Related Issues—commonly known as the Committee of Twenty—was constituted in 1972 and developing countries had nine seats on it. For the Outline of Reform see IMF, *International Monetary Reform. Documents of the Committee of Twenty,* Washington D.C., 1974.

participation of developing countries in the decision-making process regarding the reform of the system. Finally, the UNCTAD secretariat emphasized the interdependence between the problems of trade, development finance and the international monetary system.

The above-mentioned issues were discussed at UNCTAD III and were also taken up by IMF's Committee on Reform of the International Monetary System and Related Issues—commonly known as the Committee of Twenty. A series of studies prepared for this Group stressed the importance of a broad range of issues, including those involving the contribution of trading arrangements and development finance to the balance-of-payments process; expanded views on the substantive issues connected with interdependence; offered an assessment of the role that statistical indicators might play in the adjustment process, particularly as regards developing countries; and analysed the payments difficulties of developing countries, drawing attention to their incompatibility with the rules of a liberal trade and payments system.

Major studies in the area of reserve assets discussed the options for a future system of reserves and assessed how various means of dealing with outstanding balances of reserve currencies and gold, such as the establishment of a facility in IMF to substitute SDRs for such holdings, might affect the developing countries; and underlined the need for concessionality of funds provided to developing countries through the "link".

In the event, however, the Committee of Twenty's Outline of Reform fell short of these expectations in several respects: problems of commodity trade and trade barriers restricting the exports of developing countries, which exert a profound influence on their external payments, were largely ignored; the Committee's concern with swift adjustment of imbalances led it to overlook the inequality in the ability of developed and developing countries to finance deficits; the oil price increase at the end of 1973 and the resultant unprecedented imbalances in international payments caused the focus of attention to shift from "adjustment" to "financing"; this led to the establishment of IMF's Oil Facility, but developing countries were denied preferential access to it, though they did benefit from a scheme designed to reduce the interest burden of borrowing under the facility;[9] and efforts to achieve symmetry between the responsibility of "surplus" and "deficit" countries met with little success.

Concern at this failure to secure a fundamental reform of the international monetary system was reflected in the resolutions of the General Assembly of the United Nations in 1974 which constitute the foundations of the Programme of Action on a New International Economic Order.

The work of the Committee of Twenty culminated in agreement in the Interim Committee in Kingston, Jamaica in January 1976, principally on exchange rates and gold. Again, several elements considered essential by UNCTAD for an improvement of the system were, however, missing. The agreement contained no reference to a reduction in the role of gold or of reserve currencies, without which an advance in the position of SDRs could not be secured; to the establishment of a

---

[9] The idea of subsidizing interest costs on non-concessional borrowings by developing countries had first been proposed at UNCTAD I.

substitution account, either for currencies or for gold; or to the establishment of the "link".

UNCTAD V in 1979 was convened against a background fraught with problems for both developed and developing countries: the former were faced with high inflation and unemployment combined with recession; the latter with deteriorating terms of trade, large and growing payments deficits and erosion of asset values owing to exchange rate fluctuations. The UNCTAD secretariat drew attention to a number of distinctive features which could, and in fact did, have serious consequences later, among them the increasing tendency for the creation of international liquidity to be assumed by the private sector instead of IMF, and commercial bank lending to developing countries at short maturities and high interest rates; the Conference adopted resolution 128 (V) in which, *inter alia,* it invited IMF to improve the terms and utilization of the Extended Fund Facility; to study the need for a longer-term facility to help member countries carry out structural adjustment over longer periods; and to liberalize further the Compensatory Financing Facility.

The Conference further decided to establish an *ad hoc* Intergovernmental High-level Group of Experts to examine fundamental issues concerning international monetary reform.[10] The Group of Experts met in 1980 and was attended by developing countries, the socialist countries of Eastern Europe and China. The developed market-economy countries, with one exception, did not attend. The Group of Experts agreed that the existing international monetary arrangements were inadequate, inefficient and inequitable and considered the evolution of the international monetary system as an element of a new international economic order. The Group of Experts elaborated objectives and characteristics of a reformed international monetary system, among which universality of membership and equity in the decision-making process were recognized as important elements. Among other suggestions, attention was drawn to the possibility of convening, within the framework of the United Nations, a world monetary conference on international monetary issues.

The external payments position of non-oil producing developing countries sharply deteriorated once more in 1980-1982. Emphasizing that a sizeable proportion of their current account deficit was due to long-term shifts in relative prices and would not, therefore, be self-correcting with the advent of recovery in the developed countries, the UNCTAD secretariat pointed out that the structural changes in the composition of output which the developing countries needed to make could only take place in the presence of considerable external financing of a medium-term to long-term character. In the meantime, however, several countries experienced difficulties in meeting debt service payments and the private capital markets now sought to reduce their exposure and themselves became a source of payments problems for these countries. Since the official institutions, particularly IMF, were unable to counter these trends effectively, the developing countries had to adjust by cutting back imports and arresting growth. In view of the high degree of interdependence in the world economy, this retrenchment inevitably had a negative effect on the incipient recovery in the developed countries.

---

[10] See Conference resolution 128 (V), (para 11), on International Monetary Reform. The Conference adopted this resolution by 69 votes to 17, with 13 abstentions.

Global interdependence

Reiterating its thesis on global interdependence, the UNCTAD secretariat called on member countries to address the immediate financial problems of developing countries in the context of efforts to improve the performance of the world economy as a whole. To this end, three sets of mutually-supportive measures were proposed, viz. a substantial enlargement of the liquidity and financing available to developing countries; greater efforts by developing countries to increase the inflow of foreign investment and foreign-exchange earnings; and increased emphasis on the part of the developed countries on bringing down unemployment, interest rates and protective barriers.

UNCTAD VI in 1983 considered immediate measures designed to improve the financial position of developing countries and enlarge their capacity to import. These included: a shift in emphasis in IMF conditionality towards greater importance on expanding productive capacities; regular SDR allocations and the creation of a medium-term facility to channel SDRs to developing countries; gold sales by IMF for the benefit of poorer developing countries; further liberalization of the CFF; accelerated disbursements by the World Bank and a more flexible approach in its conditionality on structural adjustment lending; an increase in Official Development Assistance (ODA); and a variety of debt relief measures.

Though the immediacy and magnitude of the payments crisis called for emergency measures, the secretariat also stressed the importance of addressing the structural deficiencies in the international monetary and financial system and identified a number of priorities. The resolutions adopted by the Conference did not adequately address these concerns. There were divergent opinions expressed concerning both the analysis of the problems and the appropriate remedies. One of the major arguments concerned the extent to which the recovery in the developed countries would obviate the need for specific immediate measures to increase the flow of finance to developing countries.

Participation of developing countries in decision making

The participation of developing countries in the decision-making process within the international monetary system has been an important topic within UNCTAD throughout the past 20 years though the focus has somewhat altered in the light of changing circumstances and priorities. UNCTAD I, in 1964, recommended that international financial and monetary agencies should endeavour to increase the participation of nationals of developing countries in the process of policy formulation. This reflected the growing belief that the philosophy underlying the monetary system set up at Bretton Woods was not necessarily appropriate to the essential needs of developing countries and that developing countries had not had a say in the matter. UNCTAD II, in 1968, was able to welcome the fact that developing countries, through their representation on the Executive Board of IMF, had participated in the negotiations that led to the agreement to create SDRs. This event followed on from, and owed much to, the adoption of a United Nations General Assembly resolution on this matter, as well as to the strong position taken by the Managing Director of IMF.

When, in the latter part of 1971, it became clear that the entire structure of the international monetary system would have to be reviewed, concern regarding the decision-making process took on a new dimension. Indeed, during December of that year, the meetings of the Group of Ten [11] which led directly to the Smithsonian Agreement [12] took place outside the framework of IMF.

At the time of UNCTAD III in 1972 two issues of principle remained unresolved: first, how reform was to be negotiated; and secondly, how wide the scope of the reform should be. Underlying both these issues was the role to be played by the reformed system in promoting the trade and development of the developing countries.

As regards the negotiating process, the Conference called for the strengthening of the role of IMF as the central forum for debate and decision-making, and for the effective participation of developing countries; it also invited IMF to accept the proposal to set up a Committee of Twenty of the Board of Governors on the reform of the system and urged that developing country representation in that Committee should not be less than that existing in the Executive Board of IMF.

The Committee of Twenty was duly constituted later in 1972 and developing countries were given nine seats on it, the same number as on the Board of IMF. Moreover, the Secretary-General of UNCTAD was invited to participate in the deliberations of the Committee. In 1974, UNCTAD was invited to participate in the work of IMF Interim Committee on International Monetary Affairs on which developing countries had an equal number of seats as the developed countries, and UNCTAD also became the executing agency for a UNDP project designed to assist the Group of Twenty-Four [13] in elucidating issues under negotiation in the international monetary field. Since 1975, the Secretary-General of UNCTAD has also taken part in the work of the joint IMF/World Bank Development Committee.

Though the progress since then towards a fundamental reform of the international monetary system has fallen short of expectations, the needs and interests of developing countries have been better articulated than in the past through UNCTAD's active participation in the work of the above-mentioned Committee, which has continued to be supported by the research work of the secretariat and the monitoring role of UNCTAD's intergovernmental bodies.

FINANCIAL RESOURCES FOR DEVELOPMENT

The creation of UNCTAD coincided with a growing recognition of the development finance gap and with the emergence of a certain consensus on development

---

[11] The Group of Ten consists of the major developed market-economy countries, and now consists of 11 members—Belgium, Canada, France, the Federal Republic of Germany, Italy, Japan, the Netherlands, Sweden, the United Kingdom, the United States and Switzerland.

[12] The Smithsonian Agreement realigned the exchange rates of the major currencies, including a devaluation of the official price of the dollar in terms of gold, and was an attempt to re-establish fixed exchange rates following the unilateral suspension of dollar convertibility and the floating of several major currencies.

[13] The Group of Twenty-Four (formally the Intergovernmental Group of Twenty-Four on International Monetary Affairs), with eight members from each of the three regional groups, was established following decisions taken at the second Ministerial meeting of the Group of 77 in Lima in 1971. Its principal objective is to co-ordinate the position of developing countries on international monetary and financial issues, in particular, those under consideration in IMF and the World Bank.

objectives. UNCTAD played an important role, along with the General Assembly of the United Nations and the Development Assistance Committee (DAC) of the Organization for Economic Co-operation and Development (OECD), in laying down the foundations for international consensus on targets for the volume and terms of financial flows. In the 1960s, an important proportion of financial flows to developing countries was channelled through bilateral development assistance. In addition, bilateral private flows consisting mainly of direct investment represented, on average, about 20 per cent of total net flows. Multilateral development financial institutions, especially the World Bank, were also widely used to channel finance towards developing countries. Deliberations within UNCTAD focused mainly on quantitative targets for financial flows and on the quality of flows, especially of bilateral official flows; emphasis was also placed on the key role played by the multilateral financial institutions.

By the mid-1970s the sharp rise in bank lending, especially through the Eurocurrency markets, greatly altered the composition of flows, resulting in an overwhelming share of private bank lending in total financial flows. This has also created serious problems for developing countries, regarding both their access to capital markets and to a hardening of the terms of such finance through increases in interest rates and margins and the shortening of maturities.

Volume, terms and conditions of financial flows

GNP target of aid

In recognition of the need to augment the domestic efforts of the developing countries with external finance, the Conference, in 1964, recommended that developed countries should endeavour to supply net financial resources to developing countries at a level equivalent to 1 per cent of their national income. The terms of such external financing were also broadly defined, in particular with respect to the repayment period of loans and to the untying of flows, as well as measures to promote foreign direct investment.

Following the request contained in the Final Act of the first session of the Conference, the UNCTAD secretariat undertook detailed quantitative estimates of the capital requirements of developing countries on the basis of their "trade gap".[14] This constituted the first substantial attempt to quantify capital requirements of developing countries. Along with quantitative estimates of the volume of flows, the secretariat also examined in detail the terms and conditions of flows which would be suitable to the needs of developing countries. The results of the secretariat's findings were contained in a document presented to the second session of the Conference in 1968 in New Delhi.[15]

---

[14] The "trade gap" is defined as the excess of foreign-exchange payments (on account of imports of goods and services, including investment income) over foreign exchange earnings, while the "savings gap" is the excess of investment requirements over domestic savings. *Ex post* the two gaps are always equal, since the excess of the domestic use of resources over the domestic supply of resources cannot exceed the net transfer of resources from abroad.

[15] These estimates and the appendant analysis are contained in a large volume published in 1968: *Trade prospects and capital needs of developing countries* (TD/34/Rev.1) (United Nations publication, Sales No. E.68.II.13).

Official development assistance (ODA) target

UNCTAD II in 1968 made a further important contribution to defining basic concepts on terms and conditions of financial flows. While endorsing the 1 per cent target for total flows of financial resources (net of amortization and capital repatriation), the Conference also adopted a supplementary target for net ODA of 0.75 per cent of the GNP of developed countries. It was considered that a sub-target for official flows was useful, insofar as these flows were more responsive to government policies and were, therefore, more amenable to meaningful international agreement. This sub-target, combined with the total flow target, may be seen as also indicating the desirable balance between official and private flows.

Terms of aid

UNCTAD II also recommended that further efforts be made by donor countries to soften the terms of aid beyond the norms set out by DAC and the General Assembly and that terms be harmonized among donor countries. It was proposed that the terms of aid should be further softened by increasing the amount of aid given in the form of grant (which would be equivalent to 80 per cent or more of official aid) or by improving interest rates, maturities or grace periods of the official aid loan commitments of donor countries.

In the light of UNCTAD studies[16] on the cost of aid tying, the Conference recommended that donors should take measures to reduce the extent of tying and to mitigate any harmful effects through, *inter alia,* a greater coverage of local costs, permitting procurement in developing countries, and a widening of the range of choice among goods or services available to recipient countries under tied aid.

After UNCTAD II, the international community paid increased attention to the question of the terms of development finance. The Commission on International Development, better known as the Pearson Commission,[17] and the General Assembly, through its work on the elaboration of the International Development Strategy for the Second United Nations Development Decade, contributed to further clarification of targets, in particular, the target for ODA of 0.7 per cent of GNP of donor countries. The third session of UNCTAD in 1972 endorsed this target for ODA, in addition to the 1 per cent target for total net flows. UNCTAD III recommended measures to ensure the continuity of ODA through, for example, multi-year programming, and requested the Trade and Development Board to examine further the concepts of aid and flow targets.

A Group of Governmental Experts on the Concepts of the Present Aid and Flow Targets was established by the Board and met in 1973, 1974 and 1977 to consider the issue. The Group examined the question of definition and measurement of flows, including the question of netting out reverse flows. The Group

---

[16] See, for example, "The cost of aid tying to recipient countries" (TD/7/Supp.8) and "Report on tied credits—Chile" (TD/7/Supp.8/Add.1). Both documents are printed in *Proceedings of the United Nations Conference on Trade and Development, Second Session,* vol. IV—*Problems and Policies of Financing* (United Nations publication, Sales No. E.68.II.D.17).

[17] The Commission on International Development was set up in 1968 upon a request from the President of the World Bank to consider all aspects of problems and policies related to the development of developing countries and to make relevant recommendations. The conclusions of the Commission are contained in its report: *Partners in Development: Report of the Commission on International Development* (London, Pall Mall Press, 1969).

highlighted the importance of ODA for developing countries, especially for the least developed among them and stressed the priority of the 0.7 per cent ODA target over the 1 per cent target for total flows. It also pointed out deficiencies in statistical coverage and noted the necessity of the establishment of a comprehensive statistical reporting system.[18] There have been significant improvements in several reporting systems and efforts to make these more compatible. However, significant gaps and deficiencies remain.

The Conference, at its fifth and sixth sessions in 1979 and 1983 adopted two important resolutions concerning ODA. In these resolutions, 129 (V) and 164 (VI), the developed countries have pledged themselves to increase ODA flows so as to attain the 0.7 per cent target by 1985 or no later than the second half of the decade. They have been urged to adopt interim plans on a multi-year basis to reach this target. On the quality of aid, it has been stressed that ODA should contain the highest degree of concessionality possible, and should be provided to the least developed countries in the form of grants. Provision of aid should be made in a flexible manner, implying that it should cover more programme aid, quick disbursing funds and local cost financing. Moreover, aid should be untied and given on an increasingly assured, continuous and predictable basis. It was also felt that aid procedures should be improved by a better co-ordination between donor and recipient countries. The UNCTAD Committee on Invisibles and Financing related to Trade was given the mandate to review and monitor the measures on which agreement had been reached.

Upon a request by the General Assembly in 1979, the UNCTAD secretariat submitted to it a report on increased transfer of resources,[19] which contained a review and analysis of various proposals on an expanded volume of resource transfers to developing countries. These proposals were aimed at: (a) an improved management of the interdependence in the world economy, involving either a short-term demand stimulation or a long-term structural transformation in the world economy; (b) improving the channelling of financial resources from international capital markets for long-term investment in developing countries; (c) investment in specific economic sectors of developing countries, such as energy, food and raw material production and processing; and (d) establishing a medium-term facility to support the process of structural balance-of-payments adjustment in developing countries. The report also concluded that expanded arrangements for resource transfers should provide for an appropriate blending between resources raised on financial markets and concessional flows, in order to improve the volume, terms and distribution of non-concessional flows. In this regard, it recognised that increased use of official intermediation should be made through the setting up of such mechanisms as multilateral guarantees and interest subsidy accounts.

Broadly speaking, real achievements have been disappointing. The collective DAC ODA/GNP performance is less than half of the agreed 0.7 per cent target. Of the 17 DAC member countries, only four (Denmark, the Netherlands, Norway and

---

[18] For the report on its most recent session see TD/B/646 reproduced in *Official Records of the Trade and Development Board, Seventh Session, First Part, Annexes,* agenda item 5 (c). For the report on the second session see TD/B/493/Rev.1 (United Nations publication, Sales No. E.75.II.D.8).

[19] *"Acceleration of the transfer of real resources to developing countries: increased transfer of resources. Report of the Secretary-General"* (A/34/493), 30 October 1979.

Sweden) have reached or exceeded the target. With respect to the terms of aid, concessionality has recently tended to decline. The conditions of aid have not improved either, insofar as more than half of bilateral aid disbursements remains fully or partially tied and non-project assistance has fallen in real terms during the decade of the 1970s. In the mid 1970s member States and national and multilateral institutions of the Organization of Petroleum Exporting Countries (OPEC) began a substantial aid programme for the benefit of other developing countries. The UNCTAD secretariat undertook to compile data on these activities, and the first such report appeared in 1977. The secretariat has established a reporting system with a view to reporting on an annual basis in the field of aid co-operation of OPEC countries and institutions. It is also hoped, at a later date, to expand this system to include aid activities of other developing countries. The most recent report [20] indicates that for the nine year period 1973-1981 OPEC countries provided 2.5 per cent of their gross national product in aid to other developing countries.

Multilateral development finance

Consideration of multilateral development finance within UNCTAD has centred principally on two themes—first, consistently strong support for the role of multilateral development finance in the overall provision of development finance and second, proposals for reform of the institutions' lending programmes and policies, in particular proposals that would use the skill and prestige of those institutions to facilitate other flows through the use of guarantees or by acting as intermediaries by borrowing and on lending.

Consensus appeared to have emerged by the 1960s on a large role for IDA in the overall provision of official development assistance and for Multilateral Development Finance Institutions (MDFIs) generally in providing a substantially larger share of overall development finance. The general confidence in which MDFIs were held was further reflected in the variety of proposals to strengthen their role. At UNCTAD I, in 1964, reference was made to the possible role of a multilateral investment insurance scheme then under study in the World Bank as a means of promoting foreign private direct investment. UNCTAD II, in 1968, considered the question of a multilateral interest equalization fund. The proposal, generally known as the Horowitz proposal,[21] would have allowed an international institution to borrow funds in financial markets on commercial terms and re-lend these funds to developing countries at lower rates of interest and with longer maturities. The interest subsidies were to be covered by contributions from developed countries and from the World Bank. While there was no concrete follow-up to this proposal, the World Bank did establish, in 1975, a scheme for interest subsidization through its Third Window Interest Subsidy Fund. The Conference at its fifth session in 1979 recommended that early consideration be given to a proposal for the establishment in the World Bank of a long-term facility to finance purchases of capital goods by developing countries. Similarly, the practice of co-financing, whereby World Bank

---

[20] *Financial Solidarity for Development, 1983 Review* (TD/B/C.3/187-TD/B/C.7/63) (United Nations publication, Sales No. E.84.II.D.3).

[21] The basic proposal was made to the first session of the Conference in 1964 by Mr. Horowitz who was at that time Governor of the Bank of Israel and Head of Delegation of Israel to the Conference. (See E/CONF.46/C.3/2).

loans are associated with private finance, has been given support as has special sectoral lending, for example, for energy exploration and exploitation.

Another area of concern voiced within UNCTAD has related to measures to increase the overall capacity of MDFIs, and particularly the World Bank, to provide development finance. Support has been given to increases in the capital base and to changes in the Articles of Agreement which would allow the gearing ratio to be relaxed from its 1:1 relationship to the capital base, permitting increased lending on any given capital base.

The effectiveness of the debate within UNCTAD in terms of improvements in the ability of MDFIs to lend, or to the programmes and policies of these institutions, is difficult to assess. While the World Bank in 1975 did establish a Third Window Interest Subsidy Fund, this has now ceased to function. The World Bank implemented in 1980 a programme of structural adjustment lending and, in 1983, a Special Assistance Programme was introduced designed to respond to the current financial requirements of developing countries. Co-financing programmes have been enlarged. However, the lending capacity of multilateral institutions has been limited by resistance by developed countries to expand their capital base. The share of programme lending *vis-à-vis* project lending remains modest, and the terms of lending have hardened. Funds devoted to concessional lending to poorer countries have shrunk, exemplified by the recent experience of the Seventh Replenishment of IDA, which at $9 billion represents a significant reduction in real terms over the Sixth Replenishment.

Private flows

Recognition has been given throughout UNCTAD's 20 years to the potential of private finance in external financial support to development. The flows primarily considered have been private direct investment, export credit finance and access to, and appropriate use of private capital markets and bank finance. During the 1960s and early 1970s, the attention of the Conference and of the Committee on Invisibles and Financing related to Trade (CIFT) was on private direct investment, mechanisms involving intermediation by multilateral financial institutions to expand the use of private capital market finance (e.g. the Horowitz proposal), and the use of export credit finance available from developed countries. From the early 1970s, attention moved towards questions of direct access to the rapidly expanding Eurocurrency markets and proposals for an export credit refinancing or guarantee facility, which would assist developing countries offering export credit finance on their exports. More recently, due to the stagnation and then collapse of developing country access to capital markets, attention is being focused again on intermediation as a means of improving access and on greater use of private direct investment.

UNCTAD I, in 1964, gave emphasis to the promotion of private direct investment and the necessary supportive actions required by both investors and host countries. The second session of the CIFT, in 1966, adopted an agreed statement on problems of development which, *inter alia,* specifically addressed flows of private direct investment and in that connection referred to a multilateral investment insurance scheme then under study within the World Bank as a way of promoting the flow of private capital. The second session of the Conference, in 1968, gave recognition to the potential of private direct investment but identified many factors both positive and negative which complicated the picture and which required careful examination. Between the second session of the Conference and the fourth session of CIFT, which met in July 1970, a major study was launched by the secretariat on the balance-of-payments effects of private foreign investment. The CIFT gave further guidance to the work asking that the studies continue in order to: improve the methodology; collect additional data; and seek to quantify the domestic income and employment effects of foreign investment, including the impact on indigenous enterprises, taking into account the direct and indirect balance-of-payments effects as well as alternative ways in which foreign capital, skills and technology might be transferred.

In 1971, CIFT devoted attention to private direct investment—views among groups of countries differed as to the general net effects of such investment and the adequacy of the methodology being elaborated to examine the question, and the Conference at its third session was asked to take up the question of providing instructions for further work by the UNCTAD secretariat in that field. The Conference at its third session adopted resolution 56 (III) on foreign private investment in its relationship to development,[22] which was broadly critical of private foreign investment, and authorized the Secretary-General of UNCTAD to continue studies on private foreign investment "with a view to determining with the greatest possible accuracy the effects of foreign private investment on the development process of the developing countries".

The sixth session of CIFT, in 1973, considered a report entitled "Main findings of a study of private foreign investment in selected developing countries" (TD/B/C.3/111), the main conclusion of which was that it was not possible to draw general conclusions on the effect of private foreign investment on the economies of developing countries and that the outcome would vary from case to case. The Committee agreed that the secretariat should undertake a study that would seek to assess the impact of policies or guidelines concerning the operations of foreign private enterprises on the economies of the host countries. The substantial research effort and intensive consideration of these issues largely came to an end in 1975 at the seventh session of CIFT, when it adopted resolution 12 (VII) on the flow of financial resources which, *inter alia,* requested "the Secretary-General of UNCTAD to prepare periodically comprehensive reports on private and official flows to and from developing countries". More recently the attention of many countries has moved towards foreign private direct investment and this is likely to be reflected in a greater emphasis on this matter in future UNCTAD meetings.

Access of developing countries to capital markets

UNCTAD has examined several methods to enlarge the access of developing countries to capital markets (private bank lending and bond markets), and to assure some stability in the supply of this type of finance. These methods generally included co-financing and multilateral guarantees. The question of guarantees was examined in detail by a Group of High-Level Experts on Finance for Development

---

[22] The Conference adopted this resolution by 73 votes to 3, with 23 abstentions.

which met in Geneva in 1978.[23] In general, guarantees were opposed by multilateral institutions on the ground that, according to their charters, guarantees have to be booked against their total loanable resources in the same way as a direct loan of the same amount. Guarantees were also opposed by some large borrowers established in capital markets.

With respect to export credits the original focus had been on the use of export credits extended by developed countries as a source of finance for developing countries. Continued concern in this area became subsumed within the discussions on problems of external indebtedness. Discussion of export credits *per se* shifted in the mid-1970s to consideration of proposals for an export credit refinancing or guarantee facility which would assist developing countries by offering credit on their non-traditional exports. Basically on grounds of cost, the discussions soon focused on the elaboration of an export credit guarantee facility, which would provide its guarantee to medium- and long-term export credits granted by developing countries, so that they might more easily be refinanced on international capital markets. Extensive study has been made of the problems of export financing in developing countries in general and of the detailed technical characteristics of the facility. However, although a certain degree of agreement has been achieved on the features of such a facility, the proposal still remains on the agenda of UNCTAD.

Debt problems of developing countries

The question of debt has been intensively examined within UNCTAD since the first session of the Conference. The role of UNCTAD in working out proposals on debt relief and on guidelines on debt rescheduling has been prominent. The perspective of the secretariat is that debt has to be seen within the overall framework of terms and volume of transfers of resources for development and that the need for debt-relief measures be assessed in the context of the broad long-term development process of debtor countries.

At UNCTAD I, the report of the Secretary-General pointed out that, while the capacity of developing countries to repay their debt had been reduced by the slow growth of their exports and deterioration in their terms of trade, the burden of servicing their debt had increased as a result of a hardening of the terms of lending due to a shortening of maturities and an increase in interest rates. The Conference recommended,[24] *inter alia,* that competent United Nations bodies and/or other international financial institutions should stand ready, at the request of any developing country, to review, in co-operation with the creditor countries concerned, the external indebtedness of the developing country concerned, where appropriate, with a view to securing agreement, or consolidation of debt, with appropriate periods of grace and amortization and reasonable rates of interest.

---

[23] During the meeting of the Group, a proposal on an International Loan Insurance Fund was submitted by Mr. Xenophon Zolotas, then Governor of the Bank of Greece. The purposes of such a Fund were to stabilize the international financial markets and to enlarge access. (See the report of the Group, printed in *Official Records of the Trade and Development Board, Eighteenth Session, Annexes,* agenda item 5, document TD/B/722, annex I.)

[24] See *Proceedings of the United Nations Conference on Trade and Development,* vol. I—*Final Act and Report* (United Nations publication, Sales No. E.64.II.B.11), annex A.IV.5. The Conference adopted this recommendation by 109 votes to none with 11 abstentions.

At the second session of the Conference, in 1968, the secretariat placed additional emphasis on the institutional aspect of debt rescheduling. Shortcomings of the then prevailing process of rescheduling were highlighted. Rescheduling techniques were informal and resulted in a general agreement between the creditor and the debtor country, but required for its application further complicated bilateral arrangements between individual creditors and the debtor. This process seemed time-consuming, giving rise to a good deal of uncertainty, tending to disrupt not only trade and payments but also the inflow of capital and the whole development process.

The secretariat suggested the adoption of an early warning system within an appropriate institutional framework in order to avoid a debt crisis which would compel debtor countries to take unnecessarily drastic measures. Moreover, rescheduling criteria and procedures should not disrupt the development process of debtor countries and should be tailored to the special characteristics of the case, particularly in situations where imbalance was more of a structural than of a short-term character.

At UNCTAD III, in 1972, attention was drawn to the dangerous worsening of debt servicing problems of developing countries and to the urgent necessity of adopting measures for debt relief. It was stressed that debt relief should not be a limited response to a crisis situation but should be examined within the context of broad development goals. A multilateral framework was needed to examine the debt problems of a country in the context of its overall development plan and the requisite net transfer of resources. Other proposals were put forward by the secretariat, such as: the inclusion of a "bisque clause" whereby, under certain conditions, the debtor would be accorded some pre-agreed measure of relief in the form of postponement or waiving of amortization and interest payments; and the formulation of standards and procedures to be applied in debt renegotiation, so as to assure equal treatment of countries in similar situations.

An *ad hoc* Group of Governmental Experts on the Debt Problems of Developing Countries was established in 1974 and held three sessions. The final report of the Group in 1975 contained a set of agreed common elements for consideration in future debt renegotiations, which could provide guidance and contribute to securing equal treatment of debtor countries in similar situations.[25] Furthermore, upon recommendations of the Group, the Trade and Development Board in 1975, by resolution 132 (XV), authorized the Secretary-General of UNCTAD to provide appropriate assistance to debtor countries in relation to the holding of *ad hoc* meetings where creditor countries and the debtor developing country and a number of developing countries would examine the debtor's situation in a broad development context prior to debt renegotiations in the usual form. UNCTAD was also authorized to participate in debt renegotiation meetings in the Paris Club[26] on the same basis as other international organizations.

---

[25] See *Debt problems of developing countries. Report of the Ad hoc Group of Governmental Experts on its third session* (TD/B/545/Rev.1) (United Nations publication, Sales No. E.75.II.D.14).

[26] The Paris Club is the name given to an *ad hoc* group of official creditors which meets in Paris for the purpose of renegotiating the official or the officially-guaranteed non-concessional (principally export credits) debt of a debtor country. The meetings are organized and chaired by the French Treasury.

At UNCTAD IV, in 1976, the debt problems of the most seriously affected and the least developed countries were given prominence. The Conference adopted without dissent resolution 94 (IV), whereby the governments of the developed countries pledged themselves to respond quickly within a multilateral framework to requests arising from these countries for relief on their debt-service payments. This resolution also called upon international forums to work out features which could provide guidance in future operations relating to the debt problems of developing countries.

Subsequently, the Board, at the third part of its ninth special session meeting at Ministerial level, in March 1978, adopted resolution 165 (S-IX). In section A, developed donor countries committed themselves to provide debt relief to poorer developing countries, particularly the least developed among them, by means of an adjustment of the terms of past bilateral official development assistance to the then currently prevailing terms, or other equivalent measures, as a means of improving the net flows of ODA. Eighteen developed market-economy donor countries adopted such measures for the benefit of the poorer developing countries. The United States has applied no measure of relief in the context of this resolution, nor have the socialist countries of Eastern Europe, which have taken the view that such multilateral action is inappropriate, given the nature of their trade and economic relations with the developing countries. None the less, the relief accorded by the developed market-economy donor countries amounts to approximately $6 billion to the benefit of over 45 developing countries. Since this relief was accorded principally to the poorest developing countries, whose outstanding indebtedness was largely composed of ODA lending, it represented a substantial reduction in their total debt-service burden.

The basic principles regarding future operations relating to debt problems contained in section B of resolution 165 (S-IX) were refined and elaborated to become the detailed features contained in resolution 222 (XXI), which was adopted by the Trade and Development Board in 1980. Section A of this resolution reiterated the commitment made by developed countries to proceed to retroactive term adjustment of ODA debt of poorer countries and introduced a dynamic element whereby developed donor countries agreed "to seek to continue to adopt retroactive adjustment of terms or equivalent measures in accordance with section A of resolution 165 (S-IX), so that the improvement in current terms can be applied to outstanding official development assistance debt", and requested the Board to keep this matter under review. Section B of the resolution contained detailed features for future debt-relief operations. The objectives of such guidelines were: to assure expeditious and timely action; to enhance the development prospects of the debtor country; to restore the debtor country's capacity to service its debt in both the short term and the long term; and to protect the interests of debtors and creditors equitably. It further welcomed "in the context of Trade and Development Board resolution 132 (XV) of 15 August 1975, the invitation by the Chairman of the Paris Club to the Secretary-General of UNCTAD to participate in the meetings of that creditor group on the same basis and terms as the representatives of other international organizations". UNCTAD was also asked to review the implementation of the arrangements agreed upon.

Since 1978 the representatives of the Secretary-General of UNCTAD have participated in over 45 Paris Club meetings dealing with the debt of some

25 countries. At such meetings UNCTAD presents a statement on the economic circumstances and future prospects of the debtor country. This introduces a development focus to the consideration of the nature and extent of debt relief to be accorded. Prior to such meetings, if a debtor country so wishes, the UNCTAD secretariat provides assistance to the country in preparing its case for submission to the debt reorganization forum. The secretariat also makes available to requesting countries technical assistance on debt management, including computerized debt recording and management systems.

Concrete results arising from the proposed measures contained in resolution 222 (XXI) have been modest. With respect to debt rescheduling, the UNCTAD secretariat's review of the present arrangements for debt rescheduling pointed out that they did not fully respond to the objectives of the agreed features. The review further concluded that considerable scope for improvement existed in terms of (*a*) more timely action by debtor countries in seeking international consideration of their debt problems and in seeking assistance from multilateral institutions in the preparation of a comprehensive analysis which would guide their debt renegotiations; (*b*) ensuring availability of bridging finance to help debtors tide over severe foreign exchange shortages which tend to surface during the sometimes prolonged period of debt renegotiations; and (*c*) ensuring availability of long-term financial support needed to underpin structural adjustments aimed at restoring long-run debt-servicing capacity. The Trade and Development Board at its twenty-eighth session, in March 1984, reviewed these matters and adopted agreed conclusions. Moreover, it decided that it would conduct a major review of the debt and development problems of the poorer developing countries at its thirtieth session, in 1985, and would further review the operational effectiveness of the guidelines at its thirty-fourth session, in 1987.

Mobilization of domestic resources

UNCTAD has always stressed that the primary responsibility for the development of developing countries rested with those countries themselves and, to that end, the optimum mobilization of domestic resources was necessary. The review of the economic performance and, in particular, of efforts made by developing countries to mobilize internal resources would thus constitute an important element of an international development policy. Such reviews fall within the competence of the UNCTAD Committee on Invisibles and Financing related to Trade. The assessment would also answer the legitimate concern of countries which provide external resources, that such resources were being used effectively and constituted a supplement to, and not a substitute for, domestic efforts.

Earlier studies prepared by the UNCTAD secretariat during the period 1967-1972 were devoted to the search for indicators which would provide an objective basis for assessing genuine efforts made by developing countries to mobilize domestic resources. It was not found feasible to seek to draw a sharp distinction between genuine efforts and extraneous factors which have affected the relative success of a country. However, certain indicators which may not provide such distinction were, nevertheless, useful in focusing attention on areas in which remedial measures would be required. The approach used in later studies was to examine both the size of resources mobilized for development and the degree of efficiency with which these resources were used. Among the quantitative indicators selected, some of which reflect the combined effects of the size and efficiency of resource use, were: the rate of growth of gross domestic product (GDP), sectoral rates of growth, production structure, export performance, investment and savings rate, tax ratio and employment. The importance of qualitative factors in evaluating performance was also recognized. Education and training, adequate nutrition and health services were essential to the maintenance of an efficient labour force and were prerequisites to long-run self-sustained development. Also important was assessing the effectiveness of the planning process as well as other policies which had a bearing on development such as population, price stabilization and fiscal policies. Of course, in the evaluation of comparative performance, the wide differences among developing countries in levels of development, socio-economic structure and institutional framework had to be borne in mind.[27]

Impact of capital flows on saving

Particular attention has been given to domestic saving not only because of its major role in financing capital formation but also because it is a direct indicator of development effort. A study by the UNCTAD secretariat in 1975 did not support the common belief that capital inflows discourage savings. For deficit developing countries, there was no negative relation between the two variables. As for the supposed negative impact on saving of a more equal distribution of income, statistical evidence appears not only inconsistent with this view but even tends to support the contrary hypothesis that the long-run savings rate may be increasingly associated with more equitable distribution of personal income. The study also indicated that financial intermediation might have a significant impact on productivity and on the volume of savings and investment.[28]

The major conclusions that emerged from the secretariat studies mentioned above, was that developing countries, in general, have indeed exerted considerable efforts to mobilize and make effective use of their internal resources. This is supported by the growth attained in all the major economic variables particularly before 1970. Investment and domestic savings did not only rise in real terms, but their share in GDP also registered an impressive gain. The 5.8 per cent annual growth of GDP registered in the 1960s exceeded the 5 per cent target for the First United Nations Development Decade. Significant advances were also registered in education, health and nutrition.[29] Furthermore, except in least developed countries, a turning point had already been reached in the rapid pace of population growth.

---

[27] See the following reports by UNCTAD secretariat "The mobilization of internal resources by the developing countries" (TD/B/C.3/28); "Objectives for the mobilization of domestic resources by the developing countries" (TD/B/C.3/58 and TD/B/C.3/75/Rev.1) and "Mobilization of domestic resources for development" (TD/118/Supp.1), reproduced in *Proceedings of the United Nations Conference on Trade and Development, Third Session,* Vol. III—*Basic Documents* (United Nations publication, Sales No. E.73.II.D.6).

[28] "Saving in developing countries" (TD/B/C.3/124/Supp.1 and Corr.1) and "Domestic saving in developing countries" (TD/B/C.3/124/Supp.1 and Corr.1 and Add.1).

[29] See UNCTAD, *Trade and Development Report, 1981* (TD/B/863/Rev.1), part II, chap. 3 (United Nations publication, Sales No. E.81.II.D.9).

Planning has also come to be widely accepted as an indispensable tool for accelerating the pace of development and its quality has improved.

However, while the investment and savings ratio continued to increase after 1970, output growth remained stable or slowed slightly but in the early 1980s collapsed and in some cases turned negative. This could be largely attributed to the adverse external environment which has increasingly been a constraint on the optimum mobilization of internal resources. This situation was recognized as early as UNCTAD III with the adoption of resolution 57 (III) which recommends, that developed countries should refrain from taking any steps which interfere, either directly or indirectly, with the full and efficient mobilization of domestic resources. But important failures and shortcomings on the domestic front were also registered in a number of countries, among which were the failure of the rate of agricultural output to exceed population growth and the inability of the fast-growing industrial sector to absorb the high rate of expansion of the labour force. In addition, some countries have had difficulty in controlling very high rates of inflation. Nevertheless, an examination of the impact of international prices on the saving performance of net oil importing developing countries showed that it had improved by some 40 per cent over the period 1960-1978 in spite of deterioration in their terms of trade.

These evaluations indicate that even the best efforts by developing countries can be rendered ineffective by a hostile external environment and the international community should therefore try to come to grips with the problem of how to lead the world economy back to self-sustained growth. Developing countries should also try to correct their shortcomings and exert greater efforts to accelerate their growth. In view of the growing evidence that the behaviour of exchange rates in developed market-economy countries has a pronounced effect on the availability of external finance, and in view of the intimate connection between capital inflow and domestic saving and investment of developing countries the UNCTAD secretariat has under way a major research effort in this area.

C. Overall appraisal and tasks for the future

UNCTAD's approach to international monetary issues stemmed directly from its evaluation of the post-war monetary and trading systems, which were considered inadequate with respect to their stated objectives and irrelevant, at times even detrimental, to the interests of developing countries. UNCTAD's record of the past 20 years, therefore, is one of constant endeavours, rendered more arduous by an increasingly disturbed world economic environment, to achieve negotiated improvements in the system, to make it both more attuned to current world realities and more responsive to the needs of developing countries.

UNCTAD's role in this, as in other spheres, has been twofold: that of identifying, and securing a broader appreciation of, the major issues as it perceived them, mainly through the research activities of the secretariat; and of seeking to influence decisions at the global level, mainly through the work of its intergovernmental bodies. The outcome of these endeavours has, to a certain extent been positive.

Responding to a perceived need for the redress of imbalances in the world economy and for the correction of deficiencies in the international monetary system, UNCTAD made a major contribution to the development of such concepts as compensatory and supplementary financing, SDRs and the "link", as well as to the debate on the reform of the system and the analysis of the debt problem. In so doing, UNCTAD added impetus to the process which led the relevant multilateral institutions to adopt new policies, or to make changes in existing ones, which better corresponded to the needs which it had helped to identify. Among these developments were the expansion of the IMF and the increased range of balance-of-payments financing facilities, the corresponding improvement in the degree and terms of access, the creation of SDRs, the added importance given to programme lending by the World Bank and, more recently, the introduction of structural adjustment loans and the Special Assistance Programme. UNCTAD's efforts have also contributed to the achievement of a greater role for developing countries in the decision-making process of the system.

The process of change has not, however, moved equally fast in other areas. With regard to the SDR, little progress has been recorded towards making it the principal reserve asset of the system, partly because it has not been created on a regular basis or in sufficient quantities. Furthermore the "link" between SDR creation and development finance has not been established, nor have balance of payments financing facilities been specifically tailored to the structural adjustment needs of developing countries.

The UNCTAD secretariat and a large majority of the membership's view is that these issues should be tackled in the context of a comprehensive reform of the system involving both institutions and policies, the need for which is greater today than at any time during the past 20 years. Such a reform needs to address the major destabilizing features of the world economy, viz: the increasingly structural nature of the payments deficits of developing countries; the inadequate availability of liquidity on reasonable terms for these countries in relation to the size and nature of their external financing needs; the increased privatization of the system; and the deflationary policies and protectionist measures currently enforced by many developed countries.

From a longer-term viewpoint, a reformed international monetary system needs to take due account of the interests of, and the role played by, all categories of countries, as well as of the high degree of interdependence which characterizes the world economy today. A fundamental reform as an integral part of a restructured system of international economic co-operation is still, therefore, high on UNCTAD's list of priorities and is indeed the subject of on-going work.

Negotiations within UNCTAD in the area of transfer of resources have encountered serious difficulties, mainly because the general attitude of donor countries is to consider resource transfers as involving only costs to their budget; therefore, these transfers should be effected in such a way as to minimize the immediate financial costs and to provide reverse benefits for them in terms of strengthening bilateral political or economic links with recipient countries. Even in cases where international consensus has been achieved, some developed countries have neither implemented nor moved towards the recommendations. This failure to translate agreed goals into practical steps of implementation casts a shadow over multilateral negotiations.

None the less, a certain degree of progress has been made. One success is perhaps the recognition by the international community of economic development as a legitimate objective and a shared responsibility, with the transfer of resources as a natural corollary of this global development strategy.

With respect to debt, most developed market-economy donor countries have accorded debt relief measures on ODA loans to the poorer countries. Within UNCTAD, guidelines for future debt renegotiations have been defined and the role of UNCTAD in multilateral debt forums and in providing technical assistance to debtor countries has become established. In view of the increasing needs of the developing countries these successes must be considered modest. In spite of the guidelines the present approach to the debt problem is not uniform and is on a case-by-case basis. Solutions imposed upon debtor developing countries often imply painful downward adjustment in their economies. Relief given is of a short-term character, aiming mainly at coping with the immediate risk of lack of liquidity. Developing countries are applying increasingly sophisticated tools to improve their debt management but the root causes of the problems remain untackled, namely, the hardening of the terms on which development resources are provided, a narrowing of export markets due to global recession and protectionism, and the generally disadvantaged position of developing countries in the world trading and financial systems.

With respect to the question of transfer of resources, the volume of financial flows to developing countries, both on concessional and non-concessional terms, is stagnating or even declining. The willingness of governments of donor countries to reactivate international financial co-operation has been further weakened by world recession. The compliance with agreed recommendations contained in various resolutions, especially concerning ODA volume and terms targets, has been far from satisfactory.

It is regrettable that the many challenges facing UNCTAD today remain broadly those which were identified in the early 1960s and which provided impetus for the establishment of UNCTAD. None the less some solutions, often partial, have been found, problems have been better defined and the role of UNCTAD in providing a universal forum where all issues and their interrelationships may be examined has served the international community well. The world economy of the 1980s is in crisis and the role for UNCTAD as a sounding board for new intitiatives has never been more necessary.

III. UNCTAD'S ACTIVITIES IN TRADE AND INDUSTRIALIZATION POLICIES, WITH SPECIAL REFERENCE TO TRADE IN MANUFACTURES

A. Nature and evolution of the problems

In the early 1960s when UNCTAD was still in the making, the developed market-economy countries had achieved a substantial part of their initial post-war objectives in the international sphere. Discrimination by exchange control had been virtually abolished. Dollars were no longer being rationed in Western Europe, and the major world currencies could be freely exchanged for dollars or gold. The role of tariffs as the main instrument of trade policy was practically restored, and the successive negotiating rounds under GATT auspices made considerable progress in reducing the high tariff levels of the first post-war years, although at a noticeably slower pace after the General Agreement on Tariffs and Trade (GATT) round of trade negotiations at Torquay (1950-1951).

This encouraging picture was overshadowed, however, by the failure to liberalize trade in agriculture—a reflection of the persistent maladjustment of the agricultural sector, at both the international and the national levels, which has remained throughout the post-war period. Trade in manufactures among the developed market-economy countries was practically, though not entirely, freed of quantitative restrictions, but the "sensitiveness" of a few industries, particularly textiles, largely associated with over-investment, became evident at an early stage. During the 1951-1952 recession in Western Europe, the textile industry was the most severely affected, and it was also the first industry to feel the impact of the competition from Japan, India, and a few other Asian countries.

As regards developing countries, the international trade situation in the early 1960s, was far from encouraging. The rules of GATT were formulated in the context of post war reconstruction and in particular taking into account the experiences of the 1930s with regard to trade among developed countries. They did not take specifically into account the needs of the developing countries (part IV of the General Agreement, conceived to accommodate developing countries, was adopted in 1965, more or less concurrently with the setting-up of UNCTAD and in its spirit and letter it reflected the recommendations formulated during UNCTAD I).

Indirect benefits were accruing to developing countries from the growth effects of trade liberalization in industrial countries, but the former countries themselves remained on the margin of the development process. In the markets of the developed market-economy countries, developing countries had to reckon with differential tariffs, increasing with the degree of processing, so as to affect most severely the stage at which the benefits to producers are the highest. Non-tariff barriers of various kinds, frequently of a rather elusive nature, were imposed on a range of products of special interest to developing countries. Last but not least, formal and informal arrangements among large firms, generally in the context of complicated mechanisms operating within and among transnational corporations (TNCs) were powerful tools for barring access to markets to outsiders.

On the side of the socialist countries of Eastern Europe, the situation was also discouraging. Trade relations of the countries members of the Council for Mutual Economic Assistance (CMEA) with developing countries were limited to only a few developing countries, with imports of the former group concentrated on selected primary commodities. The methods and instruments of central planning were highly effective in keeping imports at the desired levels and in implementing a planned distribution of the sources of supplies, although the system also contained features with a potential for the expansion of trade and economic co-operation with developing countries.

Co-operation among developing countries in the framework of economic groupings was at an early stage. Some attempts were made to integrate markets, but progress was too slow to contribute effectively to the industrialization process.

This general state of affairs was one of the main reasons for the orientation of the strategies in the countries that began to industrialize in the post-war years, and those adopted and maintained after the war in countries where the process had started in the unpropitious conditions of the 1930s. As is well known, with few exceptions if any, industrialization in developing countries took an inward-looking orientation. In the circumstances, external as well as internal, this seemed to be the easier course, but in the long run it did not prove economically viable. The emerging industries required high rates of protection and various forms of aid, and, in the absence of further efforts to improve their efficiency, the well-known self-perpetuating process of reliance on the State was inevitable. Most disappointing, perhaps, the eagerly awaited savings of foreign exchange, to be obtained through the import substitution of consumer goods, fell short of expectations as a result of foreign exchange outflows related to the growing volume of required imports of capital and intermediary goods.

Clearly, the inward-looking orientation of the early industrial strategies was only one element of a much more complex story which at different points of time and with variations has been the common experience of many developing countries. The imitative character of the technologies used irrespective of the factor endowment of countries, the large concessions granted to foreign and local entrepreneurs, not always justified by their actual contributions to development objectives, the excessive concentration of modern industries in urban areas, the under-estimation of the development potential of the traditional sector often combined with inadequate attention to agriculture, etc., are well known features frequently encountered through the 1950s and 1960s.

The economic setting outlined above led to the adoption of policies which responded to a certain extent to the needs of the developing countries. In the debate surrounding the Havana Charter and leading to the conclusion of the General Agreement on Tariffs and Trade in 1947, one of the developing countries' main concerns was to secure a free hand in commercial policies to pursue their industrialization and development objectives.[1] Concern over the other aspect of the problem, namely the need for greater access to markets in developed countries, was to come at a later stage. None the less, part of their initial concern found expression in article XVIII of the General Agreement on government assistance to economic development, which permitted developing countries to modify or withdraw concessions for the protection of infant industries. Following the 1955 revision of the General Agreement, the conditions for imposing quantitative restrictions were also eased with respect to developing countries experiencing balance of payments difficulties. Developing countries invoking article XVIII were not, however, exempt from requests for compensation, or from the threat of retaliation.

In so far as inward-looking industrialization policies tended to become progressively more costly, it was inevitable that developing countries should turn their attention to markets abroad and to the need for increased export earnings to support their development programmes. However, in view of the limited prospects for the substantial expansion of traditional exports of primary commodities, their attention focused increasingly on the rapid augmentation of exports of manufactures. It was not until the end of the 1950s that the idea that the international trading community should take positive measures to assist the trade of developing countries began to gain acceptance. The theory upon which GATT was based assumed that its effective operation would, in itself, lead to the economic growth, and consequent development, of its participants. The provision of an environment in which the most efficient industries in developing countries could expand into world markets was expected to enhance the achievement of development goals. A major flaw in this theory of comparative advantage, however, was that it ignored the realities of economic power. Differences among trading countries with respect to levels of development, size of domestic markets, degree of efficiency and diversification of production, were ignored, as were the different negotiating strengths of trading partners. Furthermore, the effect of patterns and rigidities of a historical character was not taken into account. The centre-periphery theory, particularly as articulated by Raúl Prebisch, addressed these factors and provided the basis for a comprehensive new approach. Because of structural impediments of a historical nature, even the strict application of the unconditional most-favoured-nation (MFN) principle was seen as unlikely to lead to a narrowing of the gap between developed and developing countries and might have the contrary effect.[2] The most dynamic elements of world trade were the exchanges among the countries in the "centre" and, therefore, it was in the interest of the countries on the periphery to adopt export-oriented policies to be able to take account of the dynamism of the centre. Import substitution by developing countries was seen to be practical only on a regional scale.

---

[1] Stein Rossen, *Notes on rules and mechanisms governing international economic relations* (Fantoft, Norway: The Chr. Michelsen Institute, Department of Social Science and Development, 1981) (DERALP publication, No. 127, chap. I, para. 4.2 (IV)).

[2] See, *inter alia,* Dr. Prebisch's report to the first session of UNCTAD ("Towards a New Trade Policy for Development"), *Proceedings of the United Nations Conference on Trade and Development (Geneva, 23 March-16 June 1964)*, vol. II—*Policy Statements* (United Nations publication, Sales No. 64.II.B.12).

New policies were, therefore, needed to bring about the reduction or the gradual elimination of the host of tariff and non-tariff barriers facing these countries' exports in developed country markets. Both in GATT and in the United Nations the discussions became actively concerned with the reformulation of commercial policies in developed countries. In the early 1960s GATT's new emphasis on the trade problems of developing countries found expression in the Programme of Action put forward by developing countries and to which a number of developed countries agreed—subject to certain understandings.[3] Also within both organizations, it was generally accepted that in future tariff negotiations the principle of reciprocity should not necessarily apply between developed and developing countries.[4]

B. Principal policy initiatives and their results

The policy framework that emerged from UNCTAD I led to the identification of major sectoral issues in international economic relations. In the area of manufactures, the most pressing need for the newly created Organization was to find an expedient which in a relatively short time would reduce or abolish tariffs on all products of developing countries in the developed country markets, without obligations on the part of developing countries to make reciprocal concessions. The idea of a generalized system of preferences outlined by Raúl Prebisch at UNCTAD I and adopted as a principle at UNCTAD II proved to be an acceptable approach. The work on the complicated and elusive problems of restrictive business practices and non-tariff barriers was also decided upon at an early stage (UNCTAD II and UNCTAD III, respectively).

While in the initial phase, UNCTAD's programme as mentioned above, was essentially sectoral in approach, the developments in the world economy commencing from the early 1970s began to focus attention on another set of issues which cut across sectoral boundaries. First, there was a growing recognition of the interrelated character of global economic problems and the need to evolve more effective approaches for dealing with these interrelations. Second, it was becoming increasingly clear that the expansion of trade in manufactures of the developing countries depended not so much on preferential access to the markets of developed countries as on a rapid process of structural adjustment in those countries which would help to maintain an open non-discriminatory trading system. The structural transformation and industrialization of developing countries and the industrial restructuring in developed countries were perceived as interlinked parts of a global process of structural adjustment and change.

UNCTAD's responsibility in the area of trade in manufactures and semi-manufactures has been entrusted to the Committee on Manufactures and at a later

---

[3] See United Nations, "Trade Problems Between Countries at Different Stages of Development" (E/CONF.46/PC/14); and "Submission by GATT" (E/CONF.46/PC/34).

[4] See the Ministerial Declaration of GATT of 30 November 1961, GATT, *Basic Instruments and Selected Documents, Tenth Supplement* (Geneva, March 1962), p. 26, and General Assembly resolution 1707 (XVI) of 19 December 1961 on international trade as the primary instrument for economic development.

stage also to the Special Committee on Preferences. As one of the main Committees of the Trade and Development Board, the overall function of the Committee on Manufactures has been to promote consistent policies to expand and diversify the export trade of developing countries in manufactures and semi-manufactures. Initially, the activities of the Committee on Manufactures focused on the problems of access to markets. With the adoption by the General Assembly in 1974 of the Declaration and the Programme of Action on the Establishment of a New International Economic Order (NIEO) (resolutions 3201 (S-VI) and 3202 (S-VI)) and its emphasis on development issues, the Trade and Development Board in the late 1970s also became directly involved in the issues related to trade in manufactures. The principal policy initiatives undertaken by the Committee on Manufactures, the Special Committee on Preferences and by the Trade and Development Board are analysed in the following sections.

THE GENERALIZED SYSTEM OF PREFERENCES

The negotiations leading to the adoption and implementation of the generalized system of preferences (GSP) took nearly a decade. Several years had elapsed before the principle of preference received acceptance and more than two years were needed to work out the details of the various schemes of preferences. The schemes were put into effect after a certain period of delay in some cases the delay was considerable.

Agreement on the principle of preferences

Customs tariffs constituted and still constitute an important impediment to international trade. The substantial reduction of tariffs has been the main objective of the intermittent negotiations held within the framework of GATT since its inception. These negotiations, carried out on the basis of reciprocity, served mainly the interests of developed countries. With the increasing membership of GATT, in particular of developing countries, a problem arose with regard to the participation of those countries in the negotiations. The principle of reciprocity became an acute problem when, in the preparatory work for the Kennedy Round negotiations, a decision had to be made regarding the participation of the developing countries. Considerable interest was therefore expressed in the possibility of introducing preferential tariffs for the exports of developing countries in their trade with developed countries. This possibility was first formally discussed at the GATT ministerial meeting held in May 1963, and afterwards in a working party set up for this purpose. This new emphasis on the trade and development problems of developing countries culminated in a revision of the General Agreement on Tariffs and Trade in 1965 by the addition of Part IV, which, however, did not fully exempt the developing countries from reciprocity. In effect, although it is stated in paragraph 8 of article XXXVI of the Agreement that the developed countries would not expect reciprocity for commitments made by them in trade negotiations with the developing countries, a separate note to the article specified that what was meant by the article was that the developing countries were not expected to "make contributions which are inconsistent with their individual development, financial and trade needs".[5] Insistence on some kind of reciprocity in the negotiations reflected the strong determination of developed countries to uphold the MFN principle, lest it should undermine the very foundation of the Agreement. On the whole, Part IV constituted a compromise falling far short of the expectations and development needs of the developing countries. The discussion on preferences within the framework of GATT had therefore come to a standstill.

An opportunity to reopen the debate came when the United Nations Conference on Trade and Development was convened in the spring of 1964. At that session, tariff preferences in favour of developing countries formed one of the key issues in the search for effective solutions to the trade problems of developing countries. The case for tariff preferences rested on several arguments, the principal among them being that such treatment would be a means for enabling the developing countries to come closer to real equality of treatment. The traditional MFN principle was designed to establish equality of treatment among the various sellers to a particular market, but did not ensure equality of treatment in several respects of considerable importance to developing countries. First, unless the MFN tariff was zero, there was no equality of treatment with the domestic producers, nor with the producers inside the emerging regional groupings in western Europe. Second, the MFN principle did not take account of inequalities in economic structure and levels of development among countries; to treat equally countries that are economically unequal constituted equality of treatment only from a formal point of view but in fact amounted to inequality. Third, partly as a result of negotiations conducted on the basis of reciprocity and the MFN clause, typical manufactured and semi-manufactured export products of developing countries were frequently subject to higher nominal and, in most cases still higher effective duties than typical import products in intra-developed country trade. Fourth, as a result of the formation of regional groupings (the European Economic Community (EEC) and the European Free Trade Association (EFTA) much of the trade flows were carried out outside the MFN system and the formal application of the MFN clause to developing countries, in those conditions, was in fact a least-favoured-nation treatment. Preferential reductions on imports from developing countries would bring them closer to achieving equality of treatment with producers inside the national or multi-national markets, would take into account the fact that they were at a lower level of development and would correct the competitive disadvantage resulting from the creation of regional groupings.

The Conference adopted certain principles to govern international trade relations and trade policies conducive to development. General Principle Eight recommended that developed countries should accord preferential concessions in favour of developing countries without requiring any concessions in return from developing countries. The majority of the developed countries were in favour of preferences, and the others including the United States of America, were opposed to them and supported instead the application of the MFN principle in the extension of concessions by developed to developing countries. Consequently, the developed

---

[5] The same wording was later used in the Tokyo Declaration (Declaration of Ministers, approved at Tokyo on 14 September 1973). For the text of the declaration, see GATT, *Basic Instruments and Selected Documents, Twentieth Supplement* (Sales No. GATT/1974-1), p. 19.

market economy countries either abstained or voted against this Principle. In its recommendation A.III.5, the Conference recognized the urgent need for the diversification and expansion of the export trade of developing countries in manufactures and semi-manufactures and considered it desirable to obtain the widest possible agreement with respect to the extension of preferences.

For this purpose, it recommended that the Secretary-General of the United Nations make arrangements to establish a special committee of governmental representatives with a view to working out the best method of implementing such preferences on the basis of non-reciprocity from the developing countries, and to discussing further the differences of principle referred to above and reporting to the continuing machinery established following the first session of the Conference.

The divergences with regard to preferences could not overcome either within the Special Committee on Preferences set up by the Secretary-General of the United Nations in 1965 pursuant to recommendation A.III.5 of the Conference or by the Group on Preferences set up by the Trade and Development Board in 1965 as a subsidiary body of the Committee on Manufactures. A breakthrough came about following a statement made by the President of the United States at the meeting of the Latin American Heads of State at Punta del Este in April 1967. In it, the president of the United States recognized that comparable tariff treatment might not always permit developing countries to advance as rapidly as desired and that the granting of temporary tariff advantages for all developing countries by all developed countries would be one way of dealing with this question.[6] This statement unlocked the negotiations and from that time onwards progress could be made both within the Organization for Economic Co-operation and Development (OECD) and in the UNCTAD Group on Preferences. Henceforth, attention was concentrated mainly on how, rather than whether, to grant preferences.

At the second session of the Conference, held at New Delhi in 1968, the issue of preferences was at the centre of the negotiations. The Conference had before it the Charter of Algiers adopted at the Ministerial Meeting of the Group of 77 in October 1967 by the developing countries, which set out, *inter alia,* the principles to be observed in implementing a generalized system of preferences.[7] The Conference also had before it a report by the Special Group on Trade with Developing Countries of OECD[8] setting out a number of general considerations regarding temporary special tariff treatment by developed countries in favour of all developing countries.

---

[6] The shift to a favourable position was explained by the United States Assistant Secretary of State for Economic Affairs as follows: "Politically, we found ourselves virtually isolated from all the developing countries and most of the industrialized countries as well. Economically, our reservation in principle and scepticism precluded our having much influence over the proliferation of discriminatory arrangements and also reduced our influence with regard to the specific workings of a preference scheme which other industrialized countries indicated they might put into effect, whether or not the United States took part" (see United States Congress, *The Future of United States Foreign Trade Policy: Hearings before the Sub-Committee on Foreign Economic Policy of the Joint Economic Committee, Ninetieth Congress, First Session,* Vol. I (Washington, D.C., Government Printing Office, 1967), p. 79).

[7] See *Proceedings of the United Nations Conference on Trade and Development, Second Session,* vol. I—*Report and Annexes* (United Nations publication, Sales No. E.68.II.D.14), annex IX.

[8] TD/56, *Ibid.,* vol. III — *Problems and Policies of Trade in Manufactures and Semi-manufactures* (United Nations publication, Sales No. E.68.II.D.16).

These considerations encompassed certain principles on which all schemes subsequently introduced were based.

Divergences persisted at the Conference because the positions regarding the main elements of a system of preferences were far apart. The compromise reached found expression in Conference resolution 21 (II), in which the principle and objectives of preferences in favour of developing countries were formally accepted. Paragraph 1 of the resolution states that the Conference "agrees that the objectives of the generalized non-reciprocal, non-discriminatory system of preferences in favour of the developing countries, should be: (*a*) to increase their export earnings; (*b*) to promote their industrialization; (*c*) to accelerate their rates of economic growth". The Special Committee on Preferences, established by the Conference to conduct the necessary negotiations, completed its work in October 1970 when arrangements concerning the establishment of a generalized, non-discriminatory, non-reciprocal system of preferences were drawn up and agreed upon. In proclaiming the Second United Nations Development Decade, starting from 1 January 1971, the General Assembly of the United Nations, at its twenty-fifth session, included the preferential arrangements as an integral part of the International Development Strategy. By their decision of 25 June 1971 the Contracting Parties to the General Agreement on Tariffs and Trade (GATT) decided to waive the provisions of article I of the Agreement for a period of 10 years to the extent necessary to permit developed Contracting Parties to accord preferential tariff treatment to products originating in developing countries and territories.[9]

Implementation and effects

The GSP at present consists of 16 separate schemes involving 20 developed market-economy countries and six socialist countries of Eastern Europe.[10] By the end of 1972 all the schemes had been implemented, except those of Canada and the United States, whose schemes were introduced in 1974 and 1976 respectively. In 1980 the Special Committee on Preferences conducted a comprehensive review of the first 10-years of operation of the GSP and concluded that the system had played a positive role in improving the access of developing countries to the markets of developed countries. It recognized, however, that the objectives of the system had not been fully achieved and agreed therefore to extend its duration for another ten-year period or until 1990. The schemes that had been implemented at an early date had already been extended for another ten year period. Canada and the United States have taken steps to renew their schemes upon expiration. The renewal of the GSP no longer requires a GATT waiver in view of the adoption of the Enabling Clause as a result of the Tokyo Round.

---

[9] Decision of 25 June 1971 (L/3545) (GATT, *Basic Instruments and Selected Documents, Eighteenth Supplement* (Sales No. GATT/1972-1), p. 24.

[10] The preference-giving countries or groups of countries are Australia, Austria, Bulgaria, Canada, Czechoslovakia, EEC (10), Finland, Hungary, Japan, New Zealand, Norway, Poland, Sweden, Switzerland, the United States of America and the USSR. The German Democratic Republic does not have customs tariffs but, after endorsing in 1973 the joint declaration of socialist countries of Eastern Europe, it undertook to apply other economic and foreign trade measures which, as a rule, are of a preferential nature designed to expand imports from the developing countries. Poland applied its scheme as from 1976, upon the introduction of a customs tariff.

The system is a highly complex preferential arrangement but its essential elements may be described as follows: the products covered include mainly manufactures and semi-manufactures falling within chapters 25-99 of the Customs, Co-operation Council Nomenclature (CCCN) but with important exceptions, such as textiles, leather and petroleum products. Agricultural products in CCCN chapters 1-24 are included only to a limited extent. In general, manufactured products covered by the schemes enjoy duty-free treatment, while eligible agricultural products enjoy various tariff cuts. Preferential imports into the European Economic Community (EEC) and Japan are subject to safeguard mechanisms in the form of tariff quotas, ceilings and maximum country amounts. Preferential imports into the United States are limited to products for which developing countries do not demonstrate competitiveness, while preferential imports into Australia are subject not only to competitive need exclusions, but also to tariff quotas. In contrast to these schemes embodying limitations and/or exclusions, the other schemes are open-ended in the sense that they rely exclusively on the standard escape clause as the principal safeguard mechanism. This clause, which is analogous to GATT article XIX, states that preferences would be withdrawn if preferential imports enter in such a quantity that they cause or threaten to cause injury to domestic producers. In order to qualify for preferential treatment goods must also satisfy certain origin conditions. They must be transported directly from the exporting beneficiary country to the preference-giving country and must be substantially transformed in the country of origin. Substantial transformation of products is determined on the basis of complex requirements involving various qualifying and non-qualifying processes and/or certain levels of value-added.

Total imports of OECD preference-giving countries from developing countries amounted to about $267 billion in 1982. Half of these imports were dutiable but only about $63 billion were eligible for preferential treatment. Not all of these eligible imports received preferential treatment, mainly because of tariff quotas and competitive need limitations in the major schemes. It is estimated that only about $28.2 billion actually received preferential treatment. With the addition of preferential imports from two of the preference-giving socialist countries of Eastern Europe for which data is available, the total rises to $31.6 billion. Preferential imports have shown a significant increase, rising from the $12 billion achieved in 1976. In real terms estimates indicate that about a quarter of 1982 imports may be attributable to GSP induced trade expansion. After more than 12 years of operation, however, GSP induced trade expansion. After more than 12 years of operation, however, GSP imports still account for a small proportion of dutiable imports (23 per cent) and an even smaller proportion of total imports (11 per cent).

The utilization of GSP benefits varies widely as between beneficiaries as well as between schemes. Since the GSP covers mostly manufactured products and only selected agricultural products, beneficiaries with a wider industrial base and diversified industrial exports naturally stand to benefit more than those relying on exports of agricultural products and raw materials. Roughly a dozen industrially more advanced beneficiaries supply 80 per cent or more of total preferential imports. However, owing to the limitations imposed under the major schemes, the utilization rates by these major beneficiaries are comparable to those of the other beneficiaries.

In addition to its complex character, the GSP has from the start been faced with serious challenges. Since the GSP consists of tariff preferences granted by developed countries, it follows that whenever there is global tariff liberalization, the benefits of the GSP are reduced. At the recently concluded Tokyo Round of negotiations the developing countries made special efforts to safeguard these benefits. In essence they sought agreement on the binding of GSP preferential margins and on compensation in case there was an erosion of such margins as a result of MFN tariff cuts. They were naturally disappointed by the results. As UNCTAD studies show, there was an across-the-board erosion of GSP margins, while the MFN tariff cuts on the important non-GSP covered products fell short of compensating for such erosion.

With the approaching end of the initial 10-year period of the GSP, the two questions that were posed were whether or not the system should be extended and, if so, in what form. Given the important objectives of the GSP, there was a fair amount of certainty that it would be continued; there was doubt, however, that it could be extended without further encroaching on the principles on which it was based. The agreement relating to the framework for the conduct of world trade which emerged as a result of the Tokyo Round of multilateral trade negotiations (MTNs) provided the legal basis for the further extension of the system beyond its initial 10-year period. The agreement regarding what has come to be known as the "Enabling Clause"[11] allowed developed contracting parties to grant differential and more favourable treatment to developing countries without granting such treatment to other Contracting Parties, notwithstanding the provisions of article I of the General Agreement. The agreement on the "Enabling Clause", however, incorporated another clause which specified that less developed Contracting Parties would accept greater obligations with the progressive development of their economies and improvement in their trade situation. This provision implicitly seemed to provide a basis for "graduation" of developing countries. Under the GSP, graduation is accomplished by restricting or phasing out preferential treatment with respect to "competitive" developing countries. In the GATT context it is accomplished by making developing countries participate more fully in the framework of rights and obligations under the General Agreement.[12] In both cases, what is intended is a movement back towards MFN treatment.

The GSP was a major policy initiative of the 1960s. It proved to be a viable instrument for trade co-operation between developed and developing countries in the 1970s despite the slow process characterizing its improvement. In the 1980s, the GSP began to bear the brunt of the erosion of preferential margins resulting from the Tokyo Round tariff liberalization, and more important, of the policy of graduation which has caused a significant retrenchment of its benefits. Thus the issue today concerns not so much the pace of its improvement as the preservation of these benefits. In the 1970s the discussions within the Special Committee on Preferences

---

[11] See "Differential and more favourable treatment, reciprocity and fuller participation of developing countries", Decision of the Contracting Parties of 28 November 1979 (GATT, *Basic Instruments and Selected Documents, Twenty-sixth Supplement* (Sales No. GATT/1980-3), p. 203).

[12] During the Tokyo Round, the developing countries made contributions, in the form of tariff bindings or reductions, on $3.9 billion of their imports in terms of 1976 or 1977 trade. (See GATT, *The Tokyo Round of Multilateral Trade Negotiations, II: Supplementary Report* (Sales No. GATT/1980-1), p. 6.)

and in other forums centred more on specific details for improving the beneficiary lists, the product coverage, the depth of tariff cut, the safeguard mechanism and the rules of origin. Improvement as to the scope of the GSP was resisted mainly because of economic difficulties faced by the preference-giving countries. Since 1981 the process of improvement has nearly come to a halt giving way, instead, to graduation measures which constitute a direct challenge to the GSP's basic principles, in particular that of non-reciprocity.

Restrictive business practices

Restrictive business practices (RBPs) are essentially non-governmental restrictions affecting trade and development. They are employed by enterprises, acting together or individually, with the objective of regulating or influencing the prices, maketing and distribution of exports and imports and the manufacture, sale and resale of products within a country. Most developed market economy countries and a number of developing countries have enacted restrictive business practices legislation. In some countries, such as Canada and the United States, the introduction of RBP legislation dates back to the nineteenth century.

A shortcoming of existing legislation is that it is essentially inward-looking, in that it seeks to control only those practices which affect the domestic economy, but not those engaged in by enterprises within its jurisdiction which affect the economies of other countries. This in turn means that restrictive business practices in international trade adversely affecting a domestic economy are difficult to control. For example what action can a country undertake when it believes it receives collusive tenders from members of an international cartel, if all the enterprises in question are located abroad, and they do not have any assets, subsidiaries or affiliates in the country affected? Moreover, it can be very difficult in such circumstances for a country to detect and even more to prove that it is the target of collusive bids. And even if it does obtain proof of collusion, what else can it do except to reject the bids?

Allied to this issue is the problem of obtaining information and the possibility for transnational corporations in particular finding avenues to avoid controls on restrictive business practices. In particular, a transnational corporation can decide to keep information relating to its activities in countries which can prohibit its transmission abroad.

It should be pointed out that transnationals, on account of their market power nationally and internationally, are in a strong position to use restrictive business practices through, for example, the manipulation of the transfer prices for their intra-firm trade. For instance, in order to try to eliminate competition facing its subsidiary, the parent company may decide to supply the requirements of its subsidiary at an articifially low price, thus enabling the subsidiary to engage in predatory behaviour in the market for its products. Once competition has been eliminated, the transfer prices might become artificially high, in order to regain lost profits.

A further important shortcoming of domestic restrictive business practices legislation *vis-à-vis* transnational corporations is that whereas developed market-economy countries prohibit restrictive business practices engaged in collectively by independent enterprises, when enterprises form or merge into a single economic entity, such as a transnational corporation, then these countries tend to regard such practices as being outside the scope of their legislation. It is therefore likely that, far from controlling the activities of transnational corporations, existing restrictive business practices legislation in industrialized countries has often been one of the motives behind the creation or the enlargement of such corporations.

The need for action at the multilateral level and the drawing up by UNCTAD of the Set of Principles and Rules

One of the main reasons why action at the multilateral level is needed in respect of the control of restrictive business practices affecting international trade is that action has to be undertaken by all countries simultaneously, and in particular by the larger trading nations. This is because one cannot expect a country to take action unilaterally to eliminate practices such as export cartels, while its other principal trading partners allow and encourage these practices.

For the last 30 years or more, governments have recognized that restrictive business practices require action at the multilateral level. However, past efforts seeking international agreement on the manner and extent to which restrictive business practices should be controlled, have not succeeded. The most notable of such efforts was made at the time of the drawing-up of the Havana Charter for an International Trade Organization, in 1947-1948.

During the 1950s, other efforts were undertaken, particularly at the United Nations Economic and Social Council and at the GATT. The report of the *Ad hoc* Committee on Restrictive Business Practices to the Economic and Social Council contained proposals for an international code, based essentially on the principles set forth in chapter V of the Havana Charter. However, these did not obtain the support of the developed countries. The work initiated by GATT in 1955 led to the adoption in 1960 of *ad hoc* notification and consultation procedures for dealing with conflicts of interest between contracting parties in this field. The procedures have never been invoked.[13]

At the second session of the Conference (UNCTAD II), held in 1968, a tentative start was made on work in the area of restrictive business practices. The Conference called for a study on restrictive business practices by private enterprises of developed countries, with special reference to the effects of such practices on the export interests of developing countries, especially the least developed.[14] This was followed, in 1970, by the call in the International Development Strategy for the Second United Nations Development Decade for the identification of restrictive

---

[13] The reason for this apparent lack of interest in action within the GATT may have been due to subsequent action taken within the Organization for Economic Co-operation and Development (OECD), which adopted in 1967 a recommendation concerning co-operation between member countries on restrictive business practices affecting international trade, involving notification and consultation procedures in a search for mutually acceptable solutions to these problems. In 1976, the OECD Council also adopted Guidelines for Multinational Enterprises. (See R. Krishnarmurti, "UNCTAD as a Negotiating Instrument on Trade Policy: THE UNCTAD-GATT Relationship", in M. Zammit Cutajar (ed), *UNCTAD and the South-North Dialogue: The First Twenty Years* (Pergamon Press, 1985).

[14] Conference resolution 25 (II) of 27 March 1968.

business practices particularly affecting the trade and development of developing countries, with a view to consideration of appropriate remedial measures, the aim being to reach concrete and significant results early in the Decade.

In the course of the 1970s there developed a renewed awareness of the need for stengthened controls over restrictive business practices, especially in respect of international trade. This awareness resulted, in part, from concern about the use of such practices by transnational corporations, which had emerged as the principal actors in international trade, and in part from concern about the increasing resort to the use of such practices in the context of what has been called the "new protectionism".

In 1972, UNCTAD's work was significantly strengthened at the third session of the Conference in Santiago, which decided [15] *inter alia,* to establish an *ad hoc* group of experts on restrictive business practices. This Group was called upon to identify all restrictive business practices, including those of transnational corporations, which adversely affect the trade and development of developing countries. The necessity of multilateral action with respect to restrictive business practices was further recognized by governments, which recommended that the Group "shall examine the possibility of drawing up guidelines for the consideration of governments of developed and developing countries regarding restrictive business practices adversely affecting developing countries". Work at the Expert Group level led UNCTAD IV, in Nairobi in 1976, to decide that action at the international level should include negotiations with the objective of formulating a set of multilaterally agreed equitable principles and rules for the control of restrictive business practices, including those of transnational corporations, adversely affecting international trade, particularly that of developing countries and the economic development of these countries.[16]

The Third Group of Experts on Restrictive Business Practices, which was established to carry out the work on restrictive business practices, gave top priority to the negotiation of a set of principles and rules and, in 1979, at its sixth session, it prepared a draft which was ready for consideration by a negotiating conference. The United Nations Conference on Restrictive Business Practices was then covened by the General Assembly to negotiate the draft. At its second session, in April 1980, the Conference approved the Set of Multilaterally Agreed Equitable Principles and Rules for the Control of Restrictive Practices and transmitted it to the General Assembly. The adoption of the Set of Principles and Rules by the General Assembly in resolution 35/63 of 5 December 1980 was the culmination of more than a decade of work at UNCTAD in the area of restrictive business practices.

The objectives, as stated in the Set, are—among others—to ensure that restrictive business practices do not impede or negate the realization of benefits that should arise from the liberalization of tariff and non-tariff barriers affecting the trade and development of developing countries. The Set also aims at greater efficiency in international trade and development and at protecting and promoting social welfare in general and, in particular, the interests of consumers in both developed and developing countries.

---

[15] Conference resolution 73 (III) of 19 May 1972.

[16] Conference resolution 96 (IV) of 31 May 1976.

The Set of Principles and Rules represents an important first step towards the solution of the problems and shortcomings of existing controls of restrictive business practices at national, regional and international levels. Although not legally binding, its adoption by the General Assembly involves a moral undertaking by all States to recognize and apply the principles and rules contained in the document, and to collaborate to this end. The Set contains a number of provisions addressed to enterprises concerning their behaviour, and provisions addressed to governments concerning action to be taken at national, regional and international levels. At the international level, in particular, it provides for consultation procedures among governments to solve problems relating to restrictive business practices.

The Set also called for the establishment of an Intergovernmental Group of Experts on Restrictive Business Practices, operating within the framework of a Committee of UNCTAD, to provide the institutional machinery for follow-up action as well as to monitor its effective application. It was also decided by the General Assembly that five years after adoption of the Set, a conference should be convened "for the purpose of reviewing all the aspects of the Set of Principles and Rules". In this regard the Intergovernmental Group of Experts has been charged to make proposals for improvement and further development of the Set.

At its second session, in November 1983, the Intergovernmental Group stressed the serious concern of all countries about the continued resort to restrictive business practices by enterprises in international trade transactions. An important element in this respect is the increasing use of so-called "grey area" measures, such as voluntary export restraints and orderly marketing arrangements, which largely fall outside the existing rules of the international trading system. Concern was expressed—especially by developing countries—that the extent of the use of restrictive business practices was a reflection of the ineffective application of the Set of Principles and Rules. This was reflected in the resolution adopted by consensus, which underlined the importance of the adequate implementation of the Set.

The Group also decided, in resolution 2 (II), to include in the agenda for the next session (scheduled to be held from 7 to 16 November 1984), the formulation of proposals for the improvement and further development of the Set of Principles and Rules, for submission to the Review Conference to be convened in 1985. To this end, States were invited, in the resolution, to forward their views to the Secretary-General of UNCTAD.

States, in adopting the Set of Principles and Rules for the control of restrictive business practices, were no doubt aware that the adoption of the international instrument, although a considerable breakthrough, would not in itself bring to an end the adverse effects of restrictive business practices in international trade transactions. The Set established the desired norms for the control of restrictive business practices at national and regional levels, and placed on States a moral obligation to introduce and strengthen legislation in this area and to ensure that their enterprises abided by the Set. Hence, the effectiveness of the international instrument depends upon its implementation. The Set is entirely action-oriented. It is addressed both to enterprises, including transnationals, and to States at the national, regional and international levels. Action by States at each of these levels is complementary. In particular, the control of restrictive business practices nationally, through the effective enforcement of appropriate legislation, is closely related to action at the international level, including exchange of information and experience, consultations between States and, where needed, technical assistance.

NON-TARIFF MEASURES

Governmental non-tariff measures (NTMs) of various types have for many years been applied in international trade. Many of these, like quantitative restrictions, limit trade directly and in absolute terms; others tend to restrict or distort trade because of their diversity, lack of transparency and of the manner in which they are administered. The difficulties involved in following the evolution of NTMs and evaluating their effects on trade are well known. What should and should not be included in the concept is still a matter of debate. Standards, including those regarding quality, packaging and labelling regulations, while capable of facilitating trade, are, on the other hand, capable of being used in a fashion so as to restrict trade, for example by making certification of imported products more difficult than in the case of domestically produced goods. Many NTMs are of a qualitative character, so that the approaches to their liberalization are more difficult since these depend upon the characteristics and effects of the measure in question. The fact that they are very diverse in nature—including those applied for reasons other than economic ones—and of varying technical complexity and that new ones are continually being found, heightens the difficulties in dealing effectively with this question.

While the tariff policies of the developed market-economy countries have followed an uninterrupted trend towards trade liberalization ever since the early post-war years and throughout the 1960s, this has not been the case with non-tariff measures. No sooner had the liberalization process within the Organization for European Economic Co-operation (OEEC) reached its culminating point, than a number of NTMs, previously abolished, were reintroduced, albeit in new forms and especially in the form of "voluntary" export restraints. While beginning in the late 1950s, first in the trade relations of the United States and later in those of a few western European countries with Japan, with respect to the latter's exports of textiles, "voluntary" export restraints have been extended during the following decades to cover a wide range of developing countries and also an ever increasing variety of products.

The activities of the UNCTAD secretariat in the area of NTMs

Issues concerning NTMs and related problems have been of concern to UNCTAD from its inception. The final act of UNCTAD I, adopted in 1964, contains specific provisions on this subject; for instance, recommendation A.III.4 provides guidelines for non-tariff policies, including adherence to the standstill on the intensification of existing barriers, as well as on the introduction of new trade restrictions. It also provides that developed countries should, as a matter of urgency, remove quantitative restrictions on manufactured and semi-manufactured products of export interest to developing countries, as soon as possible.

From the beginning, the UNCTAD Committee on Manufactures provided a forum for study, discussion and continuing review of the issues concerning NTMs. UNCTAD secretariat studies were an important contribution to the analysis of the economic and trade aspects of such measures, particularly those affecting developing countries. In 1969, the UNCTAD secretariat defined governmental NTMs (as distinct from RBPs, which are non-governmental) and separated them into two categories: (*a*) those barriers applied purposely to limit the value of import of the product in question for certain reasons, e.g., to protect domestic producers; and (*b*) those that may not be considered as barriers *per se* but which, in view of their diversity, technical complexity and the manner by which they are administered, tend to restrict or distort international trade in the products affected. The UNCTAD secretariat further analysed the effects of NTMs and advanced suggestions for dealing with their restrictive and distorting effects on trade.

Since the early 1970s, resolutions calling upon developed countries to reduce or eliminate non-tariff barriers (or their effects on trade) and requesting the UNCTAD secretariat to collect and disseminate information on these practices, have been adopted at each of the intervening Conferences. At UNCTAD III, in 1972, the Conference adopted resolution 76 (III), which recognized the need for a continuing examination by UNCTAD of non-tariff barriers and requested all Governments of member States to co-operate fully with the UNCTAD secretariat in providing it with the appropriate information for the advancement of its work. At UNCTAD IV, Conference resolution 96 (IV) adopted in 1976, requested the developed countries to improve access to their markets, particularly through the reduction or elimination of non-tariff barriers, or where this was not appropriate, to reduce or eliminate their trade restricting or distorting effects, in particular those which applied to products of export interest to developing countries.

The multilateral trade negotiations (MTN) launched under the auspices of GATT in 1973 with the adoption of the Tokyo declaration, included as one of its main objectives the liberalization of NTMs. As a result, the activities of UNCTAD in this field were substantially slowed down in the expectation that NTMs of particular concern to developing countries would be successfully dealt with, even though the negotiations themselves covered only a very limited number of such NTMs. During the Tokyo Round, that is from 1973 to 1979, the activities of UNCTAD were limited to assisting developing countries in participating fully and effectively in the negotiations; to following closely developments in the negotiations, and to providing relevant documentation to the GATT bodies for use as they deemed appropriate. In this connection it may be mentioned that many of the specific proposals presented by the developing countries in the negotiations were derived from UNCTAD studies.

At UNCTAD V, held in 1979, the Conference adopted resolution 131 (V) on protectionism and structural adjustment, which *inter alia* called upon developed countries to move towards the reduction or elimination of quantitative restrictions and measures having similar effects, particularly in relation to products exported by the developing countries. The resolution requested the Trade and Development Board to continue to review developments involving restrictions of trade with a view to examining and formulating appropriate recommendations concerning the general problem of protectionism. Furthermore, the Secretary-General of UNCTAD was requested to continue the work of compiling and up-dating the inventory of NTMs affecting the trade of developing countries and of analysing the effects of such measures.

In response to the mandate provided by Conference resolution 131 (V) and subsequent Board decisions which further expanded this mandate, the UNCTAD secretariat prepared extensive documentation on both the theoretical and the empirical aspects of protectionism, including the impact of NTMs. In particular, it established a data base on trade measures, of which the objective was to provide basic information necessary for assessing the structure, incidence and impact of non-tariff restrictions to trade. In its current state, the computerized data base contains information on import régimes of over 40 countries. Its coverage is being extended in terms both of countries—in order to embrace all trade flows—and of governmental measures bearing upon international trade in all sectors.

Resolution 159 (VI) adopted at UNCTAD VI in 1983, saw the culmination of a process of diagnosis and of building awareness of the issues to be confronted, in particular in the area of NTMs. This resolution directed the Trade and Development Board to examine the issues relating to the phasing-out of quantitative restrictions and measures having a similar effect, the application of anti-dumping and countervailing duty laws, regulations and procedures, and requested the Board to follow-up the work on safeguards. Another aspect of the resolution was the framework it established for attacking the various facets of protectionism. The Board was given a general monitoring review function and the mandate to make recommendations in this regard. In addition, the Board's role in following the course of negotiations in GATT was confirmed, as well as its responsibility in assisting developing countries to participate in such negotiations.

STRUCTURAL ADJUSTMENT RELATED TO TRADE

Throughout the post-war period, policies designed to promote industrial objectives have been increasingly adopted in all developed market-economy countries. In itself the emergence of such policies should not have conflicted with the international adjustment of industry, including the adjustment aspects of industries of particular interest to exports of developing countries. When industrial policy is truly forward-looking, it should facilitate, and to the extent possible, anticipate the effects of market forces, such as those generated by changes in comparative advantage. During most of the expansionary period starting with the early 1950s, the forward-looking component has indeed been dominant in the policy-mix of the developed market-economy countries. However, throughout this period, these forward-looking policies were also accompanied, to a varying degree, by defensive policies applying to sectors and industries with low profitability that were experiencing difficulties in the face of import competition. Among the various policy instruments used, investment incentives—ranging from accelerated depreciation and tax-free reserves to subsidized loans and export subsidies (despite the 1962 ban, under GATT article XVI)—have proved to be the most effective.

Since in many cases the declining industries in developed countries happen to be labour-intensive and of a more traditional type, governmental assistance has often been associated with protectionist measures, generally directed against imports from developing countries. In more recent years "packages" of trade and industrial policies have gained greatly in importance; some non-tariff barriers in particular, in combination with investment incentives and similar measures, are being increasingly used to assist ranges of production in the face of competing imports from developing countries. The most disturbing aspects of such defensive policies is that they generally aim at protecting or making competitive virtually the whole industrial structure facing competition from developing countries, thus leaving practically no scope for adjustment vis-à-vis these countries. Moreover, much of what, in fact, amounts to the protection of domestic industrial interests tends to be represented as a vehicle of adjustment, as is almost invariably the case with "emergency" protection measures. "Emergency" protection is introduced on the grounds that the industry concerned needs a breathing space to adjust itself to foreign competition, but generally it tends to assume a permanent character.

The textile industry in developed countries provides a clear example of this approach. The notion of "market disruption" was the basis for the short- and long-term arrangements on cotton textiles, which were followed by the Multi-Fibre Arrangement (MFA). Under the MFA, the developed importing countries have negotiated a series of "comprehensive" bilateral agreements which restrain the entire range of textile and clothing exports from over 30 developing countries. As the network of restraint agreements expanded, its product coverage was enhanced and its permanent restrictive character tightened. Despite commitments by governments to pursue appropriate adjustment policies in this area and to phase out internationally uncompetitive lines of production, this was not done in practice. The MFA has demonstrated that effective structural adjustment cannot be seriously envisaged without a credible commitment to liberalize. These issues were addressed in a study undertaken for the tenth session of the Committee on Manufactures.[17]

The problem of structural adjustment has reached a new dimension in recent years as a result of the difficulties experienced by the world economy. The decade of the 1970s has witnessed a retardation of structural adjustment at a time when the need for structural change was greatest owing to rapid shifts in patterns of comparative advantage, especially as regards the increased export competitiveness of a number of developing countries. The defensive and protectionist policies of many developed countries have put additional obstacles in the way of the short-run adjustment process, while failing to enhance its long-run possibilities.

Activities of UNCTAD in the area of structural adjustment

The activities of the UNCTAD secretariat associated with restructuring issues—approached through the trade aspect—began in the area of adjustment assistance measures. Following recommendation A.III.6 adopted at UNCTAD I and a number of decisions by the Committee on Manufactures, the secretariat produced at regular intervals, starting in 1968, reports and studies on the evolution of adjustment policies in selected developed market-economy countries for submission to the Committee on Manufactures and the Conference. Among the numerous documents produced on the subject, a report submitted to UNCTAD III in 1972[18] deserves to be specifically mentioned since it represented the first attempt

---

[17] *International trade in textiles, with special reference to the problems faced by developing countries* (TD/B/C.2/215/Rev.1) (United Nations publication, Sales No. E.84.II.D.7).

[18] "Restrictive business practices" (TD/121/Supp.1), reproduced in *Proceedings of the United Nations Conference on Trade and Development, Third Session*, vol. II — *Merchandise Trade* (United Nations publication, Sales No. E.73.II.D.5).

within the United Nations system to quantify the effects on industrial employment in the United States, the United Kingdom and the Federal Republic of Germany of a doubling of imports of manufactures from developing countries. The findings of the study have often been quoted by international organizations to show the marginal effects of increased imports from developing countries on employment in developed market-economy countries. In noting this report, Conference resolution 72 (III) requested the developed countries "to adopt where appropriate suitable adjustment assistance policies or programmes, with a view to achieving a better allocation of resources, particularly taking into consideration trade liberalization measures for the expansion of the exports of manufactures of the developing countries".

In the preparations for UNCTAD IV, a step forward towards the elaboration of a strategy for restructuring international trade in manufactures, including the implications for the export capability of developing countries, was made by the UNCTAD secretariat in its report entitled: "A comprehensive strategy for expanding and diversifying the export trade of the developing countries in manufactures and semi-manufactures".[19] Compared with the earlier approach of UNCTAD, which largely tended to concentrate only on the access to markets, the report broke new ground: (*a*) by including the supply side of the problem and (*b*) by providing a broad framework for inter-relating a number of elements already covered by UNCTAD's activities. The report led to resolution 96 (IV), adopted in Nairobi in 1976. Among other things, the resolution called upon the developed countries to "... facilitate the development of new policies and strengthen existing policies that would encourage domestic factors of production to move progressively from the lines of production which are less competitive internationally, especially where the long-term comparative advantage lies in favour of developing countries..." The resolution did not go far enough in spelling out the practical modalities of action, but nevertheless it strongly emphasized the need for broad policy changes along the lines indicated in the secretariat's report.

By the time of the preparation for UNCTAD V, it appeared that little progress had been made, particularly by the developed countries, in implementing the provisions of resolutions 72 (III) and 96 (IV) in respect of structural adjustment. The unfavourable economic trends since the mid-1970s, and the tendency in developed countries to subordinate the long-term growth objectives to short-term considerations, have led to the revival of protectionist policies aimed in particular at limiting imports from developing countries. In such a situation, the secretariat submitted to UNCTAD V a new report[20] which developed further the ideas and policy proposals contained in the report prepared for the Nairobi Conference and also submitted a report on the implications for developing countries of the new protectionism in developed countries.[21]

---

[19] TD/185, *ibid., Fourth Session,* vol. III, *Basic Documents* (United Nations publication, Sales No. E.76.II.D.12).

[20] "Comprehensive measures required to expand and diversify the export trade of developing countries in manufactures and semi-manufactures" (TD/230, *ibid., Fifth Session,* vol. III – *Basic Documents* (United Nations publication, Sales No. E.79.II.D.16)).

[21] "Policy issues in the fields of trade, finance and money, and their relationship to structural changes at the global level" (TD/225) (*ibid.*).

It is significant in this context that resolution 131 (V), adopted at the Conference in 1979, dealt both with protectionism and structural adjustment. Within this resolution, protectionism was envisaged not as a short-term phenomenon reflecting a temporary period of recession in the industrialized countries, but rather as a symptom of a larger problem related to the way in which the world economy would evolve, particularly in the light of the industrialization of the developing countries. Regarding structural adjustment, the resolution called on the Trade and Development Board to organize "an annual review of the patterns of production and trade in the world economy... with a view to identifying elements or problems most relevant, in the light of the dynamics of comparative advantage, to the attainment of optimum overall economic growth, including the development and diversification of the economies of developing countries, and an effective international division of labour".

From the viewpoint of action, it should be noted, however, that while resolution 131 (V) marked a step forward by bringing together protectionism and structural adjustment, it did not clearly establish the link between the two issues in the search for any viable solution. Although developed market-economy countries had specifically agreed, under the terms of the above resolution, to take account of any recommendation on structural adjustment in their national policies, they were not willing to discuss interactions between this latter issue and protectionism, in a North-South context.

In its resolution 226 (XXII) of 20 March 1981, the Trade and Development Board decided to establish a sessional committee at its first annual regular session to carry out the task assigned to it by the Conference. The Board expanded further by subsequent decisions the original mandate provided in Conference resolution 131 (V); for example, it specified in its decision 250 (XXIV) of 19 March 1982, that the studies by the secretariat should give commensurate attention to the sectors of agriculture, manufactured goods and services.

The scope of the annual review is such that it has given the secretariat an opportunity to produce, since 1980, a series of studies which have contributed to and facilitated the examination of these issues at the intergovernmental level. In these studies, structural change is described as a handmaiden of economic development, and it is manifested in the changing relative importance of different sectors of production and consumption. Structural adjustment, on the other hand, is a recognition of the fact that the process of structural change may incur costs. Structural adjustment policies, therefore, are designed to regulate the speed of change, in order to minimize the costs involved in the process. These recent studies by the secretariat have stressed the fact that the complexities of the workings of the world economy are such that any discussion of the means of lubricating global structural adjustment along the lines of comparative advantage, or of facilitating the achievement of a better international division of labour, can only be productively pursued if account is taken of the inter-related nature of the problems facing the world economy. In the absence of this comprehensive approach, it is difficult to generate sound policy initiatives.

These studies by the secretariat have also underlined the advantages of positive adjustment policies over protective trade policies. However, effective adjustment assistance policies cannot be carried out in isolation and without a credible commitment to trade liberalization and respect for multilateral disciplines, reinforced by appropriate surveillance and transparency at both the national and the international levels. Respect for multilateral disciplines, trade liberalization and effective structural adjustment policies are not substitutes, but inseparable components, of any programme to resolve the crisis in international trade relations and promote world economic recovery.

In 1983, the secretariat submitted to UNCTAD VI a new report entitled: "Protectionism, trade relations and structural adjustment",[22] which suggested a comprehensive approach combining trade, adjustment and development policies. It recommended concerted efforts at the national and international levels to: (a) improve and strengthen the international trading system, while taking account of the longer-term trade and development objectives and needs of developing countries; and (b) devise and implement positive structural adjustment policies in order to provide improved market access, in particular for developing countries.

Conference resolution 159 (VI) on "Protectionism, structural adjustment and the international trading system", adopted in Belgrade in 1983, reflected to a large extent the comprehensive approach advocated by UNCTAD, and clearly recognized the existence of linkages and interactions between structural adjustment, economic growth and development and the reversal of protectionist trends. It reinforced the role of the Trade and Development Board as a forum for wide-ranging discussion and exchange of information, to promote in particular greater transparency in the process of structural adjustment. It also clearly recognized the Board's responsibilities to "... review and monitor trade developments and, where appropriate, make general policy recommendations, *inter alia,* with a view to encouraging factors of production to move progressively into lines of production where they are internationally competitive ..." Although the resolution did not go far enough in spelling out specific actions at the national and international levels which could lead to the establishment of international disciplines on protectionism and structural adjustment, it did result in a general understanding of the role of the Trade and Development Board in this area and thus removed the outstanding impediments to the launching of serious initiatives on these issues.

SERVICES

Within the United Nations system a number of organizations have been dealing with issues in specific service sectors, some of which, such as the International Telecommunication Union (ITU), have been active in the area of communications long before the establishment of the United Nations. Many United Nations organizations, such as the International Civil Aviation Organization (ICAO) and the International Maritime Organization (IMO) have a responsibility with respect to certain services, while other organizations (e.g., the World Intellectual Property Organization (WIPO) deal with issues pertinent to a variety of service sectors. Issues relating to particular services, such as transport and banking, have been addressed in the context of regional and subregional integration and in forums such as OECD.

---

[22] "Protectionism, trade relations and structural adjustment" (TD/274 and Corr.1), to be printed in *Proceedings of the United Nations Conference on Trade and Development, Sixth Session,* vol. III, *Basic Documents* (United Nations publication, Sales No. E.83.II.D.8).

Since its establishment UNCTAD has been deeply involved in specific service sectors, notably transport, insurance, tourism and financing related to trade, as well as in service issues related to the transfer of technology. This work has led to the negotiation of certain instruments in UNCTAD, particularly in the area of maritime transport,[23] as well as to resolutions and guidelines in this and other areas. The UNCTAD secretariat has also been executing technical assistance programmes with respect to these services, including those for the least developed countries. Service issues have also been addressed in the context of UNCTAD's work on restrictive business practices,[24] and are covered by the Set of Principles and Rules.

UNCTAD's role with respect to services intensified in 1982 as a result of the Trade and Development Board's decision 250 (XXIV) in which it was agreed that, when dealing with factors of relevance to the issues of protectionism and structural adjustment and policies influencing structural adjustment and trade, commensurate attention should be paid to services. The first study undertaken in this context was presented to the twenty-sixth session of the Board, namely: "Production and trade in services, policies and other underlying factors bearing upon international service transactions".[25] In turn, this led to the overall issue of services being dealt with in the documentation presented to the Conference under the item on international trade[26] and to the Board at its twenty-eighth session.[27]

Recently, however, there have been moves on the part of certain countries to place the international debate on issues pertaining to the service sector in a more general context.[28] The underlying motives would seem varied. Certain countries appear to be seeking to establish a multilateral framework for negotiating concessions with respect to regulations affecting transactions in services, including participation in the service sector of foreign countries, particularly a framework which would permit their negotiating leverage with respect to trade in goods to come into play. This would seem to be the intent of those developed countries which pressed for the inclusion of a work programme on services in the GATT ministerial declaration of 1982. While their efforts did not achieve this objective, they did succeed in including a provision in the declaration to the effect that Contracting Parties are recommended to undertake national studies on services and are invited to exchange information on such matters, *inter alia,* through international organizations such as GATT and to review the results of these examinations along with the

---

[23] See, for example, the report by the UNCTAD secretariat, "UNCTAD activities in the field of shipping" (TD/278 and Corr.1) (*ibid.*).

[24] See the report by the UNCTAD secretariat "The effects on international trade transactions of restrictive business practices in the services sector by consulting firms and the enterprises in relation to the design and manufactures of plant and equipment" (TD/B/RBP/13).

[25] TD/B/941 and Corr.1.

[26] "Protectionism, trade relations..." (TD/274).

[27] "Protectionism and structural adjustment in the world economy", Part II — "Recent developments in the context of global trends in production and trade" (TD/B/981 (Part II) and Add.1 and 2).

[28] The general service issue has been discussed in such meetings as the GATT Ministerial session of November 1982, the OECD Council, the Latin American Council, the Latin American Economic Conference (Quito, January 1984), Ministerial Meetings of the Group of 77, not to mention UNCTAD VI, from whence this specific mandate emerged.

information and comments provided by relevant international organizations at the 1984 session, to consider whether any multilateral action on these matters is appropriate and desirable.

Developing countries have sought to focus the attention of the international community on collective efforts to strengthen their service sectors and devise mechanisms for increasing their participation in international service transactions. They have examined service issues in various forums, including the fifth Ministerial Meeting of the Group of 77 and in regional groups (e.g., the Latin American Economic System (SELA). In the Buenos Aires Platform, adopted at the fifth Ministerial Meeting of the Group of 77, the developing countries sought specifically to set up a major study programme in UNCTAD to identify and establish priorities regarding services of particular importance to developing countries and to devise programmes which would enable the developing countries to have greater participation in international service transactions and make recommendations for mechanisms for multilateral co-operation to this end.[29]

Regardless of the underlying motives of the proponents, the consideration of service issues in a universal and interdisciplinary forum is welcome and timely. Recent technological developments have given rise to entirely new services and to interlinkages among services and between goods and services which may have a revolutionary impact on the production and trade of both goods and other services and on world patterns of trade and development thus justifying their examination in a universal and interdisciplinary forum, where the overall trade and development aspects could be taken into account. Its timeliness also derives from the present situation, when a reassessment of the development process, and of the international community's commitment to such a process, is under way. A closer examination of the role of services in the development process would seem to constitute an essential component of this general reassessment of development strategies at the national, regional and multilateral levels.

At Belgrade, the Conference, in its resolution 159 (VI), directed the UNCTAD secretariat to continue its studies of service issues and stated that UNCTAD should, *inter alia,* consider the role of the service sector in the development process, keeping in view the special problems of the least developed countries. The Trade and Development Board was invited to consider, at its twenty-ninth session, appropriate future work by UNCTAD on services.

In response to the mandate contained in Conference resolution 159 (VI), the secretariat embarked on a general study which should be seen as an initial effort to establish a basis for considering services in a framework of both a general and a development-oriented nature. The approach to be adopted in the general study is first to examine the situation of services in the world economy and in developing countries on an overall basis and in the context of key service sectors. The study identified definitive and statistical problems confronting further analyses and possible methods for overcoming such problems. In the light of this analysis, an attempt was made to explain such situations, using conventional theory, and to suggest elements for a methodology to measure the contribution of services to the devel-

---

[29] See the Buenos Aires Platform (TD/285), sect. IV, C (resolution on international trade in goods and services, sect. C). (For the printed text of the Buenos Aires Platform, see *Proceedings of the United Nations Conference on Trade and Development, Sixth Session,* vol. I, annex VI.)

opment process. The questions concerning the regulation of service activities, on both a domestic and an international basis, were examined in greater detail. Those issues on which current international debate on services is centred, and the questions related to the role and appropriate scope of the regulation of services, were also examined. Finally, the study made a series of recommendations aimed at establishing a development-oriented framework for future work on services.

This overall study was accompanied by a series of sectoral and other special studies. Studies on individual service sectors (maritime transport, banking, insurance, engineering and consultancy services and transborder data flows) examined, on a sectoral basis, the various issues identified in the general study, as well as the special importance of services to the least developed countries, and commented upon the "services of the future" — a look at how technological breakthroughs are creating new services and their implications for trade and development. These studies provide a major input into the general exercise, while also constituting independent studies in their own right.

In parallel to this exercise of preparing for the twenty-ninth session of the Trade and Development Board, it is envisaged that individual countries will be conducting national studies of the role of services in their own economies. A questionnaire circulated by the Secretary-General of UNCTAD in late 1983 had the dual objective of collecting information and of stimulating governments' (especially those of developing countries) interest in service issues. The UNCTAD secretariat is preparing itself to assist (in collaboration with other international bodies) developing countries, particularly the least developed countries, in this exercise.

The document submitted to the twenty-ninth session of the Trade and Development Board was only able to touch upon these issues in a preliminary fashion but clearly indicated the need for, and areas of, future work. The GATT system to govern international trade relations with respect to goods essentially ignored development considerations. While many countries considered that development would be stimulated by the effective operation of the system, it became apparent to the international community a decade later that major changes were required in the system to make it responsive to development needs and supportive of development objectives. The efforts to incorporate such changes into the GATT system have been pursued for over 20 years but with limited results and even these are in the process of being eroded.

In contrast to the situation in respect of specific service industries, such as shipping and civil aviation, no overall multilateral contractual framework exists at present for services, and there is no international consensus as to the need for such a framework let alone the principles upon which such a framework should be based.

It is not certain that discussions will even lead at the multilateral level to the drawing up of such a framework. What is clearly of crucial importance, however, is that if work directed toward the eventual establishment of such a framework is to be initiated, it must, from its inception, be cast in a development context. The speed at which the impact of technological developments on transactions in services (both old and new) and service inputs, are moving, makes such an approach imperative if overall development considerations are not to be undermined.

C. The international trading system: summary of issues and tasks for the future

One could view the establishment of UNCTAD in itself as the manifestation of the perception by the international community that the international trading system required reform. The failure to implement the Havana Charter in full meant that GATT formed the centre of the trading system which was not constructed with specific development objectives in mind. Although many of its original Contracting Parties may have believed that its effective application would encourage export-led economic development, in reality, the General Agreement focused on trade relations in a narrow sense, and thus other major issues in the Havana Charter were not dealt with. After a decade of experience with its operation, however, the international community recommended that modifications should be introduced to provide the multilateral system with a greater development orientation and an organization more committed to the development process.

At the time of the establishment of UNCTAD there existed a great variance in the views of countries as to the ways, and the extent to which, the post-war trading system should be reformed. The emergence of a consensus that developing countries required preferential tariff treatment was the first concrete achievement in this respect. Although considered by the donor countries as a temporary derogation from the General Agreement and which, in retrospect, may have fallen far short of expectations in terms of trade benefits, the generalized system of preferences (GSP) represented a major breakthrough by putting into action the theory that developing countries should be entitled to special trade measures in their favour without providing reciprocal concessions in return.

Although agreement, in principle, on the GSP was reached in 1968, as already mentioned, it took several years for the individual schemes to be put into effect. Even before some major countries had implemented their GSP schemes, new developments threatened to undermine its long awaited benefits. In early 1972 the major industrial countries decided to enter into another round of multilateral trade negotiations which could logically be expected to result in a serious erosion of the preferential tariff margins which developing countries would enjoy under the GSP. This concern of the developing countries was addressed at the UNCTAD III in Santiago in 1972, where the UNCTAD secretariat was assigned the responsibility, in Conference resolution 82 (III), of providing advice and technical assistance to developing countries in these negotiations. Developing countries' request for such assistance were based on their experience in the previous ("Kennedy") GATT multilateral round, where they had failed to obtain meaningful benefits.[30] A large technical assistance project financed by the United Nations Development Programme (UNDP) with regional and interregional components was set up to provide such assistance.

The first step in this new multilateral round was the negotiation of its objectives. The developing countries were successful in including many commitments in their favour in the Tokyo declaration, which in retrospect appear to have been the

---

[30] See *The Kennedy Round estimated effects on tariff barriers* (TD/6/Rev.1) (United Nations publication, Sales No. E.68.II.D.12).

zenith of the international community's acceptance of the "development consensus". The Tokyo declaration stated that the aims of the negotiations would include an increased share for developing countries in international trade, improved access to markets for their exports, preservation and expansion of the GSP, and "differential and more favourable treatment" with respect to non-tariff measures. It was agreed that the non-reciprocity principle (as stated in the GATT) would be upheld, and that consideration would even be given to "improvements in the international framework for the conduct of world trade".

Developing countries entered the Tokyo Round encouraged by these commitments, following the logic of the GSP, and adopted the approach of seeking to obtain special and differential treatment in all areas of trade relations. As the negotiations progressed, however, it became evident that not only did they have little chance of obtaining this objective but, in fact, risked having their basic rights obtained in previous negotiations and under the GATT itself, seriously undermined.

At UNCTAD V, which was held during the final stages of the Tokyo Round, the Trade and Development Board was requested, in Conference Resolution 132 (V), to make a global evaluation of the MTNs on the basis of a report by the Secretary-General of UNCTAD. After a number of preliminary documents, the final report focused on the effect, on the international trading system as a whole, of the results of the Tokyo Round and of other negotiations which had taken place in parallel (e.g., the negotiation of the Multifibre Agreement (MFA) and its first renewal).

The UNCTAD secretariat's preliminary assessment was that since the initiation of the Tokyo Round in 1973, considerable changes had taken place in the trading system. To a large extent these developments constituted an exacerbation of opposing trends which had existed from the early days of the post-war trading system. While there had been an impressive reduction in the level of customs duties, especially on industrial products in the developed market-economy countries, the opposing trend had resulted in sectors of trade being subject to special arrangements under which trade in these sectors took place outside the framework of the principles and rules of the General Agreement, such sectors included textiles, many agricultural products, steel, shipbuilding etc. Tariffs had become of less relevance, and were no longer considered as viable measures of protection, not only because of their lower levels, but for a variety of reasons. Among these reasons were the entry of new, competitive suppliers in the world market for a variety of products and the growing instability in exchange rates.

The secretariat felt that there was a strong tendency toward "managed trade", under which the prices and/or quantities of imports were controlled through flexible measures of protection rather than the traditional measure of the tariff. Such "management" inevitably took place against the interests of weaker trading partners, notably the developing countries. An increase in discrimination against developing countries was evident which was facilitated by the introduction of new concepts (or the resurrection of old ones) into the system to justify deviations from the basic principle of non-discrimination; such concepts included "market disruption", "selectivity", "graduation", "conditional most-favoured-nation treatment", and the like. All these measures attempted to provide legitimacy to discriminatory actions against developing countries. When discriminating measures were applied against developing countries, they were usually directed against those very sectors where developing countries had achieved a considerable success in the world market. It also pointed out that these tendencies had first surfaced in the legislation and regulations of the major trading powers, subsequently being reflected in multilateral arrangements.

The discussion provoked by the analysis presented to the twenty-third session of the Trade and Development Board led the developing countries to submit a draft resolution seeking that the Board conduct a review of "Developments in the international trading system" on an annual basis. This proposal and interlinked issues were considered at the twenty-fourth, twenty-fifth and twenty-sixth sessions of the Board, based on documentation prepared by the secretariat to assist in the deliberations.[31]

The efforts of the Trade and Development Board in this area gained even greater relevance after the disappointing outcome of the GATT Ministerial meeting in November 1982 where it proved impossible to obtain a firm commitment on the part of the Contracting Parties to take the steps necessary to counteract the pressures leading to an inevitable collapse of the multilateral system. This issue of the trading system was addressed by the developing countries at the fifth Ministerial Meeting of the Group of 77, and the Buenos Aires Platform called for the Trade and Development Board to study the rules and principles of the system with a view to establishing a new set of rules and principles leading to a system of a universal character. The secretariat's examination of the trading system was included in the background documentation for UNCTAD VI.[32]

Negotiations at UNCTAD VI in Belgrade led to the adoption of Conference resolution 159 (VI), paragraph 14 of which states that:

The Trade and Development Board should review and study in depth developments in the international trading system. The Board could, while fully respecting the principles of most-favoured nation treatment (MFN) and non-discrimination, make recommendations on principles and policies related to international trade, and make proposals as to the strengthening and improvement of the trading system with a view to giving it a more universal and dynamic character as well as to making it more responsive to the needs of developing countries and supportive of accelerated economic growth and development, particularly that of developing countries.

To support the Trade and Development Board in carrying out this mandate the secretariat has initiated a detailed analysis of developments in the trading system including the actions and policies of the major trading countries and groups of countries, to obtain an in-depth view of the problems which would have to be addressed in any attempt to strengthen and improve the trading system. In addition to this empirical approach, individuals with lengthy experience in trade policy and negotiations have been requested to prepare discussion papers with respect to specific issues that need to be confronted in this context. It is expected that the Board will consider at its thirtieth session (Spring 1985) the manner in which it will undertake this review of developments in the international trading system.

---

[31] "Multilateral trade negotiations: background notes by the UNCTAD secretariat" (TD/B/913 and Corr.1) and "Recent developments in international trade relations: note by the UNCTAD secretariat" (TD/B/948).

[32] "The current world economic crisis and perspectives for the 1980s" (TD/272), to be printed in *Proceedings of the United Nations Conference on Trade and Development, Sixth Session,* vol. III, *Basic Documents* (United Nations publication, Sales No. E.83.II.D.8).

The analyses conducted to date reveal that recent developments confirm the initial perception of the secretariat; although certain positive actions have been taken, the overall tendency has been to more managed trade, more frequent resort to "flexible" measures of protection (e.g., anti-dumping duties), introduction of non-trade and even non-economic considerations in trade, a greater reliance on bilateral approaches and increased discrimination against developing countries. The system also appears incapable of providing an adequate framework for negotiations between countries at different levels of economic development or with differing economic and social systems. The critical economic situation of many developing countries, their debt servicing burdens and the general state of disorder in the monetary and financial areas has exposed to an even greater degree, the inadequacies of the present system.

IV. SHIPPING

A. The shipping scene prior to UNCTAD I

For most of the period up to World War II international shipping tended to be controlled almost exclusively by a few maritime powers. This state of affairs largely reflected the main contours of international economic relations (balance of power, colonialism) and the importance of the role of shipping in commercial policy underlined in varying degrees by security considerations. The post-war period of 1947-1964 witnessed the birth and the struggle for independence of some 75 States. These new nations watched with deep concern the decline in their terms of trade which were being further aggravated by the serious impact of rising freight rates and the inadequacies associated with the existing institutional mechanism in shipping.

The newly independent nations became very conscious of the adverse impact on their balance of payments of the outflow of foreign exchange in payment for invisible transactions, the major one of which was shipping. The total freight charges in the trade of developing countries with developed countries in 1961 were approximately $4.7 billion. The magnitude and economic importance of those charges can best be appreciated when compared with the total imports (f.o.b.) and exports of developing countries in the same year, which amounted to $23.6 billion and $23.0 billion, respectively.[1]

Thus, prior to UNCTAD I shipping problems of developing countries ranged from complete dependence on foreign flags for the sea transport of their international trade to those of countries partly dependent and struggling to expand their national merchant marines. These are summarized below.[2]

Problems relating to developing countries with no merchant fleets giving rise to the following consequences:

The payment of the entire freight bill of the country would be in foreign exchange;

Total dependence on foreign flags for sea transport of the country's trade with the result that:

Export promotion of certain sensitive articles needing assistance would be difficult or totally dependent on foreign flags;

---

[1] Economist Intelligence Unit, "Ocean shipping and freight rates and developing countries", (E/CONF.46/27), reproduced in *Proceedings of the United Nations Conference on Trade and Development, Geneva, 23 March-16 June 1964*, vol. V—*Financing and Invisibles. Institutional Arrangements* (United Nations publication, Sales No. 64.II.B.15), p. 225, para. 16.

[2] See N. Singh, *Achievements of UNCTAD I and UNCTAD II in the field of Shipping and Invisibles*, (New Delhi: S. Chand and Co., 1969).

An inherent weakness in negotiating with liner conferences regarding the problem of reduction in freight rates or of fighting an increase in freight rates announced by the conferences;

A feeling of helplessness in relation to overseas trade policies which might give rise to a feeling of national frustration;

Loss of employment opportunities in the absence of a national shipping industry, including shipbuilding and ship repairing activity, apart from the manning of ships;

For a maritime State, in addition to the economic aspect there would be a political feeling of frustration on account of total dependence on foreign sea transport to obtain supplies in an emergency.

Shipping problems of developing countries with infant national fleets. These countries are faced with problems relating to adequate guarantee of foreign exchange needed to purchase vessels, appropriate technical and commercial know-how, adequate training facilities, adequate repair and maintenance facilities.

Conference practices. The liner conference system which has existed since 1875 illustrated very clearly the power of the traditional shipowners. This monolithic structure of closed door monopolies had become widespread and dominated every major trade route by the 1960s. Developing countries faced difficulties with respect to admission of their national shipping lines to conferences suffering the consequences of this system of unilateral fixing of freight rates, discriminatory practices, the stifling of competition by tying shippers to members of the conference and the refusal of conferences to hold meaningful consultations with shippers from developing countries.

Thus the approach of developing countries to the question of shipping which guided actions in UNCTAD in its first 20 years from UNCTAD I to UNCTAD VI was based on four main policy objectives:[3]

To influence the structure and level of freight rates in order to lessen the impact of high freight rates on their traditional and non-traditional exports;

To establish and expand their own national merchant fleets and their rights to assist such fleets in their infant stage;

To rewrite international shipping legislation and the basic framework of regulations;

To create an environment conducive to the improvement of their human resources and physical infrastructure.

W. R. Malinowski[4] summarized the justification of developing countries to seek the achievement of those objectives in stating that:

Reliance on foreign operations had certain unfavourable implications for the already serious balance of payments position of most developing countries;

---

[3] See L. M. S. Rajwar, "Trade and shipping needs of developing countries", in Rajwar *et al.*: *Shipping and Developing Countries* (Carnegie Endowment for International Peace) No. 582, March 1971.

[4] W. R. Malinowski, "Toward a change in the international distribution of shipping activity", in Rajwar *et al., op. cit.*

The group of countries which controlled shipping did so mainly because it was a profitable activity. Hence the decisions of their enterprises were more closely linked to considerations of profit than to those of service to trade;

The fact that the shipping industry was controlled by a number of developed countries was only partly the result of some basic advantages that those countries possessed and to a large extent the position of those countries was the result of their national shipping policies arising from historical and traditional factors and that it was no coincidence that several developed maritime countries had also been major colonial powers. Also, in many cases the fleets of those countries were originally established for reasons that were not entirely "economic".

In addition, on the eve of UNCTAD I two schools of thought about shipping had emerged.[5] One school of thought, the "free market", held that shipping services should be provided by private enterprise on the basis of free competition. The other school maintained that governments must take the ultimate responsibility.

The post World War II shipping environment, the concerns of newly independent developing countries, the resistance of most developed countries to change, and the interaction of these two schools of thought were to reflect the sharp difference between developed and developing countries on shipping issues and at the same time shaped the two decades of intergovernmental negotiations and actions on shipping.

Thus, when UNCTAD I met, the developed/developing countries relationship on shipping matters was characterized by a general feeling of disappointment and frustration and differences in viewpoints and sharp divergence in approach. UNCTAD I was to launch a process in order to bridge the gap in the long run.[6]

B. UNCTAD I — The launching of a process

UNCTAD I provided an opportunity to raise issues related to shipping and freight rates. This was done in the context of the impact which maritime transport had on the balance of payments of developing countries. A report was prepared by the Economic Intelligence Unit (E.I.U),[7] at the request of the Secretary-General of the Conference, in connection with the sub-item on "Measures for improving the invisible trade of developing countries through increasing receipts for services such as tourism and reducing payments for transportation, insurance and similar charges". The report suggested that recommendations could be made which could emphasize, *inter alia,* the need for the establishment of a consultation/negotiation

---

[5] Jan J. Oyevour "Technological change and the future of shipping in developing countries", in Rajwar *et al., op. cit.*

[6] E. Gold, *Maritime Transport, The Evolution of International Marine Policy and Shipping Law* (Lexington, Mass. and Toronto: D. C. Heath, 1981), p. 279. Gold describes the atmosphere prevailing as that of "vigorous opposition and almost shrill alarm in response to these demands and proposals" put forward by developing countries at UNCTAD I. In particular, the major shipping countries, all members of Group B, opposed placing any of the shipping matters on the Conference agenda.

[7] *Op. cit.* (see footnote 1).

machinery between liner conferences and national or regional shippers' councils, the desirability of development of the merchant marines of developing countries, the examination of possible regulatory measures concerning liner conferences and the need to give priority to port development.

The efforts of developing countries at UNCTAD I could go no further initially than agreeing to the "Common Measure of Understanding".[8] That Understanding is perhaps best described as the lowest tier of negotiated agreement possible. The Understanding concentrated on liner trades (which were then those services in which developing countries were largely interested) and whose operations and monopolistic practices were self-regulated by a cartel-type system of liner conferences which was felt by developing-country interests not to take enough account of their legitimate trading and shipping concerns and needs. The Understanding was addressed principally to securing closer consultations between shippers and conferences in regard to the adequacy of shipping services. It supported the idea of international financing, and of technical assistance for the improvement of port operations and connected inland transport facilities in developing countries on favourable terms and conditions. It also encouraged the development of merchant marines of developing countries on the basis of sound economic criteria[9] as an important element of an import substitution policy.

Equally important, the Understanding recognized the need for establishing a permanent organ where deliberations on shipping questions could continue. That gave birth—although not clearly envisaged at the time—to the Committee on Shipping.

The forces emanating from the first Conference and the momentum gathered by developing countries created sufficient pressure to institutionalize shipping questions in UNCTAD. Consequently, when the Trade and Development Board met at its first session in April 1965, the developing countries proposed to formulate the terms of reference of a body dealing with shipping matters. The Board, by resolution 11 (I) of 29 April 1965, decided to establish a separate Committee and not, as some had anticipated, in the form of a working group of the Committee on Invisibles and Financing related to Trade. The Committee on Shipping held its first regular session in Geneva in November 1965 and its first special session in July 1966.

The terms of reference of the Committee on Shipping stipulated, *inter alia*,[10] the need:

To promote understanding and co-operation in the field of shipping and to be available for the harmonization of shipping policies of governments and regional economic groupings which fall within the competence of the Trade and Development Board;

---

[8] The Third Committee at UNCTAD I constituted a Working Party on Shipping which, after 13 meetings and historically revealing animated deliberations, often with raised tempers, concluded an agreement that resulted in the celebrated recommendation on a "Common Measure of Understanding on Shipping Questions" (Annex A.IV.22 to the Final Act of the Conference).

[9] The term "sound economic criteria" was never clearly defined and as a consequence it was to "haunt" the negotiations in UNCTAD up to the mid-1970s.

[10] See *Rules of procedure of the Main Committees of the Trade and Development Board* (TD/B/740), annex II.

- To study and make recommendations on the ways in which and the conditions under which international shipping can most effectively contribute to the expansion of world trade, in particular of the trade of developing countries. Particular attention should be paid to economic aspects of shipping, to those shipping matters which affect the trade and balance of payments of developing countries, and to related shipping policies and legislation of governments on matters which fall within the competence of the Trade and Development Board;
- To study measures to improve port operations and connected inland transport facilities, with particular reference to those ports whose trade is of economic significance to the country in which they are situated or to world trade;
- To make recommendations designed to secure, where appropriate, the participation of shipping lines of developing countries in shipping conferences on equitable terms;
- To promote co-operation between shippers and the conferences, a well-organized consultation machinery should be established with adequate procedures for hearing and remedying complaints by the formation of shippers' councils or other suitable bodies on a national and regional basis;
- To study and make recommendations with a view to promoting the development of merchant marines, in particular of developing countries.

Subsequently, the Committee on Shipping approved, at its fourth session in 1970, is work programme.[11]

The shipping industry, prior to the creation of UNCTAD, was outside global international economic regulations or action, while trade had been subject to international regulation under the General Agreement on Tariffs and Trade (GATT).

The establishment of UNCTAD, and of its Committee on Shipping in April 1965, brought under examination the international shipping industry with the participation of all countries. Consequently, a forum was created where all parties involved in maritime transport—governments, shipowners, shippers and port authorities—could meet to discuss, negotiate and elaborate international measures to meet the concerns of the developing and developed countries. Perhaps equally important was the fact that the Committee on Shipping provided the only universal forum where developing and developed countries could meet to air their grievances and find acceptable international solutions and agreements on matters that had begun gravely to affect the shipping industries and economies of countries.

The Committee on Shipping, as an integral part of UNCTAD, moved along the policy lines and philosophy of its governing body. UNCTAD at its inception was primarily concerned with trade from the point of view of commodity price stabilization and devising support measures for the terms of trade. Thus, in the early years of the Committee on Shipping the dominant issues in its deliberation concerned the level and structure of freight rates, protection of shippers' interests, consultation machinery and other related issues such as terms of shipment.

---

[11] See the report of the Committee on Shipping on its fourth session (*Official Records of the Trade and Development Board, Tenth Session, Supplement No. 5* (TD/B/301)).

Deliberations were assisted by in-depth research carried out by the UNCTAD secretariat on issues not hitherto subject to prior investigation or research. The initial activity and explanatory studies quickly took shape in the context of UNCTAD II in New Delhi (1968). A clearer work programme was agreed upon and this led to, *inter alia,* a series of commodity-specific maritime transport studies (timber, rubber, iron ore, jute, etc.) and to a comprehensive study of the liner conference system, associated with studies on consultations, and studies on shippers' interests. In addition, related work on maritime legislation was stepped up, as was the work on the analysis of ports. An annual review was initiated for the purpose of monitoring and discussing the evolution of shipping, and of providing a compendium of statistical data. From the early 1970s UNCTAD increasingly focused its attention on developmental issues; consequently, the question of the development of national merchant marines was to gain prominence in the deliberations of the Committee on Shipping.

It was also natural for the Committee on Shipping from the start to concentrate on the liner sector. The controversy and near antagonism over liner conferences provided the impetus for the devotion of a large amount of time and effort to solving the problems and grievances that surrounded the liner conference system. The introduction of containerization led to a vast technological change in the liner sector. The Committee on Shipping reacted to this changing situation to meet the challenge of the future. Consequently, in September 1978, the terms of reference of the Committee on Shipping were expanded to include the question of international multimodal transport and the work programme of the Committee was correspondingly enlarged.[12]

C. Overall view of the development of UNCTAD activities in the field of shipping

In the early years of UNCTAD research and studies prepared by the secretariat played a limited role in the formulation of issues which could become the subject of negotiations. The first two sessions of the Committee on Shipping were devoted to the formulation and adoption of the work programme. One of the subjects, however, which was proposed by the secretariat for inclusion in the work programme, was found to be very controversial — i.e. "the route studies". The negotiations took place on this issue at a special session of the Committee on Shipping. There was even a vote because it was not possible to find a solution which would be satisfactory to all. The issue revolved around how far the liner conferences and liner shipping companies should disclose their internal information on decision making in the field of freight rates. The information was not normally available to shippers. The developing countries, the majority of which at that time represented the interests of shippers, were in favour of a better insight into the freight rate-making process. This issue, although not directly affecting the economic interest of partners, has for long demarcated the line between those who wanted to change the existing mechanism of price formation in liner shipping and those who wanted to maintain the *status quo.*

---

[12] See TD/B/740 (*op. cit.*).

Naturally, under, the direction of the Committee on Shipping, the UNCTAD secretariat was called upon to take certain initiatives in the form of research and the preparation of studies. The various studies were deliberately directed to assisting all parties interested in shipping to obtain a clearer insight into the economies of the industry. Greater transparency of its inner workings—in particular of the rate-making process and its underlying principles—was aimed at in order to dispel the general apprehension which prevailed on the subject, and to prepare the ground for greater mutual trust between the suppliers and users of shipping services in negotiations.

However, the secretariat became a catalyst that brought forth issues upon which governments began to act and the role of the documentation prepared by the UNCTAD secretariat on substantial economic matters gradually increased. It began to play a role in the formulation of positions and decisions during UNCTAD II and later during UNCTAD III, V and VI. It also played a very significant role during the preparations for the elaboration of a code of conduct for liner conferences and in the formulation of the policy on the open registries and multimodal transport.

Similarly, the research carried out by the UNCTAD secretariat contributed to the identification of topics which later became the subject of substantial debate and lengthy negotiations in UNCTAD. One of them was the question of merchant fleets under flags of convenience, which was discussed with other topics at the sixth session of the Committee on Shipping, on the basis of a research report on "Economic consequences of the existence or lack of a genuine link between vessel and flag of registry".[13]

Another illustration of the role of research and policy papers prepared by the secretariat in negotiations were those submitted to UNCTAD V on merchant fleet development.[14] They focused discussion on institutional barriers to merchant fleet development of developing countries and on the control exercised over bulk cargo movements by transnational corporations involved in vertically integrated operations and the use of flag-of-convenience fleets.

During the preparatory work in UNCTAD on the Convention on Multimodal Transport no single overall policy paper was prepared, as had been done for the code of conduct for liner conferences, but a number of papers were prepared on specific questions such as: economic consequences of multimodal transport and containerization for developing countries, liability, documentation and customs questions. That was because the basic concept of the Convention, i.e. that of the Multimodal Transport Operator responsible for the transport of goods on the whole transport route was retained from earlier discussions, held in other forums—The International Maritime Organization (IMO) and the Economic Commission for Europe (ECE). Besides, developing countries had little experience in multimodal transport, and therefore needed detailed studies to be able to formulate their position.

---

[13] TD/B/C.4/168.

[14] TD/222 and Supp.1-6 (For the printed texts of TD/222 and Supp.1-3 see *Proceedings of the United Nations Conference on Trade and Development, Fifth Session*, vol. III—*Basic Documents* (United Nations publication, Sales No. E.79.II.D.16).

The Committee on Shipping acted primarily through resolutions. These were of necessity addressed to governments, and for their effectiveness had perforce to rely on the willingness of the appropriate national authorities to accede to the requests that were made, as well as on the success of such efforts to persuade conferences and shippers to respond to the Committee's requests. The outcome of the resolutions was, in the event, found to be largely ineffective in terms of specific expectations. Persuasion and voluntary compliance having failed, the developing countries felt constrained to act through the Committee so as to bring greater concretion into its decisional procedures. Hence, a subsidiary body, the Working Group on International Shipping Legislation, was created in 1969 and from the early 1970s worked through the medium of international conventions and model rules or norms to bring about recommended changes in law or practice.

The creation of the Working Group was a landmark in the institutional restructuring of the work of the Committee. It was mandated to review "The economic and commercial aspects of international legislation and practices in the field of shipping from the standpoint of conformity with the needs of economic development, in particular of the developing countries, in order to identify areas where modifications were felt to be needed, for the drafting of legislation or other appropriate action". It was given action-oriented priority tasks to investigate the existing laws on the carriage of goods by sea (bills of lading and charter parties), conference practices, marine insurance, general average, and related maritime subjects and to draw up variants of clauses for draft international conventions and other instruments and to propose practical suggestions for adherence by the parties affected. The scope of the Committee's work was thus extended beyond shipping operations to cover the allocation of risk as between owners and shippers, and related features of maritime activities, while its move to study terms of shipment (April 1969) and to investigate cargo reservation practices (May 1970) foreshadowed the future focus of its concerns on how cargo was controlled and might be shared more equitably between world fleets. In particular, the recognition by the Committee at its fourth session (1970) of the principle that flag lines of developing countries should be admitted to full membership of liner conferences operating in their national maritime trade, and to have an increasing and substantial participation in the carriage of cargoes generated by their foreign trade, must be considered pivotal. The decision taken at the same session to transmit the secretariat study on liner conferences to the Working Group was in turn to have significant consequences for world shipping, leading as it did to the elaboration of a code of conduct for liner conferences.

From that point onwards, the work of the Committee, whether channelled through the Working Group or *ad hoc* bodies, was almost wholly taken up until the mid-1970s with drawing up a convention on a code of conduct for liner conferences, and with a new area of concern—multimodal transport. Proposals on a code of conduct were submitted to the third session of the Conference at Santiago in 1972, while the insistence by developing countries that multimodal transport be discussed within UNCTAD, so that their needs could be fully debated under its auspices, led to a recommendation by the Conference that the economic aspects of such transport be made a subject of special study within UNCTAD. Consequently, the Economic and Social Council in due course transferred consideration of this subject from other United Nations bodies to UNCTAD.

From the late 1970s onwards the developing countries took a closer interest in the working of the bulk cargo market, since bulk cargoes make up some 80 per cent of the total tonnage carried in seaborne trade, and this concern is reflected in the agendas for sessions of the Committee on Shipping to this day. The activities of UNCTAD shifted accordingly towards studying the control of transnational corporations over cargo availability and movement, and the operation of flags of convenience (FOC) or open-registry (OR) fleets. At the same time, studies commenced on formulating ways and means of promoting shipping as an industry, particularly in developing countries, and encouraging economic co-operation among States to that end. Attention was also switched to investigating the hull and cargo marine insurance markets, and most recently to the question of maritime liens and mortgages when contemplating shipbuilding or purchase. A study on maritime fraud, including piracy, was considered in an *ad hoc* group in 1984.

"UNCTAD philosophy" underlined the deliberations on shipping matters. These deliberations took place in a general atmosphere of "rich-poor" confrontations and negotiations. W. R. Malinowski[15] described such confrontations as a "situation in which the interests of various groups formulated either as demands or as defence of the *status quo*. Each participating group looks for ways and means to obtain total or at least partial satisfaction. Such a situation may lead to deadlock, to unilateral action, or to accommodation and reconciliation of interest through negotiations. Thus confrontation is the opening of the road to progress."

There was no doubt as to the international character of the deliberations of the UNCTAD Committee on Shipping. This in itself was a major accomplishment. What had always been seen as private concern industry, cloaked in secrecy and the prerogative of traditional maritime powers and private concerns, began to change. The industry was kept under an intensive spotlight and a process began towards "internationalization" of the industry by placing it under commonly agreed principles of international private and public law.

Further major UNCTAD accomplishments in this field include more widespread awareness that shipping is primarily a service industry, whose usefulness should be evaluated in relation to its service to international trade; that a simple, commercial view of the industry as a profit-oriented one is basically insufficient; that, in the last analysis, the "sound economic criteria" on which the shipping industry should be based need to be extensively broadened to include interests of national economies and economic development; and that these criteria need to be viewed in the international context of promoting world trade.

A small inventory but a large testimony to the achievements of UNCTAD in the field of shipping in the course of 20 years of its existence is the entry into force of the United Nations Convention on a Code of Conduct for Liner Conferences, the adoption of the United Nations Convention on International Multimodal Transport of Goods, the adoption of the United Nations Convention on the Carriage of Goods by Sea (the "Hamburg Rules"), the establishment of shippers' councils in developing countries, the improvements in ports of developing countries, the achievement of the 10 per cent target of world fleet for developing countries in the second United Nations Development Decade (developing countries' fleet grew

---

[15] "Shipping and the third world", *Intereconomics,* No. 1, January 1971.

from 8.1 per cent in 1964 to 10.8 per cent in 1980 to 15.8 per cent in 1983, equivalent to an increase in tonnage of 11.1 million gross registered tons (grt) in 1964, 44.7 million grt in 1980 and 66.3 million grt in 1983). These developments were steps taken by the international community towards creating a more rational basis for operating international maritime transport. They demonstrated that it was not only awareness of shortcomings in the functioning of the shipping industry that was to gain momentum but also recognition of the types of remedial measures to be sought which ultimately led, where necessary, to international regulation of the shipping industry.

Over these 20 years the path taken has not been easy. Successes, disappointments and sometimes failures could not have been avoided. The cause at times lay with lack of political will of governments or unreasonable negotiating postures of others, of issues being raised before sufficient "homework" had been undertaken. Sometimes a well-intentioned but over-enthusiastic secretariat got its signals confused and the message it attempted to convey did not find a responsive ear. At times issues were raised without sufficient sensitivity to the prevailing world economic situation. Also, when one group of countries becomes too reliant on the secretariat it becomes lax and unprepared. Such reliance leads to apathy, particularly when the secretariat, after a major breakthrough, does not bring forth innovative ideas for a period of time, leading to an intermittent loss of momentum.

The more significant sectoral activities are reviewed in detail below.

THE LINER CONFERENCE SYSTEM AND THE LINER CODE

Taking its cue from the "Common Measure of Understanding", the Committee gave priority attention during 1965-1970 to investigating the liner conference system. Its main thrust was directed towards securing full conference membership for merchant fleets of developing countries and thus to provide the framework for their vessels to operate in liner services and to share in the formulation of conference policy, and for their shippers to participate more meaningfully in consultation procedures.

After some preliminary studies, the UNCTAD secretariat prepared a major research paper on the liner conference system [16] in general. It was submitted to the fourth session of the Committee on Shipping in 1970 [17] which referred it to the Working Group on International Shipping Legislation for further detailed consideration. Subsequently, after the decision of the Working Group on International Shipping Legislation in February 1971 to include in its work programme the question of a code of conference practices, a policy paper on the subject was prepared and issued six months in advance of UNCTAD II, in order to make it available to the ministerial meeting of the Group of 77 in Lima (November 1971) and also to publish it before the Committee of European National Shipowners Associations (CENSA) completed its own code of conference practices by the end of December 1971.[18]

---

[16] TD/B/C.4/62/Rev.1 (United Nations publication, Sales No. E.70.II.D.9).

[17] Resolution 12 (IV), sect. II, para. 6.

[18] *The Regulation of Liner Conferences (a code of conduct for the liner conference system)* (TD/104/Rev.1) (United Nations publication, Sales No. E.72.II.D.13 and corrigendum).

When the Working Group met in early 1972 it had before it the UNCTAD secretariat report mentioned in the previous paragraphs.[19] By this time, however, CENSA had already adopted a self-regulation code for liner conferences.[20]

S. G. Sturmey[21] explained succinctly the developments of those pioneering days of negotiations in UNCTAD on shipping, indicating that developing countries were opposed to the CENSA code for a number of reasons, of which two were noteworthy. First, the method of its elaboration meant that the vast majority of ship-using countries, and also many ship-owning countries, particularly among the developing countries, had no part in the determination of either the content or the structure of the code and no opportunity even to make their views known. Second, the code was felt to be weak in its provisions and in its reliance on self-regulation to be almost certainly ineffective. The debate in the Working Group was relatively brief, but marked by a sharp cleavage of opinion between the countries which had been involved in the formulation of the CENSA code of practice and the other countries, which believed that a different sort of code should be formulated, in a different manner, in a different forum and with provision for outside enforcement of its requirements. The developing countries at that stage endeavoured to formulate their own code of conduct for liner conferences to put before the meeting. However, the difficulties which arose regarding the role of national legislation in relation to a code of conduct prevented an agreed position being reached within the short period of the Working Group, and two alternative developing country codes were produced—one by the African and Asian countries and the other by the Latin American countries. In their substance the two codes were extremely close and the differences were rather of a drafting nature than of substance. In the implementation sections, however, the Latin American countries tended to take a different view on the implementation provisions to that taken by the Afro-Asian countries.

Agreement had earlier been obtained that the conclusions of the Working Group could be forwarded directly to the United Nations Conference on Trade and Development, to be held at Santiago in the spring of 1972, and without having to pass through the Committee on Shipping. Consequently, the report of the Working Group, together with the two draft codes, was submitted to the Conference. Prior to UNCTAD III the developing countries met in Lima to prepare for the Conference and there they established as one of the important tasks of the Conference the formulation of a universally acceptable code of conduct. At Santiago, the developing countries unified their position and produced a full draft of a code for discussion with the countries of Groups B and D. Little debate on the subject occurred in public meetings during the Conference but there were lengthy meetings at which attempts were made to "harmonize, if that were possible, the position of all countries regarding the production of a universally acceptable code of conduct".

Conference resolution 66 (III) "Draft code of conduct for liner conferences" was adopted by a roll-call vote, with 74 countries voting in favour, (developing countries, socialist countries of Eastern Europe and China); 19 countries voting

---

[19] *Ibid.*

[20] "Code of practice for conferences" elaborated by CENSA and transmitted by the Government of the Netherlands (TD/128 and Corr.1).

[21] S. G. Sturmey, *The UNCTAD Code of Conduct for Liner Conferences,* (Bremen Institute of Shipping Economics, Lectures and Contributions, No. 7, Bremen, 1974).

against (Australia, Belgium, Canada, Denmark, Germany, Federal Republic of, Finland, France, Greece, Ireland, Italy, Japan, Netherlands, New Zealand, Norway, Spain, Sweden, Switzerland, United Kingdom, United States of America) being those of B Group; there were two abstentions (Austria, Israel). The resolution requested the General Assembly at its twenty-seventh session, to be held later that year, "to convene as early as possible in 1973 a Conference of Plenipotentiaries to adopt a Code of Conduct for Liner Conferences to be adopted by the governments of all countries and to be implemented in a manner that is binding on them and can be suitably enforced". Thus the notions of universal acceptability and legal enforceability were both forcefully presented in the resolution. Annexed to the resolution was the draft code of conduct for liner conferences which had been prepared by the developing countries and it was this code of conduct which was to form the basis for the negotiations through the two sessions of the Preparatory Committee and the first and second part of the Plenipotentiary Conference.

The General Assembly, in resolution 3035 (XXVII), called for the code of conduct to be elaborated and adopted during 1973. Passed near the end of 1972, this allowed 12 months for the job to be done. It was essential, therefore, if the deadline of end-1973 was to be met, that work start immediately after the New Year. Two sessions of the Preparatory Committee were provided for, and these were held in January and June, together with a conference of five weeks to follow.

After a long series of votes on the specific provisions of the code, the complete Convention was eventually adopted on 6 April 1974 by 74 votes to 7, with 5 abstentions.[22] It contains principles and objectives, substantive provisions and final clauses, and is accompanied by two resolutions of which one relates to non-Conference operations.

Under the Code of Conduct for Liner Conferences, practically all aspects of liner shipping services, which are controlled unilaterally by the conferences themselves, will instead be brought within the provisions of the Code. In concrete terms, this would mean more orderly institutionalization of conference services as follows:

(*a*) Membership, as per stated equitable criteria;

(*b*) Shares of cargo, preserving rights of exporting, importing and "third-flag" States;

(*c*) Freight levels determinable on the basis of publicly acknowledged criteria;

(*d*) Freight increase notifications as per specified notice periods and subject to consultation procedures;

(*e*) The institutionalization of consultation between conferences and shippers on all major aspects of liner services;

(*f*) The legal recognition of shippers and shippers' organizations as consultative parties;

---

[22] Fifty-eight developing countries voted for the Code, (as also did Turkey) and they were joined by the socialist countries of Eastern Europe, by China, and—among the developed countries—by Australia, Belgium, France, the Federal Republic of Germany and Japan. The abstentions came from Canada, Greece, Italy, Netherlands and New Zealand, while Denmark, Finland, Norway, Sweden, Switzerland, the United Kingdom and the United States voted against.

(g) A monitoring role for government authorities;

(h) A mandatory dispute settlement machinery;

(i) Regular public reporting of conference activities and practices.

At this stage it may be important to note that, although all members of Group B eventually supported the spirit of the Code and most of its provisions, it was perhaps the combination of (b) and (h) which presented the unsurmountable hurdle to the delegations which abstained or voted against.

The Convention had very stringent entry-into-force criteria. It required the ratification of at least 24 countries owning on 1 July 1973 at least 25 per cent of the world general cargo tonnage, thus ensuring that it could only enter into force through action of countries of all groups represented in UNCTAD. Almost 10 years later, on 6 October 1983, the Convention entered into force when the Federal Republic of Germany and the Netherlands ratified it, whereby the total number of countries who became contracting parties to the Convention reached 59, owning 28.68 per cent of the relevant world tonnage.

The degree of attention, analysis and agonizing over the objectives and contents of the Convention on a Code of Conduct for Liner Conferences [23] has indeed been overwhelming.

INTERNATIONAL SHIPPING LEGISLATION

At the second session of UNCTAD, held in New Delhi in 1968, it was asserted by developing countries that a large proportion of the existing body of international shipping legislation had originated at a time when the interests of the developing countries had not been taken into account. In particular, it was felt that the law and practices relating to bills of lading, charter parties, limitation of shipowners' liability and marine insurance were unsatisfactory from the standpoint of developing countries. Pursuant to this initiative and to Conference resolution 14 (II) ("International legislation on shipping"), the Working Group on International Shipping Legislation was created, by resolution 7 (III) of the Committee on Shipping. Its terms of reference include the following:

To review economic and commercial aspects of international legislation and practices in the field of shipping from the standpoint of their conformity with the needs of economic development in particular of developing countries in order to identify areas where modifications are needed ...

At its first session, the Working Group adopted the following work programme:[24] (i) bills of lading; (ii) charter parties; (iii) general average; (iv) marine insurance; and (v) economic and commercial aspects of international legislation

---

[23] For selected readings on the Code see, *inter alia:* M. J. Shah, "The dispute settlement machinery in the Convention on a Code of Conduct for Liner Conferences, *Journal of Maritime Law and Commerce,* vol. 7, No. 1, and "The implementation of the United Nations Convention on a Code of Conduct for Liner Conferences, 1974, *Journal of Maritime Law and Commerce, vol. 9, No. 1;* S. G. Sturmey *op. cit., The Code—The Next Five Years* (Bremen: Institute of Shipping Economics, Lectures and Contributions, No. 27, Bremen, 1980).

[24] See the report of the Working Group on International Shipping Legislation on its first session (*Official Records of the Trade and Development Board, Ninth Session, Third Part, annexes,* agenda item 7, document TD/B/289).

and practices in other fields of shipping.[25] Considering first the subject of bills of lading, the Working Group co-ordinated its work with the United Nations Commission on International Trade Law (UNCITRAL) and as a result the United Nations Convention on the Carriage of Goods by Sea (the Hamburg Rules) was elaborated to replace the "Brussels Convention".

The overall effect of the new Convention will be to redress the existing bias favouring shipowners in regard to liability for loss and damage to goods. Broadly speaking, shipowners will no longer be able to claim exemptions from liability to compensate shippers for loss, damage or delay to goods, unless they can prove that they took all measures that could reasonably be required to avoid the loss. The monetary limitation of such liability has also been raised to account for inflation so that it is more consonant with present day cargo values. Numerous additional changes have been made with the result that the Hamburg Rules establish a more equitable and modern legal régime governing the rights and obligations of both shipowners and shippers. The net effect of the changes will be reflected in the more orderly treatment of cargo claims and settlements, flowing from a régime in whose formulation shippers and shipowners from all countries have participated on an equal footing.

The fourth session of the Working Group considered the subject of charter parties, and requested the secretariat to carry out further studies on designated aspects of time and voyage charter parties.

Four sessions of the Working Group were dedicated to the subject of marine insurance. These sessions, which were attended by representatives of both insurers and assured, were devoted to formulating a set of standard clauses for marine, hull and cargo insurance as a non-mandatory international model, and work on them is continuing.

This initiative in marine insurance occurs in an area where at present no international rules of any kind exist and where each "market" uses either its own insurance policy terms and conditions or adopts or amends those of another leading market drawn up by insurers without formalized consultation with those assured. It is expected that when the full UNCTAD model international marine insurance policy terms and conditions are formulated, the resulting consensus of views will bring much needed harmonization to the operation of international marine insurance, and that, in particular, a more equitable and simpler contractual basis will emerge through the association of assured in its formulation.

The Committee on Shipping, at its tenth session, added the following subjects to the work programme of the Working Group:

(*a*) Maritime liens and mortgages;

(*b*) Registration of rights in respect of vessels under construction; and

(*c*) Arrest of vessels or other sanctions as appropriate.[26]

When these subjects were being considered, members of Group B were reluctant to see UNCTAD involve itself in this work. Arguments were raised as to the competence of UNCTAD *vis-à-vis* that of other organizations, such as IMO.

---

[25] See resolution 7 (III) (*Official Records of the Trade and Development Board, Ninth Session, Supplement No. 3* (TD/B/C.4/55), annex I, and Conference resolution 14 (II)).

[26] Resolution 49 (X) on international maritime legislation.

The Committee also requested the UNCTAD secretariat to update an earlier study on terms of shipment, and to investigate maritime fraud, including piracy. The secretariat was further requested to expedite its work in formulating a model code for maritime legislation as a guide to developing countries in the formulation of their national legislation.

Shippers' interests

The initial focus of the studies made on shippers' interests was to secure recognition of the principle that liner conferences should not fix rates and conditions without meaningful consultation with shippers and the provision of acceptable evidence in justification of rate increases. This principle has been embodied in the United Nations Convention on a Code of Conduct for Liner Conferences. Consultation is practised in the vast majority of liner trades.

However, shippers in developing countries complain that the "consultations" held by the liner conferences are often of a superficial character. A particular grievance is that the conferences conduct their "real" negotiations with their trading partners in developed countries. More recently shippers have also complained that liner conferences are circumventing procedures for consultations on basic freight rates by the device of increasing surcharges for bunker prices or currency adjustment factors, often under formulas which shippers claim are not comprehensible.

Complaints relating to transnational corporation control were examined by the secretariat in its report on "Relationships between shippers at both ends of a trade" (TD/B/C.4/180), and a further report—"Formation and strengthening of shippers' commodity groups—guidelines for developing countries" (TD/B/C.4/188)—recommended ways in which developing countries could gain control over their own cargo movements, and thus be in a position to force the conferences into meaningful consultations.

At the tenth session of the Committee on Shipping, the secretariat was requested, by resolution 46 (X), to prepare a report on the effectiveness of existing consultation procedures, and in particular on the methods and formulas used by conferences in calculating and imposing surcharges which the Committee on Shipping would discuss at its eleventh session, in 1984.[27] UNCTAD work on this subject over the years has encouraged and contributed markedly to the growth of shippers' organizations in developing countries which are increasingly gaining strength.

Merchant fleet development

Initial efforts were concentrated in the liner sector, as discussed earlier, mainly because of the primary engagement of developing countries in liner shipping, and the difficulties encountered by their fleets in entering the liner conferences, which were dominated by the shipping lines of their trading partner countries. These

---

[27] "The effectiveness of consultation machinery" (TD/B/C.4/260) and "Formulae and methods used for calculating and applying liner conference surcharges" (TD/B/C.4/265).

efforts resulted in acceptance of the principle, now embodied in the Code of Conduct for Liner Conferences, that the national lines of developing countries have a right to conference membership on equal terms with the lines of their trading partner countries. This principle has gained wide acceptance.

It has always been recognized within UNCTAD that the lack of finance for ship acquisition was and remains a major difficulty of developing countries in expanding their national merchant marines. The activities of UNCTAD aiming at the alleviation of this problem include, *inter alia,* the elaboration of recommendations urging more favourable financial terms for the acquisition of ships by developing countries; the examination of ways and means of providing developing countries with information regarding the availability and the terms of financial assistance for the acquisition of ships from bilateral and multilateral donors;[28] and examination of the forms of co-operation among developing countries aimed at the possible establishment of multinational shipping enterprises.

From UNCTAD V onwards, activities relating to merchant fleet development have been oriented towards the bulk sectors, which the eighth session of the Committee on Shipping identified as the sectors in which progress by developing countries had been minimal. Bulk cargoes exported and imported by developing countries appear to a large extent to be captive cargoes of transnational corporations (TNCs) which are in a position to use transfer pricing techniques to the disadvantage of developing countries.[29]

The developing countries recognized that it would not be feasible to apply the same principles in the bulk trades as in the liner trades because of the irregular nature for the most part of many bulk movements, but they sought international recognition of their right to "equitable participation" in the regular bulk trades (i.e. in trades in which bulk vessels shuttle back and forth as in the liner trades). This principle was not, however, acceptable to the developed countries, which argued that the bulk trades are "free", and open to new entrants without barriers, and as a result a resolution affirming this principle (Conference resolution 120 (V) "Participation of Developing Countries in World Shipping and the Development of their Merchant Marines" was adopted by majority vote. The countries voting against were the Group B countries and those abstaining were the Group D countries. This resolution requested the secretariat to examine the controls exercised by TNCs over the main dry bulk cargo movements. Following consideration of the secretariat report[30] at the ninth session of the Committee on Shipping there was a general consensus that "the bulk trades may not be as free as formerly supposed" and a group of experts was convened to examine practices of importers and exporters in the main dry bulk trades. The Group met twice in 1981 and presented seven unanimously agreed recommendations, but presented divided

---

[28] The fact that financing on soft terms for ships has recently been amply available does not necessarily affect the need for general improvements in financing arrangements. Financing instruments on soft terms now available are basically subsidy programmes for ailing shipbuilding industries designed as a temporary measure. Consequently, similar arrangements are not available for the purchase of second-hand tonnage. Furthermore, these instruments would no longer be available should governments of shipbuilding countries, for whatever reason, decide to cease or change the basis of subsidization.

[29] See *Control by transnational corporations over dry bulk cargo movements* (TD/B/C.4/203/Rev.1) (United Nations publication, Sales No. E.81.II.D.3).

[30] *Ibid.*

views on the vital issue of whether or not barriers existed to the entry of developing countries into dry bulk operations.[31]

At its tenth session the Committee on Shipping adopted resolution 48 (X) which noted the report of the Group of Experts, and recommended that the Group's recommendations be implemented, but requested the secretariat to prepare reports for the next two sessions on progress achieved by developing countries in developing their bulk fleets. The same resolution also called for the convening of another group of experts to examine the operations of importers, exporters, traders and providers of shipping services in the hydro-carbon trades. This Group met in 1984.

While these activities have been proceeding within UNCTAD a number of developing countries have expressed growing impatience at the slow pace with which recognition is being given to their right to participate in the bulk trades and in recent years there has been an accelerated tendency for many of them to press ahead with unilateral cargo reservation measures without waiting for further developments in UNCTAD. Indeed, some of the members of the Group of Experts expressed the view that the only developing countries which had achieved success in dry bulk shipping were those which had adopted unilateral measures.

The open registry issue

Parallel to the discussion on participation in the bulk trades, discussions have been proceeding on the flags of convenience (FOC) issue.

This issue was raised in UNCTAD as a result of concern over the fact that almost one-third of the world fleet was owned by non-national FOC owners who had little or no connection with the States whose flags their ships flew and whose precise role in world shipping was uncertain. Subsequently, secretariat reports showed that FOC operations constituted a device which enabled the traditional maritime countries to maintain ownership and control over world shipping despite the fact that they could not operate economically under their own flags, and pointed out the inherent dangers of anonymity of FOC ownership. While the subject of FOCs was first raised in UNCTAD by the developed market-economy countries, initiatives in this field were pressed by the majority of developing countries and by the socialist countries of Eastern Europe.

In 1978, the Working Group on International Shipping Legislation addressed the question of a "genuine link" for the first time and reached the unanimous conclusion that the expansion of open-registry fleets had adversely affected the expansion of other fleets, including those of developing countries. Following further

---

[31] See the Report of the Group of Experts on Problems faced by the Developing Countries in the Carriage of Bulk Cargoes on its second session (TD/B/C.4/234 - TD/B/C.4/AC.2/5). These recommendations were as follows: sales contracts to include a clause urging that favourable consideration be given to the utilization of developing countries' fleets; the provision of adequate information to enable countries to assess their ability to compete; that shipowners and operators from developing countries be given the opportunity to participate in bulk trades which provide regular employment for bulk carriers; the attention of governments to be drawn to the advantages to be gained from forming regional pools, the need for appropriate maritime legislation, for long-term shipping arrangements and for special financial arrangements to facilitate the purchase of ships.

debate on the subject, a special session of the UNCTAD Committee on Shipping met in May/June 1981 and adopted a resolution by majority vote [32] resolution 43 (S-III) calling for the establishment of an Intergovernmental Preparatory Group (IPG) to propose a set of basic principles concerning the conditions upon which vessels should be accepted on national shipping registers, with a view to preparing documents for the holding of a United Nations conference of plenipotentiaries to consider the adoption of an international agreement.

Consequently, the General Assembly, in its resolution 37/209 of 20 December 1982, decided to convene a plenipotentiary conference early in 1984, to be preceded by a preparatory committee. Pursuant to Board resolution 271 (XXVI), the Preparatory Committee met in November 1983 where the work for an international agreement on conditions for registration of vessels was further advanced. The Plenipotentiary Conference held the first part of its session in July/August 1984.

The open-registry negotiation has so far proved to be the most intricate and difficult ever to take place on shipping. The very explosive political nature of the issue, the fact that one-third of the world fleet is registered in flag-of-convenience countries, the vast commercial interests of a number of powerful developed market-economy countries, as well as the "problematiques" of the open registry, have raised a controversy as a result of which accusations and counter-accusations have been thrown back and forth between the protagonists and opponents of the system. The secretariat has not escaped the wrath of the supporters of the system. The difficulties have been compounded by the fact that among the Group of 77 are open-registry countries such as Liberia, Panama, and the Bahamas which have vigorously resisted any international action to tighten the conditions upon which vessels are accepted on national registers.

Some had envisaged that the subject could be closed after the meeting of the first Intergovernmental Group. However, initiatives on this subject continued. The secretariat produced thorough and extensively researched literature on the subject [33] particularly on the adverse economic and social implications of the system on the international community. The attempts to frustrate negotiations on the subject by drowning the secretariat in a mass of studies did not distract the developing countries, including those who supply labour to open-registry fleets, from pursuing their objectives of tightening the conditions of registration of ships. The subject and the objective of the exercise went through a fundamental change. The negotiations no longer centre on the emotive subject of "phasing out" open registries but have concentrated on the minimum conditions for accepting vessels on national registers through internationally accepted standards built into an international agreement. Undeniably, such an agreement would infuse greater transparency and ensure accountability in the operation of shipowners operating open registry fleets. On no other subject have private lobbies and commercial organizations involved in FOC operations been as active in attempting to defeat moves to restrict this system. They

---

[32] 49 in favour, 18 against and 3 abstentions. The countries voting against were 16 countries members of Group B, together with Israel and Liberia. Belgium, France and Turkey abstained.

[33] Of the many reports prepared by the secretariat it is relevant to mention the periodical report on beneficial ownership of open registry fleets. These reports trace the ownership of vessels in addition to the national owners recorded in the registers of open-registry countries as well as true managers. The latest report (1983) on this subject is to be found in TD/B/C.4/261.

played a major role in supporting and influencing positions of their governments in the negotiations. In fact, their voices appeared to drown even the most moderate members of their Group, who appeared to dissent from the very rigid attitude adopted by the classical "hard-liners" in Group B.

PORTS

Unlike most of the work of the UNCTAD secretariat, which has been produced as background material for intergovernmental debate and action, much of its work in the field of ports has largely consisted of providing guidance to governments and port authorities on ways of improving the planning, administration and operation of seaports.

It has long been established that port costs—both direct and indirect—constitute a significant proportion of the transportation costs of international shipments. Thus increased port efficiency is an important key to the lowering, or at least the containing, of transportation costs necessary for the stimulation of world trade.

Recognizing this, part of UNCTAD's work programme had been concerned with increasing the contribution which ports in developing countries could make towards more efficient maritime transport. This programme has been carried out through three different but complementary activities: namely, research, training and technical assistance.

For many years, the United Nations has rendered technical assistance to governments and port authorities on ways of improving port efficiency. There has, however, been a tendency, for many experts simply to catalogue a port's deficiencies and to propose a series of measures to improve the situation without necessarily giving the port authority concerned a clear idea of the benefits to be derived from the implementation of some particular subset of the measures proposed. The result has been that, all too often, no action was taken or, at best, only those measures which could be put into effect easily were implemented. It might turn out that measures taken, far from solving the problem, simply transferred it from one part of the port to another.

The objective of UNCTAD's research was to develop methodology for the study and solution of port problems in order to have a quantitative basis for advising governments on:

(*a*) How to obtain the maximum benefit from existing port facilities;

(*b*) How to develop, in the most economic fashion, new facilities to cope with changing volumes and types of traffic.

Studies have been carried out to advise governments and port authorities on such matters as pricing policy, port performance indicators, how to improve the throughput of general cargo berths and the impact of unitization on port operations and planning.[34] All these research studies involved the use of ports in developing

---

[34] *Berth throughput: Systematic methods for improving general cargo conditions* (TD/B/C.4/109 and Add.1), United Nations publication, Sales No. E.74.II.D.1, and *Port development—A handbook for planners in developing countries* (TD/B/C.4/175) (United Nations publication, Sales No. E.77.II.D.8 and corrigendum).

countries as case studies in order that the results would be of real, practical value to developing countries.

Although UNCTAD's research reports enjoyed a wide circulation, particularly in developing countries, it has to be recognized that port managers were often too busy with day-to-day tasks to study UNCTAD's reports in the depth required for the implementation of recommendations. Accordingly, the secretariat converted several of its research reports into material for seminars and training courses, and training programmes were conducted in developing countries in order to disseminate the results of research studies directly to port managers in a position to implement them.

After UNCTAD became a participating and executing agency of the United Nations Development Programme (UNDP) in 1969, ports have been one field in which UNCTAD has been particularly active. Experts have always been carefully briefed on UNCTAD research studies and UNDP-financed technical co-operation projects have provided a vehicle through which UNCTAD's studies have been implemented.

In the mid-1970s, when port congestion became a problem on a scale hitherto unseen, the effect of serious congestion and how it could strangle the national economy was brought home.

Early in 1976 there were, at any one time, approximately 40 per cent of general cargo vessels steaming between ports, 40 per cent being discharged and loaded in ports and 20 per cent anchored outside ports waiting for a vacant berth. This disastrous 40-40-20 situation cost shippers over $5 billion in a year—and a good deal of that was borne by shippers particularly in the developing countries. Many development projects had to be postponed or cancelled due to irregular or curtailed deliveries of capital equipment and materials. UNCTAD made an important contribution to the solution of port congestion in a number of cases by sending out port congestion task forces to assist local staff determine the real causes of the congestion, to propose specific action to deal with the problem and to help with the implementation of the measures required.

Less dramatic, perhaps, but probably making a greater long-term contribution to port efficiency in developing countries, was UNCTAD's work in the field of port management training. Having started training activities tentatively through the organization of an annual port management training course for senior port and government officials, UNCTAD is now seriously tackling the problem of training some 40,000 middle and junior managers in the ports industry. Through projects such as TRAINMAR (financed by UNDP and recipient governments) and Improving Port Performance (financed by the Swedish International Development Authority (SIDA)), UNCTAD is helping to establish and strengthen local training centres—both national and regional. Course material is being developed both centrally and in local training centres and local instructors are being specially trained to conduct these courses. As against the training of 100 managers a year in the 1970s there is now a capacity to train over 1,000 managers a year with materials developed under UNCTAD's supervision and this number should rise to some 2,000 a year in the second half of the decade.

The three port activities—research, technical assistance, and training—are inextricably interconnected. As a result of its research UNCTAD has gained clearer insights into the solution of port problems. The results of that research have been presented directly to port management through training programmes. The implementation by these managers either themselves or with technical assistance, has seen the work carried to its logical conclusion.

An important conclusion to be derived from the work of UNCTAD in the field of ports is that it has differed significantly from other activities which were generally classified as "technical assistance to developing countries".

The universal character of the contribution of UNCTAD's work in the field of ports has to be recognized. The beneficiaries of port improvements in developing countries are not only the developing countries themselves, but the whole international community. By port improvement and developments, greater port efficiency reduces sea transport costs; ships (mostly operated by foreign companies) are turned around at a faster rate and reliability in trade flows is increased. Perhaps this is one of the reasons why, in the "Common Measure of Understanding" and the work programme of the Committee on Shipping, port development has figured so prominently.

MULTIMODAL TRANSPORT AND CONTAINERIZATION

Convention on International Multimodal Transport of Goods

Efforts to set up legal rules for international multimodal transport gained considerable momentum in the late 1960s following the introduction of large-scale containerization. At that time both the International Maritime Committee (CMI) (Tokyo Rules) and the International Institute for the Unification of Private Law (UNIDROIT) had presented drafts for a convention on international multimodal transport, which were merged to form the so-called TCM (*Transport combiné des marchandises*) draft. This TCM draft served as the basis for discussion of the United Nations/InterGovernmental Maritime Consultative Organization[35] Conference on International Container Traffic in 1972. However, due to the dissatisfaction of developing countries with the draft, the TCM Convention itself was not placed on the agenda of the diplomatic conference and consequently, only a resolution was passed recognizing the need for a convention on multimodal transport.[36]

In view of the shortcomings of existing draft conventions, the Trade and Development Board, in pursuance of Economic and Social Council resolution 1734 (LIV), established an intergovernmental preparatory group of 68 countries, with the task of drafting a text of a convention on international multimodal transport, bearing in mind the special requirements of developing countries. The Intergovernmental Preparatory Group (IPG) held six sessions between October 1973 and March 1979. The UNCTAD secretariat supported the work of the Intergovernmental Preparatory Group by a number of studies relating to the problems incorporated in the draft convention.

---

[35] EC/IMCO (Now, International Maritime Organization (IMO)).

[36] For further background to the Conference see *United Nations Conference on a Convention on International Multimodal Transport,* vol. II (TD/MT/CONF/17/Add.1) (United Nations publication, Sales No. E.81.II.D.7), part one, paras 1-7.

The United Nations Conference on a Convention on International Multimodal Transport was held at Geneva from 12 to 30 November 1979 (first part of the session) and from 8 to 24 May 1980 (resumed session), and finally adopted the Convention by consensus.[37]

At that time developing countries had misgivings relating to containerization, multimodal transport and the draft TCM convention for the following reasons.

(a) Containerization would not be suitable for developing countries since it was capital-intensive and labour saving;

(b) The progress of multimodal transport operations and adoption of a multimodal convention would not only promote containerization but also would increase control of the market by multimodal transport operators from developed countries to the detriment of national carriers, shippers and the national economy of developing countries;

(c) Multimodal transport would circumvent national legislation regarding cargo reservation, customs, inland transport, insurance, currency exchange, etc.;

(d) Developing countries had not participated in the elaboration of the draft TCM convention.

Therefore, at an early stage of negotiation, some developing countries were reluctant to accelerate negotiations in order to reach agreement on an international convention and preferred that its scope be limited to traffic between developed countries. However, the Group of 77 maintained its solidarity in the recognition of the need for, and the desirability of, participating in the preparation of a multimodal transport convention in order to ensure that the new system, which was irreversible, should be applied in future under rules suited to the interests and aspirations of developing countries.

The Group of 77 insisted that the convention should contain provisions covering public law matters such as licensing of multimodal transport operators (MTOs), consultation between MTOs, shippers and competent government authorities, compatibility with the Code of Conduct for Liner Conferences and national legislation on cargo reservation, use of local manpower and insurance market, etc.

On the other hand, in the course of the early negotiations at the Intergovernmental Preparatory Group, it was pointed out that certain developed countries had been increasingly inclined towards slow progress in finalizing a draft convention on the grounds that the commercial practices based on the International Chamber of Commerce (ICC) Uniform Rules for a combined transport document were being firmly established and consequently there was no urgent need for a convention.

A breakthrough was made at the second part of the third session of the IPG, when each regional group agreed to a "Common Understanding" between all groups as regards the scope of the draft convention.[38]

Under that "Common Understanding", it was agreed that the scope of the possible draft convention should cover mainly the private law aspects such as the

---

[37] For the text of the Convention see *ibid.* vol. I (TD/MT/CONF/17 and Corr.1).

[38] This "Common Understanding" should not be confused with the Common Measure of Understanding reached on the question of shipping at UNCTAD I and discussed in Section B above.

liability of the MTO, issuance, content and effect of multimodal transport documents. With regard to public law matters, it was agreed that the draft should include appropriate guidelines for customs procedures. The IPG finally adopted a draft containing provisions enshrining the right of each State to regulate and control at the national level multimodal transport operations and MTOs (article 4) and establishing principles for customs transit (article 32).

Through the negotiations at the two sessions of the United Nations Conference, the main issues were the character of the application of the convention, namely mandatory or optional, the parties concerned and the territorial and modal scope of application. In general, the Group of 77 aimed at mandatory application and wider scope of application in order to ensure universal and effective implementation of the convention, whereas developed countries preferred optional application and a smaller scope of application in an attempt to preserve the *status quo* under modal transport conventions and commercial practices.

The liability régime was also a hotly debated issue. Developing countries, the socialist countries of Eastern Europe, the Nordic countries and China were in favour of the so-called modified uniform liability system based on the principle of presumed fault or neglect, whereas certain developed countries insisted on the so-called network system.

The successful conclusion of the work can be attributed to the spirit of cooperation of every delegation as well as the very able leadership of the President of the United Nations Conference. The UNCTAD secretariat also contributed in preparing various studies and draft texts and in facilitating the formulation of the positions of regional groups, in particular those of developing countries.

About four years have passed since the Convention was adopted, and three countries have become contracting parties to the Convention, which requires 30 countries to become contracting parties for its entry into force. Sometimes concerns are raised about the slow progress in implementing the Convention. While it may certainly be that, particularly in some developed countries, interested commercial parties might wish to delay the entry into force of the Convention in an attempt to defend established positions by maintaining the *status quo,* it has to be borne in mind that the Convention also aims at harmonizing international transport law, an aim which is reflected in the fact that many provisions are taken *verbatim* from the Hamburg Rules. While this linkage makes it advisable for countries to become contracting parties to both conventions, it is recognized that this will involve a lengthy legal process. Furthermore, the multimodal Convention has established a new philosophy in carriers' liability which has to undergo a process of acceptance, particularly in developing countries where, to a considerable extent, inland carriers still reject any liability. Another factor to be taken into consideration relates to articles 4 and 32 of the Convention. Developing countries in their enabling legislation may wish to establish regulatory principles as well as customs transit procedures in order to dispose of an embracing legal instrument, which again requires time consuming deliberations. There also appears to be a lack of awareness in some developing countries of the advantages of the Convention in the promotion of their trade.

Although the United Nations Convention on International Multimodal Transport of Goods enshrined the right of each State to regulate and control at the national level multimodal transport operations and MTOs, the desire of developing countries to include more detailed provisions in the Convention did not materialize. Meanwhile, many developing countries are in search of appropriate measures for regulating MTOs with a view to increasing participation of national MTOs in multimodal transport. Thus, there will still be a need for pursuing the question of harmonization of the relevant international policies of governments and national policy measures concerning multimodal transport and containerization in order to ensure the orderly development of international multimodal transport.

Container standards

Since there was a need to ensure optimum use of investment in ships and containers, particularly in developing countries, the Group of 77 initiated the work of examining the desirability and practicability of drawing up an international agreement on container standards and related equipment. The International Organization for Standardization (ISO) a non-governmental body, in which representatives of industries from developed countries predominated, had drawn up voluntary standards in this respect.

Pursuant to Economic and Social Council decision 6 (LVI) and to Trade and Development Board decision 118 (XIV), the *Ad Hoc* Intergovernmental Group on Container Standards was established within UNCTAD in 1974. The Group held two sessions, in November 1976 and November/December 1978. The task of this Group was, *inter alia,* to assess the desirability and practicability of drawing up an international agreement on container standards.

At its first session, the Group assessed the work done by the International Organization for Standardization on freight containers and related subjects and the economic impact of standardization in container transport, particularly on developing countries, and considered future work on container standards including the question of practicability and desirability of an international agreement. On the latter subject, however, the Group could not reach consensus, since Groups B and D were not convinced about the need for an intergovernmental agreement.

In November 1978, the Group met for a second session to determine the practicability and desirability of drawing up an international agreement on container standards. Even though wider support by Group D countries was found for such an agreement than during the first session, no unanimous agreement could be reached. It was stressed, however, that efforts should continue on an international level as the problem could not be solved by unilateral action.

Both sessions of the *Ad Hoc* Group were supported by a number of studies carried out by UNCTAD. These included a review of the work done by ISO—as based on the views expressed by various intergovernmental and non-governmental organizations—in the field of standardization of transport and handling equipment, and the identification of problem areas in respect of formulation and application of container standards for international multimodal transport and possible remedies for them.

Pursuant to Trade and Development Board decisions 157 (XVII) and 182 (S-X), the UNCTAD secretariat, in co-operation with IMO and ISO, continued reporting to the Committee on Shipping on those matters to enable the Committee to keep problems of container standards under constant review and to make recommendations whenever appropriate. The work of the Committee in this respect was later included in its programme of work. Although the Intergovernmental Group was not able to elaborate an international agreement concerning container standards, deliberation of this problem in UNCTAD helped to draw the attention of the ISO Council and induce it to decide that proposals for changing important standards of containers would be discussed with the relevant international organizations before any final decisions were taken.

It is relevant to point out that the subject of elaborating an international agreement on container standards was not pursued vigorously to a vote at the seventeenth session of the Board because a decisive choice had to be made between negotiating either the question of container standards or the flags of convenience (FOCs) which had reached a critical stage. Consequently, the Group of 77 felt that it could not pursue successfully the two issues at the same time. The FOC question had priority.

Multimodal container tariff rules

In view of the need for standardizing and simplifying existing multimodal container tariff rules applied by various multimodal transport operators the Committee on Shipping, at its tenth session (June 1982), requested the Secretary-General of UNCTAD to convene a group of experts to examine and recommend possible principles for developing model rules for multimodal container tariffs which could be utilized, as appropriate, by commercial parties in establishing the terms and conditions of carriage. The Group of Experts on Model Rules for Multimodal Container Tariffs held two sessions in 1984 and agreed on a set of basic principles for developing model rules for multimodal container tariffs.

Should model rules be developed as expected, they will facilitate consultation and negotiation between MTOs and shippers, in particular those of developing countries, and will promote international multimodal transport.

D. Problems and challenges of the future

UNCTAD VI and beyond

The sixth session of the Conference took place at a time of crisis for international shipping. The continued world-wide economic recession had reduced demand for shipping space to such as the extent that 64.5 million dead-weight tons (dwt) of shipping, representing 7.2 per cent of world tonnage, were laid up (mid-1982), and the market mechanism was no longer capable of bringing about the necessary adjustments. In conference trades the perennial problems with regard to the adequacy of services, freight levels, surcharges, dispensation, cargo share, technological innovations and changing patterns of trade, had intensified. To make matters worse fraud began to wreak havoc in the industry.

However, against this background the developing countries continued to attach high priority to shipping. This was highlighted by the fact that the International Development Strategy for the Third United Nations Development Decade called for structural change in the industry and for a 20 per cent share of world shipping for developing countries by the year 1990.

It was evident that most developing countries had made, by necessity, the political decisions to develop and expand their merchant marines not only because they had valid claims for an equitable share in shipping but also since in this context it represented the means of creating a focus of countervailing power. None the less, their performance in securing substantial participation in world shipping remains minimal. Their share of the world fleet stands at 15 per cent, representing approximately an average annual rate of growth of 13 per cent since 1971. Their share of world shipping in 1983 was divided into 23.7 per cent of world general cargo and 14.3 per cent of containership, 15.4 per cent of world dry bulk carriers and 12.3 per cent of world tankers.

In absolute terms these figures might appear impressive, but when set against the qualitative changes that had taken place in the industry through the adoption of new technologies by established traditional carriers, the effective performance and productivity of developing countries' tonnage is considerably reduced.

While the share of developing countries of world tonnage is still not commensurate with their share of world trade (as developing countries' exports account for some two-thirds of world trade), relatively good progress had been made by developing countries and the international shipping community both in dealing with the universal problems of the shipping industry and towards improving the position of developing countries in this area.

This was demonstrated by the number of conventions, resolutions, model rules, and other measures that have taken place during the last two decades during which universal concerns as well as those particular to developing countries were addressed.

The sixth session of the Conference in 1983 took stock of the situation in world shipping, reviewed the related activities of UNCTAD and unequivocally pronounced itself in resolution 144 (VI) adopted without dissent which had three discernible elements.

The first was its forward-looking approach to new areas of vital interest to developing countries and the maritime community at large which requested the secretariat to study and investigate certain areas particularly with regard to protectionism and monopolistic practices, investment behaviour and support policies in world shipping industry and to make an in-depth analysis of ship and ports financing.

The resolution also launched new processes of work and eventual intergovernmental action in the field of ports and multimodal transport such as a model agreement for feeder services and transhipment ports, modalities of foreign investment imports, rights and duties of terminal operators and users, and a standard form and model provisions from multimodal transport documents. It also mandated the secretariat to draft a programme of action for co-operation among developing countries in the fields of shipping, ports and multimodal transport.

The second element is that the Conference unanimously endorsed the mandate of UNCTAD in new areas in the field of maritime legislation which had previously been a controversial and voted mandate of the Committee on Shipping such as those in the areas of liens and mortgages and maritime fraud and piracy.

The third element is that the Conference lent its support and provided an impetus for the on-going work programme of UNCTAD in the field of shipping, ports and multimodal transport with emphasis on structural adjustment and the need to achieve the targets set in the International Development Strategy for the Third United Nations Development Decade. Particularly relevant is the section relating to the expeditious completion of the work on conditions for the registration of ships and follow-up to the implementation of the Convention on a Code of Conduct for Liner Conferences and support for the United Nations Convention on International Multimodal Transport and the Hamburg Rules.

Overall, the resolution had the following elements.

(a) Structural adjustment in the international shipping industry;

(b) Measures to increase financial flows to developing countries;

(c) Promotion of the trade and development perspective.

While instability, restrictive practices, overtonnaging in the shipping industry, and the barriers to developing countries' increased participation will, accordingly, be the most immediate problems facing governments and the industry in the current decade, the process to deal with these problems has already been set in motion. The momentum that has been gained and the relative achievements to date indicate that these problems will not be insurmountable if goodwill and dedication to international co-operation are maintained. Perhaps equally encouraging is the fact that the developing countries are now aware both of the problems that exist and of the benefits to be derived from the industry.

From the foregoing it can be seen that most of the crucial economic issues currently engaging the attention of the international maritime community are under consideration or resolution in one form or another within UNCTAD. Several conventions, decisions and recommendations addressed to remedying a wide range of problems have been adopted unanimously, by consensus or after wide agreement. At the same time, it has been noted that uncertainties raised by the delayed implementation of many of these measures, and fed by the impact of the present extended economic recession, have not only disrupted many ocean trades but have also pressured some countries into taking unilateral steps to secure their national interests, thus heightening commercial tensions between countries and invoking charges of protectionism and threats of retaliation.

Much of the ensuing disagreement between States is no doubt fuelled by lingering remnants of controversy between them over preconceived theoretical or philosophic concepts on the extent of permissible intergovernmental intervention in shipping matters. Persistence in overemphasizing a particular school of thought or one or other political or economic doctrine at the cost of overlooking practical considerations and the search for common ground will only tend to make negotiations more difficult.

In the circumstances, it hardly appears feasible in the future to leave practical problems in the field untouched, and to attempt to resolve the present difficulties by reopening large conceptual questions appertaining to the rationale of market regulation, or to the place of shipping in national plans for economic development. That would be tantamount to putting the clock back to the time when such questions were initially posed at the first and second sessions of the Conference in similarly abstract terms, but which were later translated into more practically-oriented channels of enquiry and were then pragmatically dealt with as matters of structural adjustment in UNCTAD bodies, as described above. Further, any such retrograde step to re-open now closed issues would also be in derogation of the declarations on shipping contained in the International Development Strategy for the Second and Third United Nations Development Decades and in the Programme of Action on the Establishment of a New International Economic Order.[39]

The sixth session of the Conference has contributed to defusing the existing tensions by reaffirming its faith in the supremacy of international negotiating processes for settling major points of dispute among States. By so doing it has discouraged the non-observance of international agreements and the subversion of existing mechanisms in UNCTAD for the practical solution of problems that have achieved both an appreciable element of success and also pointed the way to further progress.

---

[39] A detailed review of UNCTAD's activities in the field of shipping, as well as the approach discussed above, is to be found in the report by the UNCTAD secretariat to UNCTAD VI, "UNCTAD activities in the field of shipping" (TD/278 and Corr.1), to be printed in *Proceedings of the United Nations Conference on Trade and Development, Sixth Session,* vol. III—*Basic Documents* (United Nations publication, Sales No. E.83.II.D.8).

V. TRANSFER OF TECHNOLOGY: TECHNOLOGY ISSUES—FROM IDEAS TO ACTION IN UNCTAD (1970-1984)

A. Introduction

Technology is a relatively new subject for national and international attention. A bare 25 years ago, it did not figure as a specific subject for consideration in any discussion of national or multilateral policies, plans and strategies. Now, the scene has vastly altered, particularly in the developing countries.

Nearly 40 countries have formulated their own technology policies, plans and/or strategies. Many of them, particularly the large and the more advanced ones, have introduced laws, regulations, rules or decrees designed to regulate the transfer and development of technology. They have also established national institutional structures—Registries, Centres, Departments or Divisions—to implement their new approaches to technology. In a few of them, technology policies have been entrusted to special ministries, or to institutional arrangements directly linked to the office of the president or the prime minister.

Many currents have contributed since 1970 to bringing about this vast change. Among them, UNCTAD is perhaps the most important source for most of the initiatives on this subject. This account traces briefly the broad lines of this contribution. It begins with a brief description of the conceptual framework for UNCTAD initiatives on technology and then goes on to describe the evolution of the institutional arrangements and of the technology initiatives within UNCTAD, and the main lines of action at the threshold of the 1980s. It ends with a brief assessment of the ground covered within UNCTAD.

B. The conceptual framework for UNCTAD's initiatives on technology

There are several reasons why technology policies, unexplored before, have begun to receive such concentrated attention since 1970. Various UNCTAD studies on transfer of technology and technology policy have discussed these reasons in detail. Attention will therefore be focused here on a brief review of five major considerations which have been responsible for making technology a key issue for the developing countries as well as for the world community. They have served as the source for the evolution of the UNCTAD approach to technology issues.

The interrelationship and the distinction between science and technology

The first consideration springs from the interrelationship, as well as the distinction, between science and technology, earlier treated as one entity. The distinction between the two, however, is central to the UNCTAD approach. Science is universal, the result of the restless search of men's minds to fathom the unfathomed depths, to climb the unclimbed mountains, to perceive the unperceived. It is open. Its discoveries are publicized from the house-tops, not kept secret. There are no gains from such secrecy. Science is a very long-term phenomenon, uncertain in its outcome. It is not amenable to planning.

Technology stands out in sharp contrast. To begin with, it is product—and process—specific. Every action of an ordinary mortal—from the woman carrying bricks on her head to the scientist deciphering the images that record the walk of man in space untied to any object—involves inputs of various levels of technology. Any advance in technology is not open. It is guarded as a secret, giving its owner economic and commercial advantages.

Moreover, in contrast to science, technology is amenable to short, medium and long-term planning. It is in fact explicitly or implicitly a part of any decision that is taken by any ministry, government official or entrepreneur, whether the decision-maker is explicitly aware of this or not. Technology could therefore be made a subject of foresight, and forethought.

Constraints on access to technology

The second consideration relates to the uniqueness of technology and the constraints imposed by those who own it on the access to it by those who do not have it. It was only a few hundred years ago that scientific and technological advanced flowed from the East to the West. The last two centuries have completely reversed this flow.

The explosive development of technology since 1850 has radically altered the ability of people to produce more and varied goods and services. Productivity per person, used as a measure of technological change incorporated in the production process, could have barely doubled in the long period between the birth of Christ and 1850. But in the 130 years since then, it has increased 12 to 15 times in the industrially advanced countries. In the process, a vast treasure-house of technologies has accumulated which other nations can draw upon for their progress.

The underlying uniqueness of technology makes it amenable to such an exchange and diffusion. It is unlike any other commodity. It is the engine of man's capacity to produce all goods and services. It is the genetic code, not of one man, but of mankind itself. It has grown cumulatively over the centuries. Most nations have contributed to this growth, but fortunately no one has predominated for long. It can be transferred to persons or across national frontiers with little regard for climate, race, religion or sex. Once transferred, both its original owner and new acquirer have it; the real economic cost of its transfer is zero. Once obtained, it cannot like other commodities be used up by its consumption. Once mastered, it has a long life. Once adapted, it appreciates.

And yet, the constraints on exchanges of technology are severe. Property rights in it give its owners command over the terms, conditions and price for its exchange. The introduction of such property rights in technology is a more recent phenomenon than that in goods. Classical economists, for instance, Adam Smith, Ricardo and Marx, centred much of their work on the production and exchange of commodities, but did not concern themselves with private ownership of technology.

Technology is so very unlike land, and yet its exchange across nations resembles practices reminiscent of the feudal age. It is usually leased not sold. Under the feudal system, the tenants and sharecroppers did not enjoy fixity of tenure or of rent, independence in planning crops or improving land and methods of cultivation. Nor did they have control over marketing of their products. A fundamental restructuring of these feudal relationships had therefore to precede the modernization of both the techniques of agricultural production and management of farms, and the blossoming of the industrial revolution.

There is a certain structural parallel between lease of land under feudalism and transfer of technology now. When technology is leased, it forms part of a much larger package covering provision of finance, capital goods, equipment and intermediate products, the construction of plant and its management, and the marketing of the products. In all the arrangements and agreements dealing in one way or another with the transfer of technology, there are several restrictions or limitations: for instance, grant-back provisions; challenges to validity of patents; exclusive-dealing; and restrictions on research, use of personnel, adaptations, exports, using alternative sources of technology, goods or services, publicity; use of technology after expiration of agreements; use of technology already imported. Some 20 such restrictive practices are listed in the draft of the international code of conduct on the transfer of technology now under negotiation in UNCTAD.

Such restrictive practices, often illegal or otherwise regulated within developed countries, have been widely imposed in international transactions, especially with the developing countries. On the other hand, technology suppliers have accepted only the minimum degree of responsibility and obligation concerning the implementation of technology agreements, guaranteeing that the developing countries will reap the full benefits from their transactions.

In consequence, the developing countries have been unable to obtain the technology they need at the right price under the right terms and conditions and at the right time. They have to pay heavy direct and indirect costs. In addition, there are several hidden costs—for instance, transfer pricing, inordinate delays, wrong choice of technology—which are not even amenable to measurement. Hence the critical importance of improving the access of the developing countries to the accumulated storehouse of modern technologies.

Lack of technology options in the formation of development plans

The third consideration is of a somewhat different type, perhaps even a negative one. It relates to the question of why technological concerns have not yet moved to the centre of the stage in development planning. The profession of the economists, the wizards of magic numbers, may bear some responsibility for this. Economists are able to assign easily-understood values to all sorts of programmes and projects in development plans. In contrast, the scientists and technologists have not so far acquired a matching facility. Behind the value figures, however, are distinct technology profiles for each sector, branch, programme, project and plant. Each technology profile spans different time-scales, and relates to different sources, including the domestic ones. The technology policy-makers have not yet successfully utilized the importance of technology options in the formulation of development plans. The existence of a spectrum of technological options has pushed to the fore the idea of breaking up the development plans into their relevant components, and making investment decisions on the basis of the technological options, covering the past, the present and the future.

The central role of research and development (R and D) in adapting and diffusing technology

The fourth consideration which has brought the technology issue to the centre of the stage is the decisive change that has taken place in the role of research and development (R and D). It may be recalled that in the hey-day of Britain's march to becoming the workshop of the world in the nineteenth century, not more than 0.25 per cent of its national resources were devoted to R and D—a miniscule sum indeed. The experts, the engineers, the technicians who spearheaded the technological transformation in Great Britain numbered no more than 50,000. The position now is vastly different. There has been a move from individual gadgeteers to group research. Teams of research workers, basing themselves on what has been achieved in the past and in other places, now undertake organized research. That is what has pushed the technological frontier to farther horizons. Such R and D may be organized in an individual enterprise, or a national laboratory. But it is planned research, not old-fashioned gadgetry. In consequence, organized R and D has assumed a central role in developing as well as adopting, adapting and diffusing technologies.

The time horizons involved in decisions on technology

The fifth consideration is the time horizon involved in decisions on technology development. Technology does not come by itself in any form. It appears only vicariously, embodied in machines and human beings. The development of the capital goods industry and the advancement of the skill profile require a much longer time horizon than any other activity. Decisions to develop them, the programmes to achieve the targets set, the plans to train the engineers and skilled personnel to design the machines and equipment and to produce them, require a long period of maturity—around a quarter of a century or more. There is no way around this stubborn reality. The perception of the critical importance of a long-term time horizon, covering four to six five-year plans, has furnished the basis for adopting technology strategies interlinking several sectors of critical significance.

There are, of course, several other considerations which are relevant to determining each country's specific approach to its own technological problems. But the five points singled out here furnish much of the rationale underlying UNCTAD's work on technology. Each of the initiatives, described in paragraph 30 below, is built on one or a combination of these considerations.

C. Technology initiatives in UNCTAD: their evolution

THE SCENE IN THE EARLY 1970S

A start can be made with an examination of the setting in the early 1970s. In the 84 paragraphs of the International Development Strategy for the Second United

Nations Development Decade (IDS II), there was room for only one paragraph on transfer of technology. It read as follows:

(64) Developed and developing countries and competent international organizations will draw up and implement a programme for promoting the transfer of technology to developing countries, which will include, *inter alia,* the review of international conventions on patents, the identification and reduction of obstacles to the transfer of technology to developing countries, facilitating access to patented and non-patented technology for developing countries under fair and reasonable terms and conditions, facilitating the utilization of technology transferred to developing countries in such a manner as to assist these countries in attaining their trade and development objectives, the development of technology suited to the productive structure of developing countries and measures to accelerate the development of indigenous technology.

The policy-makers in those days had a limited perception of the need for specific approaches to technology issues. The words of the IDS II paragraph were drawn verbatim from headings of the work programme, just then being evolved in UNCTAD for submission to the first session of its Intergovernmental Group on the Transfer of Technology, held in June 1971.

Professor Raymond Vernon had just published his study *Sovereignty at Bay*.[1] A few hundred transnationals, like knights in shining armour mounted on white chargers, were to reorganize in the most efficient manner the inter-related system of world production, trade and monetary flows. If some nation States—small and not so small ones—did not like this, that was indeed too bad. They could not be expected to withstand the powerful charge.

In the third world, India and the countries of the Andean Group were struggling in a complicated manner to work out their foreign investment policies so as to leave some scope open for unpackaged technology imports. Most of the remaining countries of the third world were all, immediately after independence, formulating their national constitutions, and enacting soon thereafter laws on foreign investment, trying to induce the foreign investors with all manner of favours, to come and make a comfortable—and indeed very profitable—home in their lands. Nearly all of them formulated laws for the protection of patents and trade marks, thereby promoting in a most perverse manner (though this was not the intention) the monopolistic control of their domestic markets by foreign patent holders—the inverse of the generalized system of preferences (GSP).

Rarely did the countries raise at each stage of the decision-making process basic questions such as: does the country have the technology?; can it develop it?; can it adapt imported technology?; how long will it take?; what resources will be needed?; what are the trade-offs between importing technology now and waiting to develop it at home?; why no import now, but plan in such a fashion that there will be no more repetitive imports in the future? Apart from these strategic questions, other more simple and straightforward questions were also overlooked: for instance, how many agreements and arrangements on the transfer of technology does the country in fact have?; what are their financial implications?; what are the terms and conditions?; have alternative options been explored?; have attempts been made to unbundle the package?

---

[1] R. Vernon, *Sovereignty at Bay: the Multinational Spread of United States Enterprises* (New York: Basic Books, 1971).

Such was the setting for the active involvement of UNCTAD in technology issues and its brief expression in a solitary paragraph in IDS II. It should also be recalled here that these issues did not figure, except as purely marginal references, in the wide canvass of development issues which UNCTAD in 1964 was established to cover. The second session of the Conference (New Delhi, 1968) had before it a study which formed the basis of a long draft resolution on issues connected with science and technology, submitted by Brazil, Chile, India and Pakistan.[2] But other issues at the Conference occupied the centre of the stage. There was no time for science and technology. The draft resolution in consequence was passed on for further consideration in the regular machinery of UNCTAD. Quite clearly, UNCTAD too was, as yet, unprepared to grapple with technology questions.

UNCTAD's UNIQUE ROLE

Following the second Conference, the UNCTAD secretariat began an active consideration of the role which UNCTAD could play in promoting an examination of the issues faced by the developing countries in the transfer of technology. Elements of a programme of work for UNCTAD (TD/B/310 and Corr.1) were put together by the secretariat. The document was considered at the tenth session of the Trade and Development Board, which took place in August 1970. After protracted negotiations, lasting for a full three weeks, the Trade and Development Board adopted a resolution agreeing to establish an Intergovernmental Group on Transfer of Technology (IGGTT). Its existence was limited to only two sessions, including, as necessary, an organizational session.

Like the beginning of even the largest rivers, technology transfer had a modest beginning in UNCTAD. But with it, the first intergovernmental institutional structure was born within the United Nations system. The latent concern of the world community with transfer of technology issues found its first home base. It was still *ad hoc* in nature, and strictly limited in time. Fom then one, UNCTAD was to serve as a spearhead for a multiplicity of future initiatives, altering for ever the language of the North-South dialogue on the subject. Before turning to these initiatives, the picture of the historical evolution of the institutional arrangements in UNCTAD may be completed. In order to lighten the text, all references to sessions of various bodies of UNCTAD and the United Nations General Assembly where technology issues were discussed, and to the major studies by the secretariat are contained in part four of this book.

The IGGTT held an organizational session (14-21 June 1971), which adopted a programme of work for UNCTAD in the field of transfer of technology. From then on, UNCTAD was fully engaged in the exploration of technology issues. The Santiago Conference in 1972 (UNCTAD III) gave a strong impetus to UNCTAD's

---

[2] The study ("The transfer of technology to developing countries, with special reference to licensing and know-how agreements") (TD/28/Supp.1 and Corr.1), which was prepared by G. Oldham, C. Freeman and E. Turkcan of the Science Policy Research Unit of the University of Sussex. For the text of the draft resolution, not discussed at the second session of the Conference, see TD/II/WG.1/L.4/Rev.1 reproduced in the appendix to the report of Working Group I, *Proceedings of the United Nations Conference on Trade and Development, Second Session,* Vol. I—*Report and Annexes* (United Nations publication, Sales No. E.68.II.D.14), p. 357.

work on technology. Its resolution 39 (III) can be taken as a landmark. UNCTAD's activities on transfer of technology began to gather momentum. The next two sessions of the IGGTT achieved marked progress in delineating some of the substantive issues. The third session was of particular significance. It launched in two resolutions, adopted by roll-call votes, UNCTAD's most celebrated initiatives in the field of technology—the negotiation of an international code of conduct on the transfer of technology, and UNCTAD's contribution to the beginning of the revision of the industrial property system, including the Paris Convention for the Protection of Industrial Property. Both these negotiations are still going on.

By 1974, UNCTAD was fully involved in issues relating to the transfer of technology. It was to find recognition in the establishment by the Trade and Development Board in the autumn of 1974 of a fully fledged Committee on the Transfer of Technology (CTT). The *ad hoc* IGGTT, temporary in character, was now transformed into a permanent Committee on UNCTAD. In the years to follow, the four sessions of the CTT, with its decisions supplemented and amplified by the fourth, fifth and sixth sessions of the Conference, several sessions of the Trade and Development Board and the United Nations General Assembly, have given rise to a multiplicity of initiatives for action at the national, regional and international levels. In addition, there were negotiations on the code of conduct. Several subsidiary intergovernmental groups considered various technology questions in depth, thus enlarging their understanding and the scope for action. All these have fundamentally altered in a decade the image of technology issues in the early 1970s as described above. As the 1970s ended, technology issues were to move on to the centre of the stage of world consideration of longer-term development of the Third World.

Selected initiatives of UNCTAD on technology

In place of the small paragraph 64 in IDS II, the decade of the 1970s saw scores of pages of agreed intergovernmental resolutions[3] on various facets dealing with

---

[3] Most resolutions have been agreed to by consensus among countries of the North, the South and the East, usually after intensive and long drawn out negotiations. Only three were decided by roll-call votes within UNCTAD:

The Intergovernmental Group on Transfer of Technology, at its third session, adopted on 26 July 1974 resolution 2 (III) on the role of the patent system in the transfer of technology to developing countries, by 28 votes to 1, with 11 abstentions (*Against:* Germany, Federal Republic of. *Abstaining:* Austria; Belgium; Finland; France; Italy; Japan; Netherlands; Sweden; Switzerland; United Kingdom of Great Britain and Northern Ireland; and United States of America);

On the same date, resolution 3 (III) was adopted on the possibility and feasibility of an international code of conduct in the field of transfer of technology, by 31 votes to 4, with 4 abstentions (*Against:* Germany, Federal Republic of; Switzerland; United Kingdom of Great Britain and Northern Ireland; and United States of America. *Abstaining:* Austria; France; Italy; and Japan);

On 9 October 1981, the Trade and Development Board, at its twenty-third session, adopted resolution 240 (XXIII), inviting the Secretary-General of UNCTAD to prepare a report on common approaches to legislation and regulation dealing with the transfer, application and development of technology in developing countries, by 75 votes to 16, with 9 abstentions (*Against:* Austria; Belgium; Canada; Denmark; France; Germany, Federal Republic of; Greece; Ireland; Italy; Japan; Luxembourg; Netherlands; Sweden; Switzerland; United Kingdom of Great Britain and Northern Ireland; and United States of America. *Abstaining:* Australia; Finland; Israel; Liechtenstein; New Zealand; Norway; Portugal; Spain; and Turkey).

technology. They formed the fountainhead of the following major initiatives, aimed at reducing the technological dependence of the developing countries, strengthening their national technological capacity and accelerating their technological transformation:

A major conceptual change from concern with plain transfer of technology, shifting step by step to transfer and development of technology, strengthening national technological capacity, and finally moving on to working out the strategies for the technological transformation of developing countries;

Establishment of an international code of conduct on transfer of technology;

Revision of the industrial property system, including the Paris Convention (stopping the pendulum which through six earlier revisions had swung further and further in favour of the monopolistic rights of the patent holders); 1980 could see the pendulum push a bit in the other direction, giving the developing countries greater freedom to protect their national interests;

Beginning of a reflection of the above initiatives in national policies, plans, strategies, laws, regulations, rules, decrees, administrative practices (all these in a co-ordinated manner, integrated with over-all national development policies, plans and strategies);

Establishment of national centres, or equivalent institutional machinery in most developing countries; some, in fact, have already created special ministries for science and technology, with most of their work concentrating on technology issues;

Establishment of regional centres on transfer of technology in Asia, Africa and Latin America; the centre for West Asia is awaiting consideration pending the improvement of the political situation in the region;

A careful consideration of the adverse impact of the reverse transfer of technology from developing countries ("brain drain"), and of adequate arrangements to counteract it;

Exploration of modalities for the promotion of co-operative exchange of skilled manpower among the developing countries, thereby strengthening the capacity of these countries for collective self-reliance;

In-depth examinations of concrete technology problems faced by the developing countries in sectors of specific significance, such as pharmaceuticals, food processing, capital goods and energy and of policies aimed at strengthening their domestic technological capacity to find solutions;

Establishment in 1976, by the fourth session of the Conference, of an Advisory Service on Transfer of Technology to respond to urgent requests by developing countries for technical and operational assistance, including the organization of country missions and training programmes;

Formulation and implementation of a strategy for the technological transformation of the developing countries, weaving together the initiatives listed above and integrating technology policies, plans and strategies into the framework of a long-term comprehensive national development perspective.

It would not be fair to place all the credit for the beginning and later flowering of these initiatives on the shoulders of the UNCTAD secretariat alone. But a glance at the list of UNCTAD studies (TD/B/C.6/INF.2/Rev.4) does underline the initiatives that owe their origin to the UNCTAD secretariat's studies on these subjects. Some of its more important, or less short-lived, contributions towards launching these initiatives are listed in part four. These studies and the policy departures they proposed were then picked up by interested governments, particularly of the Group of 77.

In the process, the very language of the dialogue on the subject was altered all over the world. People no longer use the simplistic language of Vernon's *Sovereignty at Bay*. Indeed, there are some who have, perhaps a bit prematurely, written articles on transnationals at bay. Whatever characterization may fit particular concerns prevalent at particular times, the central fact remains that technology issues have now moved from the forgotten periphery of national and international concerns to the centre of the decision-making process.

Most of the initiatives listed above originated from the studies by the UNCTAD secretariat on the subjects concerned. These were then considered at governmental level in the Committee and in its subsidiary bodies, and at higher levels, such as the Trade and Development Board and sessions of the Conference, as well as the United Nations General Assembly. The negotiations on the code of conduct and the revision of the Paris Convention are still going on. While the final outcome is still in abeyance, the very process of negotiation has helped give a live shape to the issues they covered. The borderlines of international consensus are now seen more clearly than before. The process has stimulated determined national action. They have modified not only the content of the discussion on the subject but also the direction and substance of national decision-making.

After this review of UNCTAD's role in contributing to this change, it is necessary to turn to the new issues which will be dominant during the 1980s.

D. New directives for action during the 1980s

In the advancement of UNCTAD's work on technology, contributions have been made by several sources. The first and foremost was the Intergovernmental Group on Transfer of Technology and its successor the Committee on Transfer of Technology. The Committee and the Conference have played an active complementary role. Based on the documents prepared by the secretariat, the Committee usually prepared the groundwork so that the Conference itself at its highest political level could take the necessary decisions. In the taking of these decisions, it was in the final analysis the negotiations among the regional groups in UNCTAD which played the decisive role.

THE CENTRAL ROLE OF THE CONFERENCE

The third session of the Conference, held in Santiago in 1972, launched UNCTAD's work on technology. It adopted resolution 39 (III), "Transfer of Technology", which concentrated on the transfer process. This work was consolidated in the period 1972-1976.

Drawing upon this positive consolidation, the fourth session of the Conference, in Nairobi in 1976, gave the green light for a shift in emphasis—from transfer to the development of technology. It established the intergovernmental machinery to formulate the code of conduct on the transfer of technology and decided upon the basic directives for the revision of the industrial property system, including the Paris Convention. Besides initiating these two negotiating processes, the Nairobi Conference, in adopting resolution 87 (IV), ("Strengthening the technological capacity of developing countries"), moved the centre of UNCTAD's concern from the transfer process towards the policies to be pursued at the national level to reduce external dependence and to strengthen national technological capacity. The resolution adopted a comprehensive approach to this new dimension. It also established the Advisory Service on Transfer of Technology as UNCTAD's operational arm to assist the developing countries.

The fifth session of the Conference, in Manila in 1979, drew upon the past work and focused UNCTAD's future activities upon technology planning as an instrument for accelerating the technological transformation of the developing countries. It was there in Manila that the basis was also laid for weaving together the diverse threads of the work dealing with policies, laws, plans and critical sectors and areas into an overall strategy for the technological transformation of developing countries. The period between 1979 and 1982 witnessed the preparation by the UNCTAD secretariat of the draft of such a strategy, and its initial consideration at the fourth session of the Committee on Transfer of Technology.

New initiatives at UNCTAD VI (Belgrade, 1983)

The fourth session of the Committee reviewed the past work of UNCTAD in the field of technology. In a rare example of universal agreement, it noted with satisfaction the progress of this work and achievements described in the secretariat's report on this work. It adopted as many as seven resolutions and two decisions outlining as a first step the future course of UNCTAD's activities.

The stage was thus set at the sixth session of the Conference, in Belgrade in June 1983, to look back upon the past activities and give directives for the future. Although technology was one of the "basket" items at Belgrade, and therefore not at the centre of the stage, as was the trinity of issues connected with money and finance, trade and commodities, the negotiations on the technology issue lasted throughout the Conference. After intense negotiations, the Conference finally adopted resolution 143 (VI) under the bold title "Towards the technological transformation of developing countries". Here was, in more than one sense, a call of the Conference for new action aimed at the goal of technological transformation.

Above all, Conference resolution 143 (VI) set in motion the process of negotiation within UNCTAD of the strategy for the technological transformation of the developing countries. As the negotiations on the code were coming to their final conclusion, UNCTAD was thus initiating another important area of intergovernmental negotiation—the formulation and implementation of a strategy for the technological transformation of developing countries. The Conference decided that a special session of the Committee on Transfer of Technology should be convened in early 1984 to consider the secretariat report entitled "A strategy for the technological transformation of developing countries" (TD/277). These negotiations began at the special session of the Committee held in February 1984. By the close of that session, all the three regional groups (Group B, Group D and the Group of 77) had tabled their own proposals, running altogether to a total of over 30 pages, on elements which should be included in such a strategy. These negotiations are to be carried on intensively in the period ahead at the next (fifth) session of the Committee on Transfer of Technology, scheduled for December 1984.

Apart from the strategy, the Conference also stressed that the present world economic situation made even more urgent the need for coherent action towards the technological transformation of developing countries. Underlining this urgency, it emphasized the importance of restructuring the legal environment through the completion of the negotiations on the code of conduct on the transfer of technology and the revision of the Paris Convention for the Protection of Industrial Property and agreed on the need for strengthening the resources of the Advisory Service. It also decided on several new initiatives which may be summarized as follows:

To continue, as decided by General Assembly resolution 37/207, with detailed consideration at an intergovernmental level of measures to obviate the adverse consequences of the reverse transfer of technology;

To undertake new work on interregional linkages and technological cooperation among developing countries;

To request the Committee at its fifth session to decide upon intergovernmental examination of technology policies in sectors and areas of critical significance;

To carry forward the work on the role of small and medium-sized enterprises in the international transfer of technology;

To define the specific role of UNCTAD in the Administrative Committee on Co-ordination (ACC) joint project on the "Formulation of appropriate strategies for facilitating pharmaceutical supplies to the developing countries";

To prepare proposals on complementary work by UNCTAD on new and emerging technologies;

To examine the modalities for the commercialization of the results of United Nations system funded research and development;

To examine ways and means whereby developing countries can obtain the fullest and freest possible access to technology in the public domain.

Together with the negotiations on the strategy for the technological transformation of developing countries, the elements listed above open up new directions for UNCTAD's work in the field of technology in the period ahead. The sixth session of the Conference thus marked the satisfactory conclusion of the first phase, and the beginning of the second phase in UNCTAD's programme of work on technology.

E. Some concluding reflections

It is difficult to look back upon UNCTAD's 15-year involvement with technology in order to assess it critically. The period is too short. UNCTAD did not start with any intellectual inheritance—as in other areas. The opposition, both informed and uninformed, to charting a new course was formidable. Even so, some conclusions may be drawn about the overall impact without being either too self-congratulatory or too self-critical.

First, the most striking outcome of UNCTAD's involvement with technology is the world-wide emergence of a new idiom of understanding, a new language of dialogue—now used everywhere. Fifteen years ago nobody talked technology. Now all policy-makers and United Nations agencies are talking about it, but the talk itself is fortified with consensus reached, easy-to-remember facts, and well-reasoned arguments—usually from UNCTAD sources. In August 1979, this awareness was formalized in the adoption by the international community of the Vienna Programme of Action on Science and Technology for Development. Technology is no longer a game of blind man's buff. It has become a new game altogether.

Second, the impact in developing countries, to say the least, has been considerable. Nearly 40 developing countries, accounting for over 90 per cent of the output of the third world, have established a systematic framework guiding their technology approach, whether embodied in laws, regulations, rules, decrees, policies, plans or strategies. They have established institutions—Registries, Centres, Departments, Divisions, Committees, Commissions, Councils or even special Ministries—to implement their new approaches. This is a long way forward from the near total absence of any such structures 15 years ago.

UNCTAD's initiatives brought about some 80 governmental meetings, workshops, training courses covering some 200 weeks of participation if they had taken place one after another. This is equivalent to five full academic years—a marathon pedagogical undertaking indeed. The consensus reached is now embodied in 93 resolutions, decisions and recommendations—a working "bible" on technology running to nearly 300 single-spaced pages of typescript. As a fountainhead for all these, the secretariat issued over 200 studies and reports.

Third, the record is not too bright when measured by final agreements. This may be said of UNCTAD's three negotiating initiatives: the code of conduct on the transfer of technology, the revision of the Paris Convention and the industrial property system, and the reverse transfer of technology. Even there, several areas of visible impact can be identified! (*a*) The code is nearly there. Its draft provisions guide enterprises in their transactions and governments in their policies. It is quite clearly almost operational. (*b*) The Paris Convention and the industrial property system will never be the same after UNCTAD's intervention in favour of their fundamental revision in the interests of the developing countries. (*c*) Agreement is not yet in sight on the reverse transfer of technology. But even there, the policy-makers in the developing countries have now at their command well-reasoned substantive arguments and precise enough tools to measure human capital embodied in skill flows.

It may be added finally that the paucity of final agreements does not stem from the failure of intellect or from the absence of any elegant or erudite gimmickry. International agreements in an area such as technology, where the strong are so powerful and the weak so feeble, is by necessity a slow process measured in step-by-step advances—in coffee spoons—as T. S. Eliot would have said. On that ground, UNCTAD has registered many strides, when anyone looks back on the track record.

VI. NATURE AND EVOLUTION OF TRADE RELATIONS AMONG COUNTRIES HAVING DIFFERENT ECONOMIC AND SOCIAL SYSTEMS

A. Introduction

Policy issues related to trade relations among countries having different economic and social systems have been the subject of UNCTAD's work from its inception. One of its main guiding principles in this respect was formulated from the very beginning in the proposition that "world trade is an intimately interrelated network, and the repercussions of obstacles in any one part are felt inevitably in all others".[1] In trying to cope with the specific problems in the international links between developing countries and developed market-economy countries on the one hand and the socialist countries of Eastern Europe on the other, UNCTAD has played a pioneering and constructive role.

After extensive discussions, the first session of the Conference adopted a Final Act, paragraphs 25 to 29 of which were devoted to the trade of the socialist countries of Eastern Europe with both developing countries and developed market-economy countries. On the other hand, in recommendation A.VI.7, while recognizing the significance of the problems referred to in the draft recommendation submitted by Czechoslovakia,[2] the Conference decided to transmit it to the continuing United Nations trade machinery which it was proposed to establish (i.e. the permanent machinery of UNCTAD) for further consideration and action.

In this context, the Conference pointed out that efforts to solve the existing problems in this field should continue and "... result in progressively greater levels of trade between countries having different economic and social systems. It was recognized that such a development would be in the interest of world trade as a whole".

B. Principal policy initiatives undertaken in UNCTAD

UNCTAD I

General Assembly resolution 1995 (XIX) recognized the significance of trade policy issues in relations between countries with different systems of economic and

---

[1] *"Towards a new trade policy for development"* Report by the Secretary-General of UNCTAD, *Proceedings of the United Nations Conference on Trade and Development* (Geneva 23 March-16 June 1964), vol. II—*Policy Statements* (United Nations publication, Sales No. 64.II.B.12), p. 49.

[2] For text of this recommendation see *Proceedings of the United Nations Conference on Trade and Development*, vol. VIII — *Miscellaneous Documents and list of Participants* (United Nations publication, Sales No. 64.II.B.18).

social organization. The resolution stated that the principal functions of UNCTAD shall be, *inter alia* "to promote international trade, especially with a view to accelerating economic development, particularly ... between countries with different systems of economic and social organization and to make proposals for putting ... policies into effect and to take such other steps within its competence as may be relevant to this end, having regard to differences in economic systems and stages of development".

The scope and nature of the negotiations on this subject were also defined within the framework of various recommendations of UNCTAD I, *inter alia*: General Principle Two (concerning non-discrimination), and General Principle Six (governing international trade relations and trade policies conducive to development; recommendation A.II.1 on actions to be taken by developed market-economy and centrally planned economy countries in international commodity arrangements; recommendation A.III.2 on industrial branch agreements with the principal features of the agreements between developing countries and centrally planned economies; recommendation A.III.7 on measures by centrally planned economy countries for expansion and diversification of exports of manufactures and semi-manufactures by developing countries; recommendation A.VI.3 on long-term trade agreements; and recommendation A.VI.4 on direct participation by governmental trade organizations in foreign trade.

As a result, the review and assessing of trade flows between developing countries and developed market-economy countries with the socialist countries of Eastern Europe has been one of the cross-sectoral concerns of UNCTAD. During the first three sessions of the Trade and Development Board, UNCTAD's continuing forum, the socialist countries of Eastern Europe asked for action and concrete recommendations by UNCTAD on the normalization of international trade among countries having different economic and social systems, and the removal of discrimination and artificial obstacles to that trade. During the third session of the Trade and Development Board in 1966, it was agreed that on the basis of periodic reports by the UNCTAD secretariat, East-West as well as East-South trade problems would be discussed, with specific attention paid to the trade interests of developing countries and to the work of other United Nations organs in this field.

At the fifth session of the Board in 1967, substantive discussions on the relationship of inter-systems trade were initiated on the basis of the secretariat's report. The representatives of all three country groups emphasized the role which UNCTAD should play in promoting trade relations between countries having different economic and social systems, including East-West trade. One of the most important topics centred round the convergence of the approaches by trading partners of both East and West on the meaning of equal treatment, both bilateral and multilateral, "material reciprocity" between countries using different economic instruments as a qualification of the most-favoured-nation principle, mutual advantages and so on. On East-South trade issues, the secretariat report dealt at some length with financing related to trade and the conception of bilateral economic co-operation agreements between socialist and developing countries.

UNCTAD II

Conference resolution 15 (II), adopted without dissent at the second session of the Conference in New Delhi in 1968, was the first agreement on East-West-South trade issues within the UNCTAD framework. It recognized the desirability of expanding East-West trade, on the one hand, and trade between developing and socialist countries on the other. The statement of the Secretary-General of the United Nations that "it is an inevitable consequence of growing international interdependence that the constriction of any one channel of economic relationship tends to react adversely upon other channels as well,[3] contributed to enhance UNCTAD's role in the sphere of East-West trade.

The provisions concerning the recognition of the interdependence of trade flows and the request that the Trade and Development Board should convene periodically a sessional committee to deal with both East-West trade and trade with developing countries, were considered as a significant step forward in this sphere of UNCTAD's work.

The resolution recommended, *inter alia:* to countries participating in East-West trade to seek to remove the economic, administrative and trade policy obstacles to the development of their mutual trade without prejudice to developing countries; to the socialist countries of Eastern Europe—to conclude long-term agreements for the purchase of commodities from developing countries, to abolish or reduce on a preferential basis tariffs on manufactures and semi-manufactures purchased from them and to multilateralize, to the extent possible, payment arrangements with this group of countries; to developing countries—to grant the socialist countries of Eastern Europe conditions for trade not inferior to those granted normally to the developed market-economy countries.

In the light of this resolution the eighth session of the Trade and Development Board decided in February 1969 to convene, periodically, a sessional committee, in order to proceed with consultations on, and the elaboration of, proposals concerning East-West and East-South trade relations, taking into account the activities of the regional commissions.

A salient feature of the debates in Sessional Committee of the ninth session of the Trade and Development Board (1969) was a scrutiny of the preferences accorded by the socialist countries of Eastern Europe to imports from the developing countries. The question of preferential treatment for developing countries' exports should be considered within the framework of the recommendations agreed upon in Conference resolution 15 (II), including the provisions that developing countries should take into account the modalities of the foreign trade system of the socialist countries and that they should grant them treatment which would be no less favourable than that accorded to developed market-economy countries.

A joint declaration[4] by Bulgaria, Czechoslovakia, Hungary, Poland and the Soviet Union, during the second part of the fourth session of the Special Committee

---

[3] *Proceedings of the United Nations Conference on Trade and Development, Second Session,* vol. I — *Final Act and Report* (United Nations publication, Sales No. E.68.II.D.14 and Corrigendum), p. 18, para. 71.

[4] *Official Records of the Trade and Development Board, Tenth Session, Supplement No. 6A* (TD/B/329/Rev.1), para. 192.

on Preferences (September/October 1970), established the main elements of their common approach towards the fulfilment of the goals of Conference resolution 21 (II) on a generalized system of preferences. Among these elements, mention should be made of the additional preferential measures decided upon by the above-mentioned socialist countries in favour of industrial exports from developing countries, in line with the recommendations agreed upon in section II of Conference resolution 15 (II).

A group of experts on multilateral payments arrangements was convened in 1969 on problems related to multilateral payments arrangements between developing and socialist countries. In the light of the discussions the experts recognized the need for a flexible approach in payments arrangements between both groups of countries. It was agreed that in view of the specific economic circumstances the interested countries should select the most appropriate form of settlement. The conclusion was that bilateral payment arrangements continued to make positive contributions to the expansion of trade between developing countries and the socialist countries of Eastern Europe and that no uniform method of introducing multilateralization into payments relations was practical at that time.

UNCTAD III

A second important agreement was reached during the third session of the Conference in 1972, with the adoption without dissent of resolution 53 (III) on trade relations among countries having different economic and social systems. The interesting feature of the agreement reached in the above resolution lay in the bargaining process undertaken by all interested parties, supplemented by the trade policy initiatives put forward by the UNCTAD secretariat.

These initiatives took the form of an integrated approach to trade and co-operation between the socialist countries of Eastern Europe and the developing countries which recognized that trade was becoming an integral part of a more complex process of economic co-operation. The distinctive features emerging from this system of co-operation between these groups of countries are based on specific principles consistent with the principles of UNCTAD, a comprehensive array of policy measures, specific institutional machinery and a set of legal instruments.

The integrated approach should comprise mutual action in such spheres as trade and payments, economic assistance, transfer of technology and technical co-operation, trade promotion, invisibles, etc. It should take into account the need to adapt the policy measures applied to the specific needs and circumstances of the least developed among the developing countries. Mutual efforts should be guided by the idea that the various elements of this approach were interlinked and interdependent, since successful action in one of the spheres mentioned was conditional upon, and, at the same time might stimulate, progress in other spheres. The concept of an integrated approach can be implemented at different levels—at the level of concrete projects, at the level of economic sectors or industrial branches, at that of the national economy as a whole, and sometimes at the level of regional groupings. Such an approach should also take into account the fact that comprehensive trade and economic co-operation has to be carried out through convergent efforts on both sides.

The policy measures in the different spheres can be supported by the establishment of appropriate institutional machinery and by a set of legal instruments. These institutional and legal provisions can guarantee the effectiveness of commitments, offer the possibility of introducing action-oriented review and appraisal procedures and secure a continuous positive evolution of the forms and methods of co-operation. Thus, policy measures on the one side and institutional and legal provisions on the other, can form a coherent and internally consistent whole. Practical experience suggests that, while such an integrated approach could be considered as the outcome and the culmination of a gradual development of trade and economic relations, it can, in its turn, provide new stimuli for their further expansion and diversification.

During the fourteenth session of the Trade and Development Board in 1974, a further evaluation of this subject led to the adoption of resolution 112 (XIV) — agreed conclusions on trade relations among countries having different economic and social systems. The increasing expansion of trade links between the socialist countries of Eastern Europe and both developing countries and developed market-economy countries was acknowledged and welcomed.

In the context of an improved international climate and the upward trend of these trade flows, UNCTAD's permanent machinery agreed to consider more specific topics relating to the economic relations between socialist, developing and developed market-economy countries, such as long-term trade and economic policies, economic co-operation in specific areas, industrial and tripartite co-operation, and multilateralization of trade and payments.

In December 1975, a seminar on industrial specialization through various forms of multilateral co-operation was convened, pursuant to the above-mentioned agreed conclusions of the Board. The seminar concentrated on tripartite industrial co-operation between organizations from Eastern, Western and developing countries. It was agreed by the participants that this form of industrial co-operation, in particular, the setting-up of joint industrial projects, could benefit the development of developing countries, as a result of the complementary character of actions undertaken by the interested countries. The General Assembly recognized the importance of this form of co-operation for the industrialization of developing countries in resolution 3362 (S-VII) on development and international economic co-operation.

UNCTAD IV

At the fourth session of the Conference in Nairobi, a comprehensive resolution (resolution 95 (IV)) on trade relations among countries having different economic and social systems was adopted in May 1976. It covered an agreement between the parties concerned to foster East-West negotiations and to enhance the operational activities of the secretariat. It was preceded by a report in which the secretariat put forward its initiatives to the Conference[5] and thus provided the basis for the pro-

---

[5] See "Multilateral action for expanding the trade and economic relations between countries with different economic and social systems, in particular action which would contribute to the development of developing countries" (TD/193), reproduced in *Proceedings of the United Nations Conference on Trade and Development, Fourth Session,* vol. III — *Basic Documents* (United Nations publication, Sales No. E.76.II.D.12).

posals and suggestions of the Group of 77.[6] This document was supplemented by a joint statement of the socialist countries to the Conference (TD/211),[7] setting out specific proposals.

Negotiations between the socialist countries of Eastern Europe, developing countries and developed market-economy countries were concluded within the framework of multilateral action oriented to the development of the developing countries. Thus, the preambular paragraph of Conference resolution 95 (IV) recalled several resolutions of the General Assembly[8] and of the Conference dealing with international economic co-operation. It also took into account the proposals concerning East-South trade forwarded by the Group of 77 in the Manila Declaration and Programme of Action.

China expressed reservations on issues dealt with in Conference resolution 95 (IV): the formulation regarding "... international division of labour ... on a long-term stable basis...", the inclusion of recommendations to developing countries in order to create for the socialist countries conditions no worse than those normally granted to their trading partners among the developed market-economy countries and the references to the final act of the conference on security and co-operation.

Two intergovernmental groups of experts, one on trade opportunities resulting from multilateral schemes of member countries of the Council for Mutual Economic Assistance (CMEA) and a second on a multilateral system of payments between socialist and developing countries took place in the last quarter of 1977, following Trade and Development Board decisions 138 (XVI) and 139 (XVI), respectively, which established the terms of reference for those groups of experts.

The group on trade opportunities was unable to arrive at mutually acceptable recommendations. Its report included, as an annex, the draft proposal of agreed conclusions and recommendations submitted by the Group of 77.

The second group of experts' proposals to the Board, were based on the conclusion that "At this stage no final recommendation can be made concerning any single method of introducing elements of multilateralism in the existing system of payments between socialist countries of Eastern Europe and developing countries".[9] A suggestion was also formulated stating that it was for the partners concerned to adopt and apply the payments system which they considered the most appropriate for their needs, interests and stage of trade and economic co-operation.[10]

---

[6] Manila Declaration and Programme of Action, reproduced in *Proceedings of the United Nations Conference on Trade and Development, Fourth Session*, vol. I — *Report and Annexes* (United Nations publication, Sales No. E.76.II.D.10), annex V.

[7] Section G of the joint statement by Bulgaria, Byelorussian Soviet Socialist Republic, Cuba, Czechoslovakia, German Democratic Republic, Hungary, Mongolia, Poland, Ukrainian Soviet Socialist Republic and the Union of Soviet Socialist Republics. See *Proceedings ... (op. cit.)*, vol. I, annex VIII.

[8] General Assembly resolutions 1995 (XIX), 2626 (XXV), 3201 and 3202 (S-VI), 3281 (XXIX) and 3362 (S-VII).

[9] Report of the Intergovernmental Group of Experts to Study a Multilateral System of Payments between Socialist Countries of Eastern Europe and Developing Countries (TD/B/683), reproduced in *Multilateralization of payments in trade between socialist countries of Eastern Europe and developing countries. Selected documents* (TD/B/703) (United Nations publication, Sales No. E.78.II.D.4). See para. 6 of the Group's recommendations.

[10] Para. 4 of the report of the Experts, *loc. cit.*

UNCTAD V

The bargaining process between the negotiating parties gathered momentum with the preparations for the fifth session of the Conference. Thus, the position of the Group of 77 was stated in section III of the Arusha Programme for Collective Self-reliance and Framework for Negotiations [11] and the position of the socialist countries in a document on the evaluation of the world trade and economic situation.[12]

Developing countries stressed again the need that UNCTAD adopt a comprehensive programme on trade and economic relations among countries having different economic and social systems. The measures to be undertaken dealt with a wide range of topics related to East-South trade issues, including a request that assistance be provided by the socialist countries of Eastern Europe to developing countries as set out in the International Development Strategy for the Second United Nations Development Decade.

The socialist countries expressed their views on the two essentially different types of economic relationships between developed and developing countries, as reflected in the practice of principles such as equality, mutual benefits in economic relations and non-interference in internal affairs. These countries stated that the development of the economy of the CMEA member countries and their successful implementation of integrated measures would help bring about a further expansion of their economic co-operation with the developing countries on both a bilateral and multilateral basis. They also recalled the proposals of their joint statement at the fourth session of the Conference which could provide the basis for the improvement of East-South mutual relations.

Conference decision 116 (V) was the outcome of negotiations between the negotiating groups of countries during the fifth session of the Conference, in which member States and the secretariat of UNCTAD were requested "to further implement the provisions of Conference resolution 95 (IV) of 31 May 1976". It was then decided to refer the two draft resolutions submitted under this agenda item to the permanent machinery of UNCTAD.

As a result of extensive negotiations during the twenty-first session of the Trade and Development Board, considerable progress was achieved and it became possible to combine the two draft resolutions in a broad and comprehensive informal text with few outstanding points of disagreement. Under resolution 220 (XXI) of 27 September 1980 the Trade and Development Board decided to request States members of UNCTAD to continue efforts aimed at the further expansion of trade relations among countries having different economic and social systems, as well as to continue, at its twenty-third session, the consideration of the above-mentioned informal text, in conformity with the objectives of the New International Economic Order.

Three operative sections were contained in this text. In section I, the Board called upon countries participating in East-West trade in expanding their relations

---

[11] See *Proceedings of the United Nations Conference on Trade and Development, Fifth Session*, vol. I —*Report and Annexes* (United Nations publication, Sales No. E.79.II.D.14), annex VI.

[12] *Ibid.*, annex VII.

to take into account the interest of developing States. In section II, the Board recommended to the socialist countries of Eastern Europe and to the developing countries that they should give new impetus to their co-operation: extend the practice of concluding long-term intergovernmental agreements covering potential areas for trade and long-term bilateral programmes of economic, commercial and scientific technical co-operation; improve the payments arrangements; promote the establishment in developing countries of joint ventures in the fields of industry, agriculture and trade to increase the exports of manufactured and semi-manufactured products; and improve co-operation mechanisms at bilateral and multilateral levels. In section III, the Secretary-General of UNCTAD was requested to strengthen the services of the secretariat and to intensify the technical assistance activities of UNCTAD in this area.

Resolutions 243 (XXIII) and 262 (XXV) of the Board reiterated the mandate of UNCTAD in matters of trade relations between countries with different economic and social systems. They remitted and additionally improved the above-mentioned text for further consideration at the following session of the Board and at the sixth session of the Conference in 1983.

UNCTAD VI

Decision 145 (VI) of the sixth session of the Conference was the outcome of extensive negotiations on the pending resolution on trade among countries having different economic and social systems. Two provisions were adopted without dissent, first to request member States and the secretariat of UNCTAD to implement further the provisions of Conference resolution 95 (IV) of 31 May 1976 and, second, to remit to the twenty-seventh session of the Board the amended informal text referred to the Conference and annexed to the above-mentioned decision.

The preambular section of this annex included two points of disagreement between the negotiating parties: the non-discriminatory basis for development of relations between countries having different social and economic systems and the explicit reference to disarmament as an instrument for social and economic development. The first section of the provisions in the text, related to East-West trade issues, contained the following matters on which settlement could not be reached: (*a*) to remove economic, administrative, commercial and other obstacles and not to permit the introduction of new restrictions; (*b*) to eliminate imbalances in East-West trade which might be an obstacle to the expansion of imports from developing countries. Section II of the provisions concerning recommendations to developing and socialist countries included a proposal put forward by the Group of 77 at their Fourth Ministerial Meeting in Arusha on financial assistance to be provided by the socialist countries to the developing countries, a proposal which is still under negotiation. Finally, a provision regarding the establishment, within UNCTAD, of an advisory service on the development of trade between developing and socialist countries is also under negotiation.

At the twenty-seventh session of the Board, in October 1983, decision 276 (XXVII) on "trade relations among countries having different economic and social systems and all trade flows resulting therefrom" was adopted. The salient feature of this text is that it reconfirmed Conference resolutions 15 (II), 53 (III) and

95 (IV) and requested the Secretary-General of UNCTAD, first, to convene an *ad hoc* group of experts to consider ways and means of expanding trade and economic relations between countries having different economic and social systems, and, second, to ensure adequate support for the implementation of technical assistance projects and programmes in the area of trade of developing countries with the socialist countries of Eastern Europe. It was also decided to remit to the twenty-ninth session of the Board the informal text annexed to Conference resolution 145 (VI).

The developing countries and the socialist countries stressed the importance of UNCTAD's role in promoting and facilitating the adoption by member countries of measures and policies designed to develop trade relations between countries with different systems.

The outstanding issues which were the subject of negotiations during the fifth and sixth sessions of the Conference, as well as in UNCTAD's continuing forum, include the positions of the negotiating parties with regard to: first, the quantitative financial aid goals; second, the operation of the special fund of the International Investment Bank; and third, the issue concerning the respect of the principle of non-discrimination.

The Group of 77 has reiterated its position on the achievement of the 0.7 per cent target for official development assistance as set out in the International Development Strategy for the Second United Nations Development Decade and on the necessity for measures to make the special fund of the International Investment Bank effective.

Group D countries have reconfirmed their oft-repeated attitude on the above quantitative target, including reservations made during the twenty-fifth session of the General Assembly. This group of countries has stressed the need to respect the rule of non-discrimination, which represents one of the general and special principles of UNCTAD.

C. Overall evaluation

One of the prominent milestones in UNCTAD's history was its contribution to the promotion of trade among countries having different economic and social systems; it was generally recognized that this international forum had a role to play in East-West trade issues. Nevertheless, the deterioration in the world political climate during the period between the fifth and the sixth sessions of the Conference, the reservations expressed by Group B countries regarding the discussion of East-West trade problems in the Sessional Committee II of the Board and the rigidities in the positions of different groups of countries were adversely affecting the progress of negotiations on trade relations between countries with different systems.

When assessing the work of UNCTAD in this matter, it appears that differences in the viewpoints of a conceptual and substantive nature have blocked, to a considerable extent, the entire process of negotiations of inter-systems trade. The position of Group D and Mongolia at UNCTAD VI was that questions of trade and economic relations among countries having different economic and social systems should be considered in UNCTAD in all their dimensions, due regard being paid to the inter-relationships between East-West and East-South trade flows.

The socialist countries of Eastern Europe at present maintain trade relations with more than 100 developing countries, mostly on the basis of intergovernmental agreements on trade and economic co-operation. The network of these agreements is wide, covering more than 500 agreements.

The secretariat's activities on this subject were undertaken by the Division for Trade with Socialist Countries, which dealt with a number of specific features of economic links between countries having different economic and social systems.

The focus of the initial activities of this Division was centred on the examination, among others, of questions arising in connection with the establishment of long-term trade agreements, particularly those with developing countries, with agreements on industrial co-operation by branch of production and with other problems of trade expansion between the socialist countries of Eastern Europe and both the developing countries and the developed market-economy countries.

The study of problems, experiences and prospects related to the development of trade between countries having different economic and social systems was undertaken in several ways. Various questions such as foreign trade and its place in economic plans, the role of the international division of labour, the impact of State monopoly on foreign trade in socialist countries, the importance of long-term trade agreements for the development of trade and market stabilization, the role of industrial co-operation, etc. were dealt with in the annual "Review of trends and policies in trade between countries having different economic and social systems", submitted regularly to the Trade and Development Board, since its fifth session in 1967. Furthermore, case studies on several countries and geographical regions have been prepared on trade policies pursued by socialist, developed market-economy and developing countries on their mutual trade relations, with a view to drawing conclusions and suggesting ways and means for the improvement and expansion of those relations. The Division also studied specific items related to trade among countries having different economic and social systems such as various aspects of economic and industrial co-operation, tripartite co-operation, payments arrangements, and ways and means for promoting trade, etc.

The technical assistance activities for the expansion of trade relations between the developing countries and the socialist countries of Eastern Europe have been the growing sector of the operational tasks developed by this Division during the last 10 years.

Among the activities of UNCTAD for the promotion of trade and the intensification of economic co-operation among countries having different economic and social systems is that relating to the machinery for holding bilateral and multilateral consultations among interested member States. This machinery was established in response to the needs of member States and provides an opportunity for interested member countries to discuss various questions pertaining to their mutual trade, payments, economic and industrial co-operation, etc. The consultations are confidential, voluntary and non-committal in character and may be considered as complementary to the official contacts which countries maintain with their partners.

The organization of bilateral and multilateral consultations within UNCTAD between countries having different economic and social systems is provided for in different UNCTAD resolutions and decisions on this subject. The Conference, in its resolution 53 (III), *inter alia,* invited countries having different economic and social systems to make use of the established machinery for consultations within the framework of the Trade and Development Board with a view, first, to determining the long-term prospects for mutual economic co-operation in specific fields, and second, to take into mutual consideration the existing long-term economic development plans and programmes of each partner in the fields of mutual interest. The resolution also recommends that the interested countries should notify each other in advance of the intention to hold consultations and the subjects they wish to discuss and should make the necessary preliminary preparations.

With a view to improving this consultative machinery and in order to make it more effective, flexible and responsive to concrete and specific issues, the fourth session of the Conference in its resolution 95 (IV) decided that bilateral and multilateral consultations should be held in a regular manner annually and systematically both within the framework of the sessions of the Trade and Development Board, as well as outside this framework when necessary, at the request of interested parties. The Conference also decided that the UNCTAD secretariat would participate both in the technical preparation of consultations and in their various subsequent stages.

Some 350 such bilateral and multilateral consultations between interested members of UNCTAD were organized between 1969 and 1983. The number of countries which have participated in these consultations totals 95. In addition, a number of intergovernmental organizations, such as the Council for Mutual Economic Assistance (CMEA), the International Bank for Economic Co-operation (IBEC), the International Investment Bank (IIB), the Union of Banana Exporting Countries (UPEB), also participated in a number of bilateral and/or multilateral consultations.

The consultative machinery of UNCTAD is mainly being used as a forum for the exchange of views and information between countries having different economic and social systems on issues pertaining to their mutual trade and economic relations. It has provided an opportunity for consulting partners to get acquainted with the systems of trading, market potentials and the possibilities that partners can offer to each other for co-operation in different sectors of the economy. Better utilization of the existing legal basis and institutional framework as well as an intensification of promotional activities such as closer co-operation between chambers of commerce, participation in international fairs and exhibitions, etc. are among the subjects frequently discussed during the consultations. A direct follow-up of some of the consultations has resulted in exchange of economic delegations between the partners.

For the past two decades—within the existing mandate—UNCTAD has served the governments of member countries as an instrument for the promotion of trade and economic relations among countries having different economic and social systems. Measures taken within the framework of UNCTAD have made for the steady and relatively dynamic growth of trade and economic co-operation between socialist, developing and developed market-economy countries in the past two decades. In trying to cope with all world trade flows in the context of their interdependence, UNCTAD has played a pioneering and constructive role in this area.

VII. ECONOMIC CO-OPERATION AMONG DEVELOPING COUNTRIES

A. Historical evolution of UNCTAD's involvement in economic co-operation among developing countries

THE SITUATION BEFORE 1964

The concept of economic co-operation among developing countries as an explicit policy objective of independent governments can be traced back to the early 1950s. Already in those years the countries of Latin America, inspired in part by the example of the postwar European integration efforts, and having been made conscious of their peripheral status in the world economy by the intellectual pioneering work undertaken by the United Nations Economic Commission for Latin America (ECLA) banded together in a series of initiatives, which were later to coalesce into the Latin American Free Trade Association (LAFTA) and the Central American Common Market. Parallel to these developments, the major European colonial powers attempted to shape the decolonization process in such a way as to replace their regional colonial administrations by economic co-operation frameworks. In several cases these attempts included blueprints for full-fledged political federations, but most of these were still-born or broke up soon after independence. However, the economic links left behind by the colonial powers were more durable (due to the maintenance of special economic support from the former colonial powers) and constituted the starting point for Economic Co-operation among Developing Countries (ECDC) in many parts of Africa, the Caribbean and the Pacific region.

Independently of these essentially regional and subregional co-operation and integration efforts, an entirely different impulse emanated from the Non-Aligned Movement (NAM) launched at the Bandung Conference of 1955. While conceived essentially as a political force independent of the two power blocs confronting each other in the Cold War, the NAM soon extended its purview to the economic field, which provided a broader basis than the purely political sphere for common positions based on shared interests and common claims in the emerging North-South dialogue. The first concrete expression of this, then, novel style of ECDC was the Tripartite Agreement signed in 1968 by three of the leading NAM founding-members, namely Egypt, India and Yugoslavia, aiming at a preferential mutual tariff, i.e., something less than a full-fledged free trade zone, which hitherto had been considered the only valid reason for departing from the most-favoured-nation principle, the very heart of the General Agreement on Tariffs and Trade (GATT), around which the postwar rules of the game of international trade had been built.

One of the main impulses leading to the convening of the United Nations Conference on Trade and Development in Geneva in 1964 came from another initiative of the Non-Aligned Movement, namely the Conference on the Problems of Economic Development (Cairo, July 1962).

A third form of co-operation grew out of the common interests of developing countries highly dependent on the exports of particular commodities not exported by developed countries but whose price structure and marketing channels were largely controlled by companies based in the developed countries. The best known illustration was the Organization of the Petroleum Exporting Countries (OPEC), founded in 1960 to counteract a cut in the so-called "posted price" decided upon by the international oil companies without consultation with the producing countries, for most of which petroleum revenues constituted virtually their sole source of foreign exchange. Price stabilization agreements or mutual consultative machinery at the regional or inter-regional levels had already been formed prior to 1964 for several major commodities exclusively or largely exported by developing countries, e.g., coffee, rubber and tin.

It is noteworthy that the inaugural session of UNCTAD in 1964 was not used as a forum for discussing and co-ordinating pre-existing ECDC efforts *per se,* but rather provided a framework within which developing countries could agree on common positions *vis-à-vis* the North on broad international economic issues affecting their development. The grouping set up at that session of UNCTAD constituted the formal birth of the so-called Group of 77 (presently numbering well in excess of 120 countries), by far the most broadly based group of developing countries ever organized. Due to its original concentration on international economic as distinct from political issues, this group was able to encompass not only the non-aligned countries, but also those closely associated with either of the two power blocs. This form of policy co-ordination *vis-à-vis* the developed countries—both developed market-economy countries and the socialist countries of Eastern Europe—proved to be a turning point in the North-South negotiating pattern throughout the United Nations system. Chapters of the Group of 77 were gradually organized along the UNCTAD model at United Nations Headquarters, in other major United Nations agencies and—in modified form—within the international financial institutions based in Washington.

The introduction of ECDC into UNCTAD's formal work programme

UNCTAD's rationale for initiating a programme for the promotion of economic co-operation among developing countries (ECDC) in the late 1960s was based on the following main considerations:

Most developing countries were too small in terms of economic size to sustain an autonomous and prolonged development effort, particularly in the area of industrialization, where the limits of import substitution became evident even in the larger developing countries by the early 1960s;

The pronounced North-South orientation of most developing countries' trade, infrastructures and technological inspiration made them overly dependent on policies, prices and economic conditions beyond their control; and

The economic weakness of each individual developing country *vis-à-vis* their principal negotiating partners of the North (several of whom had by then coalesced in the European Economic Community framework into a single bloc for purposes of trade negotiations) made them conscious of the need to marshall their collective economic potential in order to reinforce their bargaining positions in the various areas of the North-South economic activity, such as trade, aid, private investment and transfer of technology.

UNCTAD was the first United Nations agency to recognize the need to promote ECDC as part of its regular work programme. This happened as early as 1968 as the result of a comprehensive Concerted Declaration (23-II), adopted without dissent at the second session of the Conference in New Delhi. This Declaration was followed up by the establishment of a separate organizational unit within the office of the Secretary-General of UNCTAD as from July 1968, which bore the title of "Special Programme on Trade Expansion and Economic Integration among Developing Countries". As the name indicates, the emphasis at the time was placed on helping formal integration schemes among developing countries as well as promoting new ones. The principal operational instruments for accomplishing these objectives were problem-oriented research and technical assistance. These two arms of the programmes were closely interlinked, inasmuch as research subjects were selected by the secretariat on the basis of problems encountered in the field during the course of technical assistance activities, whereas the latter were supported by the research on problems faced by several groupings, for which others had attempted or found solutions.

Technical assistance was already being rendered by the Programme even before UNCTAD had become an executing agency of the United Nations Development Programme (UNDP) in its own right. Early recipients of such assistance included the Maghreb countries and Regional Co-operation for Development (RCD), encompassing the Islamic Republic of Iran, Pakistan and Turkey, and regional programmes on trade and industrial integration were formulated for both groups. Thereafter UNCTAD provided several trade experts as part of an interdisciplinary United Nations Team which laid the basis for economic integration among the five countries members of the Association of South East Asian Nations (ASEAN).[1] In addition to these multi-sectoral integration schemes, UNCTAD was called upon to support a number of monetary co-operation schemes, initiated at a Ministerial Meeting for Asian economic co-operation (Kabul, December 1970), which led to the creation of the Asian Clearing Union. Here UNCTAD was able to draw on the long Latin American experience in the field of clearing and payments support arrangements in an early attempt at what later came to be known as technical co-operation among developing countries (TCDC).

It was soon realized that regular members of the small staff then available could not be detached as often and as long as was required to do justice to individual regional projects, without weakening the overall capacity of the Programme. On the other hand, some requests for assistance from integration groupings or from individual countries planning to intensify their regional economic efforts were of a short-term nature requiring an immediate response, rather than the time-consum-

---

[1] For the report of the Team, see *Journal of Development Planning*, No. 7 (United Nations publication, Sales No. 74.II.A.3).

ing formulation of a long-term project. Moreover, it was soon recognized that similar problems tended to arise—albeit in different forms—in integration groupings around the developing world. UNCTAD's particular strength lay in its ability to transmit the experience of the older groupings (particularly those in Latin America) to the newer ones being created in Africa, Asia and the Caribbean.

In order to give UNCTAD's technical assistance capacity the required flexibility to meet the above-mentioned needs UNDP was approached for aid in setting up a small team of highly-qualified inter-regional advisers with experience relevant to integration problems, who would be linguistically and culturally capable of working in more than one, if not all, major developing regions. At a later stage this inter-regional team was supplemented by a Latin American regional advisory service financed through a UNDP regional project. Regional advisers were never provided for the African and Asian regions as a whole, but subregional projects, such as one (still continuing at the time of writing) in support of the Economic Community of West African States (ECOWAS) was staffed for many years by a full-time adviser based in Geneva.

Intergovernmental guidance in the formulation of UNCTAD's work programme prior to 1977

From 1968 to 1977 guidance for what was then called UNCTAD's work programme on "trade expansion, economic co-operation and regional integration among developing countries" was couched in very general terms, and formed part of broad and largely uncontroversial declarations of support by the international community which were negotiated without much difficulty at the third and fourth sessions of the Conference. Beyond these quadrennial Conference resolutions and occasional deliberations by the Trade and Development Board, the Programme was the subject of only one *ad hoc* intergovernmental group, convened in November 1970, which did not, however, affect the day-to-day work of the Programme (re-christened a "Division" following UNCTAD III in 1972).

Already then the focus of intergovernmental discussions at the Conference and the Trade and Development Board was turned away from the substance of trade expansion and regional integration towards the issue of external support on the part of the international community at large, and the developed countries in particular, thereby following the general North-South mould of UNCTAD deliberations. Although this negotiating theme placed undue weight on what was probably a marginal issue for the real success of ECDC, the UNCTAD secretariat retained a broad mandate under the terms of Board resolution 53 (VIII) adopted without dissent in February 1969. This resolution permitted research to be undertaken on a wide range of relevant subjects, seminars to be organized and information to be disseminated in non-specified ways. On the operational side, the secretariat was empowered to set up advisory services and to convene working parties of potential donors for the purpose of obtaining support for valid ECDC projects. This hotly debated portion of the resolution, promoted by a handful of developed countries, has never been used, but presumably it is still available for use by those who remember its existence.

MEXICO CITY PROGRAMME ON ECDC AND THE ESTABLISHMENT
OF A COMMITTEE ON ECDC

During the 1970s the priority attached to individual elements of UNCTAD's work programme was often measured by the existence of a separate committee to deal with it. To emphasize the importance it attached to ECDC, the Third Ministerial Meeting of the Group of 77 (Manila, January/February 1976), assembled to prepare for UNCTAD IV, decided to press for the establishment of a Committee on ECDC. In contrast to previous attempts to establish new committees (Shipping, Transfer of Technology), this attempt was accepted by the Board (October 1976) with little or no opposition on the part of the developed countries. In the meantime, a conference of developing countries on ECDC had been convened by the Government of Mexico in the capital city of that country, from which an ambitious action programme emerged, but for the implementation of which no permanent machinery receiving its mandate from the developing countries existed.

At the inaugural session of the new ECDC Committee early in 1977, the developing countries submitted the Mexico City Programme of Action to serve as the guideline for UNCTAD's ECDC work programme. At this juncture a birth defect of the new Committee became readily apparent, in the sense that the developing countries interpreted the mandate of the Committee as being limited to a discussion of support measures for a work programme, the substantive contents of which were considered to lie within the exclusive jurisdiction of the countries directly concerned, i.e., the developing countries themselves. This interpretation of the Committee's terms of reference was contested by the developed countries, who insisted upon the right of the Committee to deliberate and decide on the relative merits and priorities to be attached to individual aspects of the expanded ECDC work programme upon which UNCTAD was about to embark.

In the event, it still proved possible to agree on the three following trade-related items drawn from the Mexico City Programme which were henceforth to be given special priority status by UNCTAD: (*a*) the creation of a global system of trade preferences among developing countries (GSTP); (*b*) the promotion of co-operation among State trading organizations (STOs) of developing countries; and (*c*) the establishment of multinational marketing enterprises (MMEs). These new priority areas were to be pursued alongside UNCTAD's previously established fields of work, *inter alia,* subregional, regional and inter-regional economic integration, the promotion of capital flows among developing countries and the promotion of multinational production enterprises.[2] This new work programme constituted a considerable expansion of scope as compared to the concentration on regional integration which had till then determined UNCTAD's work.

The timing of this shift of focus was not entirely fortuitous: (*a*) the euphoria which had surrounded the concept of regional integration in the wake of the historic movement towards European integration and the relatively successful records of

---

[2] Although this field is close to the field of competence of the United Nations Industrial Development Organization (UNIDO), UNCTAD's mandate in the field of integration had obliged it to acquire an expertise in the field of industrial co-operation without which trade expansion would be meaningless in the case of several groupings devoid of an industrial base.

several third world integration schemes[3] had given way to disenchantment over the failure of virtually every integration scheme to respect timetables and make progress towards stated objectives, compounded by formal liquidations,[4] effective disactivation[5] or renegotiation of old commitments[6] in the case of some; (*b*) the dramatic success achieved by an interregional grouping such as OPEC in improving its members' terms of trade through a disciplined collective negotiating stance on a single commodity appeared to outweigh by far the modest real advances achieved or likely to be made through complex multi-sectoral regional integration efforts; (*c*) calls for a New International Economic Order (NIEO), made at special sessions of the United Nations General Assembly in 1974 and 1975, appeared to have the ring of reality as far as ECDC was concerned, as members of OPEC recycled a substantial portion of their newly acquired financial wealth to certain less fortunate neighbours and other developing countries further afield; (*d*) by 1977 it had become evident that the North-South dimension of the NIEO would not lead to any concrete results, causing many developing countries to view collective self-reliance as the only feasible alternative; and (*e*) the recession, which had gripped the industrial world in the wake of the first oil crisis in 1973-1974, had turned the developing countries into the most dynamic segment of the world economy, albeit at the cost of increasing indebtedness.

During the period between the elaboration of the work programme by the first session of the ECDC Committee and the series of ECDC meetings convened at the instance of the Arusha Ministerial Meeting (see below), i.e., roughly the three-year period from early 1977 to early 1980, the UNCTAD secretariat prepared and contracted to prepare—both from regular and from UNDP-financed project funds—a vast volume of documents on the three new priority areas of GSTP, STO co-operation and MMEs, as well as on monetary and financial co-operation and multinational production enterprises. Most of these documents were issued as non-sessional documents of the ECDC Committee, but they were used as sessional documents by the developing countries at their regional meetings leading up to the inter-regional Ministerial Meeting at Arusha.

THE ARUSHA PROGRAMME FOR COLLECTIVE SELF-RELIANCE

The factors described above combined to move ECDC to the forefront of developing countries' collective international development strategy. This became evident at the fourth Ministerial Meeting of the Group of 77 (Arusha, United Republic of Tanzania, February 1979), which devoted a great deal of attention to the elaboration and revision of the Mexico City Programme into what came to be

---

[3] The number of formulae used for achieving integration is almost as large as the number of integration schemes, to wit: allocation of integration industries by the Central American Common Market, multinational sectoral planning in the Andean Group, the private sector-initiated industrial complementary agreements of the Latin American Free Trade Association, the restructuring of the East African Community supported by a common currency and a multitude of common services to take into account the special needs of its less developed members, the fiscal compensation scheme of the Central African Customs and Economic Union. These are but a few illustrations of this point.

[4] East African Community.

[5] Maghreb, Regional Co-operation for Development, Arab Common Market.

[6] Latin American Free Trade Association.

known as the Arusha Programme for Collective Self-Reliance. In contrast to the procedure adopted at previous Ministerial Meetings of this type, the document on ECDC was no longer a mere appendix of the main position paper dealing with the North-South issues on the agenda of the forthcoming session of UNCTAD, but was placed at the very outset—the centrepiece, as it were—of the report of the meeting.

The Ministerial meeting did not consider the UNCTAD documentation referred to above in any detail, but rather recommended the convening of a substantial number of follow-up meetings by the end of the year 1979, including three inter-regional meetings of governmental experts of the Group of 77 within the framework of UNCTAD to prepare recommendations on each of the three priority areas. Furthermore, the Arusha Programme for Collective Self-Reliance contained a lengthy series of recommendations on other matters falling within UNCTAD's terms of reference, such as regional integration; transfer of technology; least developed, land-locked and island developing countries; monetary and financial co-operation; multinational production enterprises; and technical co-operation among developing countries. In addition to the three above-mentioned meetings, UNCTAD was expected to convene a total of two inter-regional and an unspecified number of regional meetings of economic co-operation groupings. The practical institutional problem as to how all these recommendations were to be implemented was not addressed directly. In effect, the Arusha Programme relied on the United Nations system, and UNCTAD in particular, to undertake the work and to be guided in this respect by periodic Ministerial meetings of the Group of 77.

This inability of the Group of 77 to implement many, if not most of their recommendations requiring substantive secretariat follow-up work, served to sharpen the dilemma that began to plague UNCTAD with the creation of the ECDC Committee and which had not been entirely settled at the time of writing. Essentially, the dilemma centred around the question as to how an organization with a universal membership (and largely financed by the developed countries) could respond to the wishes of the developing countries—as articulated by the Group of 77—in an area of primary, if not exclusive, concern to the latter. While this problem had been sidetracked reasonably well by the ECDC Committee at its inaugural session through a judicious selection of certain areas of study proposed by the Mexico City Conference, the issue assumed a different and politically more sensitive dimension at the fifth session of the Conference (Manila, May 1979), where the Group of 77 attempted to obtain blanket endorsement for the Arusha Programme including its ambitious programme in terms of meetings. Therefore, the ECDC resolution that emerged from UNCTAD V[7] required much harder bargaining than any of the corresponding resolutions at the three preceding sessions of the Conference.[8] The Conference renewed and elaborated portions of the work programme that had been initiated by the ECDC Committee two years earlier by calling for the establishment of a trade information system (TIS) regarding foreign trade of developing countries; the preparation of a handbook of State Trading Organizations (STOs) of developing countries; analysis, identification and promotion of multinational marketing and production ventures among developing countries; as well as

---

[7] Resolution 127 (V).

[8] Concerted declaration 23 (II) and Conference resolutions 48 (III) and 92 (IV).

technical assistance in various forms (training seminars, consultancy services) for STOs, MMEs and in support of monetary and financial co-operation.

The most controversial issue—namely, the convening of the meetings of developing countries requested by the Arusha Programme—was resolved by an *ad hoc* compromise: a special session of the ECDC Committee was to be convened in 1980, and the Secretary-General of UNCTAD was requested "to take measures that would enable the regional groups, particularly the developing countries, to prepare for the special session". More specifically, the Secretary-General of UNCTAD was to provide technical support and other services for "three preparatory meetings of governmental experts of developing countries" and similar meetings that might be requested by "other regional groups". These meetings were to deal with each of the three priority areas identified by the Arusha Programme, namely, the global system of trade preferences among developing countries, State trading organizations and multinational marketing enterprises.

During the ensuing months, UNCTAD helped African, Asian and Latin American regional groups of the Group of 77 to secure the necessary financial support from UNDP and helped to organize regional meetings to review the above-mentioned series of studies undertaken by UNCTAD in pursuance of the Mexico City Conference programme, as endorsed by the ECDC Committee. These regional meetings produced the substantive input for what was to become a single (instead of three) inter-regional preparatory meeting of governmental experts of developing countries convened in March/April 1980 in accordance with the Manila resolution. This was the first instance in UNCTAD's history where the secretariat was mandated to issue invitations exclusively to "developing countries". The solution to this sensitive definitive question, which had previously arisen mainly in the relatively mild terms of statistical presentations, was sought and found by the terms of the resolution itself, which had referred to the developing countries as a "regional group". Since the Group of 77 constituted the only functioning group of developing countries within UNCTAD, it was to this group that invitations were extended.

UNCTAD'S DEEPENING INVOLVEMENT WITH THE GLOBAL SYSTEM OF TRADE PREFERENCES (GSTP)

Neither the Mexico City Conference nor the Arusha Programme had singled out any of the three priority areas as meriting special attention by UNCTAD, or for that matter, by the Group of 77 itself. The resolution adopted at UNCTAD V did not even mention the GSTP among the on-going activities which were to be intensified by the UNCTAD secretariat. Nevertheless, the conclusions arrived at by the March/April 1980 interregional meeting of governmental experts made it clear that henceforth the GSTP was to attract the primary attention of the Geneva chapter of the Group of 77.

This concentration of interest on the GSTP was reflected in the institutional recommendations forwarded to the special session of the ECDC Committee,[9] the most important of which was the decision to establish a GSTP Committee by July 1980 or as soon as possible thereafter. This Committee was to be open only to

---

[9] TD/B/C.7/AC.1/3.

members of the Group of 77 and implemented for their benefit, and it was to be serviced both substantively and technically by the UNCTAD secretariat, a request which the ECDC Committee was expected to endorse. The GSTP Committee's work was to be divided into a preparatory phase and a negotiating phase, the latter to start by early 1981 at the latest.

Detailed terms of reference were set out for the new Committee, whose mandate was to be far more ambitious in terms of its fields of competence and policy instruments to be covered than any international trade negotiating round ever undertaken. The "integrated" approach proposed was to cover traditional tariff concessions, non-tariff concessions and other unspecified measures in the fields of production, marketing, payments and transport. Subregional, regional and inter-regional integration groupings were to be involved both in the preparatory and negotiating phases and were to be simultaneously strengthened and linked. Special non-reciprocal measures were envisaged for least developed, land-locked and island developing countries. The policy instruments envisaged to bring all this about were equally comprehensive: they included national indicative targets for increased bilateral and multilateral trade; special negotiating techniques for achieving concessions on quantitative restrictions; direct trade measures, such as long-term contracts; sectoral negotiations; development-oriented rules of origin; safeguards clauses; protection for infant industries and against unfair competition. The product coverage of the proposed GSTP was no less comprehensive than the wide range of policy measures, covering both manufactures as well as crude and processed commodities, including agricultural products.

Last, but perhaps most important with the benefit of hindsight, was the proposal to establish a trade information system (TIS) to support the GSTP, the only portion of the vast GSTP programme which had moved from the deliberative to the operational phase at the time of writing.

Recommendations concerning the remaining two priority areas (STOs and MMEs) further encouraged the on-going work of UNCTAD in these fields.

At its twentieth session, occurring simultaneously with the above-mentioned interregional meeting, the Trade and Development Board had meanwhile approved up to four weeks of meetings for "governmental experts of regional groups, in particular of developing countries" to be allocated to ECDC. Thus, the principle of such non-universal meetings deliberating in their own right was now agreed without the pretence that they were merely to serve as preparatory meetings for the ECDC Committee as a whole.

The subsequent special session of the ECDC Committee, which met in June 1980, could not agree on a revised ECDC work programme for UNCTAD, which therefore remained formally frozen in its 1977 formulation.

The clearance given by the Board for further meetings of governmental experts of developing countries on ECDC effectively allowed the latter to promote GSTP under UNCTAD auspices, for this was the only substantive item on the agenda of the three meetings of these governmental experts held in December 1980, May 1981 and July 1982 respectively. For the first two of these meetings the UNCTAD secretariat continued to respond to requests for studies,[10] though at a somewhat

---

[10] See, for example, TD/B/C.7/36 and Add. 1-3, TD/B/C.7/42, TD/B/C.7/45, TD/B/C.7/46, TD/B/C.7/47 and Add.1 and TD/B/C.7/48.

slower rhythm than had been true prior to the March/April 1980 meeting. After the May 1981 meeting, no further substantive studies were requested or prepared. However, the UNDP-financed TIS project, originally conceived as a support mechanism for the GSTP, was formally approved in May 1982. It began to operate as early as September 1981 and has steadily improved its ability to respond to queries concerning developing countries' trade regimes, even if such queries were unrelated to the GSTP.

Substantively the long series of meetings of governmental experts had not brought the GSTP to the negotiating phase by the time of writing, although that phase was to have begun as early as January 1981. In effect, recommendations were shuttled back and forth between the experts and senior advisers in Geneva to the policy-makers meeting in New York and Caracas, adding little of substance to what had been agreed upon at the interregional meeting of March/April. A declaration drafted at the last of the three meetings of governmental experts was duly endorsed by the Ministers of Foreign Affairs of the Group of 77 (New York, October 1982).[11] This declaration formally established a GSTP Committee to be supported by the UNCTAD secretariat with roughly the same terms of reference as had been agreed to at the early 1980 meeting and called for this Committee to meet not later than April 1983.[12] The first negotiating phase was to be concluded by 1985.

Soon after the foreign ministers of the Group of 77 had given a new endorsement for the launching of the GSTP, the issue was brought before the twenty-fifth session of the Board and led to what was then the most serious confrontation on ECDC in UNCTAD's history, since the broad question of creating non-universal negotiating groups was now being addressed directly. After a consensus resolution seemed to be within reach, an earlier draft resolution of the Group of 77 was submitted to a vote and adopted.[13] This was the first time that an ECDC issue had had to be submitted to a vote in the Board. In fact, non-universal negotiating groups were never formally convened and only a non-controversial portion was implemented, which called for a special meeting comprising all members of UNCTAD to be convened, for the purpose of "enabling the developing countries participating in the negotiations on a GSTP, *inter alia,* to define the nature, scope and extent of the support requested from UNCTAD".

This meeting, whose official title comprised the entire phrase quoted in the preceding paragraph, was duly held in May 1983 and decided to relegate the entire issue to the next meeting of the ECDC Committee, which was to be convened after the sixth session of the Conference, ending five full years of dormancy since its previous regular session.

The sixth session of UNCTAD held in June 1983 produced resolution 139 (VI) without much difficulty, since it added nothing to the work programme adopted by the ECDC Committee in 1977, in expectation of the forthcoming session of that Committee.

---

[11] See A/37/544, annex.

[12] At the time of writing, the GSTP Committee had not yet been convened, nor had it met again under the old label of "meeting of governmental experts of developing countries on ECDC".

[13] The voting on resolution 264 (XXV) went along straight group lines, with most members of the Groups of 77, B and D voting for, against and abstaining, respectively.

The third session of the Committee, which met in September/October 1983, decided to put aside a resolution on the GSTP that did not seem likely to obtain agreement and to concentrate on a broader resolution dealing with the overall ECDC work programme of UNCTAD. This work programme, contained in resolution 2 (III) of the Committee, places far more emphasis on monetary and financial co-operation among developing countries than theretofore, giving this aspect of the work a status of parity with the area of trade expansion and promotion. Apart from a new emphasis on trade in foodstuffs, trade expansion was to cover the three long-standing priority areas of GSTP, STOs and MMEs, as well as multinational production enterprises and the traditional area of economic integration. The newly emphasized side of monetary and financial co-operation was considerably elaborated as compared with the 1977 resolution, in the sense that the 1983 resolution contains specific mandates on export credit and export credit guarantee schemes, a bank of developing countries, and the promotion and facilitation of capital flows among developing countries. Beyond that the resolution endorsed on-going work in the field of economic integration and called for two meetings of economic integration secretariats.

This consensus resolution by the Committee proved to be the lull before the storm that broke out barely a week later, when the Trade and Development Board was once again confronted with the GSTP issue. This time the draft resolution was brief and unambiguous: it simply requested the Secretary-General of UNCTAD to make provision for four weeks of meetings to enable developing countries to continue work towards the GSTP, which had not been named *expressis verbis* in the controversial 1982 Board resolution. This draft was also put to a vote and adopted as resolution 274 (XXVII). For the first time in UNCTAD's history, Group B was absent during the vote. Follow-up action was similar to the practice followed in the wake of resolution 264 (XXV), in the sense that only a universal "Meeting enabling the developing countries participating in the negotiations on a global system of trade preferences among developing countries to continue the necessary work towards the establishment of the system" was formally convened in May 1984. However, the usual group meetings serviced by UNCTAD, as part and parcel of its servicing of the larger formal meetings to which they are related, did permit the Group of 77 to discuss the GSTP amongst themselves and led to the circulation of a series of working papers describing in greater detail the Group's planned negotiating framework.

The Caracas Programme of Action: the decentralization of ECDC activities by the Group of 77

The increasing demands made on UNCTAD's ECDC intergovernmental machinery by the GSTP from early 1980 onwards affected not only the ECDC programme, but UNCTAD as a whole. For instance: (*a*) the attention devoted to a single ECDC sub-programme restricted UNCTAD's capacity—particularly that of its intergovernmental machinery—to make progress in other ECDC sub-programmes; (*b*) the abandonment by the Trade and Development Board of the principle of consensus in two successive years in favour of majority decisions tended to permeate the Organization as a whole with a spirit of confrontation, which had been deliberately discarded in the mid-1960s, once it had become apparent that numerous far-reaching resolutions adopted at UNCTAD I by majority vote had remained dead letters.

Up to the Ministerial Meeting of the Group of 77 (Arusha, February 1979), UNCTAD's central role in promoting ECDC in its interregional dimension was uncontested, all the more so as the parallel efforts of the Non-Aligned Movement had lost momentum for lack of a permanent central secretariat and insufficient resources. But the difficulties encountered in relation to the GSTP at UNCTAD V and during the ensuing period on UNCTAD's capacity to fulfil its role as the focal point for ECDC helped to shift the focus of the Group of 77's ECDC efforts to United Nations Headquarters. Since 1980, the New York chapter had assumed a co-ordinating role for the Group's operational activities in ECDC, whereas previously it had largely contented itself with a supporting role, consisting of political support for annual General Assembly resolutions on ECDC. The disability of the New York chapter in not having a specialized ECDC Division within the United Nations Headquarters Secretariat to rely upon was initially offset by drawing on the services of several United Nations departments and agencies (including UNCTAD) through the various chapters of the Group in Geneva, Vienna and Rome.[14] In this manner, the New York chapter of the Group of 77 was able to prepare the background documentation for the High-Level conference on ECDC, which was held in Caracas in May 1981 at the invitation of the Venezuelan Government. Having been organized and inspired by personalities and groups different from those that had guided the Mexico City and Arusha Conferences, it was not surprising that the comprehensive Action Programme that emerged from Caracas[15] restricted UNCTAD's role to the trade sector and to a modest portion of the finance sector, equating UNCTAD's ECDC role with that of several other agencies, whose ECDC experience had been of narrower scope and more recent standing. The tasks assigned to UNCTAD were essentially the continuation of on-going work in the three priority areas discussed above (GSTP, STOs and MMEs) as well as the longstanding but so far unsuccessful efforts to establish an export credit guarantee facility.[16]

In contrast to previous action plans devised by the Group of 77 on ECDC, the Caracas Programme made provisions for follow-up at both the sectoral and the inter-sectoral levels, with responsibility for certain sectors assigned to individual chapters of the Group of 77. Moreover, the Chairman of the Group in New York was given the responsibility for helping to organize the annual follow-up and co-ordination meetings. To assist him in this task, he was given a core of assistants drawn from a specified number of Permanent Missions to the United Nations in New York and limited voluntary financial support in the form of a "Group of 77 Account for ECDC" in New York.

---

[14] Moreover, the fact that Ministerial Meetings of the Group of 77 had become a regular sideline feature of the annual General Assembly sessions in New York gave the Group's New York chapter the regular political support of which the Geneva chapter had always been deprived.

[15] A/36/333 and Corr.1, annex.

[16] A trade-related initiative in the field of services was assigned to the Geneva chapter of the Group of 77 but without reference to UNCTAD. This recommendation was followed up at a meeting held in Guatemala City early in 1984 with limited support from the UNCTAD secretariat.

Meetings of the Intergovernmental Follow-up and Co-ordination Committee (IFCC) were, in fact, held in Manila and Tunis in August 1982 and September 1983, respectively. The follow-up in the field of trade was limited to a stock-taking of the progress made on the GSTP and on STO co-operation. Regarding the former, 41 States had signified their intention to participate in the negotiations,[17] while in the field of STO co-operation the IFCC was informed of the fact that statutes for the Association of State Trading Organizations (ASTRO) had been worked out and that the minimum membership application of 15 STOs from as many countries were being awaited.[18] Among other subjects falling within UNCTAD's work programme, the IFCC touched upon: (*a*) the South Bank, with regard to which UNCTAD and UNIDO were invited to complete a feasibility study undertaken by a group of experts assembled in the International Center for Public Enterprises at Ljubljana, Yugoslavia, in August/September 1983; and (*b*) the desirability of active participation by secretariats of economic co-operation and integration groupings in the Informal Contact Group which had been set up in June 1982 under UNCTAD auspices by a Working Party of such groupings.

B. Principal policy initiatives: description, results and evaluation

ECONOMIC INTEGRATION

Economic integration was the core activity at the beginning of UNCTAD's work in the field of ECDC. From its outset in 1968, the Special Programme on Trade Expansion, Economic Co-operation and Regional Integration among Developing Countries, concentrated on technical assistance to developing countries in the creation of new integration groupings or programmes, even before UNCTAD had become an executing agency of UNDP. At an early stage, a small nucleus of highly qualified technical advisers was also established to assist economic integration groupings in solving specific problems arising in matters of trade liberalization, industrial integration or monetary co-operation.

These field activities showed that there were a number of common problems of interest to several integration groupings, which warranted the conduct of intensive research and a comparison of the experiences made by some groupings with a variety of instruments and techniques tried out to solve them. Consequently, a series of studies entitled "Current problems of economic integration" were carried out in support of UNCTAD's technical assistance programme on economic integration. A study on Industrial Integration Systems[19] contained a comparative analysis of experiences made with industrial integration instruments by integration groupings of all regions; and attempted to formulate some guidelines for the solution of industrial allocation problems in regional groupings. A parallel study in the same volume dealt with the expansion of agricultural trade in groupings of devel-

---

[17] This number had risen to 51 at the same time of writing.

[18] Thirteen STOs from eight countries had applied at the time of writing.

[19] TD/B/374 (United Nations publication, Sales No. 72.II.D.6).

oping countries. Substantial emphasis in this study programme was laid on the problem of distribution of benefits and cost of economic integration, including such aspects as measurement, selective corrective measures, fiscal compensation, etc.[20] Other studies dealt with the role of institutions in regional integration[21] and a series of trade policy issues such as the role of State trading in economic integration,[22] the relations between the generalized system of preferences (GSP) and economic integration,[23] the effects of reverse preferences (which were then still being granted by some developing countries to their former metropolitan countries) on economic integration[24] and the role of transnational corporations in the Latin American integration groupings.[25] In several instances, the research results were followed up by regional seminars or were applied outright through technical assistance to individual groupings confronted with the specific problem at that juncture.

Technical assistance projects financed by the United Nations Development Programme (UNDP) were implemented in support of virtually every regional and subregional integration organization in the developing world. Such assistance included the analysis of trade liberalization schemes, studies on common external tariffs, reform of customs practices, fiscal harmonization, financial and monetary co-operation, industrial co-operation, feasibility studies on regional importation schemes as well as institutional support in the establishment and setting up of work programmes of some of the organizations or secretariats concerned.

Illustrations of on-going regional or sub-regional projects in Africa are: (*a*) a large-scale project covering several aspects of integration in support of the Economic Community of West African States (ECOWAS); (*b*) smaller projects for the West African Economic Community (CEAO), the Central African Customs and Economic Union (UDEAC), the Mano River Union (MRU); and, (*c*) more recently, assistance for the establishment of a Preferential Trade Area (PTA) among East and Southern African States which is being undertaken in co-operation with the Economic Commission for Africa (ECA). In Latin America and the Caribbean, financed with extra-budgetary funds from the United Nations Development Programme, assistance was given, particularly in the earlier years, to the Central American Common Market (CACM/SIECA); the Andean Group's Board of the Cartagena Agreement (JUNAC); the Caribbean Common Market (CARICOM) as well as the Latin American Free Trade Association (LAFTA), which subsequently became the Latin American Integration Association (ALADI). In Asia and the Pacific, the principal on-going projects are in support of the Trade Negotiations Group (TNG) and the Bangkok Agreement—both headquartered at the Economic

---

[20] See TD/B/394 (United Nations publication, Sales No. E.75.II.D.12), TD/B/517 (Sales No. E.75.II.D.10) and TD/B/322/Rev.1 (Sales No. 71.II.D.6).

[21] TD/B/422, *Current problems of economic integration—Institutional Aspects of regional integration among developing countries* (United Nations publication, Sales No. 73.II.D.10).

[22] TD/B/436, *Current problems of economic integration—State trading and regional economic integration among developing countries* (United Nations publication, Sales No. E.73.II.D.17).

[23] TD/B/471, *Current problems of economic integration—The effects of the generalized system of preferences on economic integration among developing countries* (United Nations publication, Sales No. E.74.II.D.13).

[24] TD/B/435, *Current problems of economic integration—The effects of reverse preferences on trade among developing countries,* (United Nations publication, Sales No. 73.II.D.18).

[25] See, for example, TD/B/C.7/38 and UNCTAD/ST/ECDC/19.

and Social Commission for Asia and the Pacific (ESCAP)—and the Association of South-East Asian Nations (ASEAN).

A team of regional and interregional advisers initially financed by UNDP, later by the United Nations Regular Porgramme for Technical Co-operation and finally by UNCTAD's regular budget provided rapid *ad hoc* assistance upon request in integration and economic co-operation fields both at the national level and to the regional or subregional groupings in all the geographical regions concerned. Although their assistance included the identification and promotion of new projects for financing by UNDP, their principal activity consisted in acting as a bridge between UNCTAD headquarters, where they were stationed, and the regional or subregional integration groupings, where they were able to obtain deeper insights into the inner workings and problems faced by each in trade and other integration matters. UNCTAD's co-operation with ASEAN, the Latin American Economic System (SELA), ECOWAS and the Mano River Union are but a few examples of projects deriving from the activities of UNCTAD regional and interregional advisers.

With the progressive building up of UNCTAD's activities in the other areas of ECDC and, in particular, increasing support to interregional ECDC programmes, the reduced resources available for economic integration were more oriented to specific projects while the amount of research relevant to all integration groupings was sharply curtailed. UNDP-financed technical assistance projects executed by UNCTAD shifted gradually from institution building and the creation of new groupings, as in the case of the Mano River Union, to the solution of closely defined technical problems arising in the formulation or implementation of sectoral integration measures or programmes. The specialized interregional advisory services attached to UNCTAD but originally financed by UNDP proved particularly useful for assistance to new groupings and those not covered by technical assistance projects. It was probably this type of technical advice that was most appreciated by integration groupings. It was also relatively more successful than the attempts of the early period aimed at launching new groupings or the drafting of new integration treaties. Such sectoral assistance activities have included the preparation and implementation of trade liberalization programmes, including the origin rules and other customs devices required for their implementation; the establishment of common external tariffs; customs co-operation and customs training; trade policy measures in support of industrial integration, including assistance in the harmonization of investment codes and fiscal measures; the formulation of arrangements for the promotion of industrial co-operation; and monetary and financial co-operation and integration. More recently, technical support to integration groupings has relied increasingly on expertise available within the UNCTAD secretariat as a whole and has included assistance such as feasibility studies of regional and coastal shipping lines, insurance co-operation and co-operation in the transfer and the development of technology.

Since 1981, new impulses have been given to the Programme on Economic Integration by the creation of a separate organizational unit within the ECDC Division in charge of this Programme. Since then more attention has been paid to strengthening co-operation among economic co-operation and integration groupings; a reorientation towards sectors of current priority interest for developing countries and their groupings, such as energy; a renewed interest in research on perennial problems of crucial importance to the success of economic integration; and the exploration of possible interest and benefits that groupings may derive from a more active participation in regional and interregional ECDC programmes and projects. The first result of the latter was the establishment of a Programme for Co-operation among Economic Co-operation and Integration Groupings among Developing Countries under the guidance of an Informal Contact Group of Secretariats, which was set up as an institutional mechanism to ensure follow-up,[26] and which met in 1982, 1983 and again in 1984.

In the implementation of this programme for co-operation among groupings, which is designed to promote the exchange of information and of experiences as well as mutual technical co-operation, a meeting on energy co-operation has been held; another one dealing with problems encountered in the promotion and financing of integration projects was convened in June 1984. Particular attention is also paid to the acute problems encountered by a substantial number of integration groupings at the present juncture, due to a variety of unresolved internal and external problems, some of which are largely political, but all of which are exacerbated by the international economic crisis which in turn breeds monetary and debt problems for many individual member States.

The economic integration programme has probably been the most useful contribution that UNCTAD has made in the field of ECDC in terms of (*a*) the practical implementation of intergovernmental resolutions passed over the years; (*b*) the capacity to respond to real and perceived needs for technical assistance both by established and incipient integration groupings; and (*c*) its unique ability to act as an interregional clearing house permitting it to apply experiences gathered by regional groupings in one part of the developing world to similar problems encountered elsewhere.

While the Special Programme for Trade Expansion, Economic Co-operation and Regional Integration (TEEI) concentrated its efforts on economic integration, i.e., roughly the period 1968-1975, the instruments chosen to implement it were mutually reinforcing, in the sense that research subjects were chosen in response to needs identified in the course of technical assistance work, whereas the quality of the latter in turn was enriched by the research covering a number of integration groupings, the results of which were generally submitted to groups of experts drawn from high officials of these very groupings.

The members of the interregional advisory (IRA) service, then supported by UNDP, were carefully chosen on the strength of their expertise in a particular sector, such as trade, industry or finance, rather than on the basis of geographical equilibrium among the developing regions as has been the case more recently. The ready availability and quality of the IRA services went a long way to explaining the frequent recourse made to their services by the integration groupings then in existence, and served to build up UNCTAD's reputation as the prime source for such expertise within the United Nations system and beyond.

---

[26] See the report of the Working Party on Trade and Expansion and Regional Economic Integration among Developing Countries (Geneva, 28 June-2 July 1982), TD/B/C.7/55, chap. II.

A further factor of strength in the late 1960s and early 1970s was the personal involvement of UNCTAD staff members in the research and technical assistance activities [27] of the TEEI programme. This direct participation by staff members permitted research results and experience gathered in the course of technical assistance work to accumulate within the secretariat. Such benefits no longer accrue to the same extent under the more recent practice of farming out of major research and virtually all technical assistance projects to external consultants, thereby limiting many staff members' role to the conceptualization and "management" of research and to the administrative "backstopping" for technical assistance projects.

Any evaluation of UNCTAD's efforts in the field of economic integration cannot but note the severe reduction of the human resources allocated to this sub-programme, not only in relative, but even in absolute terms.

Monetary and financial co-operation

The principal conceptual effort undertaken in this area dates back to the founding years of the organization, when the idea of monetary co-operation among a limited number of developing countries ran against the conventional wisdom that saw such groupings as a step backward from the path towards the objective of global current account convertibility enshrined in Article VIII of the Articles of Agreement of the International Monetary Fund (IMF).

The general line of the argumentation favouring payments arrangements among developing countries was summarized in the first conclusion reached by the Group of Experts, which stated: "Payments arrangements in general... could make a positive contribution in varying degrees towards the expansion of trade among developing countries".[28] The experts also expressed a preference for arrangements containing credit facilities, conscious of the implicit discrimination that such credit facilities would create over and above the accompanying trade preferences. Drawing heavily on the experience of the post-war European Payments Union (EPU), the early studies favoured the creation of central reserve funds for these payments arrangements, for which partial external financing was warmly recommended.

Since the basic objective of these arrangements was to support mutual trade expansion, and given the largely intraregional pattern of trade among developing countries at that time, it stood to reason that neither the UNCTAD secretariat nor the various groups of experts wished to pronounce themselves as categorically in favour of global payments arrangements as was to be the case in later years, e.g., by the Report of the Commission on International Development ("Pearson Commission"). More recently these ambitious pronouncements have given way to calls for links among existing payments arrangements.

While the differences of approach between UNCTAD and the IMF on the overall question of payments arrangements was more a matter of emphasis than of

---

[27] In the case of longer missions, staff members were actually seconded to, and paid by, extra-budgetary project resources.

[28] See *Payments Arrangements among the Developing Countries for Trade Expansion. Report of the Group of Experts* (TD/B/80/Rev.1) (United Nations publication, Sales No. 67.II.D.6), para. 81, and subsequent secretariat studies (TD/B/112 and TD/B/AC.10/4), *passim*.

basic principle, the seeds for a more direct confrontation were laid by the above-mentioned Group of Experts when it recommended selective quota increases for developing countries pursuing mutual trade expansion policies.[29] Another UNCTAD initiative in the same direction that was fiercely—and successfully—resisted by the Fund proposed the establishment of a "special drawing facility to meet deficits arising out of liberalization commitments that further the integration process".[30]

Another ECDC initiative involving multilateral financial institutions (MFIs) more generally was the attempt to analyse the importance that these institutions attached to the financing of multinational projects. The study[31] showed that multinational projects, even when broadly defined, constituted a small fraction of the MFIs' overall portfolios, particularly in the case of the global and regional institutions. However, even the subregional MFIs which are linked to integration groupings and whose charters enjoin them to favour multinational projects tended to allocate the bulk of their resources to purely national projects. The conclusions of this study were submitted to a meeting of representatives of the MFIs to discuss possible countermeasures that might help to overcome what were seen to be built-in obstacles impeding the identification and promotion of integration and other multinational projects. Although the Conference did include a recommendation on this subject in its resolution 92 (IV), paragraph (e), no practical follow-up occurred in the 10 subsequent years.[32] However, the matter was considered anew at a joint meeting of integration and co-operation groupings with MFIs convened by UNCTAD in mid-1984.

The accumulation of spendable and loanable funds by a certain number of oil-exporting developing countries from 1973 onwards induced the UNCTAD secretariat to undertake a major data-gathering effort on the official financial flows from the 10 main OPEC donor countries to other developing countries and MFIs, as well as the flows from MFIs controlled by these OPEC donors to developing countries. This effort was undertaken at the request and with the financial support of the OPEC Special Fund, the predecessor of the OPEC Fund for International Development (OFID). The studies, covering the periods 1973-1975[33] and 1973-1976 respectively,[34] represented the most comprehensive compilation of OPEC's aid and other official financial flows available at the time. They were designed to

---

[29] *Payments Arrangements among the Developing Countries for Trade Expansion*, para. 88.

[30] See the report by the UNCTAD secretariat, "International policies on payments arrangements among developing countries" (TD/B/AC.10/4), para. 98. The proposal was endorsed by Conference resolution 48 (III), para. 8.

[31] A. Fuentes-Mohr, "The role of multilateral financial institutions in promoting economic integration projects in developing countries" (Part two of *The role of multilateral financial institutions in promoting integration among developing countries*) (TD/B/531) (United Nations publication, Sales No. E.75.II.D.5.)

[32] Two follow-up studies were prepared between 1982 and 1984 (TD/B/C.7/64 and UNCTAD/ST/ECDC/23(2)), the latter of which estimated the share of inter-country projects and institutions financed by the World Bank and the International Development Association (IDA) at 0.5 per cent and 0.11 per cent respectively, implying little progress compared to the survey undertaken in 1973.

[33] *Financial solidarity for development—Efforts and institutions of the members of OPEC* (TD/B/627) (United Nations publication, Sales No. E.77.II.D.4).

[34] *Ibid., 1973-1976 review* (TD/B/C.7/31 (vol. I and II)) (United Nations publication, Sales No. E.79.II.D.9).

make UNCTAD the monitoring and policy co-ordination forum concerning these flows, at which both donors and recipients might be represented.[35]

Since 1978 UNCTAD's principal regular activity in the field of monetary co-operation has consisted of the substantive servicing—in its capacity as technical secretariat—of the Co-ordination Committee on Multilateral Payments Arrangements and Monetary Co-operation among Developing Countries. This Committee comprises a total of eight clearing[36] and five credit[37] arrangements. In the Arusha Programme for Collective Self-Reliance the Group of 77 issued a mandate to this Committee to promote linkages among payments arrangements. The Committee did in fact agree on the guidelines and technical arrangements for implementing such linkages at its fourth meeting.[38] Although no meaningful links existed as of 1982, negotiations were under way between the Latin American Integration Association (ALADI) and the Central American Monetary Council with a view towards enabling member countries of the latter to join the credit and clearing arrangements of the former.

In the absence of a clear allocation of responsibilities within the regular staff of the secretariat for this important part of the ECDC programme, continuity has been largely provided by the Interregional Advisory Services (IRA), which have been instrumental in promoting and advising both the Asian Clearing Union (ACU) and the West African Clearing House (WACH), the former of which is operating with a modicum of success. Moreover, UNCTAD has acted as an intermediary for transmitting the long Latin American experience in clearing and credit arrangements to similar more recent arrangements in Africa and Asia by sponsoring study missions in both directions.

At the intergovernmental level, the monetary and financial co-operation among developing countries has found its most practical expression in the large number of regional and subregional MFIs and collective central banks, the abovementioned clearing and credit arrangements and the OPEC-related institutions, some of which have an interregional function (e.g., OFID and the Islamic Development Bank), but which are nevertheless financed and controlled by a limited number of countries. Therefore, the most broadly-based forum for monetary and financial policy co-ordination among developing countries is the Group of 24, which generally meets in conjunction with the annual meetings of the Boards of Governors of the IMF and the World Bank Group. UNCTAD substantively helped

---

[35] A survey covering the period 1973-1981 was issued in 1984 and preparation for a further update covering 1982 and 1983 had begun at the time of writing.

[36] Central American Clearing House, The Latin American Integration Association (ALADI) Payments and Reciprocal Credit System, CARICOM Multilateral Clearing Facility, West Africa Clearing House, Great Lakes Economic Community Monetary Arrangement, Central African Clearing House, Regional Co-operation for Development (RCD), Union for Multilateral Payments Arrangements and Asian Clearing House for a total of 56 member countries (including double memberships).

[37] Central American Stabilization Fund, Santo Domingo Agreement, Andean Reserve Fund, Arab Monetary Fund and ASEAN Swap Arrangement for a total of 47 member countries (including overlapping membership between the Andean Reserve Fund and the Santo Domingo Agreement) and with a potential lending capacity of $2.3 billion approximately.

[38] Final Report of the Fourth Meeting of the Co-ordination Committee on Multilateral Payments Arrangements among Developing Countries, Bridgetown, Barbados, November 1981 (UNCTAD/ST/ECDC/19).

to service the meetings of the Group of 24, when the latter discussed ECDC (Toronto, September 1982) in response to recommendations contained in the Caracas High-Level Conference on ECDC.

In further response to the Caracas mandate and parallel with the discussions by the Group of 24, the Group of 77 organized open-ended meetings of experts on monetary and financial co-operation in Baghdad and Jamaica during 1982, for the latter of which an UNCTAD task force headed by a UNDP-financed consultant prepared about a dozen documents covering a wide range of monetary and financial co-operation issues and proposals on which action might be considered. The proposal receiving most—albeit not quite unanimous—support was the one envisaging the creation of a Bank of Developing Countries (South Bank). Upon governmental endorsement by the Intergovernmental Follow-up and Co-ordination Committee (IFCC) meeting (Manila, August 1982), UNCTAD proceeded to undertake the necessary feasibility study. When the ECDC Committee re-formulated UNCTAD's ECDC work programme in late 1983, confirmation of work on this project was also specifically approved. Further meetings on the South Bank were held in New York during the first half of 1984.

Of all the sub-programmes within ECDC, monetary and financial co-operation is perhaps the one where interregional action has the greatest practical scope in view of the relatively strong institutional base (i.e., the sizable number of financially autonomous MFIs controlled by developing countries) and the particularly strong interdependence of developing countries' overall economic welfare and the international monetary system. If this is so, UNCTAD—as the prime interregional forum for ECDC within the United Nations system—should have promoted this aspect of its ECDC programme with particular vigour. Although fears on the part of the developed market-economy countries that certain of these activities might impinge upon the prerogatives of the IMF could never be entirely dissipated, resolution 1 (I) agreed upon by the ECDC Committee at its first session in 1977 called upon the secretariat to intensify work on "the promotion and facilitation of capital flows among developing countries" and "the establishment of subregional, regional and interregional export credit guarantee schemes". A fair appraisal of the secretariat's response to these two mandates during the period which has elapsed would have to conclude that it has been found wanting in imagination, consistency, vigour and—above all—co-ordination. The consequences of repeated shifting of responsibility for the monitoring of financial flows as between the various secretariat units have already been mentioned. Similar intra-organizational conflicts smouldering unresolved during the preparation for, and the follow-up phase of, the above-mentioned meeting held in Jamaica, considerably weakened the potential impact that UNCTAD might have had at that crucial phase of the deliberations of the Group of 77. As a stop-gap measure a part of the regular staff responsibility was shifted to the Interregional Advisory (IRA) services, whose primary function had never been conceived to undertake or supervise research. Even the 1983 revision of the work programme as mandated by resolution 2 (III) of the ECDC Committee, which placed monetary and financial co-operation among developing countries on an equal footing with trade expansion and promotion, was not followed up by corresponding reallocation of resources. All in all, UNCTAD's impact on monetary and financial co-operation among developing countries was a good deal weaker than it might have been under more consistent direction.

The basic proposal of instituting trade preferences among developing countries—later to be termed the global system of trade preferences (GSTP)—was formally presented at the fourth session of the Conference in 1976.[39] Its objectives were stated as follows "(a) expansion and diversification of trade among the developing countries; (b) development of industrial and other forms of economic cooperation among the developing countries with a view to accelerating their industrialization and general economic growth, and strengthening their collective self-reliance; and (c) the system should also ensure trade advantages for the relatively less advanced countries".[40]

In fact the idea of such mutual trade preferences was much older. First, mutual trade preferences had lain at the heart of virtually every regional and sub-regional integration grouping established in the 1960s and early 1970s. Secondly, a group of 16 developing countries had already signed a "Protocol relating to Trade Negotiations among Developing Countries" within the framework of GATT as early as February 1973. The UNCTAD secretariat had co-serviced and supported the negotiations leading up to the signing of that Protocol. Thirdly, the idea of non-reciprocal global trade preferences by the more advanced in favour of the less advanced developing countries had been proposed, but rejected, at the second session of UNCTAD in 1968 within the context of the negotiations for the generalized system of preferences (GSP) between developed and developing countries.

The rationale for the GSTP was partly founded on that which underlay the GSP, namely, that developing countries faced special obstacles in marketing their exports, particularly the non-traditional ones; these obstacles were to be compensated through preferential market access. Furthermore, developing countries—both oil-exporting and non-oil-exporting—constituted the world's most dynamic importers during the 1970s. It stood to reason that the newly industrializing countries (NICs) should concentrate their export promotion efforts in these new and promising markets. Since many of these markets were—and indeed still are—surrounded by high barriers designed to protect their infant industries and/or their balance of payments, special measures were required to initiate new trade flows, particularly interregional ones, for which no such measures existed apart from the abovementioned GATT Protocol. Last but not least, the GSTP was designed to give concrete expression to developing countries' political commitment to the concept of collective self-reliance.

The shortcomings of the GATT Protocol had long been recognized, particularly the limited number of signatories (none of which were in sub-Saharan Africa); reliance on tariff preference to the exclusion of the multitudinous non-tariff barriers obstructing access to many developing countries' markets; and product coverage limited to manufactured goods. Some of these limitations could have been eliminated by a re-negotiation of the Protocol. If developing countries, nevertheless,

---

[39] "Economic co-operation among developing countries" (TD/192) and "Elements of a preferential system in trade among developing countries" (TD/192/Supp.2) For the printed text of TD/192 see *Proceedings of the United Nations Conference on Trade and Development, Fourth Session*, vol. III—*Basic Document*, (United Nations publication, Sales No. E.76.II.D.12).

[40] TD/191/Supp.2, para. 25.

chose to create a new preferential system that was to replace or exist side by side with the Protocol, the reason must be found first and foremost in the political context in which the GSTP was conceived, namely as a cornerstone of the concept of ECDC, which, in turn, was seen as an essential element of the New International Economic Order (NIEO). Several signatories of the Protocol were not members of the Group of 77—the broadest politically organized grouping of developing countries—and UNCTAD rather than GATT was seen as the proper forum for promoting ECDC and the NIEO. Consequently, these rather than the above-mentioned limitations were the factors determining the decision to make a new start towards a parallel, albeit a far more ambitious and encompassing, preferential trade system for developing countries.

The efforts undertaken by UNCTAD since 1979 towards the GSTP have been sketched above. At the time of writing an evaluation of the GSTP after five years of protracted disagreement must necessarily be qualified by the fact that negotiations have not even started and the likelihood that concrete results in terms of GSTP-induced trade expansion, if any, cannot be expected for several years. On the positive side of the ledger, the GSTP has served to focus attention within UNCTAD on a single issue within the amorphous complex of ECDC issues, most of which hardly lent themselves to negotiations within a universal forum. Moreover, the GSTP was the justification for establishing a trade information system (TIS) within the UNCTAD secretariat which was to serve as the United Nations system's central data bank on trade barriers of developing countries. On the negative side, the GSTP has served to lessen, if not eliminate, support for ECDC by the developed market-economy countries within UNCTAD. It has also virtually stopped progress on the GATT Protocol, which had the dual virtue of being in force and of enjoying the political support of the developed market-economy countries.

The main test for the GSTP will come when extra-budgetary resources are placed at UNCTAD's disposal to conduct what must certainly be complex negotiations among a relatively large number of countries seeking mutual concessions on a vast array of trade obstacles. With the removal of what have hitherto been the political obstacles hindering progress towards the GSTP, the economic and technical problems surrounding the GSTP will have to be surmounted. A comparison between the latter and those surrounding the multilateral trade negotiations (MTN) conducted by the major trading countries in the so-called Tokyo rounds under GATT auspices from 1973 to 1979 illustrates the challenge facing prospective GSTP negotiators and the secretariat servicing them. The major participants in the MTN were few in number; they were supported by large teams of technical specialists based at home and in Geneva with ready access to information on the trade barriers of their negotiating partners; they had fairly clear instructions on their own margins of negotiating manœuvre; emphasis was laid on quantifiable tariffs rather than on prohibitions, licensing procedures and payments obstacles; reciprocity was the rule governing the negotiations; and a sizable secretariat with a long experience in servicing trade negotiations was available to the negotiators. None of these conditions are likely to apply to the GSTP.

Given the history of the matter, it may be necessary to conduct the GSTP in a "political" manner, thereby eschewing detailed technical approaches, the solution of which might cost some countries more in terms of human and financial resources than the net economic returns to be expected from such protracted negotiations.

Co-operation among State trading organizations (STOs)

The rationale justifying the promotion of this sub-programme was based on the following propositions: (a) that the public sector constitutes a major factor in the foreign trade of virtually all developing countries; (b) that a trade policy reorientation in the direction of more South-South trade could be more readily and effectively implemented through STOs, whose decision-making was subject to governmental influence, than would be possible through passive measures, such as preferential tariffs and other incentives offered to private traders; and (c) that STOs were better placed than private traders to finance the relatively high initial costs involved in opening up new markets, which would only show returns in the medium or long terms. The sub-programme was never intended to promote the role of the public sector in developing countries' foreign trade at the expense of the private sector.

The principal activities which UNCTAD has undertaken—generally in cooperation with the International Trade Centre UNCTAD/GATT and other institutions—in furtherance of its STO co-operation programme are: (a) the publication of a handbook containing essential data on 330 STOs in 70 developing countries; (b) training courses in both English and French directed particularly at medium-level officials of African STOs; (c) promotion of technical co-operation among STOs through on-the-job training of officials from smaller and younger STOs at the headquarters of more experienced and larger STOs; (d) support for regional co-operation in Asia and Latin America, in both of which research was undertaken on possibilities for co-operation in a number of major commodities, the results of which were submitted to regional STO meetings (Lima, 1979 and Jakarta, 1982);[41] (e) research on commodities having potential for interregional trade expansion as well as on issues having particular relevance to the problems facing STOs in expanding their trade links with other developing countries (e.g. the problems posed by restrictive conditions attached to developed countries' official development assistance and the effects of counter-trade on the ability of developing countries to bid successfully in STO tenders); and (f) support for a new interregional Association of State Trading Organizations of Developing Countries (ASTRO), which is in the process of formation, with a temporary secretariat at the headquarters of the International Center for Public Enterprises in Ljubljana, Yugoslavia, and which is expected to act as the central institution guiding UNCTAD's future efforts in this area.

To the extent that STOs already existed around the developing world, this sub-programme was able to address a real and active audience and did not have to devote all its efforts to institution-building, which hampered several other ECDC sub-programmes. On the other hand, the above-mentioned propositions, on which the sub-programme had been predicated, failed to take account of: (a) the priority which the more successful STOs must attach to purely commercial considerations, which often appear to conflict with longer-term objectives set by their governments favouring more trade and co-operation with STOs of other developing countries; (b) the low level of professionalism, the lack of incentives and the high personnel turnover rate prevailing in many STOs, all of which tend to reduce the potential for

---

[41] One of these research papers, dealing with cement, led to the convening of a specialized meeting in Istanbul early in 1983, at which, in turn, it was decided to set up an Asian Cement Association.

new orientations and practices; and (c) the disenchantment with State trading in the wake of the major crisis of recent years, which in turn has led to frequent re-organization (and sometimes even the liquidation) of STOs, accompanied by a general turning away from single-channel trading.

The time may have come for UNCTAD to discard the distinction between State and private trading and to concentrate on those institutions which are most likely to bring about the new trade orientations. It must not be forgotten that STO co-operation was conceived merely as an instrument for such changes and not as an end in itself.

MULTINATIONAL MARKETING ENTERPRISES (MMEs)

The rationale behind the idea of promoting MMEs among developing countries is (a) to reduce these countries' dependence on the international firms for the marketing of their main commodities and to help them regain a measure of influence on pricing decisions of which such dependence deprives them; (b) to recoup the often excessive profit margins separating producers' prices from the prices paid by the wholesalers and retailers in the importing country; and (c) to help exporting countries diversify their markets, including other developing countries.

Some impetus in this direction has been achieved by certain Latin American exporters of bananas, fertilizers and handicraft products, for each of which MMEs have been or are about to be created, in the case of the latter two products through the efforts of *ad hoc* Action Committees established by the Latin American Economic System (SELA). The oldest among these MMEs is COMUNBANA, established in 1977 through the Union of Banana Exporting Countries (UPEB), which has attempted to find markets for its members' banana exports in Eastern Europe, but has not tried to compete in the traditional markets of North America and Western Europe. Regional and interregional meetings of developing countries have identified a long list of items which would lend themselves to similar efforts either on a regional or an interregional scale, depending on the product in question.

UNCTAD promoted the concept of MMEs through: (a) studies analysing the juridical and financial implications of such enterprises; (b) regional inventories of existing enterprises, of which the one on Latin America was published; and (c) African and Asian regional studies identifying possibilities for establishing MMEs designed to engage in joint import procurement. Beyond these research activities, the UNCTAD secretariat implemented UNDP-financed technical assistance projects in the Asian and Pacific region designed to promote the establishment of MMEs for tropical timber, fisheries, spices and natural rubber.

The promotion of MMEs requires highly specialized and on-going field work in closely defined commodity sectors, including continuous contacts with producers and exporters of these commodities in a limited number of countries at a time. By its very nature, such activity does not lend itself to interregional negotiations at the governmental level. Although intergovernmental bodies, such as the Group of 77, should be made aware of the potential interest of this sub-programme to their ECDC objectives, the principal actors to implement these schemes must be the producers and exporters of both the private and public sectors of the selected countries as well as their subregional and regional organizations. This implies substantial extra-budgetary resources for field operations but so far UNCTAD has not been able to mobilize such support to the extent required.

MULTINATIONAL PRODUCTION ENTERPRISES (MPEs) AND JOINT VENTURES (JVs)

The value of multinational production enterprises[42] flows primarily from the fact that they can facilitate the flow of capital, equipment, technology, managerial and marketing skills from countries which have these resources in relative abundance to those in need of such facilities. Multinational enterprises may also contribute towards the creation of a relatively large and efficient production and export base for a country or group of countries allowing for economies of scale to be realized and relatively greater value added shares to be earned. MPEs could also strengthen developing countries' bargaining position *vis-à-vis* the developed countries' transnational corporations in the area of technology transfers. A recent study undertaken at Harvard University[43] has identified 833 manufacturing joint ventures based in developing countries and as many as 2,000 subsidiaries. These joint ventures tend to originate in developing countries having a relatively large industrial base or capital surplus.

In compliance with its mandate, the UNCTAD secretariat prepared four regional studies on joint ventures in 1975 and convened a group of experts in the same year to consider them. In 1979-1980, consultations were undertaken with governments of developing countries to ascertain their interest in establishing MPEs in fertilizers, processed rubber products and paper products, on all of which reports had been prepared by the UNCTAD secretariat in collaboration with UNIDO and FAO with UNDP financial support. In October 1983, UNCTAD and the International Center for Public Enterprises in Developing Countries (ICPE) co-sponsored a meeting of experts on the role of public enterprise joint ventures among developing countries, which permitted a thorough review of current policies and practices regarding MPEs and helped to identify problem areas as well as the five major sources within developing countries from which project proposals usually originate.

Progress in the implementation of UNCTAD's sub-programme on MPEs has been hampered by the insufficiency of manpower and financing for research work, technical assistance and the organization and servicing of meetings. To overcome these difficulties, extra-budgetary support is being sought from UNDP and other sources of finance.

C. Problems and tasks for the future

The ECDC work programme represents a microcosm of UNCTAD's overall area of competence, inasmuch as any external economic policy objective of a

---

[42] The terms "multinational production enterprises" (MPEs) and "joint ventures" (JVs) are here used interchangeably, although the latter term is broader in scope.

[43] Professor L. T. Wells (Junior), *Farewell multinationals—The rise of foreign investment from developing countries* Cambridge: M.I.T. Press, 1983.

developing country encompasses a real or a potential South-South dimension. As with UNCTAD's overall record, the ECDC area has had strengths and weaknesses, with marked differences from one sub-programme to another. The failure to foresee emerging trends—or, to adapt to already changed circumstances in good time—could affect the capacity of UNCTAD to respond to complex problems different from those confronting developing countries 20 years ago. While a certain measure of sobering disenchantment is probably a normal symptom of a maturing organization, it must be a continuing function of management—particularly in a development-policy-oriented organization such as UNCTAD—to ensure that work programmes evolve in line with current needs of the countries which the organization is charged to serve.

To this end, research can and has played an essential role not only in determining UNCTAD's work programme on trade expansion and economic integration, but also in influencing the thinking of governments and integration secretariats. Conversely, technical assistance undertaken—rather than "backstopped"—by interregional advisers and staff members seconded to externally financed projects, made the secretariat a living link between the real world of economic integration and the international forums in which policy recommendations are formulated and deliberated. A return to this early approach might stand the wider ECDC programme of today in good stead.

The evolution of the various ECDC sub-programmes and the resources allocated to them since 1976 reflects not so much unchanged needs and possibilities of ECDC as the slowness with which new initiatives emerged through the intergovernmental machinery. If developing countries look to each other as potential sources for satisfying major areas of weakness and dependence, such as food and energy, these do not appear to have been adequately reflected in UNCTAD resolutions or in secretariat initiatives. If a growing number of developing countries are increasing the role of the private sector in their foreign trade, corresponding adjustments may be called for within the ECDC work programme. If proposals for a South Bank are met with caution by countries whose backing is important to its implementation, this has not prevented the idea from continuing to attract support within the Group of 77 as a whole.

While criticisms can justifiably be levelled at UNCTAD's performance in the ECDC area over the years, increased South-South trade and economic co-operation will undoubtedly constitute one of the major features of the world economy by the end of the century, since the largest portential growth of supply and demand must come from countries with the greatest unfulfilled wants, unutilized supply capacities and dynamic population growth. UNCTAD's early vision in this regard and heavy institutional commitment to promote such trends can be a solid building-block on which to erect a revised and forward-looking programme in tune with the needs of today and tomorrow.

VIII. UNCTAD ACTIVITIES ON BEHALF OF THE LEAST DEVELOPED, LAND-LOCKED AND ISLAND DEVELOPING COUNTRIES

A. Least developed countries

UNCTAD has played a pioneering role in efforts to provide for special measures in favour of the least developed among the developing countries. The secretariat's activities for these countries were originally undertaken by a section in the former Research Division; because of their growing importance, however, and in order to focus attention on disadvantaged countries, in 1977 the UNCTAD secretariat established the first such institutional unit within the United Nations system for them, the Special Programme for Least Developed, Land-locked and Island Developing Countries.

POLICY INITIATIVES WITHIN UNCTAD

Special attention to what were then called the "less developed" among the developing countries began at the first session of the Conference in 1964 and has gathered momentum since. However, the principle of "non-discrimination" among developing countries was simultaneously emphasized in international deliberations on this matter, reflecting a basic difficulty and ambivalence regarding any explicit differentiation among the developing countries. To developed countries the concept seemed a matter of common sense and a fact of economic life, whereas developing countries viewed differentiation as potentially harmful to their unity. The perception by the latter was understandable as it reflected negotiating stances: for instance one of the 1964 positions of the North was for a graduated and selective set of trade preferences rather than a uniform system of commercial preferences for all developing countries being sought by the South. On this and a number of other issues discussed in UNCTAD, the Group of 77 had been reluctant to accept the principle of differentiation among themselves, this being seen as contrary to the solidarity of developing countries. However, it was agreed at the second session of the Conference in 1968, that special measures should be devised in order to enable the least developed among the developing countries to derive equitable benefits from new policy measures within UNCTAD, particularly those between developing and developed countries.

The first resolution on the subject of the least developed countries was adopted at UNCTAD II in 1968 (resolution 24 (II)).[1] Provision for special measures in favour of the least developed countries (LDCs) was included in the International

---

[1] "Special measures to be taken in favour of the least developed among developing countries aimed at expanding their trade and improving their economic and social development."

Development Strategy for the Second United Nations Development Decade. A detailed description of the general situation of these countries was set out in reports by two groups of experts, in 1969 and 1971 respectively,[2] although at that point there was no agreed list of least developed countries.

It should be recalled in this context that until the mid 1960s, developing countries were considered as homogeneous with the only distinctions being the structure of their commodity exports. As such an approach was simplistic and inadequate for conceptualizing certain policy measures, the UNCTAD secretariat embarked on basic research into what was termed the "typology" of developing countries. Drawing upon UNCTAD's work on identification and classification and on the recommendations of the Committee on Development Planning (CDP) which looked into the establishment of a list of least developed countries, a task that was fraught with methodological and political problems, the General Assembly approved the list of the LDCs in 1971. After considerable debate the CDP decided to use the following criteria: per capita gross domestic product (GDP) of $100 (in 1968 United States dollars) or less; share of manufacturing in total GDP of 10 per cent or less; adult literacy rate of 20 per cent or less.

The original list included the following countries: Afghanistan, Benin, Bhutan, Botswana, Burundi, Chad, Ethiopia, Guinea, Haiti, the Lao People's Democratic Republic, Lesotho, Malawi, Maldives, Mali, Nepal, Niger, Rwanda, Somalia, Sudan, Uganda, United Republic of Tanzania, Upper Volta (now Burkina Faso), Samoa and the Yemen Arab Republic. In 1975, four countries (Bangladesh, Central African Republic, Democratic Yemen and the Gambia) were added to the list; in 1977 two other countries (Cape Verde and the Comoros) were added; in 1981 Guinea-Bissau; and in 1982 five other countries (Djibouti, Equatorial Guinea, Sao Tome and Principe, Sierra Leone and Togo). The group of 36 least developed countries thus now comprises a population of about 280 million, or about one-eighth of the population of all developing countries (excluding China).

As a result of the creation of a specific list, UNCTAD was able to begin more focused analytical work about special measures in favour of least developed countries. The first comprehensive resolution on special measures for these countries was adopted at UNCTAD III, in 1972 in resolution 62 (III),[3] and a further resolution was adopted at UNCTAD IV, in 1976, in resolution 98 (IV).[4] With United Nations Development Programme (UNDP) financing, UNCTAD carried out missions to almost all least developed countries, which represented the first major exploratory look at the field level into the economies of these countries. In addition to providing proposals for technical assistance, these missions had an important feed-back for the secretariat's work in formulating more appropriate and concrete policy proposals.

---

[2] "Report of the Group of Experts on special measures in favour of the least developed among the developing countries," (TD/B/288) and "Special measures in favour of the least developed among the developing countries" (TD/B/349/Rev.1) (United Nations publication, Sales No. E.71.II.D.1) (For the printed text of TD/B/288 see *Official Records of the Trade and Development Board, Ninth Session, Third Part (2-16 February 1970), Annexes,* agenda item 15).

[3] "Special Measures in favour of the least developed among developing countries."

[4] "Least developed among developing countries, developing island countries and developing land-locked countries."

Several UNCTAD meetings took up the question of redressing this situation and providing for much more effective action on behalf of these countries. In 1974, the Trade and Development Board recognised the need to have integrated action on behalf of the least developed countries and decided to convene an intergovernmental group to initiate intensified efforts towards the formulation, development and review and appraisal of policies and measures in their favour. The Intergovernmental Group on the Least Developed Countries met for the first time in 1975 and gave a substantial push towards the elaboration of special measures for these countries.[5] An important meeting of least developed countries and multilateral and bilateral donor agencies was sponsored in 1977 in order to discuss more appropriate modalities for assistance in these countries.[6]

During the 1970s, it became evident that least developed countries were lagging further and further behind, and in some cases moving backwards. Their average growth rates were lower in the Second United Nations Development Decade (about 0.6 per cent) than in the first (about 0.9 per cent), and much lower than those of other developing countries. As a group least developed countries recorded per capita declines in this period in each of the following key economic areas: agricultural production, manufacturing output, gross domestic investment, export purchasing power, and import volume. Thus the second session of the Intergovernmental Group, which met in 1978, requested the UNCTAD secretariat: to carry out a series of detailed studies on the overall assistance requirements of least developed countries, which were to be examined by a high-level expert group at the end of 1979;[7] and to prepare a document which would outline a programme of action for these countries. It also suggested that full consideration be given at the fifth session of the Conference to launching a coherent, sustained and effective substantial new programme of action for the 1980s.

The secretariat put forward such an outline in the form of an issues note[8] for the fifth session of the Conference, which provided the basis for resolution 122 (V)[9] launching a comprehensive and substantially expanded programme in two phases: an immediate Action Programme (1979-1981) and a Substantial New Programme of Action (SNPA) for the 1980s for the least developed countries. This resolution stressed the urgent need to reverse the poor performance of least developed countries, mostly through the infusion of vastly increased flows of foreign assistance. It also contained the first mention of the need to double aid to these countries as soon as possible.

---

[5] For the report of the Intergovernmental Group see *Official Records of the Trade and Development Board, Fifteenth Session, Annexes,* agenda item 7, document TD/B/577.

[6] For the report of the Meeting of Multilateral and Bilateral Financial and Technical Assistance Institutions with Representatives of the Least Developed Countries see *Official Records of the Trade and Development Board, Eighteenth Session (29 August-17 September 1978), Annexes,* agenda item 6, document TD/B/681.

[7] For the report of the Group of High-Level Experts on the Comprehensive New Programme of Action for the Least Developed Countries see *Official Records of the Trade and Development Board, Eleventh Special Session (14 and 20 March 1980), Annexes,* agenda item 2, document TD/B/775.

[8] Outline for a substantial new programme of action for the 1980s for the least developed countries (TD/240), reproduced in *Proceedings of the United Nations Conference on Trade and Development, Fifth Session, vol. III. Basic Documents* (United Nations publication, Sales No. E.79.II.D.16).

[9] "Comprehensive New Programme of Action for the Least Developed Countries."

The United Nations Conference on the Least Developed Countries (1981)

In view of the special importance of the SNPA, the General Assembly decided in 1979 to act upon the recommendation in Conference resolution 122 (V) to convene a United Nations Conference on the Least Developed Countries in order to finalize, adopt and support the Substantial New Programme of Action. The United Nations Conference on the Least Developed Countries was held in Paris from 1 to 14 September 1981. The Secretary-General of UNCTAD was the Secretary-General of this conference; the UNCTAD secretariat served as its secretariat, and the UNCTAD Intergovernmental Group as its Preparatory Committee.

The Substantial New Programme of Action (SNPA)

The substantial report by the Secretary-General of the Conference served as the basis for the negotiation of the SNPA.[10] This programme of action may well be considered a milestone in efforts by the international community to counteract the unacceptable rates of economic performance in these countries. The Secretary-General's report was based on a unique process whereby each least developed country presented its own priorities, problems and development programmes as well as estimates for its external assistance requirements in the 1980s. Each country presentation was reviewed by the least developed country concerned with a selected list of bilateral and multilateral development partners; these meetings occurred in five regional clusters and were organized by the UNCTAD secretariat. Based in part on this process, UNCTAD estimated that at least a doubling of external flows in real terms combined with improved domestic policies in these countries would be necessary to reverse the recent economic decline in most of the least developed countries. This report analysed in detail the characteristics of "mal-development" in these countries, placing their plight within the international context of structural disequilibrium.

The SNPA was adopted unanimously in Paris, although there was clearly a division in Group B between those donors which wished to do much more for the poorest and which so argued in public (mainly the Nordic countries, France, Canada, Austria and Japan) and those which were unwilling to commit themselves to such measures (the United States, the United Kingdom, and the Federal Republic of Germany).

The main objectives of the SNPA are: (*a*) to promote the structural changes necessary to overcome the extreme economic difficulties of the least developed countries; (*b*) to provide fully adequate and internationally accepted minimum standards for the poor; (*c*) identify and support major investment opportunities and priorities; and (*d*) to mitigate as far as possible the adverse effects of disasters. To achieve these objectives the SNPA recommends to the least developed countries action at the national level with respect to strategy, priorities, overall and sectoral targets and other action necessary for accelerated development. It also provides for measures of support to complement action at the national level through the provision of substantially more financial resources and through policies and programmes affecting the modalities of assistance, technical assistance, transfer of

---

[10] *The least developed countries and action in their favour by the international community*, Selected documents of the United Nations Conference on the Least Developed Countries (A/Conf.104/2/Rev.1) (United Nations publication, Sales No. E.83.I.6).

technology, commercial policy measures and economic and technical co-operation among developing countries.

The SNPA essentially reflected the secretariat's recommendation to pursue a two-pronged approach and to establish a "contract" between donors and least developed countries: on the one hand, more international support (including the commitment by developed countries generally to provide 0.15 per cent of gross national product (GNP) to least developed countries in the form of aid or doubling past concessional flows by 1985, with more appropriate modalities for aid disbursements) and, on the other hand, increased national efforts by the least developed countries themselves. It also contained the agreement by the international community to pursue specific follow-up at the country, regional and global levels. In particular, the agreed follow-up included the crucial provision to continue the country-by-country review and implementation arrangements that had been begun by UNCTAD as part of the preparations for the Paris Conference, although because of donor reluctance UNCTAD was not associated with country level follow-up.

The SNPA, endorsed by the General Assembly in 1981 and reaffirmed in 1982, was also reaffirmed by the sixth session of the Conference resolution 142 (VI),[11] it is intended to bring about nothing less than the long-term transformation of the economies of the least developed countries.

THE EVOLUTION IN THE PERCEPTION OF LEAST DEVELOPED COUNTRIES' PROBLEMS

The contents of the SNPA and earlier texts of resolutions illustrate the evolution in the perception of "least development" by the international community and by the UNCTAD secretariat. Despite the good intentions in earlier resolutions, they envisaged only piecemeal improvements in no way sufficient to deal with the plight of least developed countries or to change their bleak development prospects. Recommendations were not precise and no provision was made for their implementation or for review, monitoring and follow-up. A further defect of these early efforts at the global level was that their national implications were not always clear, and consequently they were seldom taken into account at the country level.

Alterations in the substantive approach to the problems of least developed countries as well as a cumulative appreciation of the nature of their development problems have taken place over time largely as a result of UNCTAD initiatives. Instead of an almost exclusive concern with foreign trade accompanied increasingly by an insistence upon external assistance, the present *problématique*, as it appears in the SNPA, has been extended to all aspects of economic and social development. Attention has been focused on the need to strengthen these countries' economies as a whole, including investment needs and overall production capacity as well as social sectors. While continuing to be seen as crucial, increased international support has been recognized as a complement to, not as a substitute for, domestic efforts by the least developed countries themselves; this emphasis has replaced the

---

[11] "Progress in the implementation of the Substantial New Programme of Action for the 1980s for the Least Developed Countries."

earlier calls to enhance the effectiveness of merely trade-related activities or to increase external assistance *per se*. At the same time, there has also been an increased sense of urgency in highlighting the acuteness of least developed countries' problems and in giving them a higher priority on the international agenda.

In general terms, the treatment of least developed countries in successive UNCTAD resolutions and in the SNPA indicates very clearly the gradual acceptance by both North and South of the legitimacy of this category of countries requiring special international measures. The earlier insistence that the problems of least developed countries should not be considered separately but viewed essentially as an integral part of the general measures on the UNCTAD agenda has been muted to some extent and has tended to give way to a more accurate view of the development process. Gradual and increased acceptance of the category has been based on the realization that least developed countries, in the short and medium term, can derive only very limited benefits from most of the general policy measures on behalf of all developing countries.

A BRIEF EVALUATION OF THE IMPACT OF UNCTAD's EFFORTS

The results of UNCTAD's work that originally led to the creation of the list of least developed countries has subsequently led to an increasing awareness of the special needs of these countries. This awareness has changed policies of countries and multilateral agencies in several important ways. There has been a shift in the share of official assistance going to this group of countries; several donor countries have not only provided an increasing share of their assistance but have also under Board resolution 165 (S-IX) "Debt and Development problems of developing countries" (1978) cancelled the debt of, or taken other debt relief measures in favour of, these countries. The shift has been particularly noticeable for major multilateral organizations, which are now providing approximately 30 per cent of their assistance to the least developed countries. This awareness has also led to a few innovations in commercial policy measures on behalf of these countries. The creation of a special sub-committee for least developed countries within GATT should be noted, as should the special provision for these countries in the Declaration of November 1982 of the Ministers of the Contracting Parties of GATT. Trade preferences, including provisions in the Lomé conventions (concluded between the European Economic Community and the African, Caribbean and Pacific Countries) and within the generalized system of preferences (GSP), have also resulted. Furthermore, donors (the OPEC Fund, the Government of Norway and the European Economic Community have offered to pay the contributions of least developed countries and certain developing countries to the Directly Contributed Capital of the Common Fund for Commodities. The international community's growing awareness has also resulted in the creation of special focal points for activities on behalf of least developed countries within many organizations of the United Nations system, which in turn have led to an increasing emphasis on them in both regular work programmes as well as in technical co-operation activities.

The efforts of the 1960s, 1970s and 1980s have thus led to the identification of a relatively small category of the very poorest and structurally weakest countries and to the acceptance by the international community that these least developed countries are deserving of special and specific attention. The actual impact of this special attention—like the impact of all resolutions in a period of global crisis—has been far from discernible in the economic performance of least developed countries or in the transfer of resources to them. The expanded assistance flows promised in 1979 at the fifth session of the Conference as part of the Immediate Action Programme (1979-1981) never materialized. In 1981, when the SNPA was adopted, it was recognized that only a substantial increase in official development assistance (ODA) in real terms would enable the least developed countries to achieve the objectives of the SNPA. Despite this, during 1981—the year of the Paris Conference and in the midst of the world economic recession—the least developed countries received approximately 15 per cent less external financial resources in current terms than in 1980. In 1982, figures indicate that 1980 levels have been reached in current terms, but this clearly constitutes a significant decline of aid in real terms—a far cry from the commitments made in 1979 and 1981.

TASKS FOR THE FUTURE

The central political task for the future is to mobilize adequate support in both the North and the South to realize the objectives and specific commitments made in the SNPA. In this context, UNCTAD has been given responsibility at the global level for review, co-ordination and monitoring of the SNPA, including the performance of both least developed countries and the international community in terms of meeting their respective commitments. A major event in this process will be the mid-term review of the SNPA scheduled for mid-1985 during which progress will be assessed and the SNPA adjusted as necessary.

However, in terms of actual influence on the course of events, UNCTAD's role should not be overestimated and is likely to be modest. On the one hand, UNCTAD has not normally been used as a forum in which the national policies of developing countries have been analysed, discussed or monitored. On the other hand, aid flows depend essentially on the political will of donor countries, a matter that is subject to a very limited extent to influence by any international body. While UNCTAD's ability to discuss national policies and to contribute to the mobilization of additional financial resources has been limited until now, this situation merits reappraisal.

A related issue is the adequacy of UNCTAD's machinery and procedures because they have not been particularly creative in leading to specific results, to specific bits of business, to specific negotiations. In this context, the desirability of applying more generally some of the lessons learned from the international negotiations process for the benefit of least developed countries merits reflection. In the case of these countries, there has been, to all intents and purposes, a reconciliation between the need expressed in 1964 at UNCTAD I through General Principle Fifteen to "take into account the individual characteristics and different stages of development of developing countries" on the one hand, and that to preserve the unity of the Group of 77, on the other. Thus, although the existence of the category of least developed countries entails a clear differentiation among the developing countries, no break-up in the coalition of developing countries has occurred. It was rather the governments of the developed market-economy countries that did not approach the negotiations as a group. A challenge for UNCTAD would be to explore the extent to which other coalitions in both North and South might be used to expand flexibly and creatively the traditional group structure, thereby facilitating more productive international negotiations rather than confrontations that have led to stalemate within international economic discussions.

Possibilities for new conceptual or policy initiatives are limited at present. While the list of least developed countries as it now stands is reasonably coherent and confirms that the original criteria were by and large sound, the need to re-examine them has become apparent. The expected benefits from the SNPA create political pressures for including new countries in the category. There has not been any general review of the list, but the Committee for Development Planning (CDP) has evaluated on an *ad hoc* basis the cases of individual countries as a result of a request from the General Assembly; and, as indicated earlier, the list has grown steadily. Some other countries feel unjustly excluded because their cases are not evaluated; and there is also a reluctance to remove any country from the list in the absence of proper and more systematic analysis.

While the question of classification raises political issues, the past analytical approach should not be considered as sacrosanct. On the one hand, data for least developed countries are scarce and often unreliable, as is to be expected of poor countries. This shortcoming applies in particular to GDP data, for instance because of the problems inherent in measuring the activities of the subsistence sector or even population size in least developed countries. Exchange rate conversions also introduce arbitrary features into such figures. While data for the share of manufacturing in GDP are available and used extensively, how close a link can be made between growth in this sector and meaningful overall development in poor countries is far from clear, although in the late 1960s it had been taken for granted that it was close. Consistent, recent, and comparable data on literacy are not available, a problem complicated in some cases by implausible variations over short periods of time. With the present approach, comprehensive consideration of the proper weighting given to indicators taken together is not possible.

Clearly countries on the list should remain there until the end of the SNPA in 1990 because a minimum period of time is required in order to benefit from its provisions. However, 15 years have passed since the original identification exercise — during which time much analytical work has taken place, better information has become available and many changes have occurred both in the economies of poor countries and in the global economy in general. It would thus appear necessary that CDP, taking into account UNCTAD's work in the field, re-evaluate both the criteria and the list of least developed countries in the light of the possibility of holding a global review of the SNPA at the end of the decade, which might take the form of a United Nations conference on the least developed countries. It has become clear that the obstacles to accelerated development in least developed countries are deep-rooted and go beyond the economy narrowly defined, into social and geographical factors. The use of criteria more fully reflecting this recognition would help ensure that the attention of the international community continues to focus on the truly poorest and most disadvantaged countries.

B. Land-locked and island developing countries

UNCTAD has also played a key role in efforts to develop a framework for special action in favour of geographically disadvantaged developing countries. Work on land-locked developing countries began at the first session of the Conference, while the third session of the Conference launched a study of the special problems of island developing countries. The secretariat has tailored its activities to the specific requirements of these two groups of countries. While UNCTAD's efforts on behalf of the least developed countries have been based on their economic and social characteristics in general, work on the other two categories of countries has focused on their specific geographical disadvantages.

LAND-LOCKED DEVELOPING COUNTRIES

Land-locked developing countries are generally among the very poorest of the developing countries—15 of the 21 countries in this category are indeed classified as least developed (and are italicized in footnote 12, which lists land-locked developing countries).[12] UNCTAD's work has concentrated on the high vulnerability of their economies resulting from the lack of territorial access to the sea; great distances to seaports; remoteness and isolation from world markets; high costs of international transport services; inadequacy of physical facilities along transit corridors and at seaports; and complications related to commercial and legal aspects of transiting a foreign territory.

Prior to 1964, international concern with the problems of land-locked developing countries was largely confined to international legal issues of transit traffic and of access to the sea. In this connection, particular reference should be made to the examination of the question of free access to the sea by the Third United Nations Conference on the Law of the Sea.

The concern about the plight of the land-locked developing countries had gathered considerable political momentum, and the first session of the Conference adopted "Eight Principles Related to Transit Trade of Land-locked Countries" and recommended the preparation of a new international convention on transit trade. Subsequently, the United Nations Conference of Plenipotentiaries on Transit Trade of Land-locked Countries adopted a new Convention on Transit Trade of Landlocked States in July 1965. The impact of this convention has, however, been limited because of insufficient ratifications. The awareness of the particular problems facing these countries continued to grow and the second session of the Conference called for special attention and special solutions to their problems in resolution 11 (II), "Special problems of the land-locked countries".

An expert group carried out in 1970 a comprehensive examination of the problems involved in the promotion of trade and in the economic development of

---

[12] *Afghanistan, Bhutan,* Bolivia, *Botswana, Burundi, Central African Republic, Chad, Lao People's Democratic Republic, Lesotho, Malawi, Mali,* Mongolia, *Nepal, Niger,* Paraguay, *Rwanda,* Swaziland, *Uganda, Upper Volta (now Burkina Faso),* Zambia, Zimbabwe.

the land-locked developing countries. Their report[13] recommended measures to remove administrative and procedural obstacles to transit transport and called for the support of the international community to develop and maintain physical transit transport infrastructure facilities and to restructure the economies of these countries, in order to adapt them to the land-locked situation.

The third session of the Conference, in 1972, adopted a comprehensive action programme and overall strategy for land-locked developing countries (resolution 63 (III));[14] and as a follow-up, the secretariat undertook a number of studies that examined in depth the need to simplify cumbersome formalities, procedures and documentation hindering international trade and transport as well as the need to conclude agreements for the improvement of port and transit facilities.

Another major follow-up by the secretariat was the work undertaken by a second expert group in 1973, whose report[15] paved the way for the present UNCTAD policy emphasis on the "integrated planning approach", which essentially aims at promoting and consolidating co-operative arrangements between land-locked countries and their transit neighbours. Such arrangements include the promotion of joint ventures in the field of transit transport, the simplification and standardization of procedures and formalities, the facilitation of the clearance of goods (preferably through joint personnel representation at ports and border points), the facilitation of road and rail traffic across national borders and the establishment of institutional mechanisms for regular review of transit transport issues. Based on this work and in order to establish a framework for mobilizing external resources to subsidize the additional transport costs of land-locked developing countries, the UNCTAD secretariat prepared two reports in 1974 and 1975, respectively, on the establishment of a special fund. In December 1976 the General Assembly adopted the statute of the Special Fund for Land-locked Developing Countries, which had been prepared by the UNCTAD secretariat. However, this fund has so far received only very limited resources, largely because of the reluctance of donors to support any new funds.

In order to foster the integrated planning approach and test its relevance in the field, UNCTAD has been carrying out technical studies within the framework of regional transit transport projects in Africa and Asia with financing from UNDP. Specific activities have included: the analysis and assessment of present and prospective demands placed upon each existing or potential transit route both by the land-locked and the transit countries; the quality of facilities, management and maintenance for each transit route, and the problems encountered in their use; the adequacy of storage capacity on each transit corridor; the procedures, regulations and rate structures for each transit route, as well as the adequacy of existing legislation, conventions and working agreements that govern international transport including transit documentation procedures; and potential alternative routes.

---

[13] Report of the Group of Experts on the special problems involved in the trade and economic development of the land-locked developing countries, reproduced in *Official Records of the Trade and Development Board, Tenth Session. First, second and third parts. Annexes,* agenda item 13, document TD/B/308.

[14] "Special measures related to the particular needs of land-locked developing countries."

[15] *A Transport Strategy for Land-locked Developing Countries* (TD/B/453/Add.1/Rev.1) (United Nations publication, Sales No. E.74.II.D.5).

UNCTAD's efforts to mobilize support in favour of land-locked developing countries have been steadfast; and Conference resolutions 98 (IV),[16] 123 (V)[17] and 137 (VI)[18] as well as the International Development Strategy for the first United Nations Development Decade reflect them. Their impact has, however, been disappointing. Reviews of progress in the implementation of special measures and specific action in favour of land-locked developing countries have been regularly undertaken by UNCTAD and clearly indicate that the response of the international community has been quite unsatisfactory. Indeed, many important donors do not have particular development assistance policies in favour of these countries, although they generally recognize that these countries do face problems because of their geographical disadvantages.

As a result of a grave concern about the continued extremely poor economic performance of the land-locked developing countries, the UNCTAD secretariat put forward a comprehensive set of policy proposals to the sixth session of the Conference, including: the rehabilitation and proper maintenance of transit-transport facilities; the training programmes for persons at all levels involved in transit-transport operations; the development of new facilities along transit corridors in the ports and at rail terminals; the improvement of transit documentation and procedures; the strengthening of regional co-operation arrangements related to transport trade and production; the appropriate restructuring of the economies, and institution building in the transit-transport sector.[19] The Conference called upon the international community to provide assistance in these areas.

The work of a recent group of experts has discussed guidelines for future work, including proposals for a more expeditious and effective implementation of the priorities and modalities of assistance already agreed upon by the international community; means to reorient donor policies with a view to giving specific and more deliberate attention to transit-transport related programmes; and innovative ways to foster greater co-operation between land-locked countries and their transit neighbours.

ISLAND DEVELOPING COUNTRIES

Although island developing countres are not, in general, among the poorest, they constitute another category of countries which have special problems. Their handicaps are basically derived from the smallness and remoteness of most of them, and include vulnerability to natural disasters, special transport problems (which are even more acute in archipelagic countries), highly limited internal markets, lack of natural resources and heavy dependence on imports. These imports in turn are

---

[16] "Least developed among the developing countries, developing island countries and developing land-locked countries" (1976).

[17] "Specific action related to the particular needs and problems of land-locked developing countries" (1979).

[18] "UNCTAD activities in the field of land-locked developing countries" (1983).

[19] "Specific action related to the particular needs and problems of land-locked and island developing countries: issues for consideration. Part one — Land-locked developing countries" (TD/279 (part I)), to be printed in *Proceedings of the United Nations Conference on Trade and Development, Sixth Session,* vol. III, *Basic Documents* (United Nations publication, Sales No. E.83.II.D.8).

financed by a small number of foreign exchange-earning activities (commodity exports, tourism or emigrant remittances for instance). Given the high per capita cost of building and maintaining economic and social infrastructure for small and isolated populations, small islands lack the critical mass to provide basic services economically for their populations.

Island developing countries tend to receive more aid per capita than other developing countries, which can usually be attributed to the "small country effect" as well as to the perceived strategic importance of most islands. The regional institutions in the South Pacific and Caribbean, where most of the island developing countries are situated, have also been well supported by the international community.

Until the early 1970s, island developing countries had received no special attention either from the international community or in academic circles. It was while studying within UNCTAD the case of countries which were particularly disadvantaged that it became apparent that the special problems of islands required further consideration. At the third session of the Conference, it was decided to convene a small panel of experts to study and identify the problems of these countries.[20] Since that time, UNCTAD has continued the study of the common problems concerning islands and has made a number of policy proposals in this respect.[21] Many of these have been incorporated in UNCTAD resolutions 98 (IV), 111 (V)[22] and 138 (VI)[23] which were each re-affirmed by the General Assembly.

The thrust of the proposals made by UNCTAD is that the international community should recognize the special characteristics and handicaps of island developing countries and provide appropriate support to them in their development efforts. Among the areas where support is considered particularly relevant are: shipping and air services, including feeder services; telecommunications; export promotion, market access and stabilization of earnings, including invisibles and emigrant remittances; disaster planning and mitigation; environment and ecology; marine and sub-marine resources; and the use of the Exclusive Economic Zone (EEZ).

The work of UNCTAD since the early 1970s has contributed significantly to a better understanding of island developing countries and has been a determining factor in assisting the international community to recognize their specific problems. A number of analytical and descriptive studies have shown that small island developing countries have characteristics distinct from those of developing countries in general. As a result, the type of development strategy regarded as appropriate in general and promoted by the United Nations may in some aspects be inappropriate for these countries in particular. The studies have also highlighted

---

[20] See *Developing Island Countries. Report of the Panel of Experts* (TD/B/443/Rev.1) (United Nations publication, Sales No. E.74.II.D.6). Also of interest are the subsequent report of the Group of Experts on Feeder and Inter-island Services by Air or Sea for Island Developing Countries (printed in *Official Records of the Trade and Development Board, Eighteenth Session, Annexes,* agenda item 6 (c), document TD/B/687) and selected papers submitted to the Group of Experts (TD/B/AC.24/2).

[21] The most recent proposals are to be found in TD/279 (Part II)—see footnote 19 above.

[22] "Specific action related to the particular needs and problems of island developing countries" (1979).

[23] "UNCTAD activities in the field of island developing countries" (1983).

certain specific handicaps facing small island countries as well as dispelling some myths concerning them.[24] A related methodological question which these studies have shown to be important is the extent to which continental developing microstates have sufficient characteristics in common with small island developing countries so that analyses of their problems would benefit from being examined jointly.

Growing recognition of the conclusions regarding island developing countries is reflected in the five resolutions passed unanimously in the General Assembly on island developing countries between 1976 and 1982, and the further discussion of this question scheduled later in 1984 for the thirty-ninth session. The International Development Strategy for the Third United Nations Development Decade specifically highlights their problems, a departure from the strategies for the 1960s and 1970s. Other organizations have also begun to focus on this group; for instance, the Commonwealth Heads of Government endorsed, in 1979, a special programme of action in favour of the smaller Commonwealth island countries, and the Lomé Conventions make special provisions for these countries.

However, a number of countries and institutions are clearly sceptical about the specificity of island developing countries, and some are against the proliferation of such special categories of developing countries. But they do not feel strongly enough to oppose resolutions or initiatives taken as long as they are relatively innocuous and do not involve the mobilization of additional resources.

One important task which remains is the drawing up of a specific threshold for size so that island developing countries below it should receive special attention from the international community. It should be noted that the Non-Aligned Movement has already taken such a step. In the absence of such a threshold within UNCTAD, it is very difficult to express an opinion as to the extent to which particular resolutions have been implemented.

A logistical question also arises regarding the need to ensure actual participation of island countries themselves in discussions of direct relevance to them. The expenses for establishing diplomatic missions or even travel to international meetings are very high in per capita terms for small island States; and thus such States are often not present in international discussions, even those that directly concern them.

Finally, a further task for the future would be to attempt to define some national measures or policies which island developing countries themselves might pursue. International support measures would probably be more effective if there were agreement on what specific national policies in the islands themselves were to be followed.

---

[24] In this context, see for instance the "World map of natural hazards in tropical oceans", in "The incidence of natural disasters in island developing countries" (TD/B/961), 1983.

IX. INSURANCE

A. Insurance in developing countries prior to 1964

The basic function of insurance is to provide protection against the financial consequences of certain losses. It involves a process whereby an individual, firm or organization can, in return for payment of a premium, transfer to an insurer the risk associated with these financial losses. Also, the insurance business is concerned essentially with spreading risks as widely as possible. By insuring a large number of similar risks, the insurer can calculate the likely claims that will be paid and the required premium for each risk that will be necessary to meet those claims.

Historically, the practice of insurance was not totally alien to the social and economic values of developing countries. As revealed by some social and anthropological studies, families, tribes and clans used to contribute, if a member of the community was struck by a misfortune, to share the loss, thus reducing and mitigating the impact on the individual. However, insurance in its contemporary form is relatively new, and was usually associated with the production methods and patterns of society imported from the developed countries.

The efforts of international insurers and reinsurers to expand their activities abroad are inspired by the need for more spread through extending their business beyond their countries of origin in order to improve the stability of the results of their underwriting. Thus, this tendency to broaden the scope of their activities is an essential part of their strategy and is often encouraged by their governments, whose balance of payments may be favourably affected as a result.

As early as the nineteenth century, most of the big internatonal insurers had established agencies and branches in Western Europe, America and other highly industrialized countries, since these countries offered a high volume of business. However, the advent of war and resulting economic depression changed the course of economic affairs, disrupting old trading patterns and ushering in an era of trade restriction which affected insurance as well. Hence the strategy of expansion of international insurers was directed toward the countries that offered fewer restrictions.

Consequently, prior to the 1960s, most developing countries' insurance markets consisted of locally licensed agencies and branches of foreign insurance companies, and a few foreign owned local insurers. These agencies and branches handled most of the domestic risks emanating from these markets except that large and complex risks were insured directly abroad.

There were several conditions which hindered the establishment and growth of genuine local insurance markets in developing countries. First, the economic base of most of these countries was extremely narrow, because of the prevalence of subsistence economy and the existence of limited industrial and commercial sectors. Second, these countries lacked sufficient capital to invest in insurance, which is an industry without prospects of immediate profitability. Third, technical and managerial skills were relatively scarce, particularly for the more complex forms of insurance. As a result of these deficiencies and weaknesses, the idea of providing local insurance was thought to be high in cost and unproductive.

Another factor contributing to the slow emergence of the local insurance sector in developing countries was the inadequate insurance regulatory frameworks. These frameworks in fact gave foreign insurers privileges while putting obstacles to the emergence of an indigenous insurance industry. Consequently, many insurance markets remained under the control of foreign companies and the domestic insurance industry lacked the incentive to develop more fully.

The result of these conditions was a fragmented, unregulated market where neither the country's overall national interest nor the interests of those of the locally insured were necessarily protected adequately. Even in countries where local companies had been operating for some time, the majority of these insurers were largely dependent on foreign reinsurers to make up for the shortage of underwriting capacity, financing and expertise.

Some domestic companies were in fact mere commission agents for international insurance and reinsurance companies. Major outflows of foreign exchange ensued either as remittance for profits or settlement of reinsurance balances or both. Consequently relatively small insurance funds were available for local investment and, hence, development. While important exceptions existed, too many of the foreign agencies, branches and companies placed little emphasis on developing technical and managerial skills among the local population.

B. The role and activities of UNCTAD in the field of insurance

It was against this background that discussions on insurance were held during the first session of the Conference in 1964. Four basic reasons were identified as to why steps should be taken to restrain the activities of foreign insurance companies operating in developing countries. These were:

The need to rationalize a chaotically fragmented market and to make supervision of the market easier;

The need, as a result of the growth of national economic consciousness, to encourage and develop an indigenous insurance industry and the skills associated with it;

The need to ensure that most of the funds generated by the insurance process were retained in the country, and to control their employment;

The need to save foreign exchange as heavy net deficits had been incurred on overall external accounts.

Accordingly, UNCTAD at its first session (1964) in its recommendation A.IV.23 acknowledged that "... a sound national insurance and reinsurance market is an essential characteristic of economic growth ...". This recommendation was addressed to developed countries and set out a number of tasks to be carried out in co-operation with the developing countries. It called upon developed countries to (a) give their full cooperation to the developing countries to encourage and strengthen their national insurance and reinsurance markets; and (b) continue and increase the technical assistance and training facilities which they provide. The recommendation further stipulated that technical reserves and guarantee deposits of insurance and reinsurance companies or institutions should be invested in the country where the premium arises and called on developed countries to encourage such investment by removing all obstacles to the achievement of this aim.

In contrast, the second important text on insurance and reinsurance, adopted without dissent at the third session of the Conference in 1972 (resolution 42 (III)), was addressed more to the developing countries and invited them to take a series of measures geared to promote two objectives. The first was the need to minimize, to the extent feasible, the dependence of developing countries on international insurers and reinsurers. Second, it was implicitly recognized that total independence of foreign insurance and reinsurance markets was not possible and, therefore, efforts should be made to secure the most appropriate terms and conditions at the lowest cost commensurate with the risks involved.

This change in emphasis is a reflection of the growing awareness in the developing countries of their own responsibility in the development process. In the field of insurance in any case, they recognized implicitly that a better utilization of their own resources and internal means could play an important role in that process.

In conformity with this strategy the UNCTAD secretariat, at the request of the Committee on Invisibles and Financing related to Trade, has carried out several studies, covering some fundamental issues with regard to the establishment and development of nationl insurance markets in developing countries and suggested measures that governments of developing countries can take to meet their goals. These main topics include:

(a) Introduction of appropriate insurance legislation and supervision;

(b) Investment of technical reserves of insurance concerns in the country where the premium arises;

(c) The principle of local insurance for local risks;

(d) Measures designed to improve the performance of insurance companies in developing countries;

(e) Reinsurance;

(f) Co-operation in insurance among developing countries; and

(g) Insurance education and training.

C. Present market structure and its evolution

At its first session, in 1964, UNCTAD recognized the importance and role of insurance in development. This importance stems not just from its role as an essential intermediate service but also from its impact on the national economy as a whole, especially as it affects the supply of capital for investment and the balance of payments.

Indeed, compared to the situation that had prevailed prior to the 1960s, most developing countries have generally made progress in their efforts to establish or strengthen their domestic insurance markets. But, despite these efforts, their domestic insurance markets still lack the size and sophistication that characterize the markets of North America, Europe and Japan.

In 1960, the world premium volume was $13 billion. In 1980 it reached $431 billion, almost 30 times the comparable amount of 1960. The premium volume generated by the insurance markets of developing countries showed a marked increase, from a mere $1 billion in 1960 to $21 billion in 1980. Even allowing for the change in currency values, this growth has by no means been unimpressive. Of course, the volume is well behind that of insurance markets of industrialized countries.

The structure of any insurance market in developing countries has been influenced by the action of the government. Government intervention has taken place at two levels. The first type of intervention was the introduction of insurance legislation and supervision, which prescribed the rules and conditions under which insurance concerns were to conduct business in the country, including rules concerning nationality of insurance concerns. This has resulted in a decrease in the number of foreign companies conducting business in many developing countries. Complementing this decrease in foreign companies has been an increase in the number of domestic insurers.

Second, government intervention in some countries took place at the operational level, including State participation in the ownership of insurance concerns, establishment of State-owned institutions that received compulsory or agreed cessions of business from the entire insurance market and State monopoly of the insurance or reinsurance business.

Measures have been taken to secure a larger volume of business for the national market. Certain risks, for example imports and property located within the country, were required to be insured locally, if local insurers could cover the risk. In a few cases, compulsory or first-refusal reinsurance cessions to domestic reinsurers were required from the domestic insurers. This was intended to increase the domestic market's capacity to retain certain risks which in turn would reduce foreign exchange outflows and enhance the development of local insurance expertise.

Whilst the 1960s and early 1970s were periods during which national insurance industries were established or strengthened in many developing countries, the main feature of the second half of the 1970s appears to be the initiation and intensification of regional and sub-regional co-operation. Co-operation among developing countries in the field of insurance and reinsurance, in line with UNCTAD recommendations in 1964 and 1972, has produced encouraging results. Co-operation has taken place at two levels: (*a*) at the institutional level by creating regional and sub-regional reinsurance corporations and pools; and (*b*) at the operational level by establishing regional insurance associations and institutes for training insurance personnel.

D. Future actions

The studies carried out by the UNCTAD secretariat and the meetings of the Committee on Invisibles and Financing related to Trade have served as a catalyst for encouraging developing countries to implement their strategy of self-reliance in insurance. This is not meant to suggest that self-reliance has been achieved or that all major problems have been solved. Much remains to be accomplished.

In the above circumstances, steps should be taken to assist member countries in:

(*a*) Continuing their efforts for a successful localization of their insurance covers through increasing their know-how and capacity;

(*b*) Increasing insurance consciousness among the peoples in these countries and providing for them the types of cover and guarantees which take into consideration their social, economic and cultural environment;

(*c*) Integrating better the insurance industry into the economy of the country, particularly with regard to appropriateness of cover and the investment of assets;

(*d*) Improving the control and supervision of the insurance business, including measures to increase the credibility and solvency of local insurance companies;

(*e*) Undertaking any needed action in respect of the problems associated with foreign reinsurance;

(*f*) Enhancing efforts in professional training of insurance personnel and providing and consolidating support services to insurance industries;

(*g*) Promoting co-operation between developing countries and the international insurance markets on an equitable basis for the common interest of all; and

(*h*) Initiating and strengthening regional and subregional co-operation in the provision of capacity, training, and insurance support services.

It is clear that the insurance sector will have an increasingly important role to play in developing countries. Improvement in the social and economic conditions of these countries will undoubtedly need the contribution of the insurance sector through the improvement of conditions of cover and its adaptation to the economic and social needs of the people.

Part Three

OTHER ACTIVITIES IN THE FIRST TWENTY YEARS

I. OPERATIONAL ACTIVITIES

A. Background

In 1964, UNCTAD was established primarily as a policy formulating and deliberative body and General Assembly resolution 1995 (XIX) establishing UNCTAD did not contain any reference to technical co-operation. However, with the new focus placed on the link between trade and development it soon became apparent that the external sector had not been given due emphasis in the past in bilateral or multilateral technical assistance programmes. Developing countries began to seek technical assistance to develop an adequate infrastructure and for the training of personnel.

At its fourth session, the Trade and Development Board[1] adopted resolution 30 (IV) in which it recommended that the Secretary-General of UNCTAD should be a member of the Inter-Agency Consultative Board of the United Nations Development Programme (UNDP)—a body which comprised all the executive heads of the participating organizations—and invited UNDP and the Secretary-General of the United Nations to give all due consideration to requests from the developing countries for technical assistance in the fields of export promotion and invisibles, including shipping, insurance and tourism. This resolution of the Board was subsequently endorsed by the General Assembly, in its resolution 2207 (XXI) of 17 December 1966.

As part of the United Nations Secretariat, the UNCTAD secretariat became involved in the substantive support of trade projects executed by the United Nations itself, in its capacity as a participating agency of UNDP. While the administrative, operational and financial functions were performed centrally by the United Nations, UNCTAD was involved in substantive evaluation of project requests received, in identification, selection and briefing of project staff, provision of technical guidance to experts and consultants, evaluation of technical reports, and participation in training activities, whether individual (fellowships) or collective (training courses, seminars, workshops, etc.).

However, the provision of administrative and substantive support from New York and Geneva respectively was not a satisfactory solution from a purely management point of view, and resulted in unavoidable delays in the delivery of project inputs. At the second session of the Conference, developing countries expressed their dissatisfaction with the existing arrangements. The Trade and Development Board decided, at its seventh session, in resolution 44 (VII) of 21 September 1968, to recommend to the General Assembly that UNCTAD should become a fully-fledged participating and executing agency of UNDP. A recommendation endorsed

---

[1] See TD/B/97 and Add.1.

by the General Assembly at its twenty-third session, in resolution 2401 (XXIII) of 13 December 1968, four years after the creation of UNCTAD.

In assuming this new responsibility the UNCTAD secretariat devoted particular attention to two areas of immediate interest—the organizational and the substantive aspects of technical co-operation. From the organizational point of view, management and working procedures were developed to ensure a harmonious combination of effective substantive backstopping and efficient administrative and financial support of relevant UNCTAD technical co-operation activities. This called for the establishment of a complex network of relationships with governments, UNDP headquarters and field offices, the then United Nations Technical Assistance Recruitment Service (TARS), and the regional commissions, as well as with other participating and executing agencies and organizations of the United Nations system.

A Technical Assistance Co-ordination Unit was established in the UNCTAD secretariat, forming part of the Office of the Secretary-General of UNCTAD, to assume overall responsibility for UNCTAD's technical co-operation activities, with the following terms of reference: (*a*) To formulate and provide policy direction for the technical co-operation activities of UNCTAD; (*b*) To ensure co-ordination and liaison with other executing agencies and organizational units in connection with the above; (*c*) To consolidate and ensure UNCTAD's participation in UNDP country and inter-country programming activities; (*d*) To assist in the formulation and development of UNCTAD operational projects financed by the United Nations regular programme of technical co-operation, UNDP and other extra-budgetary sources; (*e*) To provide overall management for the execution of technical co-operation projects entrusted to UNCTAD; (*f*) To maintain liaison with GATT in respect of the operation of the International Trade Centre UNCTAD/GATT (ITC).

In 1976, when the Division for Programme Support Services was created, this Unit was renamed the Technical Co-operation Service (TCS) and was integrated into the new Division. The Chief of TCS continued to be responsible for the overall management of the programme, whereas policy aspects were referred to the Director of the Division for Programme Support Services, who also performed the functions of Liaison Officer with The International Trade Centre (UNCTAD/GATT) (ITC).

From a substantive point of view the programme started with the transfer of a limited number of on-going projects in the field of trade and invisibles which were previously included in the United Nations technical assistance programmes. Particular attention was given to the identification of new types of technical co-operation activities, aimed at responding to the needs of the various countries and regions. In 1970, a decision of the UNDP Governing Council known as the "Consensus" of 1970,[2] emphasized, *inter alia,* the prerogatives of governments of developing countries to determine, on the basis of their development plans, the priorities for assistance through the process of country programming; the same principle was extended to inter-country programmes. Thus the development of a dynamic programme in the areas of competence of UNCTAD was dependent on the awareness

---

[2] For the text of the Consensus see General Assembly resolution 2688 (XXV) of 11 December 1970, annex.

of governments of the possibilities which existed for technical assistance in the field of international trade and invisibles and of the assitance that they could obtain for the actual formulation of projects in a new field in which little or no experience had yet been acquired.

Against this background, one has to bear in mind the fact that UNCTAD, by any standards of a participating and executing agency of UNDP, was a small agency which had no field establishment of its own and no regular budget for technical co-operation. Although the Resident Representatives of UNDP performed the function of representatives of the United Nations system, including UNCTAD, they did not ensure, (nor were they expected so to do), the international presence at the country level necessary to inform and help governments in the preparation of requests for technical co-operation in the areas of responsibility of UNCTAD. The new country programming procedures required the active participation of representatives of the executing agencies in the countries concerned during the programming exercise for an overall consideration of the priorities of the governments for UNDP assistance.

Interregional advisers

As regular staff resources could be used only to a very modest extent to perform these new tasks, a small number of posts were established within the UNCTAD technical co-operation programme for interregional advisers who assisted in dealing to some extent with this situation. The main tasks of these advisers were to render short-term advisory services to governments at their request; as in the case of all other interregional technical co-operation projects, their posts were established with the specific support of several governments. The nature of their services was often linked to the study of situations and the elucidation of issues which were conducive to the formulation of requests for assistance on a larger scale. Originally, these posts of interregional advisers were funded by UNDP and the United Nations regular programme of technical co-operation. Over the years, most posts funded by UNDP had to be phased out and UNCTAD found it difficult to secure alternative sources of financing.

In 1979, a special allocation from the UNDP sectoral support programme permitted the recruitment of three sectoral support advisers, whose main function was to aid governments in the assessment of their requirements for technical co-operation in the various areas of UNCTAD's responsibility and to assist in the formulation of related programmes and projects. However, this allocation has been progressively reduced and the number of sectoral support advisers declined to two in 1982 and to one in 1983.

Thus, the introduction by UNDP of the country programmes and the strong orientation towards field programming constituted from the outset an environment within which it was difficult for a small agency without any field establishment, no active on-going technical co-operation programme and with a globally oriented mandate, to develop a meaningful programme at the country level when there were other agencies in a more favourable position to participate in the country programming process. This explains why much of the technical co-operation programme of UNCTAD has traditionally consisted of projects of an inter-country nature, which are more in line with the natural vocation of UNCTAD itself and also afford greater opportunities to spread scarce support resources among a large number of developing countries.

The substantive content, of the technical co-operation programme of UNCTAD is closely linked with its research, policy, analysis and negotiation tasks, ensuring to the maximum possible extent a cross-fertilization between these two activities of the secretariat. This allows not only for policy and practice to be brought closely together, but also for the translation of policy guidance emanating from the Conference and its subsidiary organs into operational terms for field-level use.

The substantive content of the various subprogrammes and their evolution over time is briefly described below.

B. Main fields of operational activities

Trade policy and trade in manufactures

Through this programme UNCTAD has assisted many developing countries in expanding and diversifying their exports of manufactures and semi-manufactures.

The generalized system of preferences

Less than a year after the launching of the first scheme under the generalized system of preferences (GSP) in 1971, a technical co-operation programme on the GSP was put into effect. During the early years the number of schemes in operation multiplied, requiring much technical guidance in order to acquaint the preference-receiving countries with the complexities of the various schemes. The activities of the programme consisted of advisory missions to preference-receiving countries; training activities in those countries through seminars and workshops; preparation of GSP manuals; and the carrying out of special studies. It soon became apparent that such technical assistance would be required on a continuing basis because of continued changes in the various schemes. Such demands for technical co-operation will continue in the light of the recent extension of the GSP schemes for a further ten years. The future introduction of the Harmonized Commodity Description and Coding System in January 1987 will have important implications for the GSP and will need to be covered by the programme. In this context, Conference resolution 159 (VI) calls for the expansion of the scope of the programme to cover other laws, regulations and procedures of the preference-giving countries which affect the exports of developing countries. This new and important discussion of the programme is an expression of the broadening requirements of developing countries for technical cooperation in this area.

The multilateral trade negotiations

In a resolution adopted at UNCTAD's third session in 1972, it was decided that technical assistance should be provided to developing countries to foster their participation in the new round of multilateral trade negotiations (Tokyo Round) being prepared at that time under the auspices of GATT. This assistance was considered necessary on account of the prevailing view that developing countries had failed to obtain significant benefits from the preceding Kennedy Round of negotiations mainly because of their inadequate acquaintance with the legal and technical intricacies involved and lack of access to statistical and other factual data, both of which were required for effective participation in this highly involved and complex kind of negotiation. Participation in these negotiations was important for developing countries, as developed countries generally declined to enter into any discussion on the lowering of trade barriers or improvement of the conditions of access, except within the framework of negotiations in the context of the General Agreement on Tariffs and Trade (GATT). A technical co-operation programme was set up in 1973, which assisted the developing countries in having their interest clearly reflected in language written into the Tokyo Declaration adopted in September 1973, which was to form the basis of this entire round of multilateral negotiations. During the negotiations, the programme responded to requests by governments and by country groupings.

The services offered by the programme included: the provision of computerized data on trade flows, tariffs and non-tariff barriers: requests and offers made in the multilateral trade negotiations (MTN): provision of technical notes for meetings of the MTN negotiating groups, for use *inter alia* by small delegations unable to attend all the numerous meetings: provision of documentation in the form of technical briefs on various negotiating issues, the holding of seminars and workshops where Government officials had the opportunity to review the status of negotiations in various areas, discuss their common negotiating problems, and hear the views of outside experts, and the preparation of specific MTN-related studies for individual countries and particular groupings. The services provided by the programme have, by general recognition, made significantly more effective the participation of developing countries in the MTNs, even if the outcome of the Tokyo Round was deemed to fall short of expectations. After the conclusion of the Tokyo Round, and in the light of the experience acquired through the programme, assistance continued to be provided, albeit on a reduced scale, to developing countries on the application and utilization of the codes agreed upon during the negotiations as well as on the areas where final agreements were still under negotiation.

In addition, the UNCTAD secretariat responded and continued to respond to requests for technical co-operation in the areas of external sector planning, export financing, export credit guarantee and export credit insurance schemes, export processing free zones, international sub-contracting and other forms of intra-industry complementarity arrangements, identification of tariff and non-tariff barriers, improvement of customs administration, etc.

Restrictive business practices

A new area for technical co-operation in trade policy is that of restrictive business practices, where advisory services and training are specifically provided for in the Set of Multilaterally Agreed Equitable Principles and Rules for the Control of Restrictive Business Practices adopted in 1980 by the General Assembly.[3] In more general terms, many developing countries are not in a position to counteract

---

[3] TD/RBP/CONF/10/Rev.1 (United Nations publication, Sales No. E.81.II.D.5).

prevailing protectionist trends, not only because their individual economic potential is still too weak to enter into an escalation of protective measures, but also because the full implication of the protectionist measures has yet to be identified and properly assessed. Technical co-operation is certainly an essential instrument in filling this gap through technical advice to requesting governments and continuous training of officials from developing countries involved in the formulation and implementation of trade policies.

Trade expansion and economic co-operation among developing countries

Since 1970, assistance has been given to a large number of economic integration and co-operation groupings from all regions. This has included assistance in the formulation and implementation of integration/co-operation schemes, support for attempts to overcome obstacles encountered in the integration process and exploration of the possibilities for including new areas of co-operation in the programmes of such groupings. Substantive areas in which technical assistance was frequently extended include evaluation and preparation of trade liberalization schemes and common external tariffs, co-operation in customs matters, including harmonization of customs procedures and documents; subregional customs training schemes; statistical co-operation; computerization of foreign trade statistics; fiscal harmonization, including harmonization of investment codes; financial and monetary integration, including clearing arrangements and payments support schemes; industrial, technological and transport co-operation; joint insurance and reinsurance schemes; and legal co-operation, including preparation of legal instruments related to "integration" industries and to administrative institutions common to a grouping. Technical support was also extended to a number of commodity producers' associations.

The growing recognition of the importance of economic cooperation among developing countries (ECDC) through the Mexico City Conference (1976), the Arusha Plan of Action (1979) and the Caracas Programme of Action (1981) gave rise to new requirements of technical co-operation in selected priority areas. To fill the information gap on trade relations among developing countries, a large-scale project was launched with the overall objective of establishing a mechanism for assembling, processing and analysing data on trade of developing countries, to serve as an instrument for strengthening their capacity to implement arrangements for expanding mutual trade. The main purpose of this project is to develop a stock of computerized data providing a link between trade flows, for both countries and products, and the corresponding customs import charges, non-tariff barriers, customs receipts and other relevant information required for the formulation of commercial policy. This body of information is intended to become a major tool in support of trade negotiations among developing countries, and in particular for establishing the global system of trade preferences (GSTP).

Through another technical co-operation project, the UNCTAD secretariat assisted in the preparation of technical documentation for an Expert Group which met in Jamaica in 1982 to propose, in pursuance of the Caracas Programme of Action, concrete measures for financial co-operation in the field of development financing, including the establishment of a bank for developing countries (South Bank).

Another priority area concerns co-operation among State Trading Organizations (STOs) of developing countries. A first step was the preparation of a Handbook providing basic information on as many STOs as possible. Support was also given to the preparation and organization in 1982 of an International Symposium of STOs, which recommended the establishment of an Association of State Trading Organizations of Developing Countries as a permanent institutional framework to promote STO co-operation. Other operational activities in this area aimed at the strengthening of the capacity of STOs, especially in less advanced countries, through appropriate training and exchange of experience among STOs in various countries.

For the future, technical co-operation in ECDC is likely to develop further in the following directions: technical support to GSTP negotiations; promotion of multinational production enterprises (MPEs) and multinational marketing enterprises (MMEs), development of co-operation between economic co-operation and integration groupings; support to monetary and financial co-operation efforts, and sectoral co-operation in such areas as food, energy and services.

Shipping, ports and multimodal transport

UNCTAD's operational activities in these areas have aimed at reducing the outflow of foreign exchange and the dependency of developing countries on foreign shipping, and at fostering the development of trade through lower transport costs and adequate shipping services, port facilities and related services, including multimodal transport of goods. The assistance given covered the economic, commercial, operational, administrative and legal aspects of maritime and multimodal transport. Increasing support was given to subregional and regional co-operation in maritime transport, as the reduction of the maritime dependency of many developing countries is more easily attainable through a pooling of efforts, especially in the areas of protection of shippers' interests, including freight analysis, cargo aggregation and cargo booking, and of shipping development. In a number of subregional or country projects, the three interrelated areas of shipping, ports and protection of shippers' interests were dealt with in an integrated manner so that decisions concerning each subsector could be based on an overall assessment of the maritime situation of the country or subregion.

One important feature of the programme is the emphasis put on training activities to assist in the formulation and implementation of maritime transport policies and in the commercial management of shipping companies, port authorities and multimodal transport firms. In addition to the traditional methods of training, two major innovative training programmes have been launched in recent years: the Training Development in the field of Maritime Transport (TRAINMAR), in which emphasis is put on the preparation of training material by national or regional institutions for local delivery to middle and junior managers, and the promotion of co-operation among training institutions through the interchange of instructors and training material; and the port training programme on Improving Port performance (IPP), which concentrates on the preparation of training material by specialized institutions for worldwide dissemination to senior port managers.

Technology

The operational activities of UNCTAD in the area of technology aim at strengthening the technological capacity of developing countries and accelerating their technological transformation. Assistance is provided through the Advisory Service on Transfer of Technology (ASTT), established within the UNCTAD secretariat pursuant to Conference resolution 87 (IV). Assistance has been rendered to many developing countries and to regional or subregional organizations in the formulation and implementation of technology plans, including technology policies and plans for specific sectors of critical importance to developing countries, such as pharmaceuticals, food processing, energy and capital goods; the formation of an integrated set of policies, laws, regulations and procedures as a means of implementing strategies aiming at the technological transformation of developing countries; the establishment or strengthening of institutional infrastructures, including technology centres and other arrangements at the national, subregional, regional and sectoral levels, so that their linkages with the productive sectors can be improved and the needs of technology users met through the provision of services, training and advice in the productive utilization of technology; and the training of personnel and exchange of experience among developing countries in the field of transfer and development of technology. ASTT has organized at regular intervals in-house training sessions for small groups of government officials. Many regional, subregional and national workshops and training programmes on general or specific aspects of technology have also been organized. UNCTAD, through ASTT, acts as lead agency within the United Nations system for projects and activities concerning the utilization and commercialization of technology and results from R and D funded or supported by the United Nations system, as well as similar activities supported or financed by governments or the public sector. In line with Conference resolution 143 (VI), ASTT is evolving suitable projects and activities concerning interlinkages and co-operative arrangements among developing countries in the field of technology.

Commodities

The main focus of UNCTAD operational activities in this area has been on support for the Integrated Programme for Commodities (IPC). In a first phase, a series of interregional seminars was held on individual commodities with a view to providing developing countries exporters of these commodities with a clear appreciation of the issues and mechanisms relating to international agreements and the mutual concessions which may be required. As of 1980, when the Agreement establishing the Common Fund for Commodities was adopted, attention turned to certain developmental aspects of the Programme, particularly in connection with the processing, marketing and distribution of primary commodities.

Assistance was also provided to food-importing developing countries in improving their procurement of major food items through improved market knowledge, and skilful trading and import management. Advice was therefore given on procurement methods, tendering procedures, sources of supply, market information and subregional co-operation in imports, and training of personnel responsible for import procurement was organized through individual fellowships and workshops. Training material was assembled with a view to preparing a handbook on import procurement of food commodities. In 1980, a feasibility study was made for the establishment of a market information service to be used by food importing developing countries.

Insurance and reinsurance

Through this subprogramme, UNCTAD has assisted many developing countries, in their efforts to reduce their dependence on foreign-based insurance and reinsurance companies and the corresponding outflows of foreign exchange through appropriate legislation and regulations, the promotion of domestic insurance markets, the establishment of national insurance/reinsurance institutions and the promotion of subregional and regional co-operation in the field of insurance. In addition, a vast training effort was undertaken in view of the severe shortage of skills in this field in developing countries. Direct support was provided to several insurance training institutes located in developing countries; seminars and workshops were organized on selected insurance subjects of particular importance for participating countries, and individual fellowships were awarded to senior and middle-level insurance managers and government officials.

Least developed, land-locked and island developing countries

When the group of least developed countries (LDCs) was first identified in the early 1970s, specific trade policy projects were designed and implemented with a view to strengthening the external sector of the LDCs by expanding their export earnings, minimizing the procurement costs of imports and promoting import substitution; improving the system of formulation and management of price policy, as well as the structure of distribution, particularly as regards basic commodities, and ensuring the effective use of international, regional and subregional potential in order better to achieve self-sustained economic growth. This part of the programme included regional advisory services, country projects and training activities. A new impetus was given to the assistance to LDCs with the launching of the Substantial New Programme of Action (SNPA) in pursuance of Conference resolution 122 (V). After the adoption of SNPA at the United Nations Conference on the Least Developed Countries (Paris, 1981), similar assistance was sought for the substantive preparation of individual country reviews, mainly in the areas of trade and of aid modalities.

Assistance in the field of transport was also given to many land-locked developing countries to facilitate their access to the sea and to world markets. An integrated planning approach which permitted identification of action required with regard to the main transport and communications bottlenecks. Transit corridors and transport modes in most land-locked subregions were systematically investigated in order to identify the most cost-effective ones and to reduce the real cost of access to the sea, since the development and improvement of transport and communications systems are essential for facilitating trade and economic co-operation among developing countries on a regional or subregional basis. These activities, promoted co-operation between land-locked countries and their transit neighbours for the development of transit infrastructures and for the facilitation of the movement of goods in transit.

The specific needs of island developing countries, such as the development or improvement of inter-island and feeder transport services or the identification of viable alternative economic activities, have been reflected in the programme, as well as in aspects of technical co-operation in other areas such as shipping and economic co-operation among developing countries.

Trade with the socialist countries of Eastern Europe

In conformity with Conference resolution 95 (IV), a comprehensive programme of technical assistance for the development of trade between the socialist countries of Eastern Europe and developing countries was launched in 1979. Under this programme, training events such as seminars, workshops and seminars-*cum*-study tours were organized at the interregional, regional or national level to familiarize government officials and representatives of the business sector in developing countries with the trade policies and practices and the trading system of the socialist countries of Eastern Europe, and their relationship to the overall management of the economy, as well as to make better known the opportunities for East-South trade. Technical advice was also provided, on request, to governments of developing countries on specific matters relating to their present and potential trade with the socialist countries of Eastern Europe. Information was published and disseminated on: trade policies and modalities of trade and economic co-operation between the socialist countries of Eastern Europe and developing countries; the main characteristics of the trade flows involved in imports and exports, with particular reference to their commodity composition; commercial legislation, the institutional framework of such trade, including trade and economic agreements, mixed commissions, foreign trade organizations, chambers of commerce, trade fairs, etc.

Trade facilitation

UNCTAD became engaged in technical co-operation in the field of trade facilitation as early as 1970; the main purpose of this activity has been to advise governments and subregional organizations on matters related to the simplification and harmonization of trade formalities and procedures and the standardization of documents used in international trade; the programme, known as the Special Programme on Trade Facilitation (FALPRO), through its advisory service, assisted many national trade facilitation committees and similar bodies in their work towards establishing regional or national systems of aligned documents conforming to agreed international standards and recommendations. FALPRO has also co-operated in the implementation of other technical co-operation projects as far as trade facilitation matters are concerned (e.g., transit-transport projects for land-locked countries, subregional integration projects, trade promotion projects, and customs administration projects). (A more detailed account of FALPRO is contained in Section II below.)

Money, finance and development

Technical co-operation in the area of monetary and financial issues started in 1976 with a project of technical support to the Intergovernmental Group of 24 on

International Monetary Affairs.[4] The main focus of this project was the preparation of action-oriented studies on monetary issues currently under consideration in the International Monetary Fund's Interim Committee, the joint World Bank/IMF Development Committee and in other bodies as appropriate. These studies covered such subjects as the role of special drawing rights (SDRs); trade barriers and the balance-of-payments adjustment process; reserve assets and exchange rate systems; and options for international monetary reform.

More recently, the growing importance of international financial markets as a source of external finance for developing countries, coupled with mounting difficulty in relation to external debt servicing, has increased the demand for specialized advisory services in external financing, planning and management. For several years UNCTAD has been providing such services to an increasing number of developing countries through technical co-operation. These services cover assistance in establishing and running computerized debt management systems; evaluation of future borrowing requirements which may form the basis for seminars on alternative paths of economic development; advice on improving existing debt management procedures and systems; assistance in debt renegotiations and assistance in the formulation of policy in external financial planning and management.

Research and training programme

In the late 1970s, the experience gained by the UNCTAD secretariat through the execution of technical co-operation projects in support of the generalized system of preferences (GSP), the multilateral trade negotiations and the Integrated Programme for Commodities showed that, apart from the requisite political will and convergence of objectives, progress is largely determined by the extent to which relevant technical skills, factual data, analytical material and other necessary tools are available to the parties involved. It was felt that a greater and more systematic recourse to technical co-operation in this area might speed up the negotiating process in fostering the capacity of developing countries for gathering, processing or analysing the necessary technical data for conducting negotiations. At the same time, there has been growing concern about the basic assumptions regarding the functioning of the world economic system on which the work and initiatives of UNCTAD had been based since its inception. A new thrust was justified to reappraise and recast the conceptual framework in which the interrelationship between the different components of the system could be assessed in a coherent manner. Such an effort would in turn give a new impetus to the negotiating function of UNCTAD through the identification of structural changes and issues amenable to negotiation. In response to these two complementary needs, a Research and Training Programme was launched with the joint financial support of UNDP and the OPEC Special Fund. To date eight workshops have been held under this programme, of which two were devoted to international commodity issues and the remainder to: restrictive business practices; negotiations on international trade in textiles; international trade negotiations; co-operation among developing countries on monetary and financial issues; legal aspects of the transfer and development of

---

[4] Generally known as the Group of 24. The Group is composed of developing countries, operating within the framework of the International Monetary Fund.

technology; and trade policy issues in general. A Register of Research on Trade and Development Issues was published and up-dated. In 1984, a comprehensive study on South-South trade was undertaken. However, the pursuit of this programme on a more permanent and regular basis requires an assurance of a much larger volume of extra-budgetary funds.

Assistance to national liberation movements

In pursuance of pertinent resolutions adopted by the General Assembly and the Economic and Social Council inviting the United Nations agencies to provide adequate support to national liberation movements recognized by the Organization of African Unity, the Conference and the Trade and Development Board have on several occasions requested the UNCTAD secretariat to initiate a programme of operational activities in this area. However, owing to difficulties in mobilizing adequate extra-budgetary resources, the only technical co-operation project implemented by UNCTAD so far has been the Economic and Social Survey of Zimbabwe, prepared and published shortly before the independence of that country.

Dimension of the overall programme

The various operational activities described above reflect the complexity of the trade problems faced by developing countries. Technical co-operation by UNCTAD is, however, only a very small part of the total of multilateral co-operation for development. This is evident, for example, from the fact that the expenditures of UNCTAD financed by UNDP represented in 1982 1.8 per cent of total UNDP expenditure and that in the same year UNCTAD accounted for only about 1 per cent of total technical co-operation expenditures incurred by the United Nations development system. In terms of annual expenditures, the UNCTAD programme increased from $0.9 million in 1971 to $15.3 million in 1981 and then declined to $11.8 million in 1982 and to $10.2 million in 1983. The share financed by UNDP has always been prominent, varying between 80.3 per cent and 93.0 per cent over the period 1971-1983. The sharp reduction in UNCTAD's programme expenditure in 1982 and 1983, which is expected to worsen in 1984, was mainly caused by the drastic reduction in UNDP financial resources, which resulted in severe disruptions to the project planning and implementation process of Governments and executing agencies. UNCTAD has been particularly affected by this situation in view of its heavy dependence on UNDP financing and is finding it increasingly difficult to meet the growing requirements of developing countries for technical co-operation. A diversification of the sources of finance for UNCTAD's operational activities could help to alleviate the situation.

The International Trade Centre (UNCTAD/GATT)

This brief history of UNCTAD as an operational agency would not be complete without some reference to the parallel and complementary role of the International Trade Centre UNCTAD/GATT (ITC) in trade promotion. Up to 1967, technical assistance in export promotion was provided by several units and agencies of the United Nations system, including GATT, the regional commissions, UNIDO and FAO. In order to ensure an appropriate co-ordination of these activities and to avoid duplication, several of these units agreed to join their efforts in a United Nations Export Promotion Programme open to all agencies of the United Nations system. At this stage, UNCTAD and GATT were considering ways and means of harmonizing their participation in this programme, and the two secretariats concluded that the best solution might be to pool their resources in a joint centre. A proposal along these lines was submitted to and endorsed by the Trade and Development Board at its fifth session and the contracting parties to GATT. The agreement between UNCTAD and GATT on the establishment of the International Trade Centre was approved by the General Assembly and came into effect in January 1968. Under the legislative authority granted, the Centre was operated jointly by GATT and UNCTAD, and its budget and work programme were approved by the Trade and Development Board and the contracting parties to GATT on the basis of recommendations made by a Joint Advisory Group (JAG) on the International Trade Centre, whose participation was open to all UNCTAD and GATT members. The Centre helps developing countries to formulate and implement trade promotion programmes and activities, and to build up the necessary institutional infrastructure in this area. It assists in the creation of specialized services for trade promotion and international marketing and in the identification of export market opportunities. UNCTAD (through the United Nations budget) and GATT each contribute 50 per cent of its regular budget, and its operational activities are financed mostly through bilateral contributions and to a lesser extent by UNDP. While the Centre enjoyed full autonomy in respect of the execution of bilaterally-funded projects, its legislative authority to execute UNDP-funded projects was effected through UNCTAD until January 1984, when UNDP granted ITC the status of an Executing Agency.

Prospects

Through its operational programme, UNCTAD has provided a significant measure of support to developing countries in meeting their development priorities and objectives and in their efforts to achieve economic self-reliance individually and collectively. UNCTAD's technical co-operation activities, which developed at a fairly regular pace during the decade 1971-1981, declined for two consecutive years in 1982 and 1983, a trend which is likely to become even more pronounced in 1984 and 1985. UNCTAD finds itself in the difficult position of not being able to meet the technical co-operation requirements of the developing countries, despite the substantive technical backstopping capacity available in the secretariat, because extra-budgetary resources are too small. Failure to compensate for the expected shortfall in financial resources would indeed be greatly detrimental to the development efforts of the developing countries, in view of the important role of technical co-operation in their development efforts and the type of technical co-operation that UNCTAD does and could provide.

II. SPECIAL PROGRAMME ON TRADE FACILITATION (FALPRO)

A. Nature and evolution of trade facilitation

Nature of trade facilitation

It has been estimated that one quarter of everything produced in the world is traded over national borders. The goods traded have to be physically moved over these borders and any such movement is subject to an array of complex formalities, procedures and paperwork.

Available estimates indicate that the costs of trade procedures and documentation amount to about 10 per cent of the value of the goods traded. This is a very important cost factor, and a serious impediment to the expansion of international trade. Moreover, means of transport are often kept idle at borders or in ports while customs or other formalities are completed. The resulting addition of direct and indirect costs amounts to a hidden tax which is eventually borne by the final consumer.

This situation can be remedied through an organized and systematic effort to rationalize trade procedures and documentation, or what is now known as trade facilitation. International trade facilitation brings about direct gains in the form of cost reduction, speeding up of movement of goods and increased reliability of trade and transport data. Indirectly, easier procedures also help to reduce port congestion and encourage potential traders to engage in external trade, etc.

Evolution from a European approach to world-wide application

The United Nations became engaged in the international trade facilitation effort in 1960 through an initiative within the Economic Commission for Europe (ECE). Since 1970, UNCTAD has provided a forum for technical co-operation on trade facilitation for developing countries which gradually developed and, in 1975, became a separate secretariat unit, the Special Programme on Trade Facilitation (FALPRO).

The background to this development dates back to the late 1950s, when some countries became acutely aware of the obstacles to trade caused by complicated procedures and paperwork, but also found ways of reducing these obstacles through rather simple facilitation measures. It was soon realized that real progress in the field of trade facilitation could only be achieved through international co-operation, and this led in 1960 to the creation within ECE of a special Working Party which in 1963 adopted what is now known as the "United Nations layout key for trade documents". Since then, a large number of trade and transport documents, international as well as national, have been aligned to that key. This harmonization has considerably reduced some practical obstacles to international trade; it represents an indirect, but efficient, method of trade promotion.

In 1969, ECE agreed on the need for facilitation work to be co-ordinated on a worldwide basis and for the existing technical function of the United Nations Secretariat to be strengthened to further this aim. The matter was brought to the attention of the Executive Secretaries of the regional commissions, who agreed that the most appropriate formula for a global approach in this field would be the establishment, within the framework of the United Nations Development Programme (UNDP), of an interregional project to be attached to UNCTAD. In April 1970, a trade facilitation project prepared by UNCTAD was approved by UNDP.

With the expansion of work in the following years, it became clear that a distinction would have to be made between UNDP-financed technical assistance activities and substantive secretariat work. In June 1973, the executive heads of UNCTAD and ECE agreed that UNCTAD would assume responsibility for the provision of secretariat technical expertise on a worldwide basis.

With the establishment of the Special Programme on Trade Facilitation (FALPRO) as a separate UNCTAD secretariat unit, the United Nations trade facilitation activity obtained a platform for the global extension of this work.

FALPRO does not report to any of the bodies within UNCTAD's permanent machinery and therefore is not part of the policy or negotiation oriented "mainstream" activity of the Organization. However, the attachment to UNCTAD enables FALPRO to act as a natural focal point in a global "trade facilitation network", through co-operative arrangements with the regional commissions and the International Trade Centre UNCTAD/GATT (ITC), with specialized agencies of the United Nations and with other international bodies concerned. In this context, FALPRO can claim to play a unique role within the system.

FALPRO's mandate and terms of reference

The legislative mandate for FALPRO, reaffirmed by the Trade and Development Board in 1979 through decision 187 (XIX), reads as follows:

... the work on facilitation of trade procedures and documentation undertaken through the Special Programme on Trade Facilitation should be continued and intensified, within the framework of the resources made available to UNCTAD, ensuring the full participation of developing countries in this effort.

The terms of reference for FALPRO were originally established in the United Nations programme budget for 1976-1977. They can be summarized as follows:

Action on formalities, procedures and documents in international trade, including technical backstopping to UNDP-financed facilitation projects, harmonized formalities and standardized documents for transit procedures, preparation of an inventory and presentation of data requirements in international trade, etc;

Co-ordination of facilitation measures to be undertaken jointly with ECE and the other regional commissions and aiming at covering all facilitation efforts carried out within these and other international bodies;

Development of new data processing and data communication methods in international trade;

Information on trade facilitation measures to be provided in the form of continued collection and dissemination of information on facilitation measures and preparation and maintenance of a technical manual on facilitation matters.

Functions within UNCTAD

FALPRO has a cross-sectoral function in UNCTAD, dealing with facilitation matters globally in co-operation with other UNCTAD programmes. Examples include: documentation for commodity agreements; procedures and documentation for regional integration projects, for the generalized system of preferences and for ports, shipping and multimodal transport; preparation of guidelines and of drafts for transit agreements; harmonization of customs procedures; various statistical and coding projects.

B. Main results of FALPRO's activities

More than 100 countries—most of them developing countries—are now involved in trade facilitation, which encompasses a wide variety of measures to make trade easier by removing obstacles in the form of documents and procedures and by developing new and rational methods for directing and monitoring the flow of goods and money in trade. This is an important achievement, as much of the facilitation effort would be wasted if improved procedures were to apply only in a limited number of countries, with traditional procedures prevailing in the rest of the world. Co-operation with developing countries in their effort to keep abreast of progress in the facilitation field is now a very important part of FALPRO's work.

Work on development of new facilitation measures and technical solutions is carried out through day-to-day co-operation between FALPRO and ECE and its Working Party and groups of experts. Among the more relevant results of this co-operation are 19 recommendations adopted by the Working Party which provide the basic standards in international trade facilitation. Moreover, two important publications have been prepared jointly by UNCTAD and ECE for worldwide application: a *Trade data elements directory* and a *Trade data interchange directory;* a *Trade facilitation manual* is under preparation.

In many countries the introduction of simplified and aligned trade documents has reduced direct documentation costs by 50-75 per cent and has indirectly provided the basis for a common understanding of the data requirements in trade and for the recent agreements on standard data elements and on guidelines for the exchange of trade data. The introducition of new technology for information processing and transmission makes it possible to document trade transactions by teletransmitted data; goods can be cleared through customs and released on receipt of a simple message passed through interlinked computers in different parts of the world, to give but one example.

FALPRO has carried out a particularly onerous task in compiling the United Nations LOCODE, a code system for ports, airports and other locations in the world which are important in international trade. In implementing an ECE recommendation, this work also involves the Economic Commission for Latin America and the Caribbean (ECLAC), the Economic and Social Commission for Asia and the Pacific (ESCAP) and a number of other organizations.

Furthermore, for the last 10 years, FALPRO has been engaged in research and development work on particular administrative and procedural problems related to transit transport. This has led to the preparation of a reference document "Guidelines for drafting of transit agreements", intended to help countries negotiating such agreements by providing a legal and administrative framework from which relevant provisions can be selected. Although equally applicable for all countries, these guidelines may be particularly useful when land-locked countries and neighbouring coastal countries have to agree upon rules for the surface transit of goods between sea ports and the hinterland.

As a result of FALPRO's work, national trade facilitation bodies have been set up in several developing countries. One of FALPRO's regular tasks is to keep in contact with these bodies, train their staff in the country concerned or in Geneva and encourage their participation in the international facilitation work, often in the form of technical co-operation between developing countries.

C. Problems faced in carrying out trade facilitation

Selection of target countries

The facilitation work was initiated in industrialized countries where high manpower costs and lack of labour were the main reasons for the interest in rationalization of procedures and documents. A considerable intellectual and financial investment has been made in the development of new techniques in this field. It is now highly desirable to extend the use of such new technology globally, and to engage developing countries actively in international facilitation work, not only to help them to benefit from improvements in procedures and paperwork, but also to avoid the introduction of methods which are too sophisticated or otherwise unsuitable for the less developed countries.

FALPRO's field work has mainly been financed by UNDP or donor countries which have laid down certain conditions, directing activities towards land-locked or least developed countries. Neither category is suited for the introduction of more sophisticated procedures and data transmission methods as alternatives to traditional document practices. A number of other developing countries, with greater potential in this respect, can be served by FALPRO only exceptionally, if at all. This is an unsatisfactory state of affairs since many of the technical standards and solutions developed within ECE can only attain their real value if applied worldwide. The best way to extend their application would be by introducing them in some developing countries which are particularly important in international trade. It is likely that the so-called newly industrializing countries would be the most suitable target group.

Resistance to change

Many developing countries have retained trade regulations and procedures from the time before independence. This situation is often compounded by a certain administrative inertia and a reluctance to change among officials who are ensconsed in traditional habits and practices. Another important obstacle is that in many cases the simplification of trade procedures entails a reduction of the number of staff employed in office work, or loss of certain privileged positions through changes of responsibilities of the officials involved. These factors are often responsible for a certain lack of enthusiasm regarding the simplification of trade procedures.

However, this is not a phenomenon restricted to governmental functions. More often than not, commercial practices are even more difficult to change, despite the fact that the commercial parties are the main, direct beneficiaries of trade facilitation.

It is therefore necessary to ensure that all parties concerned in each country are informed, are interested and take a positive view of trade facilitation as an overall national economic reform. While there is often a recognition of this fact at the policy-making level, what is required is to convince officials at the operational level of the desirability of reform, to explain the consequences of such reforms on their own functions, and to show how trade facilitation can also result in a better allocation of human resources.

Another important aspect in trade facilitation work—and one which creates a resource problem—is the need to train officials from participating countries so as to enable them to carry out facilitation programmes in their own countries, in cooperation with FALPRO, the regional commissions and other bodies concerned.

D. Tasks for the future

The UNCTAD medium-term plan for 1980-1983 envisaged that, by the end of 1979, FALPRO would have completed the first part of an overall action plan for the systematic reduction of trade formalities, in the form of basic intergovernmental agreements on a methodology for data transmission, including a complete study and proposals on sets of data elements and syntax rules, as a substitute for paper documentation in trade; the completion of a Trade Facilitation Manual, and the implementation by 10 to 12 developing countries of facilitation measures recommended by FALPRO. The major thrust for the biennium 1982-1983 was the implementation of basic agreements on new methods for data communication, the refinement of these methods and the planning of further facilitation measures.

The plan has been implemented through the preparation and publication of the two Directories, respectively on Trade Data Elements and on Trade Data Interchange (to be seen as the first instalments of the Trade Facilitation Manual), and through other results, already mentioned.

FALPRO's work will now focus on implementation of trade facilitation measures in those developing countries where work has already started, and in initiating such work in other countries. In the near future some developing countries will probably be ready for a "second generation" of more sophisticated measures, based on the introduction of new technology. Technological progress will have to be monitored and—if possible—influenced in order to develop solutions which are suitable for all trading countries in the world. A great deal of effort will be needed in order to involve more developing countries actively in the work.

FALPRO works in an area where it is possible to offer practical service for the operation of trade, and where the only significant problems are those of obtaining resources sufficient to meet the demand for such services, and of keeping abreast with technological progress. As trade facilitation work will succeed through perseverance rather than through massive short-term action, it is hoped that means will be available for continuous and systematic activity in this field.

III. UNCTAD AND DISARMAMENT

The United Nations, in accordance with the Charter, has a central role and primary responsibility in the sphere of disarmament. The first special session of the General Assembly devoted to disarmament adopted a final document which outlines a global strategy for disarmament and could be said to constitute a "Disarmament Charter" of the United Nations.[1] This document stresses that the United Nations should play a more active role in the field of disarmament and that, "in order to discharge its functions effectively, the United Nations should facilitate and encourage all disarmament measures—unilateral, bilateral, regional or multilateral ...".[2] The Final Document also laid the foundations for the existing international disarmament machinery, consisting of deliberating and negotiating bodies, as well as of those bodies, specialized agencies and other institutions and programmes within the United Nations system that are responsible for study, research and information or other disarmament-related activities.

UNCTAD together with other organizations, has made its contribution to the common efforts for strengthening peace and arms limitation, concentrating on the trade and economic aspects of disarmament and the relationship between expenditure on armaments and economic and social development.

The diversion of vast resources—financial, material and human—to ever-expanding military expenditure, is an important factor in the current world economic crisis. An environment of international tensions and the threat to the very existence of the human race itself is hardly a propitious one in which to solve the problems facing the world economy, particularly those confronting the developing countries.

At its very first session in 1964, the Conference adopted without dissent recommendation A.VI.10 on the "Elaboration of trade aspects of the Economic Programme of Disarmament", in which it deemed it necessary that "in pursuing studies and working out proposals, within the framework of the United Nations, on the economic and social consequences of disarmament... due attention be paid to the trade aspects of the economic programme of disarmament".

In reporting to the Conference at that session the Secretary-General of UNCTAD stated that worldwide disarmament would open up enormous possibilities for realizing resources for the development of the developing countries. He indicated that, "if part of the resources released by disarmament were used to increase the productive investment of industrial countries, this would give a greater impetus to their own growth and to the demand for imports from the developing

---

[1] General Assembly resolution S-10/2 of 30 June 1978 (Final Document of the Tenth Special Session of the General Assembly).

[2] *Ibid.*, para. 114.

countries and help to accelerate the flow of these imports".[3] General Principle Twelve adopted by the Conference declared that "All countries recognize that a significant portion of resources released in successive stages as a result of the conclusion of an agreement on general and complete disarmament under effective international control should be allocated to the promotion of economic development in developing countries".

At its third session (Santiago, 1972) the Conference adopted by a vote of 87 to none, with 9 abstentions, resolution 44 (III) on "Trade and economic aspects of disarmament", in which it requested the Secretary-General of UNCTAD to continue studies on the positive effects of disarmament on international trade and economic relations and decided that the Trade and Development Board should keep the trade and economic aspects of disarmament under continuous review.

The trade and development aspects of disarmament were not included as a separate agenda item at the sixth session of the Conference (Belgrade, 1983), as it was understood that the matter could be discussed under the item relating to the world economic situation, with special emphasis on development.

In his general report to the Conference, the Secretary-General of UNCTAD noted that "An economic perspective for the 1980s cannot be separated from the political context and from the evolution of international economic relations. A world of rising political tension and of rising armaments expenditure, not to speak of conflicts, is not compatible with or supportive of the process of world trade and development or the resurgence of national economies. Unfortunately, heavy armaments expenditure is a strain on many economies today. It is a factor underlying the present world economic crisis. The possible scenarios for the 1980s—for the developed market-economy countries, for the socialist countries, as well as for the developing countries—will be deeply influenced by the future course of spending on armaments. Needless to say, a failure to arrest the present arms race would render invalid the positive scenario for the future. It would make a reality of and justify the negative one."[4]

The discussion at the Conference clearly showed that many participants were concerned by the increasing threat to peace and international security. In the second Raul Prebisch Lecture, held during the Conference, the late Mrs. Indira Gandhi, Prime Minister of India, said: "The high level of military expenditure in advanced economies has contributed greatly to the economic crisis. It impinges on other elements like cost, supply, demand, rate of accumulation of the reproductive capital, claims on research capacity and human skills, and the entire scheme of national priorities. For every hundredfold rise in productive capacity, there seems to be a thousandfold increase in destructive capacity."[5] She also noted: "Some governments say 'arm today, disarm tomorrow'. But today's arms can deny us our tomorrows."

---

[3] "Towards a New Trade Policy for Development" reproduced in *Proceedings of the United Nations Conference on Trade and Development, Geneva, 23 March-16 June 1964,* vol. II—*Policy Statements* (United Nations publication, Sales No. E.64.II.B.12), p 58.

[4] *Development and recovery: The realities of the new interdependence* (TD/271/Rev.1) (United Nations publication, Sales No. E.84.II.D.4), para. 68.

[5] *Peace and Development* delivered by H. E. Mrs. Indira Gandhi, Prime Minister of India, p. 5.

Sweden's Prime Minister, Olof Palme, said that "although the existing nuclear arsenals are sufficient to destroy mankind many times over, they continue to grow at a high rate. During the last decade military spending in the world has been doubled. Today the world's military spending is nearly 20 times the amount of spending for development assistance. Every minute mankind spends more than $1.3 million on military purposes. During the same minute 30 children die in the world, mainly in the developing countries, many of them dying of malnutrition and starvation".[6]

In its statement on the world economic situation, the Conference stated that "Durable peace can be best assured by narrowing the economic disparity between nations. Sustained global development and a viable international economic order in turn require an atmosphere of peace, harmony and co-operation, the halting of the arms race, and the adoption of disarmament measures that will release sorely needed resources for development."[7]

In accordance with the provisions of Conference resolution 44 (III), the Trade and Development Board regularly reviews UNCTAD activities in the area of trade and economic aspects of disarmament. In this connection, special mention should be made of the eighteenth, the twenty-first and twenty-fifth sessions of the Board which paid considerable attention to the problem of effective disarmament measures for economic and social development. In considering the main features of the future work of UNCTAD on the trade and development aspects of disarmament, the Board at its twenty-fifth session took into account the decisions, conclusions and recommendations of the General Assembly on disarmament contained in the Concluding Document of the twelfth special session (second special session on disarmament), held from 7 June to 10 July 1982. The Secretariat urged that, within the limits of its competence and available resources, UNCTAD should participate in the World Disarmament Campaign which was to contribute, through better information and education, to the mobilization of public opinion in favour of disarmament and the strengthening of international peace and security. The socialist countries of Eastern Europe and several developing countries urged UNCTAD to co-operate with the competent United Nations bodies and continue keeping this question under review.

At its twenty-seventh, twenty-eighth and twenty-ninth sessions the Board discussed the possibility of including a special item on the trade and economic aspects of disarmament in the provisional agenda for a subsequent session but could not reach an agreement on this matter. It was decided to consider this matter again at the thirtieth session (March 1985), when once more the matter will be discussed.

UNCTAD has actively participated in a number of conferences, seminars, working groups, etc., devoted to the trade and economic aspects of disarmament. The UNCTAD secretariat participated as an observer in the work of the United

---

[6] TD/306, 20 June 1983, p. 3.

[7] Paragraph 13 of the statement *Proceedings of the United Nations Conference on Trade and Development, Sixth Session*, vol. I — *Final Act and Report* (United Nations publication, Sales No. E.83.II.D.6), part one, sect. A.

Nations Group of Governmental Experts on the Relationship between Disarmament and Development; at the second International Conference on "Dialogue for Disarmament and Détente", held in Vienna in 1983, and at the Conference on the Role of Non-alignment, Development and the New Economic Order (New Delhi, 1984); at the "International Dialogue on the United Nations and Peace Forces—Ways to strengthen Co-operation", organized by the International Liaison Forum of Peace Forces (Geneva 10-12 September 1984); and at the Meeting of the World Peace Council's Working Commission on Development and Disarmament (Budapest 29-31 January 1985).

In its *Trade and Development Report 1982*[8] the UNCTAD secretariat devoted a special chapter to "Armaments expenditure and disarmament: some consequences for development", drawing, *inter alia,* on the report entitled *The relationship between disarmament and development* which was prepared by a group of governmental experts, appointed by the Secretary-General of the United Nations. The chapter discussed the direct and indirect harmful consequences for developing countries of their growing armaments expenditure and the favourable prospects which disarmament would open for the acceleration of growth in the world economy as a whole and in developing countries in particular. It noted that in "a relaxation of international tension and of the arms race and the redirection of armaments expenditure to civilian use could play an important role in revitalizing the world economy and accelerating the development of developing countries".

In its resolutions 37/16 of 16 November 1982, 38/56 of 7 December 1983, and resolution 49/10 of 8 November 1984 concerning the International Year of Peace the General Assembly invited all organizations within the United Nations system to co-operate with the Secretary-General in achieving the objectives of the Year.

The Trade and Development Board will no doubt consider the contribution which can be made by UNCTAD to attainment of the objectives of the International Year of Peace when it takes up the subject of the trade and economic aspects of disarmament.

---

[8] United Nations publication, Sales No. E.82.II.D.12.

IV. ASSISTANCE TO NATIONAL LIBERATION MOVEMENTS

A. Introduction

UNCTAD's activities in the field of assistance to national liberation movements recognized by regional intergovernmental organizations should be viewed against the background of the political trend that emerged during the latter part of the 1970s within the United Nations system on assistance to the peoples and countries still living under colonial domination and foreign occupation and to their liberation movements. Until the early 1970s the debate on the nature of this assistance was confined to the General Assembly of the United Nations, though many of the resolutions adopted by the General Assembly on the subject also called on the Executive Heads of the organizations and specialized agencies of the United Nations to pay particular attention, in the context of their work, to the programme of assistance to national liberation movements recognized by regional intergovernmental organizations. However, with the increased political recognition of the national liberation movements and the participation of representatives of these movements as observers in different organizations of the United Nations, there emerged in the latter part of the 1970s a growing emphasis on assistance to national liberation movements in intergovernmental deliberations.

B. Economic and Social Survey of Zimbabwe

The first major activity to be undertaken in UNCTAD in this area was the preparation of the Economic and Social Survey of Zimbabwe.[1] This was the result of a project requested in July 1978 by the co-leaders of the Patriotic Front of Zimbabwe and financed by the United Nations Development Programme (UNDP) in accordance with relevant resolutions of the General Assembly and of the Governing Council of UNDP.

This survey, conducted by UNCTAD as executing agency, was intended to assist the peoples of Zimbabwe in their new struggle, which was envisaged to begin after the achievement of political independence. In this context, the immediate objective of the survey was "to prepare the ground for the decisive passage of Zimbabwe from colonialism to self-sustained economic development", a passage that would imply a transition from war to peace, from a European settler-dominated society to one that would care about its African population, and from an imposed economic autarky to a system firmly oriented towards regional and inter-

---

[1] *Zimbabwe: Towards a New Order: An Economic and Social Survey* United Nations, 1980 (UNCTAD/UNDP project).

national economic co-operation. Beyond this, it was envisaged that, on the basis of a sound analysis of the structural features of the economy of Zimbabwe and of its main social and economic characteristics, the survey would examine the future prospects and point to the main direction of long-term development policy.

In retrospect, this initiative seemed to have been taken at the most opportune moment because by the time the survey was completed in 1980, the people of Zimbabwe had achieved their political independence.

C. UNCTAD V

While the conduct of the economic and social survey of Zimbabwe was in progress, an initiative was taken by the Group of 77 at the fifth session of the Conference held in Manila in 1979. This initiative led to the adoption of resolution 109 (V), by vote, on assistance to national liberation movements recognized by regional intergovernmental organizations.[2] In that resolution the Conference requested the Secretary-General of UNCTAD, within the context of the International Development Strategy for the Third United Nations Development Decade, to initiate studies, within the competence of UNCTAD, as regards those peoples and countries still living under colonial domination or foreign occupation (i.e. Namibia, Palestine, South Africa and Zimbabwe). These studies were to be undertaken in collaboration with the respective national liberation movements recognized by regional intergovernmental organizations.

Pursuant to this resolution, the UNCTAD secretariat prepared, with the assistance of consultants, two studies—one on the review of economic conditions in Namibia and South Africa, and the other on the review of the economic conditions of the Palestinian people in the occupied Arab territories.

As regards assistance to the peoples of Namibia and South Africa and their national liberation movements, the first study[3] emphasized two major conclusions emerging from a review of their economic conditions. The first concerned the need for manpower development, which appeared to have acquired particular importance in the case of Namibia. The second related to the need for further in-depth examination of economic issues that would arise in the transition to majority rule. In this context, the study considered international support for transition to majority rule in Namibia to be a matter of urgency and stressed the need to prepare a comprehensive social and economic survey of Namibia, along the lines of the study on Zimbabwe.

The study on assistance to the Palestinian people[4] sought to provide a background review of the economic condition of the Palestinian people in the occupied

---

[2] The resolution was adopted by a roll-call vote of 91 to 16, with 14 abstentions. Those *against* were Australia; Austria; Belgium; Canada; Denmark; France; Germany, Federal Republic of; Israel; Italy; Luxembourg; Netherlands; New Zealand; Norway; Switzerland; United Kingdom; United States. Those *abstaining* were Chile; Costa Rica; El Salvador; Fiji; Finland; Greece; Guatemala; Ireland; Japan; Malawi; Portugal; Spain; Sweden; Uruguay.

[3] TD/B/869 and Add.1.

[4] TD/B/870.

Arab territories; to identify the main economic problems facing the Palestinian people; and to make suggestions for a programme of action designed to overcome those problems. While the study outlined a number of recommendations on measures for the stabilization and strengthening of the local economies of the occupied Arab territories, as well as for improving the social and economic situation of the Palestinian population living in those territories, it also stressed the need for carrying out further in-depth sectoral studies.

By the time these two studies were submitted to the Trade and Development Board in October 1981, the economic and social survey of Zimbabwe had been received and commended by the international community in general, and by the newly-elected Government of independent Zimbabwe in particular as a major contribution to assistance to the peoples of Zimbabwe in their new struggle for transition from colonialism to self-sustained economic and social development. The recognition of the importance and relevance of the study on Zimbabwe perhaps played a part in shaping the nature of the demand of the Group of 77 for action by the Trade and Development Board in the field of assistance to national liberation movements.

The Trade and Development Board, on 9 October 1981, after considering the two studies, adopted, by vote, two resolutions which respectively requested the Secretary-General of UNCTAD, within the context of the International Development Strategy for the Third United Nations Development Decade, to consult and prepare with other United Nations agencies and bodies, in collaboration with the South West African People's Organization (SWAPO), a comprehensive and in-depth social and economic survey of Namibia along the lines of the study on Zimbabwe and to prepare a comprehensive and in-depth survey of the state of the economy of the Palestinian people in the occupied Palestinian territories, as well as an elaborate analysis of the potentials for its development in the various sectors, and to formulate proposals for alternative development strategies in collaboration with the Palestine Liberation Organization (PLO). In these resolutions,[5] the Board invited UNDP to make available to UNCTAD additional resources for preparing these surveys.

While it has not yet been possible to secure additional resources for conducting the in-depth surveys mentioned above, a report was prepared in 1983 by consultants at the request of the UNCTAD secretariat and submitted to the Trade and Development Board. This report[6] contains a broad evaluation of the potential for, and constraints on, the economic and social development of the Palestinian people, while providing a framework and direction for the in-depth sectoral studies that would be required in preparing the comprehensive surveys. The inability of

---

[5] Resolution 238 (XXIII) on Namibia and South Africa was adopted by a roll-call vote of 75 to 1, with 21 abstentions; and resolution 239 (XXIII) on Palestine was adopted by a roll-call vote of 75 to 2, with 20 abstentions. The United States voted against resolution 238 (XXIII) and the following countries abstained: Australia; Austria; Belgium; Canada; Denmark; Finland; France; Germany, Federal Republic of; Greece; Ireland; Italy; Japan; Liechtenstein; Luxembourg; Netherlands; New Zealand; Norway; Portugal; Sweden; Switzerland; United Kingdom. Israel and the United States voted against resolution 239 (XXIII). The following countries abstained: Australia; Belgium; Canada; Denmark; Finland; France; Germany, Federal Republic of; Greece; Ireland; Italy; Japan; Liechtenstein; Luxembourg; Netherlands; New Zealand; Norway; Portugal; Sweden; Switzerland; United Kingdom.

[6] TD/B/960 and Corr.1.

UNCTAD to secure the additional resources can perhaps be explained by two factors. First, there has been a sharp deterioration in recent years in the overall resource situation of UNDP, and second, there has been no consensus within UNCTAD on its role in the field of assistance to national liberation movements.

D. UNCTAD VI

In the context of the preparation for the sixth session of the Conference, there emerged, within the Group of 77, a new idea as regards assistance to the Palestinian people. This was concerned with seeking to establish a special economic unit within UNCTAD which would monitor, investigate and report periodically on the economic situation and on the policies pursued in development of the Palestinian occupied territories.

As a result of preparatory work within the Group of 77 prior to UNCTAD VI, the Group of 77 submitted a draft resolution at Belgrade (resolution 146 (VI)) which was adopted by a vote.[7] The resolution requested the Secretary-General of UNCTAD to set up a special economic unit to monitor and investigate the policies of the Israeli-occupying authorities hampering the economic development of the occupied Palestinian territories and to report periodically to the Trade and Development Board and to the General Assembly, through the Economic and Social Council, on the implementation of this resolution. The unit was established in December 1984.

On that occasion the Conference also adopted another resolution (147 (VI)), by vote,[8] on assistance to the peoples of Namibia and South Africa. In that resolution it requested the Secretary-General of UNCTAD to prepare, in consultation with the Organization of African Unity (OAU), a comprehensive economic and social survey of the oppressed people of South Africa as well as to co-operate with the United Nations Institute for Namibia, through the provision of appropriate technical expertise, in the preparation of a comprehensive document on all aspects of economic planning and development in an independent Namibia in accordance with the relevant resolution of the General Assembly. The Conference also urged UNDP to provide adequate resources to the UNCTAD secretariat for carrying out its survey.

---

[7] The roll-call vote was 84 to 2, with 20 abstentions. Israel and the United States voted against the resolution. The following countries abstained: Australia; Belgium; Canada; Denmark; Dominican Republic; Finland; France; Germany, Federal Republic of; Ireland; Italy; Japan; Luxembourg; Netherlands; New Zealand; Norway; Papua New Guinea; Portugal; Switzerland; United Kingdom; Uruguay.

[8] The roll-call vote was 84 to 1, with 19 abstentions. The United States voted against. The following countries abstained: Australia; Belgium; Canada; Denmark; France; Germany, Federal Republic of; Greece; Ireland; Israel; Italy; Japan; Luxembourg; Netherlands; New Zealand; Norway; Portugal; Switzerland; United Kingdom; Uruguay.

E. Concluding remarks

It should be noted that in recent years, with the increased participation, in accordance with resolutions of the General Assembly, of the national liberation movements as observers in different bodies and agencies of the United Nations, within UNCTAD—as in other bodies and agencies of the United Nations—increased attention has been paid to the development problems of the peoples and countries still living under colonial domination and foreign occupation. But this development has also given rise to a new controversy within UNCTAD (and exceptional resort to roll-call votes) because some developed countries have questioned the competence and appropriateness of UNCTAD dealing with this subject which, in their view, is political and should, therefore, be dealt with in other United Nations forums, such as the General Assembly.

V. UNCTAD AND ENVIRONMENTAL PROBLEMS

Starting in the 1970s when the international community was preparing for the United Nations Conference on the Human Environment, UNCTAD has played an active role in efforts to find solutions to problems stemming from the complex interaction of man and nature, especially in the field of decision-making processes and studies on the relationship between environment and trade and development.

In June 1971, as part of the preparatory work for the Conference, a panel of experts on development and the environment met at Founex, Switzerland. The panel examined the interactions between environment and development and, in particular, the impact of environmental issues on international trade and capital flow. The recommendations made at the Founex Seminar made a significant contribution to the work on the trade and development aspects of environmental problems in the United Nations system and in UNCTAD in particular.[1]

In reflecting the rapidly growing role of environmental problems throughout the world, the Trade and Development Board at its eleventh session in September 1971 decided to include, as a separate item of the agenda for UNCTAD III the topic "Impact of environment policies on trade and development, in particular of the developing countries".[2]

This decision was followed by the adoption of General Assembly resolution 2849 (XXVI) requesting the Secretary-General of UNCTAD to prepare a comprehensive study on the effects of environmental policies of developed countries which might adversely affect present and future development possibilities of developing countries by creating additional obstacles, such as new non-tariff measures leading to a new type of protectionism, and by a decrease in the inflow of international development assistance and a deterioration of its terms and conditions.

The conclusions reached in the subsequent secretariat report made it clear that environmental measures used by developed countries might have a profound and multiple impact on the growth and external economic relations of developing countries.[3] The report stressed that measures for the protection of the environment of developed countries, such as restrictions on the use of imports of certain commodities, the imposition of regulations, standards and other non-tariff barriers on

---

[1] See "Report of a panel of experts convened by the Secretary-General of the United Nations Conference on the Human Environment" (Founex, Switzerland, 4-12 June 1971), *Development and Environment (subject area V): report by the Secretary-General* (A/CONF. 48/10).

[2] *Official records of the General Assembly, Twenty-sixth session, Supplement No. 15* (A/8415/Rev.1), Part three, Annex I, decision 83 (II).

[3] "Impact of environmental policies in trade and development, in particular of the developing countries" (TD/130), reproduced in *Proceedings... Third Session*, vol. III, *General Review and Special Issues* (United Nations publication, Sales No. 73.II.D.7).

imports, as well as increased production costs reflected in higher export prices, might have a negative effect on developing countries' export potential and on their terms of trade. The report recommended that every effort should be made to avoid, or to attenuate, the application of tariff and non-tariff barriers to developing countries designed to protect industries incurring higher costs by reason of environmental measures.

The third session of the Conference (Santiago, 1972) considered the report and adopted without dissent resolution 47 (III) on "Impact of environment policies on trade and development, in particular of the developing countries". Under this resolution recommendations were made to the forthcoming United Nations Conference on the Human Environment to bear in mind the relationship between environment and the trade and development of all countries, particularly the trade and development problems of the developing countries, and to give special attention to the report on the impact of environmental policies on trade and development submitted by the UNCTAD secretariat to UNCTAD III. The resolution also requested the Secretary-General of UNCTAD "to continue studies on the impact of environmental policies on trade and development, particularly of developing countries, taking duly into account the recommendations that may be adopted by the United Nations Conference on the Human Environment".

The United Nations Conference on the Human Environment (Stockholm, 1972) adopted a Declaration setting forth principles for the preservation and enhancement of the human environment, and an Action Plan for the human environment, consisting of recommendations for environmental action at the international level.[4]

Recommendation 103 of the Stockholm Conference called for action by governments to ensure that countries do not invoke environmental concerns as a pretext for discriminatory trade policies or for reduced access to markets. Recommendation 104 provided that appropriate steps should be taken by existing United Nations organizations to identify the major threat to exports, particularly those of developing countries, that arise from environmental causes, their character and severity, and the remedial action that might be envisaged. Recommendation 105 stated that "UNCTAD, GATT, and other international bodies, as appropriate, should, within their respective fields of competence, consider undertaking to monitor, assess and regularly report the emergence of tariff and non-tariff barriers to trade as a result of environmental policies".

The General Assembly at its twenty-seventh session considered the report of the Conference and 11 resolutions were adopted concerning various aspects of the environment. The General Assembly also established the Governing Council of the United Nations Environment Programme (UNEP), an Environment Secretariat, the Environment Fund and the Environment Co-ordination Board. Under its resolution 2997 (XXVII) the General Assembly invited organizations of the United Nations system, regional commissions, as well as intergovernmental organizations and non-governmental organizations, to intensify their efforts in the environment field and co-operate in the new institutional machinery.

---

[4] *Report of the United Nations Conference on the human environment* (A/CONF.48/14/Rev.1) (United Nations publication, Sales No. E.73.II.A.14).

In 1974, the UNCTAD secretaiat organized a special UNEP/UNCTAD Symposium on "Patterns of resources use, environment and development strategies", which was held at Cocoyoc, Mexico.

The Cocoyoc Declaration emphasized the need to redefine the purpose of development, pointed out the diversity of development, stressed the importance of self-reliance and made suggestions for action. It stated that development should not be limited to the satisfaction of basic needs, but should also include other goals and values, including freedom of expression and impression, the right to give and to receive ideas and stimulus, the realization of the need to participate in shaping the basis of one's own existence, and the right to work.

Participants also discussed the compatibility of the twin goals of self-reliance and increasing international trade, and of ways to develop alternative technologies to those prevalent in industrialized countries. Wider participation in decision-making at both national and international levels was felt to be important in rationalizing world resource use, along with the need for changes in economic, social and political structures.

Suggestions for action included: use of common property resources such as the oceans for the benefit of the poorest nations; exploration of the possibilities for international taxation; the stimulation of new styles of life, including alternative consumption patterns, alternative technologies for production, and alternative forms of human settlements; the need to locate industries more carefully so as to induce development equitably among nations. The Symposium stressed the importance of the efforts of UNEP to design strategies and assist projects for ecologically sound socio-economic development (eco-development) at the local and regional level.

The General Assembly took note of the Cocoyoc Declaration (resolution 3326 (XXIX)) at its twenty-ninth session.[5] The Cocoyoc symposium opened up a new stage in the work programme of UNCTAD in the field of environmental studies. Since then close co-operation and co-ordination has existed between UNCTAD and UNEP.

A number of meetings, consultations and seminars have taken place to assess the results achieved and to define priorities for further work. These meetings stressed, *inter alia:*

The importance of elaborating and promoting alternative strategies and patterns of development directed at meeting the basic needs of the majority of the population and compatible with vital environmental considerations;

Social evaluation, use and management of renewable and non-renewable natural resources;

Industrialization strategies and trade in manufactures based on a fuller recognition of environmental considerations;

The technological dependence of the developing countries and its implications for the transfer and development of environmentally sound and appropriate technologies.

---

[5] A/C.2/292, November 1974.

Below is a brief summary of some of the projects undertaken by UNCTAD in relation to environment and development.

One of the first UNCTAD projects devoted to this subject related to the impact of environmental issues on the International Development Strategy. Its aim was to provide an ongoing evaluation of the situation, and a stocktaking of the results of more specific projects on environment and development and at pinpointing areas for future work in the field of environment-development-trade.

Proposals and suggestions relating to the mid-term review and appraisal of the International Development Strategy for the Second United Nations Development Decade were set forth in a special chapter in the UNCTAD secretariat report "New Directions in International Trade and Development Policies".[6]

An UNCTAD/UNEP project "The environmental component in the social evaluation and pricing of natural resources" aimed at providing a conceptual framework to examine existing and alternative mechanisms for the social evaluation and pricing of natural resources, with particular reference to the implications of environmental considerations and the impact on trade and development.

A series of studies were undertaken to analyse the shortcomings in determining the way in which natural resource prices were formed, how these prices differed from norms such as the cost of extraction, how they related to the actual net benefits to developing countries, the extent to which social and environmental factors were inadequately reflected in prices, and the possible methods for introducing these neglected factors into the control of resources, through either price or non-price mechanisms. Attention was drawn to the role which the existing economic structure—the distribution of world income and economic power—played in this process.

Environment and foreign trade strategies

The main objectives of another UNCTAD/UNEP project, "The impact of environmental issues on the foreign trade strategies of developing countries" were to analyse alternative strategies of resource use in the development process of developing countries, taking specifically into account the implications of basic-needs-oriented strategies, to study the relative economic and environmental advantages and disadvantages of strategies oriented towards exporting local resources as compared to strategies aimed at conserving existing resources and/or using them directly in developing local industry and agriculture and to compare the economic, social and environmental results of strategies aimed at differing degrees of processing of natural resources.

One of the major results of the project was to provide developing countries with specific suggestions on the planning of their foreign trade sector, to take account of environmental issues.

These two projects resulted in a number of monographs some of which were either published commercially (with acknowledgment to the work done for UNCTAD), or were issued as UNCTAD documents.

---

[6] TD/B/530/Add.1.

Under topics devoted to the social evaluation and pricing of natural resources mention may be made of *The control of resources* by Partha Dasgupta,[7] which continues to be of great importance in many countries as a basic text for planning work on environmental issues. Another interesting study under the same topic was issued as a research memorandum of the UNCTAD secretariat: *Social shadow prices, externalities and depletion of natural resources exported by developing countries*.[8] This study examined the particular evaluation problem facing developing countries exploiting resources, especially where transnational corporations were involved.

Market structure, bargaining power and resource price formation[9] dealt with the problem of formation of natural resource prices and the scope for reflecting environmental considerations in these prices.

Environmental provisions in developing country mining agreements[10] reviewed 21 mining agreements in developing countries for evidence of the way in which pollution control had been dealt with in the negotiations between transnational mining companies and host-country governments.

The impact of environmental issues and the exploitation of natural resources in the foreign trade strategies of developing countries were explored in a number of studies. *Copper-dependent development*[11] examined it from the point of view of one commodity, while *Interaction between the resource commodity sector, the developing economy and the environment: the case of Malaysia*[12] examined it from the point of view of a country exploiting a variety of natural resources.

Self-reliant mobilization[13] elaborates a development strategy very different from those practised in most developing countries, but with far-reaching implications for the environment. This novel conceptual study was part of UNCTAD's efforts within these projects to consider a wide range of foreign trade strategies for developing countries and their environmental implications. *Self-reliance in a benign environment: the case of the South Pacific*[14] explored the implications of and the stresses upon self-reliance in one part of the world where it is a living tradition. The main conclusions of these two UNCTAD/UNEP studies were presented in *Resources, environment and foreign Trade*.[15]

Environmental considerations have an immediate and widespread impact on the foreign trade strategies and performance of island developing countries. These issues have been the subject of particular attention in the context of UNCTAD's specific action in favour of island developing countries (see also part two, section

---

[7] Oxford: Blackwell, 1982.

[8] UNCTAD/LDC/37, UNCTAD Research Memorandum No. 62.

[9] W. Labys, Lexington, Mass.: Lexington Books, D. C. Heath and Co., 1980.

[10] UNCTAD/LDC/15, Research Memorandum No. 61.

[11] UNCTAD/LDC/11, Research Memorandum No. 59.

[12] UNCTAD/LDC/13, Research Memorandum No. 60.

[13] UNCTAD/RD/123.

[14] In Galtung, Johan, Peter O'Brien and Ray Preiswerk, *Self-reliance — a strategy for development* (London: Bogle-L'Ouverture, 1980).

[15] UNCTAD/LDC/43.

VIII, B). UNCTAD's work on these questions arose from Conference resolutions 98 (IV) paragraph 61 ("The human geography of small islands") and III (V), paragraphs 4 and 5.

This has resulted in a study of the *Viability of small island states*,[16] and of *The incidence of natural disasters in island developing countries: A study, carried out jointly with UNDRO*.[17] UNCTAD is continuing its work on the role of environmental considerations in the development strategies of small island developing countries.

The UNCTAD secretariat is charged with the global monitoring of the Substantial New Programme of Action for the 1980s for the Least Developed Countries (SNPA). (See section VIII... in part two). The SNPA specifically refers to environmental issues in a number of paragraphs. UNCTAD therefore monitors events touching on environmental issues and collaborates in particular with UNEP, as well as with the office of the United Nations Disaster Relief Co-ordinator (UNDRO).

Trade barriers resulting from environmental policies

Another important aspect of UNCTAD activity in environmental studies commenced with the project "UNEP/UNCTAD collaboration arrangements for study on trade barriers and restrictions resulting from environmental policies".

The long-term objective of this arrangement was to facilitate governmental efforts, particularly of the developing countries, aimed at overcoming non-tariff barriers to international trade which arise as a result of regulations designed for protection of the environment.

Under phase I (July 1974 to March 1977) of the mutual arrangements between UNCTAD and UNEP a series of studies and other activities were initiated and completed. The first study, entitled *Implication for the trade and development of developing countries of United States environmental controls*,[18] was a pioneering effort to estimate the cost of pollution control measures in the United States, and to evaluate their effects on access to the United States market for exports from developing countries.

The second study, *Environmental policies and their implications for trade and development: a case study of India*,[19] was an innovative analysis of environmental control policies in India and their impact on Indian foreign trade, including market access, and opportunities for expansion of exports in the light of environmental considerations.

A case study of the trade effects of pollution control in veneer, plywood, hardboard and furniture industries analyses the economic and environmental aspects of exports of these products both in the developed and the developing countries.

---

[16] TD/B/950, July 1983.
[17] TD/B/961, September 1983.
[18] TD/B/C.2/150/Add.1/Rev.1 (United Nations publication, Sales No. E.76.II.D.5).
[19] UNCTAD/ST/MD/10.

A preliminary feasibility study on the creation of a global early warning system intended to collect and disseminate information on environmental regulations which may affect international trade, particularly of developing countries, was prepared in February 1977. This study, taking into account related early warning systems conducted under UNEP and the Organisation for Economic Co-operation and Development (OECD) auspices, concluded that it was feasible, and would be useful, to create such a trade-oriented system which could provide a basis for measures to overcome certain trade obstacles which may result from environmental regulations.

In preparing the above-mentioned studies, in particular those involving the collection of information and related data on trade barriers and other relevant restrictions due to environmental considerations, the UNCTAD secretariat was assisted by States members of UNCTAD in response to the UNCTAD questionnaire on environmental measures and products affected by such measures.

A meeting of experts on the international trade effects of environmental policies and measures was organized under joint UNEP/UNCTAD auspices in February 1977 to review the progress made since 1974, and to plan further work.[20] To assist the experts, the UNCTAD secretariat prepared a note on *Trade and development aspects of environmental policies and measures.* The meeting discussed trade and related problems stemming from current and prospective environmental policies and measures (market access for exports from developing countries, re-deployment of industries to developing countries, etc.) as well as further action which should be taken in the UNCTAD framework, especially under phase II of the mutual UNEP/UNCTAD arrangement.

Studies under this particular phase continued on the identification of market access problems and opportunities arising from environmental policies and measures, especially problems of trade in manufactures and semi-manufactures of export interest to developing countries, with a view to assisting in the examination of appropriate remedial action. Further country studies were undertaken on environmental regulations and their implications for trade and development of the developing countries: *Environmental controls in the Federal Republic of Germany and their implications for the developed countries,*[21] and *Philippine environmental policies: their implications for trade and development.*[22]

Another study, *Environmental policies and their trade implications for developing countries, with special reference to fish and shellfish, fruit and vegetables,* was published in 1982.[23]

Environmental problems in the transfer of technology

The pivotal role of technology, both in the process of development and as a powerful influence on the quality of the human environment, led UNCTAD and

---

[20] Report of the UNEP/UNCTAD informal meeting of experts on trade aspects of environmental policies and measures (UNCTAD/ST/MD/11).
[21] UNCTAD/ST/MD/24.
[22] UNCTAD/ST/MD/27.
[23] UNCTAD/ST/MD/26.

UNEP to initiate another joint project under the general heading "Transfer of technology and interrelated environmental problems". The aims of this project were:

To clarify the interrelationship which exists between technological patterns in developing countries and environmental issues, inasmuch as this has an impact on the overall process of transfer of technology;

To assess the role that environmental factors have played and should play in the development, selection and transfer of technology;

To develop recommendations for new principles and practices for the transfer, adaptation and indigenous development of environmentally sound technologies.

The broad approach underlying UNEP/UNCTAD co-operation was considered at the fourth session of the Conference in Nairobi. The decisions of the Conference were embodied in section IV of resolution 87 (IV).

Since the formal initiation of the project on 1 July 1975, and as part of the first exploratory phase of its work, UNCTAD has prepared a study entitled *Transfer of technology: its implications for development and environment.*[24] In addition, and at the request of the UNCTAD secretariat, professor Johan Galtung, of the University of Oslo, prepared a study entitled *Development, environment and technology: towards a technology for self-reliance.*[25] Both these studies discuss ways in which technology affects the environment, particularly in developing countries, and offer alternative, more self-reliant approaches to the formulation of technological strategies designed to meet more fully the material and non-material needs of the people.

In order to assist the formulation of the conceptual framework, studies on some selected topics have been carried out. These include: *Development, environment and technology: some non-economic aspects; The supply of fertilizer technology and final products to less developed countries and their impact on environment;* and an outline of an approach to studying *Transfer of technology and environment in the international food processing industry in developing countries.*

Other UNCTAD reports and studies have been prepared relating indirectly to technology and the environment: *Technological dependence: its nature, consequences and policy implications,*[26] prepared for the fourth session of the Conference; *Major issues in transfer of technology to developing countries: a case study of the pharmaceutical industry,*[27] and *The role of trademarks in developing countries,*[28] prepared for an UNCTAD group of governmental experts which met in October 1977 to examine the economic, commercial and developmental aspects of the industrial property system.

The second empirical phase of the study involved six country case studies, which explored the implications of technology transfer in particular sections. These

---

[24] TD/B/C.6/22 (United Nations publication, Sales No. E.78.II.D.10).

[25] TD/B/C.6/23/Rev.1 (United Nations publication, Sales No. E.78.II.D.11).

[26] TD/190, reproduced in *Proceedings of the United Nations Conference on Trade and Development, Fourth Session,* vol. III, *Basic Documents* (United Nations publication, Sales No. E.76.II.D.12).

[27] TD/B/C.6/4.

[28] TD/B/C.6/AC.3/3/Rev.1 (United Nations publication, Sales No. E.79.II.D.5).

included *Health and educational technology in Cuba,* [29] prepared by the UNCTAD secretariat which described the steps taken by the Government of Cuba to transfer technology to the most important segment of its services sector. It was found that the redistribution and increase of health and educational resources to ensure that they reached the relatively underprivileged rural population had a significant impact on the human environment both directly, by eliminating diseases, and indirectly, by giving the population the intellectual means to understand and utilize the environment rationally for the improvement of the quality of life. *The social and economic implications of technology transfer in Jamaican Tourism* [30] (prepared by Professor John Ohiorhenuan of the University of Ibadan, Nigeria) described the main features of the Jamaican tourist industry, as it has evolved from pre-independence times up to the mid-1970s, with particular emphasis on the impact of government policies.

A further three studies focused on the effects of technology transfer on the social and economic environment. These are: *Technology, development and environment: a case study of two resettlement programmes in Hamedan, Iran;* [31] "Technology trade and transnational corporations in the food processing of Mexico;" [32] and *Technology, development and environment: modern and traditional medicine in Senegal.* [33]

The policy paper *Technology, development and environment: suggested guidelines for the preparation of a report on technology policy instruments* [34] was prepared by the UNCTAD secretariat under the final phase of the joint project between UNCTAD and UNEP. Its purpose was to develop a framework for introducing environmental discussions on technology planning, with emphasis on the reduction of poverty and the strengthening of domestic technological innovative capabilities.

Commodity agreements with ecological dimensions

The important innovative feature of UNCTAD activities in recent years is connected with its efforts to work out and establish international agreements on commodities which take the ecological dimension into account. One example is the International Tropical Timber Agreement, 1983 negotiated under the aegis of UNCTAD, which provides for encouraging reforestation and forest management activities, as well as for development of national policies aimed at sustainable utilization and conservation of tropical forest and their genetic resources, and at maintaining the ecological balance in the regions concerned. [35]

---

[29] TD/B/C.6/46 and Corr.1.
[30] TD/B/C.6/49.
[31] TD/B/C.6/83.
[32] TD/B/C.6/75, TD/B/C.6/AC.6/2.
[33] TD/B/C.6/86.
[34] TD/B/C.6/88.
[35] TD/TIMBER/11/Rev.1 (United Nations publication, Sales No. E.84.II.D.5).

General evaluation of the contribution of UNCTAD

In evaluating the achievements of the projects under UNEP/UNCTAD co-operation it can be said that they have played a considerable role in facilitating governmental efforts, particularly those of developing countries, aimed at overcoming the negative consequences of environmental problems on trade and development.

Bearing in mind that environmental management is increasingly influencing trade and development, consideration might be given to the continuation of efforts between UNEP and UNCTAD concerning the implications of environmental policies and measures affecting international trade and development, particularly of the developing countries, together with other similar problems.

In evaluating the mutual co-operation between the two organizations, the Executive Director of UNEP in his message on the occasion of the 20th anniversary of the United Nations Conference on Trade and Development, pointed out that "The close co-operation which has existed between the two organizations since UNEP's own establishment has contributed greatly to enabling the world community better to understand and act on the relationships between environment and development. UNCTAD's efforts at creating greater international understanding, co-operation and agreement, and in particular its contribution to resolving the problems of development, have made UNCTAD's success a matter of the greatest significance to all. Sustainable and environmentally sound development is made more possible by the efforts of UNCTAD, and we look forward to fruitful co-operation over the next decade as in the last".[36]

---

[36] TD/B/1026, Annex V.

Part Four
ANNEXES

I. ORGANIZATIONAL CHART OF THE INSTITUTIONAL MACHINERY OF UNCTAD

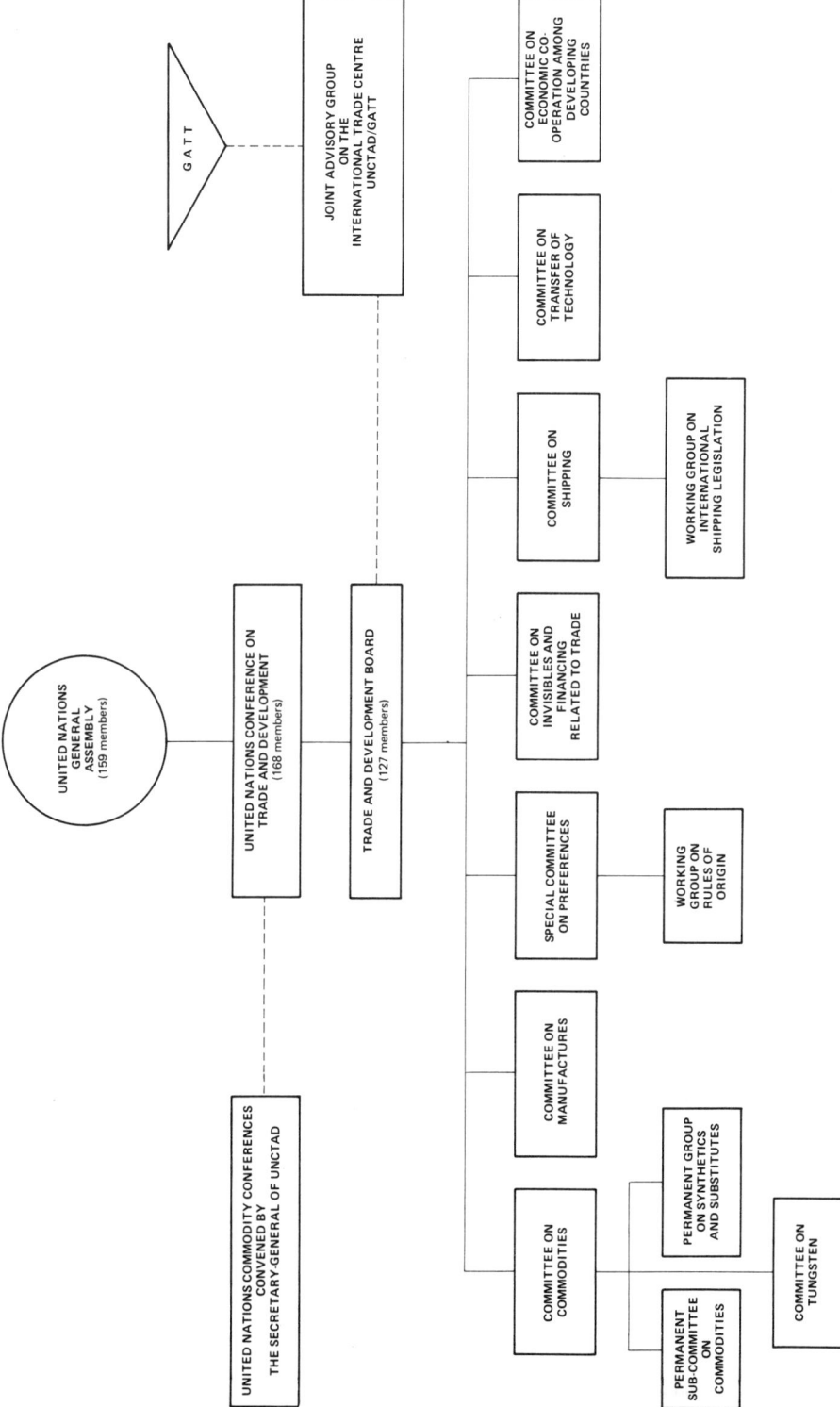

II. SELECTED LIST OF UNCTAD MEETINGS*

Commodities

Meeting	Dates	Report or final document symbol
Committee on Commodities, first session	19 July-7 Aug. 1965	TD/B/21/Rev.1
Committee on Commodities, third session	28 Oct.-8 Nov. 1986	TD/B/202/Rev.1
United Nations Cocoa Conference, 1972		TD/COCOA.3/9
First part	6-28 Mar. 1972	
Second part	11-21 Oct. 1972	
Committee on Commodities, eighth session		TD/B/543
First part	10-21 Feb. 1975	TD/B/596
Second part	21-25 July 1975	
Third part	8-19 Dec. 1975	
United Nations Negotiating Conference on a Common Fund under the Integrated Programme for Commodities		
First session	7 Mar.-2 Apr. 1977	TD/IPC/CF/CONF/8
Second session	7 Nov.-1 Dec. 1977	TD/B/IPC/CF/CONF/14 (Part I)
Resumed second session	14-30 Nov. 1978	TD/B/IPC/CF/CONF/14 (Part II)
Third session	12-19 Mar. 1979	TD/IPC/CF/CONF/19
Fourth session	5-27 June 1980	TD/IPC/CF/CONF/26
United Nations Conference on Natural Rubber, 1978		
First part	13 Nov.-9 Dec. 1978	No report
Second session	27 Mar.-12 Apr. 1979	TD/RUBBER/R.5
Third session	25 June-13 July 1979	TD/RUBBER/R.6
Fourth session	24 Sept.-6 Oct. 1979	TD/RUBBER/15/Rev.a and corrigendum
Sixth Preparatory Meeting on Copper	26 Feb.-2 Mar. 1979	TD/B/IPC/COPPER/16
United Nations Conference on Jute and Jute Products, 1981		
First part	12-30 Jan. 1981	TD/JUTE/R.5 & Corr.1
Second part	11-22 May 1981	TD/JUTE/8
Third part	20 Sept.-1 Oct. 1982	TD/JUTE/11/Rev.1
United Nations Conference on Tropical Timber, 1983		
First part	14-31 Mar. 1983	TD/TIMBER/8
Second part	7-18 Nov. 1983	TD/TIMBER/11/Rev.1

* For a full list of meetings see "Consolidated list of UNCTAD meetings 1964-1984" (TD/B/INF.133).

Money, finance and development

INTERNATIONAL MONETARY ISSUES

Meeting	Dates	Report or final document symbol
Expert Group International Monetary Issues (New York)		
First session	11-29 Oct. 1965	TD/B/32
Second session	20 June-3 July 1966	TD/B/80 and Corr.1
Expert Group on International Monetary Issues (New York)	17-25 Sept. 1969	TD/B/285/Rev.1
Ad hoc Intergovernmental High-Level Group of Experts on the Evolution of the International Monetary System, first session	28 July-1 Aug. 1980	TD/B/823/Rev.1, TD/B/AC.32/Rev.1

INFLATION

Meeting	Dates	Report or final document symbol
Expert Group on Inflationary Processes in the International Economy and their Impact on Developing Countries	28 July-1 Aug. 1975	TD/B/579
Group of High-level Governmental Experts on the Effects of the World Inflationary Phenomenon on the Development Process	24 July-4 Aug. 1978	TD/B/704, TD/B/AC.26/1 and Corr.2

INTERDEPENDENCE

Meeting	Dates	Report or final document symbol
Meeting of Governmental Experts on Interdependence of Problems of Trade, Development Finance and the International Monetary System	19-22 June 1978	No report
Meeting of Governmental Experts on Interdependence of Problems of Trade, Development Finance and the International Monetary System	21-23 May 1980	No report

DEBT

Meeting	Dates	Report or final document symbol
Ad hoc Group of Governmental Experts on the Debt Problems of Developing Countries		
First session	6-10 May 1974	TD/B/485, TD/B/C.3/118, TD/B/C.3/AC.8/4
Second session	11-17 Dec. 1974	TD/B/C.3/AC.8/11
Third session	25 Feb.-7 Mar. 1975	TD/B/545/Rev.1
Intergovernmental Group of Experts on the External Indebtedness of Developing Countries, first session	18-22 July 1977	TD/B/670, TD/B/AC.7
Trade and Development Board, ninth special session, first part (at the level of senior officials)	5-10 Sept. 1977	A/32/15, vol. II

Meeting	Dates	Report or final document symbol
Intergovernmental Group of Experts on the External Indebtedness of Developing Countries, second session	5-16 Dec. 1977	TD/B/685, TD/AC.2/10 and Corr.1 and Add.1, Add.1/Corr.1, Add.2, Add.2/Corr.1 and Add.3
Trade and Development Board, ninth special session, second part (at the level of senior officials)	23-27 Jan. 1978	A/33/15, vol. I
Intergovernmental Group of Experts on Debt and Development Problems of Developing Countries	2-11 Oct. 1978	TD/B/730, TD/B/AC.28/3
Trade and Development Board, ninth special session, third part (at Ministerial level)	6-11 Mar. 1978	A/33/15, vol. I
Trade and Development Board, twenty-first session	15-27 Sept. 1980	A/35/15, vol. II

AID

Meeting	Dates	Report or final document symbol
Expert Group on the Horowitz Proposal (New York)	25-29 Apr. 1966	TD/B/C.3/23 and Corr.2
Group of Governmental Experts on the Concepts of the Present Aid and Flow Targets		
First session	26-29 June 1973	TD/B/467
Second session	13-16 May 1974	TD/B/493/Rev.1
Third session (New York)	7-16 Mar. 1977	TD/B/646, TD/B/C.3/135, TD/B/C.3/AC.7/10
Group of High-Level Experts on Finance for Development	7-11 Aug. 1978	TD/B/722, TD/B/AC.27/1

Trade and industrialization policies with special reference to trade in manufactures

THE GENERALIZED SYSTEM OF PREFERENCES

Meeting	Dates	Report or final document symbol
Special Committee on Preferences, first session	29 Nov.-6 Dec. 1968	TD/B/218/Rev.1
Special Committee on Preferences, fourth session, second part	21 Sept.-12 Oct. 1970	TD/B/329/Rev.1
Trade and Development Board, fourth special session	12-13 Oct. 1970	A/8015/Rev.1 and corrigendum, part three

RESTRICTIVE BUSINESS PRACTICES

Meeting	Dates	Report or final document symbol
Ad hoc Group of Experts on Restrictive Business Practices	19-30 Mar. 1973	TD/B/C.2/119/Rev.1 (Sales No. E.74.II.D.11)

Meeting	Dates	Report or final document symbol
Third *Ad hoc* Group of Experts on Restrictive Business Practices, sixth session	17-27 Apr. 1979	TD/250 and Corr.1
United Nations Conference on Restrictive Business Practices, first session	19 Nov.-8 Dec. 1979	TD/RBP/CONF/8
United Nations Conference on Restrictive Businesss Practices, second session	8-22 Apr. 1980	TD/RBP/CONF/10/Rev.1 TD/RBP/CONF/11

PROTECTIONISM AND STRUCTURAL ADJUSTMENT

Meeting	Dates	Report or final document symbol
Trade and Development Board, twenty-fourth session, first part	8-24 Mar. 1982	A/37/15, Vol. I, part one
Trade and Development Board, twenty-eighth session	26 Mar.-6 Apr. 1984	TD/B/997 (Vol. II)

Shipping

Meeting	Dates	Report or final document symbol
Committee on Shipping, first session	8-23 Nov. 1965	TD/B/36 and Add.1
Committee on Shipping, tenth session	14-25 June 1982	TD/B/921

CODE OF CONDUCT FOR LINER CONFERENCES

Meeting	Dates	Report or final document symbol
Preparatory Committee of the United Nations Conference on a Code of Conduct for Liner Conferences, first session	8-26 Jan. 1973	TD/CODE/1
United Nations Conference of Plenipotentiaries on a Code of Conduct for Liner Conferences, first part	12 Nov.- 15 Dec. 1973	TD/CODE/13 (Sales No. E.75.II.D.11)
United Nations Conference of Plenipotentiaries on a Code of Conduct for Liner Conferences, second part	11 Mar.-6 Apr. 1974	

INTERNATIONAL MULTIMODAL TRANSPORT OF GOODS

Meeting	Dates	Report or final document symbol
Intergovernmental Preparatory Group on a Convention on International Intermodal Transport, first session	29 Oct.-2 Nov. 1973	TD/B/477
Intergovernmental Preparatory Group on a Convention on International Multimodal Transport, sixth session	21 Feb.-9 Mar. 1979	TD/MT/CONF/1/Add.1
United Nations Conference on a Convention on International Multimodal Transport, first part of the session	12-30 Nov. 1979	TD/MT/CONF/17/Add.1 (Sales No. E.81.II.D.7 (Vol. II))
United Nations Conference on a Convention on International Multimodal Transport, resumed session	8-24 May 1980	

CONDITIONS FOR REGISTRATION OF SHIPS

Meeting	Dates	Report or final document symbol
Ad hoc Intergovernmental Working Group on the Economic Consequences of the Existence or Lack of a Genuine Link between Vessel and Flag of Registry, first session	6-10 Feb. 1978	TD/B/C.4/177
Intergovernmental Preparatory Group on Conditions for Registration of Ships, first session	13-30 Apr. 1982	TD/B/904
Report of the United Nations Conference on Conditions for Registration of Ships, first part of the session	16 July- 30 Aug. 1984	TD/RS/CONF/10 and Add.1-2

INTERNATIONAL SHIPPING LEGISLATION

Meeting	Dates	Report or final document symbol
Working Group on International Shipping Legislation, first session	1-2 Dec. 1969	TD/B/289
Working Group on International Shipping Legislation, tenth session	25 Sept.-5 Oct. 1984	TD/B/C.4/283

CONTAINER STANDARDS

Meeting	Dates	Report or final document symbol
Ad hoc Intergovernmental Group on Container Standards for International Multimodal Transport, second session	20 Nov.-1 Dec. 1978	TD/B/734

BULK CARGO

Meeting	Dates	Report or final document symbol
Group of Experts on problems faced by the Developing Countries in the Carriage of Bulk Cargoes, second session	30 Nov.-4 Dec. 1981	TD/B/C.4/234
Group of Experts on International Sea Transport of Liquid Hydrocarbons in Bulk, second session	30 Jan.-3 Feb. 1984	TD/B/C.4/263

PORTS

Meeting	Dates	Report or final document symbol
Expert Group on Port Congestion	26-29 Apr. 1976	TD/B/C.4/152 and Add.1

MISCELLANEOUS

Meeting	Dates	Report or final document symbol
Group of Experts on Improved Methods of Financing Ship Acquisition by Developing Countries	29 May-2 June 1978	TD/B/C.4/179

Transfer of technology

Meeting	Dates	Report or final document symbol
Intergovernmental Group on Transfer of Technology—three sessions		
First session	June 1971	TD/B/365
Second session	Jan.-Feb. 1973	TD/B/424
Third session	July 1974	TD/B/520
Committee on Transfer of Technology—four regular sessions		
First session	Nov./Dec. 1975	TD/B/593
Second session	Dec. 1978	TD/B/736
Third session	Nov. 1980	TD/B/836
Fourth session	Nov./Dec. 1982	TD/B/936
First special session	Feb. 1984	TD/B/986
Intergovernmental Group of Experts on a Code of Conduct on Transfer of Technology	May 1975	TD/B/C.6/1
Intergovernmental Group of Experts on an International Code of Conduct on Transfer of Technology—six sessions		
First session	Nov. 1976	TD/AC.1/4
Second session	Mar./Apr. 1977	TD/AC.1/7
Third session	July/Aug. 1977	TD/AC.1/9
Fourth session	Oct./Nov. 1977	TD/AC.1/11
Fifth session	Feb. 1978	TD/AC.1/15
Sixth session	June/July 1978	TD/AC.1/18
United Nations Conference on an International Code of Conduct on the Transfer of Technology—five sessions		
First session	Oct./Nov. 1978 and Feb./Mar. 1979	TD/CODE TOT/9 and Corr.1, TD/CODE TOT/14
Second session	Oct./Nov. 1979	TD/CODE TOT/20
Third session	Apr./May 1980	TD/CODE TOT/25
Fourth session	Mar./Apr. 1981	TD/CODE TOT/33
Fifth session	Oct./Nov. 1983	TD/CODE TOT/41
Group of Governmental Experts on the Role of the Industrial Property System in the Transfer of Technology—three meetings	Sept. 1975
Oct. 1977
Feb. 1982	TD/B/C.6/8
TD/B/C.6/24
TD/B/C.6/76
Meetings of Governmental Experts on Transfer, Application and Development of Technology		
Food Processing Sector	June 1982	TD/B/C.6/78
Capital Goods and Industrial Machinery Sector	July 1982	TD/B/C.6/82
Energy Sector	Oct./Nov. 1982	TD/B/C.6/94
Meetings of Governmental Experts on Reverse Transfer of Technology—three meetings	Feb./Mar. 1978
Aug./Sept. 1982
Aug./Sept. 1983	TD/B/C.6/28
TD/B/C.6/89
TD/B/969

Meeting	Dates	Report or final document symbol
Intergovernmental Group of Experts on the Feasibility of Measuring Human Resource Flows	Aug./Sept. 1982	TD/B/C.6/89

Four training courses, seven workshops, five training programmes and four seminars on various technology-related issues, including transfer and development of technology, technology policies and planning, planning and contracting of projects, pharmaceutical sector policies and legal aspects of transfer of technology.

In-house training groups and programmes (Geneva): 27 of three to seven government officials each on technology policy issues; two to three weeks each.

Nature and evolution of trade relations among countries having different economic and social systems

TRADE AND DEVELOPMENT BOARD

At the following regular sessions of the Board, in accordance with Conference resolutions 15 (II) and 95 (IV), a special sessional committee was established to deal exclusively with the subject of trade relations among countries having different economic and social systems and all trade flows resulting therefrom

Meeting	Dates	Report or final document symbol
Trade and Development Board		
Ninth session, first part	26 Aug.-15 Sept. 1969	A/7616 and Corr.2, part three
Tenth session, first part	26 Aug.-18 Sept. and 24 Sept. 1970	A/8015/Rev.1 and Corr.1, part two
Thirteenth session	21 Aug.-11 Sept. 1973	A/9015/Rev.1, part three
Fourteenth session, first part	20 Aug.-13 Sept. 1974	A/9615/Rev.1
Sixteenth session, first part	5-23 Oct. 1976	A/31/15, vol. II
Seventeenth session, first part	23 Aug.-2 Sept. 1977	A/32/15 and Corr.1, vol. II, part two
Eighteenth session	29 Aug.-17 Sept. 1978	A/33/15, vol. II
Nineteenth session, first part	8-20 Oct. 1979	A/34/15, vol. II
Twenty-first session	15-27 Sept. 1980	A/35/15, vol. II
Twenty-third session, first part	28 Sept.-12 Oct. 1981	A/36/15 and Corr.1, part three
Twenty-fifth session, first part	6-23 Sept. 1982	A/37/15, vol. II, part one
Twenty-seventh session	3-20 Oct. 1983 and 2 Nov.	TD/B/973, vol. II

Multilateral payments arrangements

Meeting	Dates	Report or final document symbol
Group of Experts on Multilateral Payments Arrangements, first session	22 Sept.-2 Oct. 1969	TD/B/284 and Corr.1
Intergovernmental Group of Experts to Study a Multilateral System of Payments between Socialist Countries of Eastern Europe and Developing Countries	28 Nov.-2 Dec. 1977	TD/B/683, TD/B/703 (Sales No. E.78.II.D.4)

Industrial specialization

Meeting	Dates	Report or final document symbol
Seminar on Industrial Specialization through Various Forms of Multilateral Co-operation	2-5 Dec. 1975	TD/B/599 and Corr.1

Miscellaneous

Meeting	Dates	Report or final document symbol
Interregional Seminar on the Planning of the Foreign Trade Sector	21 Sept.-5 Oct. 1970	No report
Expert Group on Measures of Support of Socialist Countries to Integration Groupings	28 Oct.-1 Nov. 1974	TD/B/539
Intergovernmental Group of Experts on Trade Opportunities resulting from Multilateral Schemes of Countries Members of CMEA	17-22 Oct. 1977	TD/B/680
Ad hoc Group of Experts to Consider Ways and Means of Expanding Trade and Economic Relations	28 May-1 June 1984	TD/B/1001

Economic co-operation among developing countries

Committee on Economic Co-operation among Developing Countries

Meeting	Dates	Report or final document symbol
Committee on Economic Co-operation among Developing Countries, first session, second part	2-9 May 1977	TD/B/652
Committee on Economic Co-operation among Developing Countries, third session	12-23 Sept. 1983 and 6 Oct. 1983	TD/B/974

Expert group meetings

Meeting	Dates	Report or final document symbol
Groups of Experts on Economic Co-operation among Developing Countries	27 Oct.-4 Nov. 1975	TD/B/AC.19/1
Preparatory Meeting of Governmental Experts of Developing Countries on Economic Co-operation among Developing Countries	17 Mar.-8 Apr. 1980	TD/B/C.7/39

TRADE EXPANSION AND REGIONAL ECONOMIC INTEGRATION

Meeting	Dates	Report or final document symbol
Intergovernmental Group on Trade Expansion, Economic Co-operation and Regional Integration among Developing Countries	2-19 Nov. 1970	TD/B/333
Ad hoc Group on Role of Multilateral Financial Institutions in Promoting Integration among Developing Countries	4-11 Mar. 1974	TD/B/516 and Corr.1
Working Party on Trade Expansion and Regional Economic Integration among Developing Countries, first session	10-18 Apr. 1978	TD/B/702
Working Party on Trade Expansion and Regional Economic Integration among Developing Countries, second session	28 June-2 July 1982	TD/B/C.7/55
Meeting of Secretariats of Economic Co-operation and Integration Groupings of Developing Countries and Multilateral Development Finance Institutions to Examine the Problems of Promoting and Financing Integration Projects, first session	4-8 June 1984	TD/B/C.7/67

Least developed, land-locked and island developing countries

LEAST DEVELOPED COUNTRIES

Expert Groups

Meeting	Dates	Report or final document symbol
Group of Experts on Special Measures in favour of the Least Developed among Developing Countries	24 Nov.-5 Dec. 1969	TD/B/288
Ad hoc Group of Experts on Special Measures in favour of the Least Developed among Developing Countries	26 Apr.-5 May 1971	TD/B/349
Third Expert Group on Special Measures in favour of the Least Developed among the Developing Countries	13-21 Dec. 1971	TD/135, Annex I
Group of High-Level Experts on the Comprehensive New Programme of Action for the Least Developed Countries during the 1980s	26-30 Nov. 1979	TD/B/775, TD/B/AC.17/13

Intergovernmental Groups

Intergovernmental Group on the Least Developed Countries		
First session	7-18 July 1975	TD/B/577
Second session	17-28 July 1978	TD/B/719, TD/B/AC.17/10

Meeting	Dates	Report or final document symbol
Third session (Preparatory Committee for the United Nations Conference on Least Developed Countries)	4-16 Feb. 1980	TD/B/787

United Nations Conference on the Least Developed Countries

Meeting	Dates	Report or final document symbol
Preparatory Committee for the United Nations Conference		
First session	4-16 Feb. 1980	A/35/45
Second session	9-17 Oct. 1980	
Third session	29 June-10 July 1981	A/36/45
United Nations Conference on the Least Developed Countries: Country review meetings		
Asia and Pacific (Vienna)	30 Mar.-10 Apr. 1981	A/CONF.104/3
Eastern Africa (Addis Ababa)	4-14 May 1981	A/CONF.104/4
Western and Central Africa, and Somalia (The Hague)	25 May-5 June 1981	A/CONF.104/5 and Corr.1
Southern Africa, Guinea-Bissau and Haiti	22-26 June 1981	A/CONF.104/6
United Nations Conference on the Least Developed Countries—Pre-Conference Consultation among Senior Officials (Paris)	27-28 Aug. 1981	A/CONF.104/13
United Nations Conference on the Least Developed Countries (Paris)	1-14 Sept. 1981	A/CONF.104/22/Rev.1

Miscellaneous

Meeting	Dates	Report or final document symbol
Meeting of Multilateral and Bilateral Financial and Technical Assistance Institutions with Representatives of the Least Developed Countries		
First meeting	31 Oct.-8 Nov. 1977	TD/B/681, TD/B/AC.21/7 and Add.1
Second meeting	11-20 Oct. 1982	TD/B/933, TD/B/AC.21/12

LAND-LOCKED DEVELOPING COUNTRIES

Meeting	Dates	Report or final document symbol
United Nations Conference on Transit Trade of Land-locked Countries (New York)	7 June-8 July 1965	TD/TRANSIT/10
Group of Experts on the Special Problems Involved in the Trade and Economic Development of the Land-locked Developing Countries		
First session	19-22 May 1969	TD/B/308
Second session	11 May-4 June 1970	

Meeting	Dates	Report or final document symbol
Group of Experts on the Transport Infrastructure for Land-locked Developing Countries	14-23 May 1973	TD/B/453/Add.1/Rev.1
Ad hoc Group of Experts to Study Ways and Means of Improving Transit-Transport Infrastructure and Services for Land-locked Developing Countries	4-8 June 1984	TD/B/1002

ISLAND DEVELOPING COUNTRIES

Meeting	Dates	Report or final document symbol
Panel of Experts on Developing Island Countries	19-27 Mar. 1973	TD/B/443/Rev.1
Group of Experts on Feeder and Inter-Island Services by Air or Sea for Island Developing Countries	13-21 Oct. 1977	TD/B/687, TD/B/AC.24/1 and Corr.1

Insurance

Meeting	Dates	Report or final document symbol
Expert Group on Reinsurance	26 Sept.-6 Oct. 1966	TD/B/C.3/29
Expert Group on Insurance Statistics	7-14 Oct. 1970	No report
Expert Group on Insurance Legislation and Supervision in Developing Countries	19-30 July 1971	TD/B/C.3/90
Expert Group on Reinsurance	22-26 Jan. 1973	No report
Expert Group on Marine Insurance	3-7 Mar. 1975	No report
Expert Group on Insurance of Large Industrial Risks	31 Jan.-4 Feb. 1977	TD/B/C.3/137
Expert Group on Agricultural Insurance	9-13 Jan. 1978	No report
Expert Group on methods used for increasing the local retention of insurance business. Regional and national pools	5-9 Mar. 1979	No report
Expert Group on motor insurance in developing countries: Search for alternative legal systems	11-16 Mar. 1984	No report

The subject of insurance was discussed in special sessional committees of the Committee on Invisibles and Financing related to Trade up to the seventh session. At subsequent sessions of the Committee separate parts were devoted to insurance, as follows:

Meeting	Dates	Report or final document symbol
Committee on Invisibles and Financing related to Trade, eighth session, first part	5-9 Dec. 1977	TD/B/684
Committee on Invisibles and Financing related to Trade, ninth session, second part	29 Sept.-3 Oct. 1980	TD/B/833
Committee on Invisibles and Financing related to Trade, tenth session, first part	13-17 Dec. 1982	TD/B/937

Disarmament, environment

(List of meetings at which these subjects were discussed as specific items of a broader agenda)

DISARMAMENT

Sessions of the Conference

Meeting	Dates	Report or final document symbol
UNCTAD I	23 Mar.-16 June 1964	United Nations Conference on Trade and Development, first session, Geneva, Switzerland, 23 March-16 June 1964, Vol. I.
UNCTAD III, Santiago, (1972), Agenda item 8 (*d*) "Trade and economic aspects of disarmament"		United Nations Conference on Trade and Development, third session, Santiago, Chile, 13 April-21 May 1972, Vol. IV, p. 39.
105th plenary meeting	4 May 1972	
107th plenary meeting	17 May 1972	

UNCTAD — Trade and Development Board

Nineteenth session, 1979, agenda item 9 (*c*) "Trade and economic aspects of disarmament"

523rd meeting   TD/B/SR.523

Twenty-first session, 1980, agenda item 10 (*c*) "Trade and economic aspects of disarmament"

544th meeting   TD/B/SR.544

Twenty-third session, 1981, agenda item 10 (*c*) "Trade and economic aspects of disarmament"

565th meeting   TD/B/SR.565
566th meeting   TD/B/SR.566

Twenty-fifth session, 1982, agenda item 10 (*c*) "Trade and economic aspects of disarmament"

590th meeting
596th meeting   TD/B/SR.582-602
598th meeting

ENVIRONMENT

Sessions of the Conference

UNCTAD III, Santiago (1972), agenda item 8 (*e*) "Impact of environment policies on trade and development, in particular of the developing countries"

| Meeting | Dates | Report or final document symbol |

UNCTAD IV, Nairobi (1976), agenda item 12 "Action to strengthen the technological capacity of developing countries"

Trade and Development Board

Seventeenth session, 1977, agenda item 6 (*e*), "Impact of environmental policies on trade and development, in particular of the developing countries"
470th meeting

Other meetings

Special UNEP/UNCTAD Symposium on "Patterns of resources use, environment and development strategies", Cocoyoc, Mexico — 8-12 Oct. 1974

UNCTAD/UNEP informal meeting of experts on trade aspects of environmental policies and measures Geneva — Feb. 1977

III. SELECTED LIST OF REPORTS AND STUDIES

Commodities

Title	Document No.
Stabilization of international commodity markets	E/CONF.46/8. Printed in *Proceedings of the United Nations Conference on Trade and Development,* vol. III, *Commodity Trade* (United Nations publication, Sales No. 64.II.B.13)
International compensatory financing of the effects of change in the terms of trade	E/CONF.46/10
International commodity agreements: note by Prof. J. E. Meade	E/CONF.46/P/1/Rev.1. Printed in *Proceedings of the United Nations Conference on Trade and Development,* vol. III, *Commodity Trade* (United Nations publication, Sales No. 64.II.B.13)
The case for an international commodity reserve currency (Profs. A. G. Hart, N. Kaldor and J. Tinbergen)	E/CONF.46/P/7/Corr.1 and Add.1. Printed in *Proceedings of the United Nations Conference on Trade and Development,* vol. III, *Commodity Trade* (United Nations publication, Sales No. 64.II.B.13)
The development of an international commodity policy: study by the UNCTAD secretariat	TD/8/Supp.1. *Ibid., Second Session,* vol. II, *Commodity Problems and Policies* (United Nations publication, Sales No. E.68.II.D.15)
The development of international commodity policy: progress report by the UNCTAD secretariat	TD/113. *Ibid., Third Session,* vol. II, *Merchandise Trade* (United Nations publication, Sales No. E.73.II.D.5)
An Integrated Programme for Commodities: report by the Secretary-General of UNCTAD	TD/B/C.1/166
Idem: The role of international commodity stocks: report by the UNCTAD secretariat	TD/B/C.1/166/Supp.1 and Supp.1/Add.1
Idem: A common fund for the financing of commodity stocks: report by the Secretary-General of UNCTAD	TD/B/C.1/166/Supp.2 and Corr.1
Idem: The role of multilateral commitments in commodity trade: report by the Secretary-General of UNCTAD	TD/B/C.1/166/Supp.3
Idem: Compensatory financing of export fluctuations in commodity trade: report by the Secretary-General of UNCTAD	TD/B/C.1/166/Supp.4
Idem: Trade measures to expand processing of primary commodities in developing countries: report by the Secretary-General of UNCTAD	TD/B/C.1/166/Supp.5

Title	Document No.
Action on commodities, including decisions on an integrated programme, in the light of the need for change in the world commodity economy: report by the UNCTAD secretariat	TD/184. Printed in *Proceedings of the United Nations Conference on Trade and Development, Fourth session*, vol. III, *Basic Documents* (United Nations publication, Sales No. E.76.II.D.12)
A common fund title for the financing of commodity stocks: suitability stocking of individual commodities, country contributions and burden-sharing and some operating principles: report by the Secretary-General of UNCTAD	TD/B/C.1/196 and Add.1
Common fund: financial requirements (29 December 1976)	TD/B/IPC/CF/L.2
Action on export earnings stabilization and developmental aspects of commodity policy: report by the UNCTAD secretariat	TD/229. Printed in *Proceedings of the United Nations Conference on Trade and Development, Fifth session*, vol. III, *Basic Documents* (United Nations publication, Sales No. E.79.II.D.16)
Commodity issues: a review and proposals for further action: report by the UNCTAD secretariat	TD/273. *Ibid., Sixth session*, vol. III, *Basic Documents* (United Nations publication, Sales No. E.83.II.D.8)

Money, finance and development

Trade prospects and capital needs of developing countries: report by the UNCTAD secretariat	TD/34/Rev.1 (Sales No. 68.II.D.13)
The link: report by UNCTAD secretariat	TD/118/Supp.4. Revised version of TD/B/356. Printed in *Proceedings of the United Nations Conference on Trade and Development, Third session*, vol. III, *Financing and Invisibles* (Sales No. E.73.II.D.6)
The link: some further issues for consideration: note by UNCTAD secretariat	UNCTAD/FIN/5
The transfer of real resources and the link: note by UNCTAD secretariat	UNCTAD/FIN/8. Reproduced in *Money, finance and development. Papers on international monetary reform* (TD/B/479) (Sales No. E.74.II.D.15)
Debt problems in the context of development: report by UNCTAD secretariat	TD/B/C.3/109
Main findings of a study of private foreign investment in selected developing countries: report prepared by Mr. P. Streeten	TD/B/C.3/111 and Corr.1
Money, finance and development: papers on international monetary reform. A collection of papers (including TD/B/459) prepared by the UNCTAD secretariat for submission to the IMF Committee of Twenty	TD/B/479 (Sales No. E.74.II.D.15)

Title	Document No.
Interdependence of problems of trade, development finance and the international monetary system: report by the Secretary-General of UNCTAD	TD/B/495 and Add.1 and Add.1 (Annexes)
The external debt experience of developing countries: economic developments following multilateral debt renegotiation in selected developing countries. Report by UNCTAD secretariat	TD/B/C.3/AC.8/9
Ways and means of accelerating the transfer of real resources to developing countries on a predictable, assured and continuous basis. Report by the Secretary-General of the United Nations	A/31/186
Long-term problems of interdependence and the current world economic situation. Report by the Secretary-General of UNCTAD	TD/B/712
Finance for development: report by the Secretary-General of the United Nations. Includes report of the High-Level Group of Experts on Finance for Development (7-11 August 1978)	A/33/280
Acceleration of the transfer of real resources to developing countries. Note prepared by UNCTAD secretariat at the request of the General Assembly	A/33/301
International monetary issues: report by the UNCTAD secretariat	TD/233. Printed in *Proceedings of the United Nations Conference on Trade and Development, Fifth session,* vol. III. *Basic Documents* (Sales No. E.74.II.D.16)
International financial co-operation for development: Current policy issues. Report by UNCTAD secretariat	TD/234. *Ibid.*
Compensatory financing for export fluctuations. Note by UNCTAD secretariat	TD/B/C.3/152/Rev.1
Handbook of international trade and development statistics, 1983	TD/STAT.11 (Sales No. E/F.83.II.D.2)
World inflation and the development process. Report by the Secretary-General of UNCTAD	TD/B/914 and Corr.1
Review of the implementation of Trade and Development Board resolution 222 (XXI), section B. Report by UNCTAD secretariat	TD/B/945
Trade and Development Report (reports by the UNCTAD secretariat)	
1981	TD/B/863/Rev.1 (Sales No. E.81.II.D.9)
1982	UNCTAD/TDR/2/Rev.1 (Sales No. E.82.II.D.12)
1983	UNCTAD/TDR/3/Rev.1 (Sales No. E.83.II.D.13 and corrigendum)
1984	UNCTAD/TDR/4/Rev.1 (Sales No. E.84.II.D.23)

Trade and industrialization policies with special reference to trade in manufactures

THE GENERALIZED SYSTEM OF PREFERENCES

Title	Document No.
Comprehensive review of the generalized system of preferences: report by the UNCTAD secretariat	TD/B/C.5/63. Reproduced in *Operation and effects of the generalized system of preferences. Selected studies submitted to the Special Committee on Preferences at its ninth session* (TD/B/C.5/71) (Sales No. E.81.II.D.6)
Assessment of the results of the multilateral trade negotiations: Report by the Secretary-General of UNCTAD Part II— Implications of the tariff reductions resulting from the multilateral trade negotiations for the trade of developing countries	TD/B/778/Rev.1 (Sales No. E.82.II.D.1)
Evaluation of the trade effects of the generalized system of preferences: study by Craig R. McPhee	TD/B/C.5/87

RESTRICTIVE BUSINESS PRACTICES

Title	Document No.
The Set of Multilaterally Agreed Equitable Principles and Rules and Rules for the Control of Restrictive Business Practices	TD/RBP/CONF/10/Rev.1 (Sales No. E.81.II.D.5)
The role of transnational corporations in the marketing and distribution of exports and imports of developing countries: report by the UNCTAD secretariat	TD/B/C.2/197
Collusive tendering: study by the UNCTAD secretariat	TD/B/RBP/12/Rev.1. To be issued also as a United Nations publication
Elements for provisions of a model law on restrictive business practices: prepared by the UNCTAD secretariat	TD/B/RBP/15/Rev.1 and Corr.1 and 2

NON-TARIFF MEASURES

Title	Document No.
Implications for developing countries of the new protectionism in developed countries: report by the UNCTAD secretariat	TD/226. Reproduced in *Proceedings of the United Nations Conference on Trade and Development, Sixth session,* vol. III, *Basic Documents* (United Nations publication, Sales No. E.83.II.D.8)
Multilateral trade negotiations: report by the UNCTAD secretariat	TD/B/861
Non-tariff barriers affecting the trade of developing countries and transparency in world trading conditions: the inventory of non-tariff barriers: report by the UNCTAD secretariat	TD/B/940
International trade in textiles, with special reference to the problems faced by developing countries: report by the UNCTAD secretariat	TD/B/C.2/215/Rev.1 (Sales No. E.84.II.D.7)

STRUCTURAL ADJUSTMENT RELATED TO TRADE

Title	Document No.
Comprehensive measures required to expand and diversify the export trade of developing countries in manufactures and semi-manufactures: report by the UNCTAD secretariat	TD/230. Reproduced in *Proceedings of the United Nations Conference on Trade and Development, Fifth session*, vol. III, *Basic Documents* (United Nations publication, Sales No. E.79.II.D.16)
Structural adjustment related to trade: issues and policies: report by the UNCTAD secretariat	TD/B/805
Protectionism and structural adjustment in the world economy: report by the UNCTAD secretariat	TD/B/888/Rev.1 (Sales No. E.82.II.D.14)
Protectionism, trade relations and structural adjustment: report by the UNCTAD secretariat	TD/274 and Corr.1. Reproduced in *Proceedings of the United Nations Conference on Trade and Development, Sixth session*, vol. III, *Basic Documents* (United Nations publication, Sales No. E.83.II.D.8)

SERVICES

Production and trade in services, policies and their underlying factors bearing upon international services transactions: report by the UNCTAD secretariat	TD/B/941 and Corr.1

Shipping

Consultation in shipping	TD/B/C.4/20/Rev.1 (Sales No. E.68.II.D.1)
The liner conference system	TD/B/C.4/62/Rev.1 (Sales No. E.70.II.D.9)
Unitization of Cargo	TD/B/C.4/75 (Sales No. E.71.II.D.2)
Berth throughput	TD/B/C.4/109 and Add.1 (Sales No. E.74.II.D.1)
Charter parties	TD/B/C.4/ISL/13 (Sales No. E.74.II.D.12)
United Nations Conference of Plenipotentiaries on a Code of Conduct for Liner Conferences. Volume II: *Final Act (including the Convention and resolutions) and tonnage requirements*	TD/CODE/13/Add.1 (Sales No. E.75.II.D.12)
Port Development—Handbook for Planners in Developing Countries	TD/B/C.4/175 (Sales No. E.77.II.D.8 and corrigendum)
Economic consequences of the existence or lack of a genuine link between vessels and flag of registry	TD/B/C.4/168 and Add.1 and Corr.1
Legal and documentary aspects of the marine insurance contract	TD/B/C.4/ISL/27/Rev.1 (Sales No. E.82.II.D.5)
Protection of Shipper Interests: Guidelines for developing countries	TD/B/C.4/176 (Sales No. E.78.II.D.7)

Title	Document No.
Merchant fleet development	TD/222. Reproduced in *Proceedings of the United Nations Conference on Trade and Development, Fifth session,* vol. III, *Basic Documents* (Sales No. E.79.II.D.16)
Control by transnational corporations over dry bulk cargo movements	TD/B/C.4/203/Rev.1 (Sales No. E.81.II.D.3)
United Nations Conference on a Convention on International Multimodal Transport, volume I: *Final Act and Convention on International Multimodal Transport of Foods*	TD/MT/CONF/17 (Sales No. E.81.II.D.7 (Vol. I) and corrigendum)
UNCTAD activities in the field of shipping	TD/278. Reproduced in *Proceedings of the United Nations Conference on Trade and Development, Sixth session,* vol. III, *Basic Documents* (Sales No. E.83.II.D.8)

Transfer of technology

Guidelines for the study of the transfer of technology to developing countries. A study by the UNCTAD secretariat	TD/B/AC.11/9 (Sales No. E.72.II.D.19)
The role of the patent system in the transfer of technology to developing countries. Report prepared jointly by the United Nations Department of Economic and Social Affairs, the UNCTAD secretariat and the International Bureau of the World Intellectual Property Organization	TD/B/AC.11/19/Rev.1 (Sales No. E.75.II.D.6)
An international code of conduct on transfer of technology. Report by the UNCTAD secretariat	TD/B/C.6/AC.2/Supp.1/Rev.1 (Sales No. E.75.II.D.15)
Technological dependence: Its nature, consequences and policy implications. Report by the UNCTAD secretariat	TD/190. Reproduced in *Proceedings of the United Nations Conference on Trade and Development, Fourth session,* vol. III, *Basic Documents* (United Nations publication, Sales No. E.76.II.D.12)
Handbook on the acquisition of technology by developing countries. Prepared by the UNCTAD secretariat	UNCTAD/TT/AS/5 and Corr.1 (Sales No. E.78.II.D.15)
The reverse transfer of technology: A survey of its main features, causes and policy implications. Study by the UNCTAD secretariat	TD/B/C.6/47 (Sales No. E.79.II.D.1)
The role of trade marks in developing countries. Report by the UNCTAD secretariat	TD/B/C.6/AC.3/3/Rev.1 (Sales No. E.79.II.D.5)
The food processing sector in developing countries: some recent trends in the transfer and development of technology. Report by the UNCTAD secretariat	TD/B/C.6/66
Energy supplies for developing countries: issues in transfer and development of technology. Study by the UNCTAD secretariat	TD/B/C.6/31/Rev.1 (Sales No. E.80.II.D.3)

Trade relations among countries having different economic and social systems

GENERAL STUDIES

Title	Document No.
Review of trade relations among countries having different economic and social systems	TD/B/128 and Add.1-3
Expansion of trade and economic co-operation between the socialist countries of Eastern Europe and the developing countries (an integrated approach)	TD/126. Reproduced in *Proceedings of the United Nations Conference on Trade and Development, Third session.* vol. IV, *General Review and Special Issues* (United Nations publication, Sales No. E.73.II.D.7)
Multilateral action for expanding trade and economic relations between countries with different economic and social systems, in particular action which would contribute to the development of developing countries	TD/193. *Ibid., Fourth session*, vol. III, *Basic Documents* (United Nations publication, Sales No. E.76.II.D.12)
The co-operation mechanism among countries having different economic and social systems	TD/243/Supp.3
Ways and means of expanding trade and economic relations between countries having different economic and social systems	TD/B/AC.38/2 and Corr.1

STUDIES ON SPECIFIC ISSUES

Innovations in the practice of trade and economic co-operation between socialist countries of Eastern Europe and developing countries	TD/B/238
Motivations, patterns, problems and prospects in industrial co-operation between enterprises of socialist and developing countries	TD/B/490/Supp.1
Tripartite industrial co-operation	TAD/E.1/SEM 1/2
Multilateralization of payments in trade between socialist countries of Eastern Europe and developing countries. Selected documents	TD/B/703 (Sales No. E.78.II.D.4)
Trade and economic relations between Latin American countries and countries members of the Council for Mutual Economic Assistance	TD/243/Supp.2
Trade and economic relations between some Asian developing countries and the socialist countries of Eastern Europe	TD/B/857 and Corr.1
Trade and economic co-operation among African countries and the socialist countries of Eastern Europe	TD/B/920

Economic co-operation among developing countries

Trade expansion and economic integration among developing countries	TD/B/85/Rev.1 (Sales No. 67.II.D.20)
Current problems of economic integration—Agricultural and industrial co-operation among developing countries	TD/B/374 (Sales No. E.72.II.D.6)

Title	Document No.
Current problems of economic integration — The distribution of benefits and costs in integration among developing countries	TD/B/394 (Sales No. 73.II.D.12)
Current problems of economic integration — The role of institutions in regional integration among developing countries	TD/B/422 (Sales No. E.73.II.D.10)
Current problems of economic integration — The role of multinational financial institutions in promoting integration among developing countries	TD/B/531 (Sales No. E.75.II.D.5)
International policies on payments arrangements among developing countries	TD/B/AC.10/4
Juridical aspects of the establishment of multinational marketing enterprises among developing countries	TD/B/C.7/28/Rev.1 (Sales No. E.82.II.D.9)
Financial solidarity for development — Efforts and institutions of the members of OPEC, 1973-1976 review	TD/B/C.7/31 (Sales No. E.79.II.D.9)
A global system of trade preferences among developing countries (GSTP) — Issues for consideration in preparing for GSTP negotiations	TD/B/C.7/42
Economic co-operation and integration among developing countries — A review of recent developments in subregional, regional and interregional organizations and arrangements	TD/B/C.7/51 (Parts I, II and III)

Least developed, land-locked and island developing countries

Least developed countries

Report of the Group of Experts on special measures in favour of the least developed among the developing countries (1969)	TD/B/288
Special measures in favour of the least developed among the developing countries. Report of the Ad hoc Group of Experts	TD/B/349/Rev.1 (Sales No. E.71.II.D.11)
Report of the Intergovernmental Group on the Least Developed Countries (1975)	TD/B/577
Report of the Meeting of Multilateral and Bilateral Financial and Technical Assistance Institutions with Representatives of the Least Developed Countries (1977)	TD/B/681, TD/B/AC.21/7
Outline of a substantial new programme of action for the 1980s for the least developed countries. Report by the Secretary-General of UNCTAD	TD/240. Printed in *Proceedings of the United Nations Conference on Trade and Development, Fifth session,* vol. III, *Basic Documents* (Sales No. E.79.II.D.16)
The least developed countries and action in their favour by the international community. Selected documents of the United Nations Conference on the Least Developed Countries (Paris, 1-14 September 1981)	A/CONF.104/2/Rev.1 (Sales No. E.83.I.6)

ISLAND DEVELOPING COUNTRIES

Title	Document No.
Developing island countries. Report of the Panel of Experts	TD/B/443/Rev.1 (Sales No. E.74.II.D.6)
Report of the Group of Experts on Feeder and Interisland Services by Air or Sea for Island Developing Countries (1978)	TD/B/687, TD/B/AC.24/1 and 2
Specific action related to the particular needs and problems of island developing countries. Issues for consideration. Report by the UNCTAD secretariat	TD/279 (Part II). Printed in *Proceedings of the United Nations Conference on Trade and Development, Sixth session*, vol. III, *Basic Documents* (Sales No. E.83.II.D.8)

LAND-LOCKED DEVELOPING COUNTRIES

Report of the Group of Experts on the special problems involved in the trade and economic development of the land-locked developing countries	TD/B/308
A transport strategy for land-locked developing countries. Report of the Group of Experts on the Transport Infrastructure for Land-locked Developing Countries	TD/B/453/Add.1/Rev.1 (Sales No. E.74.II.D.5)
Specific action related to the particular needs and problems of land-locked developing countries: Issues for consideration. Report by the UNCTAD secretariat	TD/279 (Part I). Printed in *Proceedings of the United Nations Conference on Trade and Development, Sixth session*, vol. III, *Basic Documents* (Sales No. E.83.II.D.8)

Insurance

Establishment of a unified international system of insurance statistics	TD/B/C.3/85/Rev.1 (Sales No. E.72.II.D.9)
Insurance legislation and supervision in developing countries	TD/B/393 and Corr.1 and Add.1 (Sales No. E.72.II.D.4)
Reinsurance problems in developing countries	TD/B/C.3/106/Rev.1 (Sales No. E.74.II.D.2)
Marine cargo insurance	TD/B/C.3/120
Insurance education for developing countries	TD/B/C.3/121 and Supp.1
Insurance of large risks in developing countries	TD/B/C.3/137
Cargo insurance problems in land-locked developing countries	TD/B/C.3/140
Crop insurance for developing countries	TD/B/C.3/163/Rev.1 (Sales No. E.81.II.D.2)
Problems of motor insurance in developing countries	TD/B/C.3/176
Problems of developing countries in the field of motor insurance: study by Mr. A. R. B. Amerasinghe	TD/B/C.3/176/Supp.1
Insurance in developing countries: developments in 1980-1981	TD/B/C.3/178

Operational activities

Title	Document No.
Project INT/78/022—*Register of Research on Trade and Development Issues: 1981 Edition.* A list of current and planned research on trade and development issues, compiled from a survey of projects in development research centres	United Nations publication (Sales No. E.82.II.D.7)
Project INT/80/007—*Handbook of State Trading Organizations of Developing Countries.* Compilation of information on STOs of developing countries	United Nations publication (Sales No. A/E/F/S.83.II.D.5)
Project INT/77/015—Manual on "International Grain Procurement" (1984)	
Project RLA/80/001—Manual Sobre "La Commercialización Internacional de Azucar" (1981)	

Special Programme on Trade Facilitation (FALPRO)

Code for ports and other locations	TD/B/FAL/INF.66
United Nations Layout Key for Trade Documents	TD/B/FAL/INF.74
Trade Data Elements Directory (UNTDED)	TD/B/FAL/INF.76
Trade Data Interchange Directory (UNTDID)	TD/B/FAL/INF.77
Trade document names and functions	TD/B/FAL/INF.84
Facilitation measures related to international trade procedures	TD/B/FAL/INF.85
Aligned invoice layout key for international trade	TD/B/FAL/INF.90
Facts about the working Party on Facilitation of International Trade Procedures. First Revision, 1983	TD/B/FAL/INF.91
Special Programme on Trade Facilitation—FALPRO	UNCTAD/FALPRO/141

Assistance to national liberation movements

Zimbabwe: towards a new order—an economic and social survey (New York, 1980)	
Review of the economic and social conditions in Namibia and South Africa: report prepared by J. H. Mensah (1981)	TD/B/869 and Add.1
Review of the economic conditions of the Palestinian people in the occupied Arab territories: report prepared by M. W. Khouja and P. G. Sadler (1981)	TD/B/870
Palestine: Options for development: report prepared by P. G. Sadler and B. Abu Kishk (1981)	TD/B/960 and Corr.1

Disarmament and development

Trade and Development Report, 1982 (Part IV, chapter 3, "Armaments expenditure and disarmament: some consequences for development")	UNCTAD/TDR/2/Rev.1 (United Nations publication, Sales No. E.82.II.D.12)

Environmental problems

SESSIONS OF THE CONFERENCE

Title	Document No.
UNCTAD III (Santiago, 1972). Impact of environment policies on trade and development, in particular of the developing countries: report by the UNCTAD secretariat	TD/130. Reproduced in *Proceedings of the United Nations Conference on Trade and Development, Fourth session*, vol. IV—*General Review and Special Issues* (United Nations publication, Sales No. E.73.II.D.7)
UNCTAD IV (Nairobi 1976). Technological dependence: its nature, consequences and policy implications: report by the UNCTAD secretariat	TD/190. *Ibid., Fourth session,* vol. III—*Basic Documentation* (United Nations publication, Sales No. E.76.II.D.12)
Action to strengthen the technological capacity of developing countries, policies and institutions: report by the UNCTAD secretariat	TD/190/Supp.1 *Ibid.*

TRADE AND DEVELOPMENT BOARD AND ITS MAIN COMMITTEES

Seventeenth session of the Board (September 1977). Impact of environment policies on trade and development, in particular of the developing countries: progress report by the UNCTAD secretariat	TD/B/658
Committee on Manufactures, Seventh session (1975). Effects of environmental policies on trade in manufactures and semi-manufactures of developing countries: report by the UNCTAD secretariat	TD/B/C.2/150 (1975)
Committee on Manufactures, Ninth session (1980). Effects of environmental policies relating to trade in manufactures and semi-manufactures: report by the UNCTAD secretariat	TD/B/C.2/191
Committee on Transfer of Technology	
Environmental aspects of the transfer and development of technology: progress report by the UNCTAD secretariat	TD/B/C.6/61
Technology, development and environment: suggested guidelines for the preparation of a report on technology policy instruments: note prepared by the UNCTAD secretariat with the substantive and financial support of the UNEP	TD/B/C.6/88

OTHERS

Effects of environmental policies on trade in manufactures and semi-manufactures of developing countries: note by the UNCTAD secretariat	TD/B/C.2/128
The Cocoyoc Declaration adopted by the participants in the UNEP/UNCTAD symposium on "Pattern of Resource use, environment and development strategies" held at Cocoyoc, Mexico, from 8 to 12 October 1974	A/C.2/292, 1 Nov. 1974

Title	Document No.
Review of international trade and development 1975, part one, chap. III, "Impact of environmental issues on trade and development"	TD/B/530/Add.1/Rev.1 (United Nations publication, Sales No. E.76.II.D.2)
The impact of environmental issues on development and international economic relations: report by UNCTAD secretariat	UNCTAD/RD/114 (1976)
Summary of major themes discussed by expert groups on the interaction between development and environment and its significance for international economic relations; report by the UNCTAD secretariat	UNCTAD/RD/116 (1976)
Self-reliant mobilization, by R. Anisur Rahman	UNCTAD/RD/123 (1976)